READING & LEARNING
STRATEGIES

fourth edition

MIDDLE

GRADES

THROUGH

HIGH

SCHOOL

Susan LENSKI
Portland State University

Jerry JOHNS, Emeritus
Northern Illinois University

Mary Ann WHAM, Emerita
University of Wisconsin-Whitewater

Micki CASKEY
Portland State University

Kendall Hunt
publishing company

Book Team

Chairman and Chief Executive Officer   Mark C. Falb
President and Chief Operating Officer   Chad M. Chandlee
Vice President, Higher Education   David L. Tart
Director of Publishing Partnerships   Paul B. Carty
Editorial Manager   Georgia Botsford
Developmental Editor   Melissa M. Tittle
Vice President, Operations   Timothy J. Beitzel
Assistant Vice President, Production Services   Christine E. O'Brien
Senior Production Editor   Sheri Hosek
Permissions Editor   Caroline Kieler
Cover Designer   Mallory Blondin

Author Addresses for Correspondence and Workshops

Susan Davis Lenski
Portland State University
E-mail: *sjlenski@pdx.edu*

Mary Ann Wham
E-mail: *marywham@aol.com*

Jerry L. Johns
Consultant in Reading
E-mail: *jjohns@niu.edu*

Micki M. Caskey
Portland State University
E-mail: *caskeym@pdx.edu*

Ordering Information

Address: Kendall Hunt Publishing Company
           4050 Westmark Drive
           Dubuque, IA 52004
Telephone: 800-247-3458, ext. 4
Website: www.kendallhunt.com
Fax: 800-772-9165

Previously titled *Reading & Learning Strategies for Middle & High School Students*

Cover image © Shutterstock, Inc.

Printed in the United States of America
10 9 8 7 6 5 4 3 2

Contents

Preface, ix
About the Authors, xiv
Acknowledgments, xvi

CHAPTER **1**

Learning with Texts, 1

Learning Goals, 1
Questions to Consider, 1
OVERVIEW, 1
Demands of Content Area Texts, 2
Literacy in the Disciplines, 2
Instructing Students in Your Discipline, 3
Reading as a Sociocultural Activity, 3
Transactional Theory of Reading, 4
Your Students: A Cultural Mix, 4
English Language Learners (ELLs), 5
Struggling Readers, 6
Text Complexity, 7
Lexile Framework for Reading, 7
Contexts of Instruction, 8
Content Area Strategies, 9
Contexts for Assessment, 10
Conclusion, 10
Activities and Journal Entries for Teacher Educators, 11

CHAPTER **2**

Fostering Motivation and Reading Engagement, 13

Learning Goals, 13
Questions to Consider, 13
OVERVIEW, 13
2.1 Creating Interest, 16
2.2 Promoting Positive Attitudes, 25
2.3 Arousing Curiosity for Topics, 33
2.4 Fostering Motivation, 39
Activities and Journal Entries for Teacher Educators, 47

CHAPTER **3**

Building Vocabulary, 49

Learning Goals, 49
Questions to Consider, 49
OVERVIEW, 49

3.1 Linking Vocabulary to Background Knowledge, 51
3.2 Defining Words, 56
3.3 Understanding Relationships among Words, 63
3.4 Developing Independence in Vocabulary Acquisition, 69
3.5 Using Words Effectively, 72
Activities and Journal Entries for Teacher Educators, 76

CHAPTER **4**

Word Study, 77

Learning Goals, 77
Questions to Consider, 77
OVERVIEW, 77
4.1 Using Context, 80
4.2 Decoding and Meaning, 91
4.3 Using Reference Sources, 101
4.4 Using Greek and Latin Roots, 110
Activities and Journal Entries for Teacher Educators, 119

CHAPTER **5**

Comprehending Literary Texts, 121

Learning Goals, 121
Questions to Consider, 121
OVERVIEW, 121
5.1 Accessing Prior Knowledge, 123
5.2 Studying Aspects of Characterization, 127
5.3 Recognizing Story Structure Features, 131
5.4 Enhancing Learning with Literature, 136
Activities and Journal Entries for Teacher Educators, 140

CHAPTER **6**

Understanding Informational Texts, 141

Learning Goals, 141
Questions to Consider, 141
OVERVIEW, 141
6.1 Demonstrating General Understanding, 144
6.2 Using Text Structure, 150
6.3 Developing an Interpretation, 155
6.4 Questioning Texts, 160
6.5 Making Connections, 165
6.6 Using Text Features, 170
Activities and Journal Entries for Teacher Educators, 177

CHAPTER 7

Reading Critically, 179

Learning Goals, 179
Questions to Consider, 179
OVERVIEW, 179
7.1 Determining Authors' Qualifications, Perspectives, and Purposes, 183
7.2 Considering Alternative Views, 189
7.3 Developing Informed Opinions, 194
7.4 Promoting Critical Literacy, 200
Activities and Journal Entries for Teacher Educators, 208

CHAPTER 8

Studying, 209

Learning Goals, 209
Questions to Consider, 209
OVERVIEW, 209
8.1 Learning to Study, 212
8.2 Understanding Textbook Features, 217
8.3 Reading Flexibly, 222
8.4 Summarizing Content Information, 228
8.5 Taking Notes, 235
Activities and Journal Entries for Teacher Educators, 242

References, 243
Index, 257

Web Contents

Section 2.1
STRATEGY 1
Anticipation Guide Reproducible, 1
Anticipation Guide Consumer Education Example, 2
Anticipation Guide Driver's Education (Illinois) Example, 3
Anticipation Guide Health Example, 4
Anticipation Guide Social Studies Example, 5

STRATEGY 2
People Search Reproducible, 6
People Search History Example, 7
People Search Science Example, 8
People Search Math Example, 9
People Search Music Example, 10

STRATEGY 3
Problematic Situation Reproducible, 11
Problematic Situation History Example, 12
Problematic Situation Science Example, 13

STRATEGY 4
Predict-O-Gram Reproducible, 14
Predict-O-Gram Literature Example #1, 15
Predict-O-Gram Literature Example #2, 16

STRATEGY 5
That Was Then . . . This Is Now Reproducible, 17
That Was Then . . . This Is Now Social Studies Example, 18
That Was Then . . . This Is Now Science (Energy Sources) Example, 19

Section 2.2
STRATEGY 6
Autobiography Math Example, 20
Autobiography Carpentry Example, 21

STRATEGY 7
Opinionnaire/Questionnaire Science Example #1, 22
Opinionnaire/Questionnaire Science Example #2, 23

STRATEGY 8
Sustained Silent Reading (SSR) Log Reproducible, 24

STRATEGY 9
Content Area Picture Books: Language Arts, Mathematics, Science, the Arts, and Social Studies, 25–28

Section 2.3
STRATEGY 11
Creating Sentences Reproducible, 29
Creating Sentences Literature Example, 30

STRATEGY 12
Probable Passages Reproducible, 31
Probable Passages Social Studies Example, 32

STRATEGY 13
Content Predict-O-Gram Reproducible, 33
Content Predict-O-Gram: Social Studies Reproducible, 34
Content Predict-O-Gram Social Studies Example, 35
Content Predict-O-Gram Government Example, 36
Content Predict-O-Gram Literature Example, 37

STRATEGY 14
Poetry Prowess Resources: Language Arts, Mathematics, Physical Fitness and Health, Social Studies, Science, 38–39

Poetry Prowess Websites: Poetry, Presentation, General Poetry, Social Studies, Science, 40

Section 2.4

STRATEGY 15
K-W-L Reproducible, 41
K-W-L Industrial Arts Example, 42
K-W-L Government Example, 43

STRATEGY 16
The Imposter Art Example, 44
The Imposter Chemistry Example, 45
The Imposter Literature Example, 46

STRATEGY 17
DRAW Driver's Education Example, 47
DRAW Math Example, 48
DRAW Science Example, 49

Section 3.1

STRATEGY 1
Knowledge Rating Scale Reproducible, 1
Knowledge Rating Scale Math Example, 2

STRATEGY 2
Exclusion Brainstorming Reproducible, 3
Exclusion Brainstorming Science Example, 4

STRATEGY 3
Imagine That! Reproducible, 5

Section 3.2

STRATEGY 4
Magic Square Reproducible, 6
Magic Square Statistics Example, 7

STRATEGY 5
Graphic Organizer Reproducible, 8

STRATEGY 6
Four Square Reproducible, 9
Four Square Literature Example, 10

STRATEGY 7
Word Storm Reproducible, 11
Word Storm English Example, 12

STRATEGY 8
Word Web Reproducible, 13
Word Web English Example, 14

Section 3.3

STRATEGY 9
Semantic Feature Analysis Chart Reproducible, 15
Semantic Feature Analysis Reproducible, 16
Semantic Feature Analysis Government Example, 17
Semantic Feature Analysis Art (Spanish) Example, 18
Semantic Feature Analysis Mathematics (Spanish) Example, 19

STRATEGY 10
Closed Word Sort Reproducible, 20
Closed Word Sort Science Example, 21

STRATEGY 11
Magnet Words Reproducible, 22
Magnet Words Science Example, 23

Section 3.4

STRATEGY 13
Vocabulary Self-Collection Reproducible, 24

Section 3.5

STRATEGY 15
Identifying Figurative Language Reproducible, 25
Identifying Figurative Language Language Arts Examples, 26

STRATEGY 16
Sensing Similes and Metaphors Reproducible, 27

STRATEGY 17
Choosing Stronger Connotations Reproducible, 28
Choosing Stronger Connotations Language Arts Examples, 29

STRATEGY 18
Positive or Negative Connotations? Reproducible, 30
Positive or Negative Connotations? Language Arts Examples, 31

Section 4.1

STRATEGY 5
Predictions, Definitions, and Connections Reproducible, 1
Predictions, Definitions, and Connections Art Example, 2

STRATEGY 7
Word Questioning Reproducible, 3
Word Questioning Art Example, 4
Word Questioning Geometry Example, 5
Word Questioning Government Example, 6
Word Questioning Literature Example, 7

Section 4.2

STRATEGY 8
Repeated Readings Record Sheet Reproducible, 8–9

STRATEGY 9
Two Questions Reproducible, 10

STRATEGY 12
Foreign Words and Phrases Reproducible, 11
Foreign Abbreviations, Words, and Phrases, 12–13

Section 4.3

STRATEGY 16
Dictionary Challenge Reproducible, 14

STRATEGY 19
Word Map Reproducible, 15
Word Map Literature Example, 16

Section 4.4
STRATEGY 21
Word Spine Reproducible, 17
Word Tree Reproducible, 18
Word Tree Example, 19

Section 5.1
STRATEGY 1
Story Impressions Reproducible, 1
Story Impressions Poetry Example, 2

STRATEGY 2
Anticipation Guide Reproducible, 3
Anticipation Guide Literature Example, 4

STRATEGY 3
Character Quotes Reproducible, 5
Character Quotes Literature Example, 6

Section 5.2
STRATEGY 4
Biopoem Reproducible, 7
Biopoem Poetry Example, 8

STRATEGY 5
Missing Person's Report Reproducible, 9
Missing Person's Report Literature Example, 10

STRATEGY 6
Attribute Web Reproducible, 11
Attribute Web Literature Example #1, 12
Attribute Web Literature Example #2, 13

Section 5.3
STRATEGY 7
Story Map Reproducible, 14
Story Map Literature Example, 15

STRATEGY 8
Conflict-Resolution Paradigm Reproducible, 16
Conflict-Resolution Paradigm Literature Example, 17

STRATEGY 9
What's Your Perspective Reproducible, 18
What's Your Perspective Literature Example, 19

Section 5.4
STRATEGY 10
Locating Literary Devices Reproducible, 20
Locating Literary Devices Literature Example, 21

STRATEGY 11
Connecting Fact and Historical Fiction Reproducible, 22
Connecting Fact and Historical Fiction Literature
    Example, 23
Historical Literature for Selected Topics, 24–25

Section 6.1
STRATEGY 1
Idea Web Assessment Health/Science Example, 1
Prereading Plan (PreP) Reproducible, 2
Prereading Plan (PreP) Math Example, 3

STRATEGY 2
Anticipation/Reaction Guide Reproducible, 4
Anticipation/Reaction Guide Language Arts Example, 5
Anticipation/Reaction Guide Social Studies Example, 6

STRATEGY 3
Think, Predict, Read, Connect (TPRC) Reproducible, 7
Think, Predict, Read, Connect (TPRC) Social Studies
    Example, 8

STRATEGY 4
GIST Reproducible, 9
GIST Music Example, 10

Section 6.2
STRATEGY 5
Compare-Contrast Graphic Organizer Reproducible, 11
Compare-Contrast Graphic Organizer Physical Education
    Example, 12
Description Graphic Organizer Reproducible, 13
Description Graphic Organizer Math Example, 14
Sequence Graphic Organizer Reproducible, 15
Sequence Graphic Organizer Science Example, 16
Cause and Effect Graphic Organizer Reproducible, 17
Cause and Effect Graphic Organizer Social Studies
    Example, 18
Problem and Solution Graphic Organizer Reproducible, 19
Problem and Solution Graphic Organizer Consumer
    Education Example, 20

STRATEGY 6
Sequence Idea-Map Reproducible, 21
Sequence Idea-Map Music Example, 22
Description Idea-Map Reproducible, 23
Description Idea-Map Literature Example, 24
Compare and Contrast Idea-Map Reproducible, 25
Compare and Contrast Idea-Map Science Example, 26
Cause and Effect Idea-Map Reproducible, 27
Cause and Effect Idea-Map Science Example, 28
Problem and Solution Idea-Map Reproducible, 29
Problem and Solution Idea-Map Business Example, 30

STRATEGY 7
Signal Words Reproducible, 31

Section 6.3
STRATEGY 8
It Says—I Say—And So Reproducible, 32
It Says—I Say—And So Social Studies Example, 33

STRATEGY 9
ReQuest Reproducible, 34
ReQuest Driver's Education Example, 35

STRATEGY 10
Inference Chart Reproducible, 36
Inference Chart Art Example, 37

STRATEGY 11
Three-Level Guide Reproducible, 38
Three-Level Guide Literature Example, 39

Section 6.4
STRATEGY 12
Questioning the Author (QtA) Reproducible, 40

STRATEGY 13
Question Answer Relationship (QAR) Reproducible, 41

STRATEGY 14
Inquiry Questions (IQs) Reproducible, 42

Section 6.5
STRATEGY 15
Connections Chart Reproducible, 43
Connections Chart Social Studies Example, 44
Connections Chart Technology Example, 45

STRATEGY 16
Share What You Know (SWYK) Reproducible, 46
Share What You Know (SWYK) Language Arts
    Example, 47

STRATEGY 17
Intra-Act Reproducible, 48
Intra-Act Math Example, 49

Section 6.6
STRATEGY 18
Text Preview Reproducible, 50–51

STRATEGY 19
In the Feature, but Not in the Text Reproducible, 52

STRATEGY 20
Bar Graph Physical Education Example, 53

STRATEGY 21
Timeline Reproducible, 54
Timeline Social Studies Example, 55
Timeline School Memories Reproducible, 56

Section 7.1
STRATEGY 1
Consider the Source Reproducible, 1
Consider the Source Math Example, 2
Consider the Source Science Example, 3

STRATEGY 2
Perspective Guide Reproducible, 4
Perspective Guide Health Example, 5
Perspective Guide Social Studies Example, 6

STRATEGY 3
Ask the Author Reproducible, 7
Ask the Author Literature Example, 8
Ask the Author Science Example, 9

STRATEGY 4
Determining Authors' Purposes Reproducible, 10
Determining Authors' Purposes Literature Example, 11
Determining Authors' Purposes Social Studies Example, 12

Section 7.2
STRATEGY 5
Discussion Web Reproducible, 13
Discussion Web Health Example, 14

STRATEGY 6
Discussion Continuum Reproducible, 15
Discussion Continuum Social Studies Example, 16

STRATEGY 7
Options Guide Reproducible, 17
Options Guide Science Example, 18

STRATEGY 8
Questioning Editorial Perspectives Reproducible, 19

Section 7.3
STRATEGY 9
State-Question-Read-Conclude (SQRC) Reproducible, 20
State-Question-Read-Conclude (SQRC) Language Arts
    Example, 21

STRATEGY 10
Opinion-Proof Reproducible, 22
Opinion-Proof Essay Evaluation Scoring Guide
    Reproducible, 23

STRATEGY 11
Support Your Position (SYP) Reproducible, 24
Support Your Position (SYP) Science Example, 25

STRATEGY 12
Truman Document Excerpt History Example, 26
SOAPS + Claim Reproducible, 27
SOAPS + Claim Sentence Frames Reproducible, 28

Section 7.4
STRATEGY 13
Reciprocal Teaching Plus Reproducible, 29
Reciprocal Teaching Plus Language Arts Example, 30
Reciprocal Teaching Plus Math Example, 31

STRATEGY 14
Critical Literacy Response Reproducible, 32
Critical Literacy Response Physical Education Example, 33
Critical Literacy Response Science Example, 34

STRATEGY 15
Power Graph Reproducible, 35
Power Graph Social Studies Example, 36

STRATEGY 16
Looking at Language Reproducible, 37
Looking at Language Music Example, 38

STRATEGY 17
Problematizing Texts Reproducible, 39

STRATEGY 18
Taking Social Action Reproducible, 40

Section 8.1
STRATEGY 1
Preplan-List-Activate-Evaluate (PLAE) Study Plan
    Reproducible, 1
Preplan-List-Activate-Evaluate (PLAE) Study Plan Social
    Studies Example, 2

STRATEGY 3
Study Skills Self-Assessment Reproducible, 3

STRATEGY 4
Project Journal Reproducible, 4

Section 8.2
STRATEGY 6
Textbook Survey Reproducible, 5

STRATEGY 7
Textbook Scavenger Hunt Reproducible, 6
Textbook Scavenger Hunt Math Example, 7

STRATEGY 8
THIEVES Reproducible, 8
THIEVES Science Example, 9

Section 8.3
STRATEGY 11
SCAN and RUN Reproducible, 10

Section 8.4
STRATEGY 14
REAP Reproducible, 11
REAP Science Example, 12

Section 8.5
STRATEGY 19
REST English Example, 13

STRATEGY 20
Cornell Note-Taking Reproducible, 14
Cornell Note-Taking Science Example, 15

STRATEGY 21
Power Notes Visual Arts Example, 16

STRATEGY 22
Double Entry Diary Reproducible, 17
Double Entry Diary Language Arts Example, 18
Double Entry Diary Social Studies Example, 19

Purpose of This Book

Reading and Learning Strategies: Middle Grades through High School (4th ed.) is a user-friendly, practical book grounded in solid knowledge about reading. It is intended for use in undergraduate and graduate secondary and content area reading courses as well as for workshops and professional development for teachers in middle and high schools. Reading teachers, reading specialists, and literacy coaches will embrace it as a valuable resource for their personal libraries.

What's Different about This Book?

The characteristics of *Reading and Learning Strategies: Middle Grades through High School* (4th ed.) that make it a content book different from the ones already on your shelves are as follows.

- Straightforward organizational scheme
- Clear writing
- Useful strategies
- Helpful examples
- Content area examples
- Assessment ideas
- Ideas for teacher educators
- Reproducible classroom resources
- Website with more than 225 reproducibles and examples

Alignment with 2010 IRA Standards for Reading Professionals

Reading and Learning Strategies: Middle Grades through High School (4th ed.) is based on the Professional Standards developed by the International Reading Association (IRA). The standards were developed for all reading professionals, including paraprofessionals, elementary teachers, middle and high school content classroom teachers, middle and high school reading teachers, reading specialists, and teacher educators. Since the major audience for this book is middle and high school teachers, we based the material in the book on the standards for Middle and High School Content Classroom Teachers. This book would also be of interest to middle and high school reading teachers and reading specialists.

At the beginning of each chapter, we list the IRA standards that are addressed in the chapter. We have attempted to address each of the standards in the 2010 document, and we recognize that some have been covered more thoroughly than others. We have focused much more intensely on Standard #2, Curriculum and Instruction, than we have on the others, and we recognize that teacher learning occurs outside the pages of our book and that some standards are better taught in other venues.

You can find the entire list of the 2010 Standards for Reading Professionals on the IRA website (www.reading.org). The following are the standards for Middle and High School Content Classroom Teachers upon which we based this edition.

Standards 2010: Middle and High School Content Classroom Teacher

A Middle and High School Content Classroom Teacher is a professional responsible for teaching one of the content or academic areas (e.g. science, mathematics, social studies, or English) at either the middle or high school level. These teachers must teach the content of the discipline and have responsibility for helping students engage in and learn not only the content but also the reading and writing demands of the discipline. Middle and High School Content Classroom Teachers collaborate with *reading specialists and other professionals* to improve instruction and to modify the physical and social environments as needed.

Standard 1: Foundational Knowledge
Middle and High School Content Classroom Teacher Candidates understand the theoretical and evidence-based foundations of reading and writing processes and instruction.

	Ch 1	Ch 2	Ch 3	Ch 4	Ch 5	Ch 6	Ch 7	Ch 8
1.1: Understand major theories and empirical research that describe the cognitive, linguistic, motivational, and sociocultural foundations of reading and writing development, processes, and components, including word recognition, language comprehension, strategic knowledge, and reading–writing connections.	X	X	X	X	X	X	X	X
1.2: Understand the historically shared knowledge of the profession and changes over time in the perceptions of reading and writing development, processes, and components.	X		X	X	X	X	X	
1.3: Understand the role of professional judgment and practical knowledge for improving all students' reading development and achievement.	X		X	X	X	X	X	

Standard 2: Curriculum and Instruction
Candidates use instructional approaches, materials, and an integrated, comprehensive, balanced curriculum to support student learning in reading and writing.

	Ch 1	Ch 2	Ch 3	Ch 4	Ch 5	Ch 6	Ch 7	Ch 8
2.1: Use foundational knowledge to design or implement an integrated, comprehensive, and balanced curriculum.	X	X	X	X	X	X	X	X
2.2: Use appropriate and varied instructional approaches, including those that develop word recognition, language comprehension, strategic knowledge, and reading–writing connections.		X	X	X	X	X	X	X
2.3: Use a wide range of texts (e.g., narrative, expository, and poetry) from traditional print, digital, and online resources.		X	X	X	X	X	X	

Standard 3: Assessment and Evaluation
Candidates use a variety of assessment tools and practices to plan and evaluate effective reading and writing instruction.

	Ch 1	Ch 2	Ch 3	Ch 4	Ch 5	Ch 6	Ch 7	Ch 8
3.1: Understand types of assessments and their purposes, strengths, and limitations.	X		X		X			
3.2: Select, develop, administer, and interpret assessments, both traditional print and electronic, for specific purposes.			X		X			
3.3: Use assessment information to plan and evaluate instruction.		X		X		X	X	
3.4: Communicate assessment results and implications to a variety of audiences.								

(continued)

Standards 2010: Middle and High School Content Classroom Teacher (continued)

Standard 4: Diversity

Candidates create and engage their students in literacy practices that develop awareness, understanding, respect, and a valuing of differences in our society.

	Ch 1	Ch 2	Ch 3	Ch 4	Ch 5	Ch 6	Ch 7	Ch 8
4.1: Recognize, understand, and value the forms of diversity that exist in society and their importance in learning to read and write.	X			X	X	X	X	
4.2: Use a literacy curriculum and engage in instructional practices that positively impact students' knowledge, beliefs, and engagement with the features of diversity.	X	X	X	X	X	X	X	X
4.3: Develop and implement strategies to advocate for equity.	X		X			X	X	

Standard 5: Literate Environment

Candidates create a literate environment that fosters reading and writing by integrating foundational knowledge, instructional practices, approaches and methods, curriculum materials, and the appropriate use of assessments.

	Ch 1	Ch 2	Ch 3	Ch 4	Ch 5	Ch 6	Ch 7	Ch 8
5.1: Design the physical environment to optimize students' use of traditional print, digital, and online resources in reading and writing instruction.			X	X	X			
5.2: Design a social environment that is low risk and includes choice, motivation, and scaffolded support to optimize students' opportunities for learning to read and write.		X			X	X	X	
5.3: Use routines to support reading and writing instruction (e.g., time allocation, transitions from one activity to another; discussions, and peer feedback).			X	X	X	X	X	X
5.4: Use a variety of classroom configurations (i.e, whole class, small group, and individual) to differentiate instruction.				X	X	X	X	

Standard 6: Professional Learning and Leadership

Candidates recognize the importance of, demonstrate, and facilitate professional learning and leadership as a career-long effort and responsibility.

	Ch 1	Ch 2	Ch 3	Ch 4	Ch 5	Ch 6	Ch 7	Ch 8
6.1: Demonstrate foundational knowledge of adult learning theories and related research about organizational change, professional development, and school culture.	X							
6.2: Display positive dispositions related to their own reading and writing and the teaching of reading and writing, and pursue the development of individual professional knowledge and behaviors.			X	X	X	X	X	
6.3: Participate in, design, facilitate, lead, and evaluate effective and differentiated professional development programs.								
6.4: Understand and influence local, state, or national policy decisions.	X					X	X	

International Reading Association. (2010). Standards for Reading Professionals–Revised 2010. A Reference for the Preparation of Educators in the United States. Reprinted with permission of the International Reading Association. www.reading.org

Content Area Strategies

There is at least one content area example for most strategies presented in this book; many strategies have examples gleaned from more than one subject. Additional examples for many strategies can be found on the website. We tried to vary the content examples in each chapter so that you could see for yourself how to apply the strategies to your classroom instruction. However, there will be strategies with examples from middle and high school subjects other than your own. For those strategies that have examples from other subject areas, we urge you to adapt the strategies to fit your particular content and classroom. Virtually all of the strategies presented in this book can be applied to each of the subjects taught in schools.

Word to the Wise Teacher

Please use and adapt these strategies to make your instruction more responsive to the needs of your students. Through your thoughtful and conscientious use of this book, we know that your students will become more effective readers and learners—the base for knowledge learned throughout their lives.

How to Use This Book

Take a few minutes to get acquainted with *Reading and Learning Strategies: Middle Grades through High School* (4th ed.).

A **Quick Reference Guide** is placed on the inside front cover. Beneath each chapter title are four to six goals for students.

Go ahead—choose a specific goal and find it on the page number listed.

You will see that each chapter is arranged in the same format.

- Overview
- Numbered section heading
- Student learning goal
- Background information
- Numbered instructional strategies

    There is a **numbered section** heading (e.g., 2.1 Creating Interest).

The **goal** for the section is identified.

Background information is given to aid in reaching the goal.

Instructional strategies form the heart of this book. These strategies are carefully described and use examples from various content areas. For each goal, you will find several strategies.

Resources are listed with some sections as a reference tool.

Surf the Web features website addresses pertinent to some sections. Please note that websites are accurate at the time of publication. We cannot guarantee how long these sites will remain online.

 denotes **Group Activities**.

Readers Needing Additional Support provides ideas for adapting the strategy for readers who struggle.

Assessing Student Learning offers suggestions for assessing the teaching goal.

Website contains more than 225 resources:

- *reproducibles* to accompany many of the instructional strategies
- *additional content area examples*, all keyed to strategies in the book.

Students may access bonus material at http://webcom3.grtxle.com/ancillary and use username: *lenski* and password: *lenski* for access.

SUSAN LENSKI is a professor at Portland State University in Oregon. Before joining the faculty at PSU, Dr. Lenski taught in public schools for 20 years and at Illinois State University for 11 years. Her teaching experiences include working with children from kindergarten through high school. Dr. Lenski currently teaches graduate reading and language arts courses.

Dr. Lenski has been recognized by several organizations for her commitment to education. Among her numerous awards, Dr. Lenski was presented with the Nila Banton Smith Award from the International Reading Association; she was instrumental in her school receiving an Exemplary Reading Program Award from the International Reading Association; and she was inducted into the Illinois Reading Hall of Fame. She was also on the International Reading Association Board of Directors (2004–2007).

Dr. Lenski's research interests focus on strategic reading and writing and adolescent literacy. She also conducts research on preparing teacher candidates. Dr. Lenski has conducted numerous presentations in the United States, Canada, Guatemala, the Philippines, and Panama and has presented at many state and national conferences. Dr. Lenski has published over 60 articles and 16 books.

MARY ANN WHAM is Professor Emerita at the University of Wisconsin—Whitewater. She has taught undergraduate and graduate courses related to reading and the language arts. Prior to her position in Whitewater, Dr. Wham was director of the Rockford College Reading Clinic in Rockford, IL, where she worked with middle and high school students involved in reading improvement.

Dr. Wham is a former member of the editorial board of *The Reading Teacher* and has served on the Board of Directors of the Mid-Western Educational Research Association. She has conducted inservices and workshops for practicing teachers and has made frequent presentations at regional and national reading conferences. Dr. Wham has contributed a number of articles to reading journals regarding effective classroom literacy instruction. Currently, she is an adjunct professor at Northern Illinois University.

JERRY JOHNS has been recognized as a distinguished teacher, writer, outstanding teacher educator, and popular professional development speaker for schools, school districts, and conferences. His more than 700 presentations have involved travel throughout the United States and 13 countries. He has taught students from kindergarten through graduate school and also served as a reading teacher. Professor Johns spent his career at Northern Illinois University. He was also a Visiting Professor at Western Washington University and the University of Victoria in British Columbia.

Professor Johns served in leadership positions at the local, state, national, and international levels. He has been president of the International Reading Association, the Illinois Reading Council, the Association of Literacy Educators and Researchers, and the Northern Illinois Reading Council. He also served on the Board of Directors for each of these organizations as well as the American Reading Forum. In addition, Dr. Johns has served on numerous committees of the International Reading Association and other professional organizations.

Dr. Johns has authored or coauthored nearly 300 articles, monographs, and research studies as well as numerous professional books. His *Basic Reading Inventory*, now in the tenth edition, is widely used in undergraduate and graduate classes as well as by practicing teachers. Among his more than 20 coauthored books to help teachers strengthen their reading instruction are *Improving Reading: Interventions, Strategies, and Resources, Strategies for Content Area Learning, Teaching Reading Pre-K–Grade 3, Spanish Reading Inventory,* and *Comprehension and Vocabulary Strategies for the Elementary Grades*. Professor Johns currently serves on the editorial advisory boards for *Reading Psychology* and the *Illinois Reading Council Journal*.

Dr. Johns has been the recipient of numerous awards for his contributions to the profession. The Illinois Reading Council honored him with the induction into the Reading Hall of Fame. Other recognitions include the Alpha Delta Literacy Award for Scholarship, Leadership, and Service to Adult Learners and the A.B. Herr Award for outstanding contributions to the field of reading. He also received the Outstanding Teacher Educator in Reading Award presented by the International Reading Association, the Champion for Children Award presented by the HOSTS Corporation, and the Laureate Award from the Association of Literacy Educators and Researchers for life-long contributors to the field of reading.

MICKI CASKEY is a professor in the Department of Curriculum and Instruction in the Graduate School of Education at Portland State University. She holds a Ph.D. in Curriculum and Instruction with a specialization in Interdisciplinary Education from the University of South Florida. She draws on more than 20 years of teaching in both middle and high schools in inner-city schools. Her areas of specialization include content area literacy, learning strategies and content enhancements, middle grades education, teacher education, and action research. She is Chair of the National Middle School Association's (NMSA) Research Advisory Board; Editor of *Research in Middle Level Education Online,* an international peer-reviewed journal; and Immediate Past Chair of Middle Level Education Research—a Special Interest Group of the American Educational Research Association (AERA). Additionally, she is a Strategic Instruction Model (SIM) professional developer for the Center for Research on Learning (University of Kansas), and board member for the Oregon Middle Level Consortium of Teacher Educators and Oregon Association of Teacher Educators. Her publication record includes eight books, six chapters, four encyclopedia entries, and numerous journal articles. Her awards include the Distinguished Research in Teacher Education Award (2004) from the Association of Teacher Educators; the Scholarship of Teaching and Learning with Technology Awards (1999, 2002) from Portland State University, a Fellowship to the American Memory Program at the Library of Congress (1999), and Teacher of the Year (1996) in the Hillsborough County School District.

Acknowledgments

We are grateful to colleagues, teachers, and other professionals who have assisted us with the preparation of this book. Our special thanks go to Sheri Hosek, our superb editor, for her assistance throughout the process.

A number of teachers and graduate students were willing to share their resources, provide content examples, react to drafts of our writing, and assist in various ways that strengthened the book. We are pleased to acknowledge the excellent assistance of these wonderful individuals.

Carolyn Bailey, Rockford, IL

Jennifer Bolander, Illinois State University

Linda Bookout, Streator District #44

Kathy Byron, University of Wisconsin–Whitewater

Jane Dickinson, Sante Fe, New Mexico

Nicole Couture, Portland State University

Nancy Drake, University of Wisconsin–Whitewater

Mary Engleken, Wheeling District #21

Lou Ferroli, Rockford College

Fred M. Fox III, Portland State University

Aaron Green-Mitchell, Portland State University

Charles Johannson, Rockford, IL

LaVonne Knapstein, Wheeling District #21

Ken Kubycheck, Elgin District #46

John Liedtke, Jefferson Middle School

Janelle Lone, University of Wisconsin–Whitewater

Nellie McLean, Portland State University

Peggy Nink, Streator District #44

Marsha Riss, Metcalf Laboratory School

Mark Wyant Schell, Portland State University

J. Suzanne Oliver Sheets, Westview Elementary School

Ellen Spycher, Illinois State University

Carolyn Strzok, Huntley Middle School

Sara Trakselis, Portland State University

Christine Wolff, Wheeling District #21

Roslyn Wylie, Illinois State University

Sue, Mary Ann, Jerry, and Micki

Learning with Texts

Learning Goals

The reader of this chapter will:

- Learn about the complex demands of texts for middle and high school students
- Understand how literacy is used in your discipline
- Learn how sociocultural and transactional theories underpin disciplinary literacies
- Understand why some students have trouble reading in your discipline
- Learn how to determine text complexity
- Understand the importance of strategy instruction in developing literacy competence
- Learn about types of assessments that you can use in your classroom

Questions to Consider

1. What kinds of literacy processes are important in your discipline?
2. How do you determine whether a text is appropriate for your students?
3. Why do some students struggle with reading?
4. How can the use of literacy strategies help your students learn content?
5. What kinds of assessments should you use to support student learning?

OVERVIEW

Reading is an essential skill in our society. We encounter print in all aspects of our lives, and we often take being able to read for granted. This morning, for example, you may have read the newspaper during breakfast. If you watched morning television, you may have encountered print during commercial breaks or as a moving text at the bottom of the screen. If you drove to work, you probably read road and street signs, and during work you constantly made use of print by reading memos, e-mails, students' papers, and so on. Reading is one of the fundamental skills for the 21st century.

The majority of your students will be able to do the types of functional reading described previously. According to the 2009 National Assessment of Educational Progress (NAEP), 75% of eighth graders and 73% of twelfth graders can read at or above the Basic level (http://nces.ed. gov/nationsreportcard/). This means that most of your students will be able to read grade-level materials in your subject at a literal level. However, the same test indicates that only one-third of these students will be able to read at a Proficient or Advanced level. This finding means that only some of your students will be able to read class materials with the kind of comprehension you expect in middle and high school.

You might wonder why so many of your students cannot read assigned texts with deep comprehension, and you might also wonder whether elementary teachers have been teaching reading. That's a common thought. The fact is that students in elementary schools have been learning to read, but in middle and high school, there is a much greater emphasis on reading to learn. We know from research that even strong early readers may not be able to read the literature, science, social studies, and mathematics textbooks found in your classroom (Shanahan & Shanahan,

2008). Even though educators had hoped that strong reading programs in the K–3 grades would result in better reading in later years, this has not occurred. Snow and Moje (2010) call it an "inoculation fallacy." What educators have learned from Reading First is that the reading gains in primary years do not necessarily mean students will read better once they begin reading content area texts.

Demands of Content Area Texts

Reading breaks down for many students in intermediate grades or in middle school because the requirements of reading change once students begin having classes in the content areas such as science and social studies (Jacobs, 2008). It's one thing to read stories, which are the primary kinds of texts that are taught in early elementary grades, and it's quite another thing to read and learn from a science textbook.

According to the Carnegie Corporation of New York's Council on Advancing Adolescent Literacy (2010), the texts that are used in middle and high school are much more demanding than those found in elementary school. Texts become longer, word complexity increases, sentence and structural complexity increases, graphic representations become more important, conceptual challenge increases, and texts begin to vary widely across content areas. An example of two passages, one from an elementary science book and a second one from a high school biology book follow.

 Elementary Science

Growing Green Plants

You've probably eaten many different kinds of seeds. Beans, peas, and corn are seeds. So are nuts such as acorns. You know apples and oranges have seeds. But you probably don't know that some pine cones have seeds. Perhaps you've puffed on a dandelion and blown some of the seeds away. What might have happened to the seeds?

From *Science and technology: Changes we make.* (1985). San Diego, CA: Coronado, p. 202.

EXAMPLE

High School Biology

Flowering Plants May Appear Very Different

Flowering plants are divided into two large classes—the monocots and the dicots. In monocots, the embryo contains a single cotyledon. The monocots include grasses and grain-producing plants such as wheat, rice, and corn—the chief food plants of the world. The pasture grasses that feed cattle, another source of human food, are also monocots. Without monocots, the human population never could have reached its present state.

From *BSCS Biology: An ecological approach.* (1998). Dubuque, IA: Kendall Hunt, p. 330.

EXAMPLE

In the elementary passage, notice that the vocabulary is simple, the sentences are short, the text is personalized, and the ideas are basic. As you look at the example from the high school biology text, you'll notice the complexity of the language and thoughts. Students need to have more highly developed reading skills to read this text, skills that do not necessarily come without high-quality instruction.

Literacy in the Disciplines

The texts that middle and high school students read are more demanding, but that's not the only reason secondary students have difficulty reading the texts in your classroom.

First, most students have had few experiences reading informational texts. Elementary schools typically emphasize narrative text over informational text (e.g., Duke, 2000). Furthermore, despite two decades of research on reading comprehension, the National Reading Panel (2000) reported that content area teachers generally do not teach the strategies that students need to use when reading textbooks. That may be because many teachers don't know which strategies help students comprehend informational texts (Spor & Schneider, 1999). Some students, therefore, do not comprehend complex texts, and most teachers are not providing the instruction necessary for them to do so.

Another reason why secondary students have difficulty reading content area texts is that the texts students encounter in the middle grades through high school are far more complex than content texts in the earlier grades. Furthermore, some teachers believe that when students are faced with more difficult texts, they should be able to read without difficulty. This assumption seems logical, but it is unrealistic. An analogy illustrates how complex skills need to be taught. Imagine that you (or a son, daughter, or friend) learned how to do a front dive from a one-meter diving board. You might be able to do a front dive on a higher board without much trouble. But being able to dive does not automatically mean you can accomplish a more difficult one—say a back somersault. To learn this new skill, you would have to learn a new set of more complicated physical moves.

A third reason is one that we've stated earlier: the kinds of texts that students read in middle and high school begin to vary widely. The literacy demands of each discipline (e.g., science, mathematics, social studies, language arts) are specific to each content area and the transfer of comprehension skills is not automatic (Deshler, Palincsar, Biancarosa, & Nair, 2007). Recently, adolescent literacy educators have begun to examine the different kinds of reading necessary for each of the disciplines. Some reading skills are generalizable to all content areas, such as prediction and questioning; but for middle and high school students to read proficiently, they need specific skills that match the demands of each content area.

Literacy is unique to each of the disciplines. According to Moje (2008) and Lee and Spratley (2010), historians study researchable problems systematically in the context of the time period in which the ideas are situated. They may read primary source documents that have complex rhetorical constructions and are situated in a specific time period that represents a particular point of view. Mathematicians are problem solvers who work through the logic of a problem to arrive at a claim. Mathematics is a language as well as a form of communication. Furthermore, some mathematics textbooks and tests emphasize mathematics problems set in a context (i.e., story problems). Science looks at researchable problems that are carefully defined and studied before claims are made. Science texts often have a great deal of technical vocabulary and difficult syntax. Readers of literature analyze texts looking for ways to interpret and solve problems. Literature takes the form of novels, short stories, and poetry and are the most familiar kind of reading for students. However, the kinds of literature that is read in middle and high school appropriates rhetorical features and literary devices that make the text more complex. For example, texts in middle and high school may have more symbolism, figures of speech, and foreshadowing than students have seen previously.

Instructing Students in Your Discipline

You may have heard the saying, "every teacher is a teacher of reading." We're not going to say that. We agree with Fisher and Ivey (2005) who write about literacy being an "access skill" that is necessary for students to learn your discipline. They suggest that you consider the ways you are "capitalizing on reading and writing" rather than teaching reading and writing. The fact is that students need to read the texts in your discipline in order to learn the content you want to teach. When you want students to learn about polymers, for example, you might tell them the information, or you could ask students to read about polymers from their textbook. The beauty of reading (rather than listening) is that the student is in charge of the flow of information. Readers can speed up, slow down, or stop at any time. Readers can also look for additional information or look up the meaning of vocabulary words to help them derive meaning. Readers that already have a good working knowledge of the subject can read the text quickly. Readers for whom the subject is new might read more slowly. Reading is an important learning tool for students in your discipline.

Reading as a Sociocultural Activity

Reading is an important tool for your students because we rely on the printed word because so much of what we learn is through language. Reading and writing are complex cognitive processes whose development is facilitated by social interactions in cultural contexts. This sociocultural view of reading and writing implies that literacy learning is acquired and developed through purposeful transactions with texts in meaningful social groups. These transactions are literacy events from which the reader or writer can apply strategies that support independent processing (Almasi, 2003). On the surface, reading and writing may seem to be solitary acts, but in reality they are learned and practiced through social interactions. As students engage in reading and writing, they construct meaning in language-oriented situations (Wertsch, 1991). When students read, they rely on their backgrounds of language-rich situations for knowledge about the content of texts, ways texts are organized, vocabulary and concept knowledge, and intersecting texts; all of this knowledge about language is present as students read. In addition, language (and consequently reading and writing) is grounded in social interactions (Vygotsky, 1978).

Sociocultural views of reading also posit that learning and construction of meaning is contextual. Understanding reading from a sociocultural perspective involves viewing readers as constructing meaning within a specific social context (Bean, 2000; Bloome & Egan-Robertson, 1993). It also takes the teacher's perspective away from a deficit orientation (Vasuderon & Campano, 2009). From this perspective, schools and classrooms are contexts in which students develop reading competencies through interactions with language, instructional practices and settings, peers, and other features that constitute a learning environment. Comprehension of texts becomes a complex activity because it involves readers negotiating their background knowledge and the phonemic, syntactic, semantic, and pragmatic elements of a text as they construct an understanding of what they read. This complexity deepens as students move into secondary schools where there is a greater demand for content area reading that requires more sophisticated background knowledge and vocabulary. In short, learning content is impacted by language facility (Draper, Smith, Hall, & Siebert, 2005).

Transactional Theory of Reading

As students read informational texts, they need to approach them in a different manner than they do fictional texts. Readers need to take a specific stance toward texts when they read to learn. Rosenblatt (1978, 1994) theorized that readers read for different purposes, and as they read, they adopt a stance toward that text. The stance a reader could take varies across a continuum from efferent to aesthetic. When reading informational texts to learn, readers approach texts from an efferent stance. (In contrast, readers of fiction typically read from an aesthetic perspective.) According to transactional theory, whether or not readers approach informational texts from an efferent stance has an impact on the depth of their comprehension.

Teachers tend to spend much more time explaining to students how to read fictional texts from an aesthetic viewpoint than they do instructing students on ways to read informational texts (Ogle & Blachowicz, 2002). For example, elementary teachers spend a great deal of time teaching students how to read novels, explaining how to identify the plot, setting, theme, and characters. Many teachers also give students the opportunity to respond to the story through discussions and writing. However, few teachers help students approach informational texts, especially content area texts, from the efferent stance. Students are frequently left on their own to try to construct meaning as they read.

Informational texts, however, have had a renewed focus in the field of education. Educators now recognize that students need to be surrounded by informational texts at all levels of difficulty (Ivey & Fisher, 2006) and that students need the skills to read informational texts. The National Assessment of Educational Progress (NAEP) is reflecting this shift in priorities (American Institutes for Research, 2005). It has increased the percentage of informational passages that students need to read in order to reflect the kind of reading that secondary students do in schools and need to continue to do after they have completed their high school education.

Your Students: A Cultural Mix

The students in your class will likely be from a variety of cultures. Most middle and high school teachers may have a total of 150 or more students in the classes they teach. According to national averages, 105 of those students will have difficulty reading grade-level texts, 91 of the students will be white, 24 black, 24 Hispanic, 9 Asian/Pacific Islanders, and 2 Native American/Alaskan Native students. Of the 150 students, 54 will be poor enough to qualify for free or reduced-price lunches (NAEP, 2007).

Students from the majority culture come to school with what Bourdieu and Passeron (1977) have termed "cultural capital"; that is, these students possess culturally valued advantages as a result of family backgrounds or life experiences. Cultural capital is respected and reproduced in schooling, and in the United States, the cultural capital of the European-American middle class is given greater value in schools than the cultural capital of other groups, even in schools that have students predominantly from minority races (Banks & Banks, 2001).

Cultural capital influences and is influenced by school-based knowledges. Reading and writing, school-based knowledges, are cultural practices. These cultural practices can be considered a secondary discourse (Gee, 1993). To explain, most children acquire language, their primary discourse, through natural social interaction with adults (Holdaway, 1979). However, secondary discourses such as reading and writing in content areas may not be similar to a student's primary discourse and need to be learned in order for students to be successful in school. For example, students from the mainstream culture have had many more experiences with expository textual patterns than students from minority cultures; when students listen to adults talking, they hear information through a series of factual statements that are linked together. Conversely, students from some minority cultures have heard very few of these types of discussion patterns (Au, 1993).

Some students from minority cultures, therefore, may be unfamiliar with the discourse that predominates in schooling. Just as readers interpret reading tasks based on social and cultural influences, the decisions that teachers make about instruction are embedded in their cultural contexts. Gay (2000) states that teachers must make adaptations to cultural settings in order to be culturally responsive and, therefore, to begin to face the achievement gap between students in the majority culture and students in minority cultures. When students have not acquired the discourse of schools, they need instructional support and may need more explicit instruction in the discourse of schooling before they will become successful (e.g., Delpit, 1992). Instructional implementations, therefore, need to be studied in different cultural contexts and adapted to fit cultural needs.

Furthermore, many educators believe that classroom practices to which students from diverse cultural groups are exposed reflect mainstream cultural values. According to researchers on cultural diversity, students socialized into the major cultural groups share certain characteristics (Tyler et al., 2008). Although it would be a mistake to stereotype individual students from cultural groups, researchers suggest that teachers who have students from diverse groups organize their instruction so that it includes the characteristics of the groups represented in the classroom.

- Europeans: individualism, competition
- African American: communalism, movement, verve
- Asian American: collectivism, conformity to norms, emotional self-control, humility, family recognition through achievement, filial piety, and deference to authority
- Latino: collectivism, interconnectedness, spaciotemporal fluidity
- Native American: sharing and cooperation, noninterference, harmony with nature, present-time orientation, deep respect for elders

English Language Learners (ELLs)

Depending on where you teach, you will very likely have many ELLs in your classroom. Using national averages, of your 150 students, 59 will be ELLs. Some of your classes may be predominantly ELLs and others may have just a few. You may think that all ELLs are similar, but it's important to know that they can be a widely heterogeneous mix. Some ELLs may find themselves immersed in two languages and cultures simultaneously; others could be in contact primarily with their new language and culture. You could have some newcomers to your school, or the families of the ELLs could have been in the United States for generations. The important thing for you to remember is that all of your ELLs will need support to develop academic competence.

Academic competence is a term used for the knowledge and skills students need to find success in school (Fillmore, 2005). You will be introducing your students to the academic language of your discipline. Learning an academic language is different from learning a first language. If you have seen infants learning language, you know that exposing them to the words and syntax of the language with scaffolded repetitions is pretty much all babies need. Unlike the process of learning a first language, students learning the academic language in your discipline will need more explicit instruction (Ehlers-Zavala, 2008). Although none of your students will be native speakers of your specific academic language, ELLs will need extra instruction in some of the text and sentence structures used in your discipline. (See Chapter 6 for informational text structures.)

According to ELL experts, it may take students five to 10 years to acquire academic language proficiency (Cummins, 1979). This may surprise you because some of your students will seem to be able to speak excellent English. Most ELLs acquire basic interpersonal communicative skills (BICS) in the first few years they are in the country. Students who have acquired BICS will be able to talk with their peers, contribute to class discussion, and even read at a basic level. Being able to communicate in English, however, doesn't mean that the student has acquired cognitive academic language proficiency (CALP). It typically takes years for ELLs to develop the background in academic languages to be able to read and write in your discipline (Cummins, 1979).

There are several theoretical approaches that describe how students learn academic language. We espouse the critical socioliterate approach in which learners are engaged in understanding the culture in which texts are written and read (Johns, 1997). In this case, we believe that the culture is based on your discipline. Academic vocabulary and language are specific to each discipline. For example, those of you who are language arts teachers talk with students about foreshadowing, theme, mood, and symbolism. In this case, your students, especially the ELLs, need to understand the culture of a reader and writer. These terms will probably not be prominent in science, social studies, and mathematics, and the culture of the discipline also will be different. Furthermore, using the critical socioliterate approach as a foundation, you will be teaching students how to interrogate the language and practices of your discipline. These ideas are compatible with Freire's idea that learners need to develop literacy to "read the world." (See Chapter 7 for details about Reading Critically.)

Using the critical socioliterate approach as a foundation, you can help students develop the domain knowledge necessary to be academically competent. As you develop specific lessons, Watkings and Lindahl (2010) recommend that you ask yourselves the following questions.

- What **background knowledge** do my students already have? What background knowledge do my students need?
- How can I increase my students' **motivation and interest** to exert effort in comprehending the text?
- What are the reading abilities of my students? What parts of the text will cause them the most difficulty or challenges? How can I fill in those gaps to aid **reading comprehension**?
- How can I adapt or modify the activities/texts to help my students **access the information and read for comprehension**? What scaffolding or support can I provide during reading?
- What **vocabulary** do my students need to be able to comprehend the text, access the content, or complete the planned activities/assignments?
- How can I provide my students with opportunities to develop **oral fluency** while discussing content?
- How can I facilitate my students' responses to text through **writing** as they are learning to compose in English?

Struggling Readers

As stated earlier, NAEP data indicate that a great number of your students could be considered struggling readers. The term "struggling readers" is an artifact of schooling and is often defined as students who have difficulty with school-based reading (Franzak, 2006). According to Lenski (2008), there are many reasons why students have trouble reading the texts in your discipline.

- Students may not be able to read academic writing.
- Students may have a special learning need.
- Students may have had limited prior instruction in reading in your discipline.
- Students may be reading texts that are too difficult and complex for their ability.
- Students may not be motivated to read.
- Students may be feeling the effects of poverty.

Teaching reading and thinking strategies can help students who are unfamiliar with school discourse. Edmonds and colleagues (2009) did a meta-analysis of research on interventional studies and found that although some students may need to improve their ability to decode words, they need more focused attention on reading comprehension and strategy learning. Some students, however, will still have a difficult time reading textbooks even with the assistance of these strategies. When students have difficulty reading, they are at-risk for school failure and for losing interest in school (Smith & Wilhelm, 2006).

Text Complexity

Texts are written with varying degrees of difficulty. Consider the following sentence from a chemistry book: "An electron carries exactly one unit of negative charge and its mass is 1/1840 the mass of a hydrogen atom." Note the length of the sentence, the vocabulary, and the density of concepts. These are some of the factors that can have an impact on the difficulty of a text.

According to the Common Core Standards (http://www.corestandards.org/), students should be able to read increasingly complex texts through their school years. To determine the level of text complexity, the Common Core Standards (Appendix A in the CCS) suggest that teachers combine three measures to figure out a reading level.

The first part to determining text complexity is a quantitative measure. One of the ways to get a quantitative measure is through a readability formula. The first readability formula was published in 1923 (Klare, 1963). Since that time, over 100 readability formulas have been published. A few of the more popular formulas include the Dale-Chall, Spache, Flesch, and Fry readability formulas. Most readability formulas use sentence and word length to determine a reading level, such as 9.2 (ninth grade, second month). Many computers have readability formulas in their word processing programs.

The second part of determining text complexity is a qualitative measure. The qualitative dimensions refer to the following aspects of a text.

- Whether the text has single or multiple levels of meaning
- Whether the purpose is explicitly stated or implicit
- Whether the text structure is simple or complex
- Whether the language is 1) literal, clear, contemporary, conversational; or 2) figurative, ambiguous, archaic; or 3) domain-specific
- Whether the themes are simple or sophisticated
- Whether there are single or multiple perspectives
- Whether the text's perspectives are like the reader's or different
- Whether the genre structures are familiar
- Whether there is low or high intertextuality

The third dimension of text complexity is reader considerations. Reader variables can include reading level, motivation, background knowledge, interests, engagement, intellectual abilities, and topic familiarity.

Using three measures of text complexity is not new for teachers. They have done this automatically to help decide which texts are appropriate for their students. Before the Common Core Standards were introduced in 2010, however, it was customary for teachers and curriculum directors to only pay attention to quantitative measures, such as reading levels measured by readability formulas and Lexile measures. Now we recommend that you use all three measures to determine whether a text is appropriate for your classroom instruction.

Lexile Framework for Reading

Some states have adopted an alternative method of determining a text's quantitative reading level called the Lexile Framework. Lexiles are an educational tool that give a readability measure to a piece of text. Lexiles are determined by a formula that addresses syntactic complexity such as the number of words per sentence and semantic difficulty, such as the frequency of the words in the text. Lexiles do not address reader variables such as interest and age appropriateness or text variables such as text support or text quality. Lexile scores range from 200–1700. Books are given scores on a 10-point interval, such as 410, 420, 430, and so on. Examples of the Lexile scores for benchmark books follow.

Title	Lexile Score
Danny and the Dinosaur	200
Clifford's Manners	300
Frog and Toad are Friends	400
The Magic School Bus Inside the Earth	500
A Baby Sister for Frances	600
Bunnicula: A Rabbit Tale of Mystery	700
The Adventures of Pinocchio	800
Tom Swift in the Land of Wonders	900
Black Beauty	1000
Pride and Prejudice	1100
War and Peace	1200
Brown vs. Board of Education 1954	1300
The Scarlet Letter	1400
On Ancient Medicine	1500
Fundamental Principles of the Metaphysics of Morals	1600
Discourse on the Method and Meditations of First Philosophy	1700

According to the Lexile website http://www.lexile.com/, Lexile scores can be used to determine whether students are reading at their grade level. The Lexile Framework indicates that students in first grade should read in the 200–400 range, students in the second grade should read in the 300–500 range, and so on. All of the major norm referenced tests are linked to Lexiles, so students are also given a Lexile range in which they should be able to read independently. Once students are given a Lexile score, they can be matched with books that have a Lexile score attached. At the time of this writing, more than 50,000 books and 70 million articles have been given a Lexile score. The Lexile website includes a Lexile calculator that can determine the Lexile score for a given book. Nine states have adopted the Lexile Framework so far. For more information about the Lexile Framework for Reading, consult the website.

SURF THE WEB
LEXILE FRAMEWORK
Describes the Lexile Framework and links to a database of books with Lexile scores.
http://www.lexile.com/

Contexts of Instruction

The purpose of this book is to provide specific recommendations for reading and learning strategies to use in different classroom contexts. Experts in the field of adolescent literacy suggest that, at the bare minimum, middle and high school teachers should possess a working knowledge of

- how literacy demands change with age and grade,
- how students vary in literacy strengths and needs,
- how texts in a given content area raise specific literacy challenges,
- how to recognize and address literacy difficulties, and
- how to adapt and develop teaching skills over time (Carnegie Council on Advancing Adolescent Literacy, 2010, p. 20).

Among the teaching skills you need to know are strategies that have a moderate to strong research base (Kamil et al., 2008) such as vocabulary and comprehension instruction and increased motivation and engagement. In addition, having an understanding of how to use content area strategies is helpful.

Content Area Strategies

When students read and write, they use strategies either to make sense of texts while reading or to produce texts while writing. A strategy is a sequence of cognitive steps to accomplish a specific goal (Snow & Moje, 2010). Even though all students use strategies to some extent, students who experience difficulty with reading and writing apply strategies differently than do good readers and writers. Proficient readers and writers selectively and flexibly apply a vast array of strategies to every reading or writing event (Pressley, 1995). In contrast, students who are experiencing difficulty with reading and writing typically use fewer strategies and their strategy use tends to be rigid rather than flexible. The judicious, flexible use of strategies when reading and writing, therefore, is a prime characteristic of expert readers and writers and should be an instructional goal for every teacher.

Comprehension strategies can be defined as "specific, learned procedures that foster active, competent, self-regulated, and intentional reading" (Trabasso & Bouchard, 2002, p. 177). Although some readers "figure out" strategies for themselves, most students need to be taught reading strategies explicitly because they are much more likely to learn how to be strategic readers with instruction (Trabasso & Bouchard, 2002). Reading and writing strategies can be acquired intuitively from experience or can be learned deliberately through instructional interventions (Lenski & Nierstheimer, 2002).

For instructional interventions to be effective, teachers need to model the strategies in authentic situations (Duffy, 2002). For this type of instruction to occur, teachers need to know that reading is an interaction between the reader, the text, and the activity, and they need to know how to select appropriate strategies to facilitate comprehension. Unfortunately, most secondary teachers have not had training in teaching reading strategies, nor can we assume that teachers who have been taught strategies in preservice programs automatically use them in their classrooms (Jackson & Davis, 2000; Nourie & Lenski, 1998). Also, the teachers who teach strategies tend to design strategy lessons using traditional teacher-centered instruction (Stevens, 2001).

Content area teachers do not need to be teachers of reading to use strategies in their teaching (Fisher & Ivey, 2005). When secondary teachers develop lessons that use the reading, thinking, and studying strategies that are detailed in this book, for example, they are helping students use the kinds of literacy strategies that make texts accessible. As students continue to use these strategies, they begin to internalize strategic processes and use them independently.

In order for students to become independent strategy users, Langer (2002, 2004) suggests that teachers explicitly state the goal of the strategy. For example, if you want students to develop a general understanding of texts, you could have students use the strategy Think, Predict, Read, Connect (TPRC) as they read. As you model the strategy, explaining *why* you've selected it, you help students understand how the strategy can be used to further their own knowledge and literacy. Telling students the goal for using the strategy is the first step to having students become strategic readers in your content area and in creating a culture of literacy in your classroom (National Association of Secondary School Principals, 2005).

Contexts for Assessment

You will learn about assessment in many different contexts. For the purpose of this book, we'd like you to think about how to assess the literacy goals that we've listed on the inside cover of the book. When you are teaching, you will organize instruction so that you are addressing the content standards in your discipline. We'd like you also to consider addressing literacy standards for content areas. You can find them through professional organizations (e.g., National Council for the Social Studies), from your state's standards, and also from this book. We have identified the kinds of literacy goals that you can integrate with your content standards.

Most of the time you will want to conduct formative assessments of the goals. The purpose of formative assessment is to provide detailed achievement information that teachers and students can use to improve learning. According to the National Institute for Literacy (2007), the most common kind of formative assessment you will use is classroom questioning. We have provided many other ideas of formative assessment throughout this book.

Other types of assessment include summative and performance assessment (Roe, Stoodt-Hill, & Burns, 2011). Summative assessment is frequently used to show levels of performance for the purposes of grading, accountability, and comparisons of schools, and is typically administered at the end of a teaching cycle. These kinds of assessments might include unit tests in your content area or a standardized test of reading. You can gain a sense of how much students have achieved through summative assessments. Additionally, standardized reading tests yield information on your students' ability to read grade-level material (Morsy, Kieffer, & Snow, 2010).

A third type of assessment is a performance assessment. Performance assessments measure how well a student can complete a task. Brookhart (2010) states that many teacher-made tests measure mostly students' recall of material. According to Pinkus (2009), performance assessments are much more likely to assess higher-level thinking. Some states use performance assessments as state tests. Some of the examples we share in this book could be considered performance assessments.

As a teacher, you will be conducting ongoing assessment of your students' learning and of their literacy progress. We encourage you to make assessment a part of your teaching routine and to use the assessments to inform your instruction.

Conclusion

You are an important part of your students' lives, not only as their content area teacher but also as a disciplinary expert that models how literacy is used in your subject. You can show your students how to use literacy as a tool for learning your content by using the goals and strategies in this book. As you do, your students will learn more and will become better able to read and write in your discipline.

Activities *and* Journal Entries *for* Teacher Educators

Activities

1. Divide the class into content area groups. Have the students identify several texts that they use in their classroom. Have them determine text complexity based on quantitative, qualitative, and reader considerations. Then ask students to decide if the texts are appropriate for their students.

2. Look at the goal statements in the inside cover of this book. Copy them and cut them into strips with one statement on each strip. Have students in disciplinary groups prioritize the goal statements as they are needed in their content area.

3. Have students brainstorm ideas for assessment that they have seen in schools or have read about from other sources. Have them identify whether the assessments are primarily summative or formative.

Journal Entries

1. How did you become interested in your content area? Why did you decide to become an expert in this area?

2. Think about all of the ways scientists (replace with your discipline) need literacy to learn. Develop a scenario of a scientist accomplishing work without literacy.

3. How do you use literacy strategies in your learning?

2 Fostering Motivation and Reading Engagement

Learning Goals

The reader of this chapter will:

- Understand the theories and research on motivation
- Understand how reading motivation relates to engagement
- Understand the importance of reading motivation and engagement in the disciplines
- Recognize the importance of student choice in the disciplines
- Learn instructional strategies that foster motivation and engagement

Questions to Consider

1. What are the theories and research on motivation that relate to your discipline?
2. What is the connection between reading motivation and reading engagement?
3. Why is it critical to consider student motivation for reading?
4. How can you address reading motivation and engagement in your discipline?
5. How is student choice relevant to your discipline?

OVERVIEW

Fostering motivation continues to be one of the most pressing challenges for content area teachers. Motivation and engagement play a principal role in students' ability to comprehend text (Biancarosa & Snow, 2006; Kamil, 2003; Wigfield, 2004). However, students' motivation to engage in reading for school-related tasks declines as they transition to higher grades (Guthrie & Knowles, 2001; Guthrie & Wigfield, 2000; Unrau & Schlackman, 2006). Struggling readers start to disengage from reading and competent readers begin to dislike reading school textbooks (O'Brien & Dillon, 2008). Many students avoid reading and rely on teachers' lectures, class notes, or discussions to learn the course content. Teachers, however, are well positioned to influence and support student motivation (Wigfield, 2004).

According to a panel of literacy leaders, motivation and engagement are important issues in literacy (Cassidy, Valadez, Garrett, & Barrera, 2010). While not rated as a "hot topic," 75% of the surveyed panelists agreed that motivation and engagement should be a "hot" topic or priority. While motivation and engagement are related and often discussed in tandem, they are not synonymous. Motivation is a precursor to engagement (Meltzer & Hamann, 2004). When students are motivated to read, they are willing to engage in reading tasks and construct meaning from text. As a content area teacher, you also need to consider motivation as a critical component of your content area instruction.

Literacy experts note the importance of motivation in recent reports and guides about adolescent literacy. Motivation was identified as an essential element for improving middle and high school literacy achievement in *Reading Next—A Vision for Action and Research in Middle and High School Literacy* (Biancarosa & Snow, 2006). "Motivation and self-directed learning, which includes building motivation to read and learn and providing students with the instruction and supports needed for independent learning tasks they will face after graduation" (p. 4). Similarly, increasing student motivation and engagement in literacy learning is one of five recommendations advanced in *Improving Adolescent Literacy: Effective Classroom and Intervention Practices: A Practice Guide* (Kamil, Borman, Dole, Kral, Salinger, & Torgesen, 2008).

> To foster improvement in adolescent literacy, teachers should use strategies to enhance students' motivation to read and engagement in the learning process. Teachers should help students build confidence in their ability to comprehend and learn from content area texts. They should provide a supportive environment that views mistakes as growth opportunities, encourages self-determination, and provides informational feedback about the usefulness of reading strategies and how the strategies can be modified to fit various tasks. Teachers should also make literacy experiences more relevant to students' interests, everyday life, or important current events. (p. 26)

In both of these documents, the experts based their conclusions and recommendations on the salient research in adolescent literacy.

After reviewing numerous research studies on motivation, Edmunds and Bauserman (2006) reported that student motivation is an important concern for teachers; moreover, a "lack of motivation is at the root of many of the problems they face in teaching" (p. 414). Reading motivation also has ramifications for developing lifelong readers. Research by Wang and Guthrie (2004) revealed that students who spend more time reading are better readers than students who spend little time reading. They are also more likely to become lifelong readers. Additionally, motivation is significant for reading comprehension (Wang & Guthrie, 2004) and reading achievement (Unrau & Schlackman, 2006).

Researchers often focus their attention on intrinsic (internal) and extrinsic (external) motivation. Ryan and Deci (2000) defined intrinsic motivation as "the doing of an activity for its inherent satisfactions rather than for some separable consequence" (p. 56). In other words, intrinsic motivation involves engaging in a task for the enjoyment of the task itself. While intrinsic motivation is an important and pervasive form of motivation among humans, it also becomes weaker as students progress through the grades. In contrast, extrinsic motivation is doing an activity "in order to attain some separable outcome" (p. 60). Simply stated, extrinsic motivation involves engaging in a task for rewards associated with the task. In schools, these external rewards may take the form of grades, goal attainment, and recognition. School-based educational activities, according to Ryan and Deci, have not been designed to be intrinsically motivating. For this reason, teachers must find ways to motivate students to value and complete the activities on their own.

In terms of reading motivation, students who are internally motivated read because they find reading itself rewarding. Reading may help students to satisfy their own interests, curiosity, or quest for challenge or competence. These satisfactions often lead students to invest more time in reading. On the other hand, students oriented toward extrinsic motivation engage in reading to receive a reward. Some reading incentive programs use external motivation in an attempt to stimulate students' engagement in reading for personal satisfaction. When the primary motivator is external, interest and curiosity do not play much of a role in reading. Instead, students read for recognition, grades, competition, or compliance with external demands rather than enjoyment of reading. Some teachers try to prompt students' internal motivation by using external sources of motivation (e.g., incentives for reading a certain number of books, accumulating points to exchange for prizes or purchases). However, researchers suggest that intrinsic motivation rather than extrinsic motivation results in long-term engagement and deeper learning (Guthrie & Knowles, 2001; Wigfield, 2004). If students are to become lifelong readers and learners, they need to find reading to be internally rewarding.

Reading motivation is multifaceted. In a recent study, Guthrie and colleagues (2007) investigated motivational constructs as well as text genres, specific and general context, and self and outside sources of motivation. Motivational constructs include

1. interest regarding the students' personal investment;
2. perceived control referring to students' choices and decisions about reading;
3. collaboration involving interactions among peers;
4. involvement entailing students' immersion and experiences with reading; and
5. self-efficacy as a student's belief in his or her ability to perform a task.

These constructs, also known as students' internal motivations, are well documented in the research literature and central to reading engagement.

In their study of adolescents' reading engagement, Hughes-Hassell and Rodge (2007) examined aspects of urban youths' leisure reading. They found that 72% of the students engaged in reading as a leisure activity. Reasons for reading in their spare time included

1. fun and relaxation,
2. to learn new things, and
3. because they were bored.

Based on the findings, Hughes-Hassell and Rodge offered several recommendations for teachers and librarians.

- Provide the types of reading materials students prefer.
- Respect students' culture and heritage.
- Talk to students.
- Give students time during the school day to read.
- Provide adequate funds for school and classroom libraries in low-income urban communities.
- Be passionate about your love of reading.

While content area teachers may not be empowered to provide funds for classroom libraries, they are well positioned to champion the other recommendations for their adolescent students.

The way in which lessons are structured and presented can help to motivate and engage readers. The kinds of solutions needed to enhance student motivation and engagement must go "beyond the technical domain (e.g., the content standards curriculum) and organizational domain (e.g., management structures, decision-making strategies, and policies) to focus on the personal domain (e.g., beliefs, assumptions, interpersonal relationships)" (McCombs & Barton, 2001, p. 77).

Teachers can help students become motivated and engaged by creating interest in content area topics (Schiefele, 1992; Schraw, Bruning, & Svoboda, 1995), promoting positive attitudes, arousing curiosity for areas of study, providing a wide range of materials at an appropriate level of difficulty (Johns, 2008), offering choice, and encouraging collaboration. At the heart of motivation and engagement there should be an extensive variety of reading materials used for instruction. These materials should include, but are not limited to, texts, newspapers, magazines, reference materials, electronic databases, websites, and literary works. It is imperative that teachers do not rely solely on textbooks and whole class literature for reading, because these may not address the array of students' interests (Pitcher et al., 2007). Instead, teachers must consider students' preferences when selecting reading materials. One way to help estimate the difficulty of instructional materials is to use readability formulas or the Lexile Framework (see www.lexile.com).

The strategies in this chapter offer ways for content area teachers to use class materials to help foster motivation and promote reading engagement by capitalizing on active student involvement, personal response, social collaboration, and peer interactions. The overarching goal of motivation is more effective student learning.

Creating Interest

GOAL

To help students develop an interest in a topic

BACKGROUND

Developing students' interest in a topic is critically important for content area teachers. Based on germane research literature, Hidi and Renninger (2006) theorized a four-stage model for the development and deepening of learner interest. During *triggered situational interest*, the first phase, interest is elicited by short-term changes in environment or text features that build a connection to the content. Interest may be triggered by "incongruous, surprising information; character identification or personal relevance; and intensity" (p. 114). In the second phase, *maintained situational interest*, focused attention is sustained over a period of time. Interest persists due to the "meaningfulness of tasks and/or personal involvement" (p. 114) which are typical in project-based learning or collaborative group work. In the *emerging individual interest* phase, the learner begins to seek reengagement with the content. This third phase is when the learner starts to "regularly generate his or her own 'curiosity' questions" about the content (p. 115). In the fourth phase, *well-developed individual interest*, the learner prolongs his or her interest and values reengagement with the content over time. Hidi and Renninger's model has implications for content area teachers. They concluded that teachers can "(a) help students sustain attention for tasks even when tasks are challenging . . .; (b) provide opportunities for students to ask curiosity questions; and (c) select or create resources that promote problem solving and strategy generation" (p. 121).

Because adolescents are expected to learn new words, facts, and ideas from reading as well as to summarize, interpret, and critique their text (Carnegie Council on Advancing Adolescent Literacy, 2010), teachers must provide opportunities for engagement with discipline-specific texts. "One crucial element in getting students to read with greater focus is to create interest in the reading material" (Curran & Smith, 2005, p. 186). When content area teachers capitalize on their students' interests, they tend to be motivated to learn more about a topic, have improved attitudes toward a topic, and show increased levels of reading engagement. While adolescent students may be capable readers, they may choose not to read their textbooks or other content-specific text. Teachers can increase the extent of their involvement with text by focusing on their students' interests. One way to improve student attitudes and create interest simultaneously is by personalizing the content. Such personalization sends a message to students that learning is related to their world. The challenge is to tap into students' existing knowledge about a topic and arouse their interest in the topic. Students who are interested in a particular topic are more likely to be motivated to seek additional information about the topic. The following strategies are designed to develop students' interest in a topic.

Section **2.1** INSTRUCTIONAL STRATEGY 1

Anticipation Guide

The purpose of an Anticipation Guide (Herber, 1978) is to activate students' thoughts and opinions about a topic and to link their prior knowledge to the new material. Because Anticipation Guides are flexible strategies, they can be used effectively with any content area text as well as with nonprint media such as videos. Anticipation Guides provide an excellent springboard for class discussion and lead students into their reading or viewing with a sense of curiosity about the topic. Although an Anticipation Guide can be completed individually, assigning it to a small group promotes the collaborative aspect of learning.

Directions

1. Identify the major concepts that you want your students to learn from text materials and think about what your students may already know or believe to be true about the topic. For example, when beginning a chapter on pollution in your science text, think about your students' existing knowledge related to pollution and about the concepts you want them to learn from the text. You might consider the following aspects of the chapter to be important.

   The implication of human activities on the environment;
   The major types of pollution and their impact on human health; and
   The effects of acid rain on people, plants, water, and materials.

2. Create a series of statements relating to the major concepts of the chapter or text. The most effective statements are those about which students have some knowledge but do not have complete understanding. Write the statements where they can be seen by the entire class and present the Anticipation Guide as in the following example.

   _____ 1. Because of water pollution, some fish do not have enough oxygen to survive.
   _____ 2. Most pollution is caused by legal, everyday activities such as brushing your teeth.
   _____ 3. The coal producing factories in the Midwest are responsible for much of the acid rain.
   _____ 4. Every year more than 40,000 people in the United States die from diseases related to air pollution.

3. Explain to students that they are about to read a new section of text. Then say the following.

   Before you read the text, I want you to respond to a series of statements based on the text material. As you read the statements, put a check mark next to those that you believe to be true or with which you agree.

4. After students have completed the Anticipation Guide, proceed with class discussion. Urge students to share their opinions about the validity of the statements based on their prior knowledge.

5. Have students read the text selection. Return to the Anticipation Guide after reading, and revisit the statements. Have students discuss the statements in small groups or with the entire class. Students should be encouraged to correct any statements that were initially incorrect.

SECTION 2.1

CHAPTER 2

web resources

Anticipation Guide
   Reproducible, 1
Consumer Education Example, 2
Driver's Education Example, 3
Health Example, 4
Social Studies Example, 5

Readers Needing Additional Support

> Carefully select the words used for the statements to help ensure that students will be able to read the statements. You might also read the statements aloud to the class before students respond independently.

SURF THE WEB

LESSON USING AN ANTICIPATION GUIDE
Offers an instructional plan and multiday lesson using an Anticipation Guide that can be adapted for older students. After using an Anticipation Guide, students are invited to create an Anticipation Guide and share it with a partner.
www.readwritethink.org/lessons/lesson_view.asp?id=226

People Search

People Search (Hemmrich, Lim, & Neel, 1994) is a strategy designed to promote collaboration among the students in your classroom. It uses an interview technique for implementation and creates interest in a topic as it increases students' motivation to learn more about a topic. Additionally, it supports social interaction and helps foster positive attitudes toward learning. This interaction among students is a source of enjoyment and is an excellent way to introduce a new unit of study. It has also been used effectively as a way of reviewing concepts developed during a topic of study.

Directions

1. Decide on the topic or theme of your People Search. This strategy can be implemented as a way of introducing a new course, as the beginning of a unit, as an introduction to a new chapter of study, or as a review technique.

2. Prepare 10 to 20 relevant statements or questions about the topic. If you are introducing a new subject to your students, your statements might be more general. For example, if you are beginning a study of the United States government, you might use the following statement.

     Find someone who . . .
     can name the vice president of the United States.

   If, however, you are continuing a unit of study about the United States government, your statements might be more specific. An example of this type of statement follows.

     Find someone who . . .
     can name the main job of the vice president.

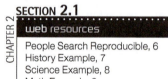

SECTION 2.1

web resources

CHAPTER 2

People Search Reproducible, 6
History Example, 7
Science Example, 8
Math Example, 9
Music Example, 10

3. Write the statements on the People Search reproducible, duplicate it, and distribute a copy to each student.

4. Have students walk around the room and interview their classmates to find someone who can answer the questions or perform the required tasks.
   Tell them that once someone has answered a question or responded to a statement in the appropriate space, they are to ask the person to sign his or her name next to the answer. Remind them that they must have as many different signatures as possible.

5. Set a time limit of 10 to 15 minutes for completion of the People Search.

6. Have students share the success of their People Search at the end of the allotted time as a whole class activity or in small groups.

7. The example on the following page is based on a geography text.

Geography

People Search

Find someone who ...   Name

1. knows the name of an economic system in which businesses and factories
    are owned by individuals.

    _____

2. knows to which nation most of Canada's exports go.

    _____

3. can name the three major river systems of Latin America.

    _____

4. knows the country of the *mestizos.*

    _____

5. can identify Pablo Neruda's "claim to fame."

    _____

EXAMPLE

Readers Needing Additional Support

Before students begin their People Search, read the statements aloud or have partners read the statements together to possibly find one statement each can sign for his or her partner.

Section **2.1** INSTRUCTIONAL STRATEGY 3

Problematic Situation

Mathison (1989) suggests that asking students to solve a paradox or a problem is one of the primary elements in sparking students' interest about a topic. A Problematic Situation (Vacca & Vacca, 2002) promotes lively classroom discussions as it compels students to delve into their prior experiences and share their knowledge with their classmates, thus increasing their interest in a topic and promoting collaboration. As teachers, you can design problematic situations specifically related to a particular text or other reading material. By creating a problem to be solved, you can develop an exciting and imaginative introduction to text material. This particular strategy provides an avenue for arousing students' natural curiosity and prepares them for texts in which a problem/solution scenario exists or can be developed by the teacher.

Directions

1. Identify a topic from your content area about which you can develop a problematic situation for students to analyze. Prepare a short paragraph describing the problem or use the example from a geography text that follows.

2. Place students into mixed ability groups and read the problematic situation to them. Then present a written copy of the problem to each group of students. This may be done by distributing copies of the reproducible on the website with the Problematic Situation on it or by writing the problem where it can be seen by the entire class. An example of a problem follows.

    A revolution or a coup against the Perons is developing. You have been asked to join the effort to overthrow the Perons, whom you have come to believe are corrupt. What will you do? Will you continue to live as you are, knowing that some of your money is being misused? Or will you become part of the revolt that is brewing? Upon what will you base your decision? How will it impact your family? What will happen if you decide not to join the revolt and the revolution is successful?

3. Instruct students, within their groups, to generate possible solutions to the problem. Tell them to imagine that they are the persons facing the dilemma in the problematic situation. Be sure to provide them with

enough information so that they will focus their attention on the key concepts within the text as they discuss and develop their solutions. One possible solution follows.

> I think I'll take my family and leave the country. I can't stand living where dishonest people rule. I want my family to be safe and my children to grow up in an environment that gives them good values.

4. Have each group record all of their responses on the Problematic Situation reproducible as they discuss them. As students make their lists, encourage them to discuss the merits and difficulties of each presented solution, as in the following example.

> Leaving the country is not going to be easy. Where will we go? How will we get extra money for travel?

5. Encourage whole class sharing of the solutions after the small groups have completed their assigned task. After completing a Problematic Situation, students are ready to read their texts and supplement their existing information with additional material.

6. Ask students to read the text passage, looking for information that supports their solutions during reading. Encourage students to modify their proposed solutions if they discover new information that influences their original decisions.

7. Have the class discuss the merits of each group's revised solutions.

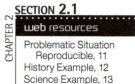

SECTION 2.1

CHAPTER 2

web resources

Problematic Situation
  Reproducible, 11
History Example, 12
Science Example, 13

Geography

Problematic Situation

The year is 1946 and you are a citizen of Argentina. Your country is ruled by a dictator whose name is Juan Peron. He has maintained power by creating labor unions, schools, and new industries. His wife, Eva Peron, has helped him by encouraging workers to give money to the government's programs. However, with his power as a dictator, Peron has taken control of the press, businesses, labor unions, and the army. Sometimes people are arrested and killed without cause. If people are seen as enemies of the government, they frequently "disappear." Some opposition to the Perons is developing. People you know have reason to believe that the Perons are stealing money that the workers have given to the government. But life is better than it used to be. Although you are poor, you're not as poor as you once were because you have a job.

What Will You Do?

Problem(s)	Solutions/Questions/Concerns
1. *A possible revolution is developing.*	*Will I stay? Will I leave?* *Will I become part of the revolution?*
2. *Life will be unstable.*	*If I leave, how will I get extra money for travel? Perhaps I'll contact a relative outside the country. I must make plans fairly*
3.	*quickly.*

EXAMPLE

Consider placing a variety of readers who struggle in the same group. Join their group and help guide the process by asking questions and encouraging students to elaborate their ideas about the problem(s).

Section **2.1** INSTRUCTIONAL STRATEGY 4

Predict-O-Gram

A Predict-O-Gram (Blachowicz, 1986) can be used to create interest in a narrative, introduce vocabulary, and motivate students to make predictions about a narrative using five story elements (i.e., character, setting, problem, action, solution) as categories. Students write each vocabulary word in one of the categories listed on the Predict-O-Gram. At the conclusion of their reading, students revisit their predictions about the vocabulary words and make necessary changes to reflect the selection read.

Directions

1. Prior to introducing the Predict-O-Gram, select 12 to 15 words from a story that are new to students. The words should relate to the setting, characters, actions, goal or problem, and solution or resolution. Make a copy of the Predict-O-Gram reproducible found on the website.

2. Place the title of the selection at the top of the reproducible and write the words you selected on the lines. The particular words you select will help determine the difficulty of completing the Predict-O-Gram. Duplicate sufficient copies for your students and distribute them. An example of words selected for "Silent World" is listed below.

Kamal	pantomimed	deaf
allergic	woods	hiking
finger spelling	brush	poison oak
gesture	Caroline	communicate
Mr. Soong	anger	

3. Introduce the Predict-O-Gram by highlighting and reviewing the basic story elements in the chart. Invite students to predict what will happen in the story by placing words on the lines in the most appropriate part of the chart. For example, the proper noun *Kamal* might be placed in the *Setting*, *Characters*, or even *Goal* or *Problem*. Students can work individually, with a partner, or in a small group to complete the Predict-O-Gram.

4. Have students share their predictions for the story. Expect and encourage a variety of predictions. In addition, there will probably be some common predictions. Write their predictions where they can be seen by the entire class to help students see the range of predictions and diversity of thinking. Some possible predictions for "Silent World" are listed below.

   The story takes place in the <u>woods</u> of <u>Kamal</u>.
   <u>Kamal</u> is <u>deaf</u>, so he or she uses <u>finger spelling</u> to <u>communicate</u>.
   <u>Mr. Soong</u> is <u>hiking</u> in the <u>woods</u> and gets into <u>poison oak</u> in the <u>brush</u>.

5. Following sufficient discussion, invite students to read the story. Remind them to keep their predictions in mind.

6. After the story has been read, tell students to revisit their Predict-O-Gram and use arrows to move words to a more appropriate category in the Predict-O-Gram. Encourage small group and whole class discussions.

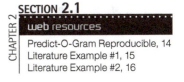

SECTION 2.1
web resources
Predict-O-Gram Reproducible, 14
Literature Example #1, 15
Literature Example #2, 16

7. Use a blank Predict-O-Gram to help students plan and structure a short story. Words can be written in the various categories and crossed off as they are used to draft the story.

Readers Needing Additional Support

When introducing the words, be sure students understand their meanings. After students have placed the words on the Predict-O-Gram, invite initial predictions from students who are English learners and/or students who struggle in reading.

Section **2.1** INSTRUCTIONAL STRATEGY 5

That Was Then . . . This Is Now

That Was Then . . . This Is Now (McLaughlin & Allen, 2002) is a strategy that requires students to sketch and label what they know about a topic before and after reading a text. Students record their images and a summary statement on the That Was Then side prior to reading the text, thereby creating an interest in the topic and establishing a purpose for reading. After the reading is completed, students sketch and summarize the information from the text on the This Is Now side of the reproducible.

Directions

1. Duplicate the That Was Then . . . This Is Now reproducible found on the website and distribute a copy to each student.

2. Identify a topic that you will be teaching in your content area. Introduce the topic to students. In this example for middle school social studies, the contributions and legacy of ancient Greece provide the basis for the students' reading. Engage students in discussion to activate their background knowledge.

3. On the That Was Then side of the sheet, have students sketch some of the things we have as a result of the ancient Greek civilization. Initially, students might recall and draw images related to the Olympics or Greek mythology.

4. Direct students to write a summary statement after completing their sketches on the That Was Then side. A sample summary statement might read, "The Olympic games were started by the Greeks. The Greeks also wrote stories about the Greek gods and goddesses like Zeus and Athena."

5. Have students read the appropriate text selection. Encourage them to create mental images as they read about the contributions of ancient Greece.

6. Tell students to develop a sketch on the This Is Now side. The new sketch should be related to the information conveyed in the text. For this social studies text selection, students might now include images related to *The Iliad* and *The Odyssey* by Homer, theater with its comedies and tragedies, philosophy, and/or sculpture.

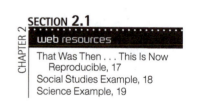

SECTION 2.1

CHAPTER 2

web resources

That Was Then . . . This Is Now
  Reproducible, 17
Social Studies Example, 18
Science Example, 19

7. Have students write summary statements reflecting the information contained in their This is Now sketches.

8. Have students compare and contrast their before- and after-reading sketches in small groups or with a partner. Students can also share their summaries. A social studies example is shown on the following page.

Social Studies

That Was Then . . . This Is Now

That was then . . .

Summary The Olympic games were started by the Greeks. The Greeks also wrote stories about the Greek gods and goddesses.

This is now . . .

Summary Greece contributed to many fields: theater, literature, philosophy (Socrates), and architecture.

Assessing Student Learning

Take a Three-Minute Pulse

Goal: *To help students develop an interest in a topic.*   Developing and sustaining student interest in content area topics can be challenging. To help students develop interest in a topic, you can use questioning strategies to prompt higher-level thinking (Marzano & Pickering, 1997) and personalization. You can also use questioning strategies as an informal type of assessment. To assess the degree to which students are interested in a selection of content area text, you might use a technique called Take a Three-Minute Pulse (Tuttle, 2009). After students have been reading a text selection for 10 to 15 minutes, have them pause and reflect on the reading. Then, ask students to respond quickly to a question or two designed to tap their thinking. Marzano and Pickering (1997, p. 400) suggested the following type of prompts.

- How does this information relate to you?
- How does what we've just learned relate to . . .?
- How is what we've just learned similar to or different from . . .?
- Identify one thing you already knew and something that was new to you.

Have students write their answers on a card (e.g., 3 x 5 or 4 x 6 card) so that you can scan them quickly to get a sense of students' responses. Once you have reviewed their reflections, consider instruction that builds on their interests, connections, and understandings of the topic.

Promoting Positive Attitudes

GOAL

To help students develop positive attitudes toward content area topics

BACKGROUND

Attitudes have been defined as "those feelings that cause a reader to approach or avoid a reading situation" (Readence, Bean, & Baldwin, 2004, p. 117). Attitudes toward reading are connected with feelings about reading. It stands to reason that students' feelings about reading will probably correlate positively with the amount of reading they are willing to do. By providing activities for students that are enjoyable as well as challenging and manageable, you can encourage students to have positive attitudes toward reading and your content area. For learning to occur within your classroom, students need to have positive attitudes about themselves as learners and must believe that they are capable of succeeding academically (Graves, Juel, & Graves, 2003).

The old adage "nothing succeeds like success" can be applied to your classroom. Try to offer activities to your students that virtually ensure some successful experiences in the course. Students must experience success in the vast majority of activities in which they participate if they are to progress academically (Brophy, 1986).

Activities that allow students to participate in aspects of self-expression can help develop positive attitudes toward your content area. Written, oral, and artistic self-expression activities are all avenues that promote students' sense of being valued within their classrooms. Marzano (1992) has presented four ways that can help you foster positive attitudes among students: instill in students feelings of acceptance; provide a classroom that is comfortable and orderly; involve students in activities that they value; and explain with clarity what you expect them to do.

Positive attitudes often go hand in hand with self-awareness and self-expression. By acknowledging that students' feelings and opinions are important, you are empowering them as learners. The following strategies are designed to build positive attitudes toward content material while communicating to students that you value their thoughts and opinions.

Section **2.2** INSTRUCTIONAL STRATEGY 6

Writing an Autobiography

Writing an Autobiography (Countryman, 1992) can easily and effectively be applied to any content area. All students bring some background to every subject. For example, in social studies, all students have experienced interactions with other people; in history, all students have families with a unique personal background; and in math, everyone has a math autobiography because all of us use math in our everyday lives.

Writing an autobiography enhances engagement among students because it enables them to assume more responsibility for what goes on in their classrooms. Even students for whom mathematics may have been a negative experience feel empowered as they write about themselves in relationship to the subject matter. Suddenly, the impersonal world of mathematics becomes one that engenders feelings. Students often are surprised to find that their classmates share many similar experiences and attitudes toward a subject (Countryman, 1992).

Another benefit of this strategy is that teachers learn about their students in a personal, individual way. For example, autobiographies reveal information about confidence levels, self-esteem, and attitudes. Most important, autobiographies bring laughter into the classroom as students share their experiences. When learning becomes engaging, teachers are on their way to producing learners who are enthusiastic and willing to be active participants in the academic journey.

Students may be interested and benefit from reading biographies. The Internet offers a number of biography databases.

SURF THE WEB

BIOGRAPHIES
Short biographies of famous people.
www.biography.com

More than 30,000 biographies.
www.infoplease.com/people.html

More than 19,000 biographies on notable people from ancient times to the present day.
www.s9.com

More than 25,000 biographies with some multimedia. Also links to other biography databases.
www.libraryspot.com/biographies

Biographies of hundreds of women who helped to shape the course of history.
www.distinguishedwomen.com

Directions

1. Introduce and discuss the idea of writing autobiographies. Tell students that an autobiography is an author's account of his or her own life. Use the following example or adapt it to fit your content area.

   Today we are going to focus on one aspect of your life—your experience with mathematics. I want you to tell me about your successes with math. How have they been important in your life? Consider what you like about learning math. What do you not like? If you could teach this class for one day, what would you teach your classmates? What would you personally like to learn this year in the area of mathematics?

2. Model writing your own content area autobiography and read it to the class. In addition to being presented with a model, your students will enjoy knowing that you, too, have feelings about your experiences with your content area.

3. Give your students ample time to complete their autobiographies. Perhaps one class period can be devoted to writing rough drafts and another period used for revisions.

4. Place students in small groups after the autobiographies have been completed. Ask them to share their autobiographies with their group members. Some of your students may be comfortable sharing their writing with the entire class.

5. Collect the autobiographies and read them to gain insights about your students and their attitudes toward the subjects you are teaching. An example of a mathematics autobiography follows.

SECTION 2.2
CHAPTER 2
web resources
Autobiography Math Example, 20
Carpentry Example, 21

Mathematics

Autobiography

When I was in junior high school, I sort of liked math. I liked it because everything made sense and seemed to fit together very neatly. Then I met Mrs. Brynwood in eighth-grade algebra. Nothing has been the same for me since then as far as math is concerned. I still don't get the abstract principles that she tried to teach us. And besides, who needs to know the value of *x* in real life? Last semester, however, I took geometry from Mr. Phillips. He is cool and so is his class. He really makes learning fun, and if I didn't get it, he figured out a different way to help me understand it.

If I could teach this class for one day, I would teach the students how to figure out the cost of going to college. Like how do you know how much you should pay for tuition? And if you only go part-time do you just pay a percentage of the tuition? These are things I'd like to learn about this semester.

EXAMPLE

Readers Needing Additional Support

Provide a series of guiding questions that will aid students in writing their autobiographies. Some possible questions are presented below.

- What do you first remember about the subject?
- How old were you or what grade were you in?
- Was there a special teacher you remember?
- What do you like about the subject?
- What do you dislike about the subject?
- How have you used or not used what you were taught?
- What problems have you encountered with the subject?
- What would you do if you were the teacher of the subject?
- What are some things you would like to learn about the subject this year?

Section **2.2** INSTRUCTIONAL STRATEGY 7

Opinionnaire/Questionnaire

Opinionnaire/Questionnaire (Reasoner, 1976) is designed to examine students' attitudes and experiences related to selected issues. In addition to encouraging students to examine their own attitudes towards a subject or event, this strategy enables students to interact with their classmates as they interview them. Opinionnaire/Questionnaire is another strategy that promotes social interaction among your students, thereby helping to promote positive attitudes toward learning while developing interest and increased motivation.

Directions

1. Survey your text and identify ideas or events on which you wish to focus your instruction. Write a series of questions designed to tap students' opinions, attitudes, and prior knowledge related to the subject.
2. Use an example from your content area or the following example. It is designed to generate information about students' attitudes towards the Holocaust in a high school literature class reading *Anne Frank: Diary of a Young Girl* (1995) and studying the Holocaust in world history.
3. Tell students that they are going to survey their classmates to find out their opinions and knowledge about the topic.
4. Provide all students with a copy of the Opinionnaire/Questionnaire you develop and ask them to interview their classmates.

Literature and History

Opinionnaire/Questionnaire

Directions: Respond to the following questions. You may choose more than one response to each question.

1. What words would you use to describe concentration camps?

   _____ death factories   _____ relocation facilities

   _____ hard labor camps   _____ historical fiction

   _____ jails   _____ punishment

                                               _____ other

2. Why do you think that the Nazis hated Jewish people?

   _____ They were afraid of them.   _____ Nazis were just naturally mean.

   _____ The Nazis felt superior to the Jews.   _____ The Nazis didn't hate the Jews. They were just following orders.

3. Which of the following statements do you believe to be true?

   _____ Auschwitz was the largest Nazi-operated camp.

   _____ One hundred individuals were reduced to ashes each day.

   _____ Prisoners who worked hard were allowed to go free.

   _____ There was usually enough food to go around in the concentration camps.

   _____ Blue-eyed blonds were spared.

EXAMPLE

5. Divide the class into small groups and ask them to share and compare their responses.

6. Ask each group to write a summary for each part of the Opinionnaire/Questionnaire, incorporating elements of summary writing.

7. Collect the summaries and develop a class summary or book that can be reviewed at the end of the unit. Students will enjoy seeing how their attitudes and knowledge have changed during their course of study.

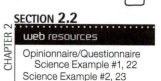

SECTION 2.2

CHAPTER 2

web resources

Opinionnaire/Questionnaire
Science Example #1, 22
Science Example #2, 23

Readers Needing Additional Support

Assign pairs of students to conduct the Opinionnaire/Questionnaire survey. The student who is the better reader can preview the survey with the student needing support and assist with difficult words. Each student can select a portion of the survey to present based on his or her comfort level.

SURF THE WEB

THIS DAY IN HISTORY
Choose the month and day to learn about events that happened throughout history.
www.historychannel.com/this-day-in-history

Section **2.2** INSTRUCTIONAL STRATEGY 8

Sustained Silent Reading (SSR)

Sustained Silent Reading (Berglund & Johns, 1983; Hunt, 1970; Ivey & Broaddus, 2000, 2001) encourages students to read self-selected materials during a designated time in the school day. Although the self-selection of reading material has long been reported as a motivating factor for students at all levels, the traditional school model provides only limited opportunities for students to self-select reading material (Mercurio, 2005). Many research studies have shown relationships between the amount of independent reading students engage in and reading achievement (Wu & Samuels, 2004). You should provide students with ample opportunities to engage in self-selected reading in and out of school. Ivey and Broaddus (2001) found that over 60% of middle school students in their study valued independent reading. Such reading has been referred to as free reading, silent reading, or Sustained Silent Reading. You may need to work with colleagues to help establish workable Sustained Silent Reading programs. Mercurio (2005) noted that seventh graders' negative attitudes about reading were reduced from 37% to 19% in a self-selected reading class. Time students spent reading also increased. Recently, Garan and DeVoogd (2008) confirmed the positive benefits of Sustained Silent Reading for students.

Directions

1. Begin by telling students that they will be given an opportunity to choose something that they would like to read and to read it for a specified period of time. Invite students to suggest possible names for the reading period. Johns and Lenski (2010) list many names that have been used to characterize the period (e.g., Drop Everything and Read [DEAR], Read in Peace [RIP], Students and Faculty All Read Independently [SAFARI]).

2. Have students develop a procedure for selecting a name for the SSR period. Once a name is selected, designate a specific time when everyone will participate in the SSR period.

3. Help students establish a set of procedures and guidelines that will characterize the SSR period. Some possible items could include selections from the following list.

   - Find a comfortable place to read.
   - Have more to read than you think you will need.
   - Have your materials with you.
   - Stay quiet and read during the entire time.

   Guide students in selecting just-right books. Katz, Polkoff, and Gurvitz (2005) suggest scaffolded independent-level reading. At the independent level, students can recognize approximately 99% of the words and understand what was read (Johns, 2008). Gradually, more difficult materials can be selected. The goal is to help students select books at an appropriate level of difficulty that will engage them because of the topic or genre.

4. Begin SSR with a period that is relatively short and increase the time as students demonstrate a readiness to read for longer periods. When students ask to continue reading after the time is up, you may want to consider increasing the SSR period in the near future.

5. Model the process by reading your self-selected materials as students engage in their reading. Be prepared for students to ask you about what you are reading.

6. Allow students to achieve their own purposes during the period. Refrain from quizzing students or turning the period into a lesson of some sort. You may want to give students an opportunity to record their thoughts on a SSR Log (reading log).

7. Have materials available for students who do not have anything to read or who run short of materials before the period ends. Ivey and Broaddus (2001) found the 10 most popular types of reading materials were the following (beginning with the most popular).

   - Magazines
   - Adventure books
   - Mysteries
   - Scary stories
   - Joke books
   - Animals (informational books)
   - Comic books
   - Series books

- Sports (informational books)
- Books about people their age

8. Encourage students to find materials for their independent reading in the public library, a bookstore, the school library, or at home.

Readers Needing Additional Support

Ensure that the reading materials vary widely in difficulty, interest, and length. Help students select materials that are at an appropriate level of difficulty. Generally, students should be able to identify approximately 95% of the words on a page of text (Johns, 2008). Provide several appropriate choices and have students survey the materials and then make a selection. Encourage students to discontinue reading materials that are too difficult or not of interest and have them make a more appropriate choice.

Section **2.2** INSTRUCTIONAL STRATEGY 9

Picture Books

Picture books, alphabet books, wordless books, narrative picture books, and informational picture books can be used in content areas to increase motivation, help students understand concepts, appeal to visual learners, and provide easier reading materials for students who struggle with reading (Carr, Buchanan, Wentz, Weiss, & Grant, 2001; Hibbing & Rankin-Erickson, 2003). Generally, books read aloud to middle and high school students should contain provocative issues and moral dilemmas to stimulate critical thinking, promote thoughtful discussion, and help students collaborate in the construction of meaning (Carr et al., 2001; Richardson, 2000). Guidelines can help teachers select books for their specific content areas (Costello & Kolodziej, 2006). Fortunately, a bibliography of picture books for secondary content area teachers has been compiled (Carr et al., 2001) to provide possible resources. In addition, Tiedt (2000) offers many ideas for using picture books with older students.

Directions

1. Survey the book lists on the website resources to locate a particular picture book that might be appropriate for a topic in your curriculum. Other books may be recommended by colleagues or librarians in your school system.

2. After selecting a book, read it to determine whether it is appropriate for the topic or unit being taught.

3. Decide whether the book should be read aloud or offered to students for independent reading. For example, *Starry Messenger* (Sis, 1996) tells the story of Galileo "in simple language but with rich illustrations" (Carr et al., 2001, p. 152). Reading it aloud to students may help them appreciate this talented individual. The book also contains some of the words written by Galileo on the perimeters of the pages, and it might be a useful introduction to the world of this scientist.

SECTION **2.2**
CHAPTER 2
web resources
Content Area Picture Books:
Language Arts, Mathematics,
Science, the Arts, and Social
Studies, 25–28

4. By sharing quality picture books with students, along with your genuine pleasure in such books, you help students expand their opportunities for learning.

SURF THE WEB
A list of picture books for high school students.
www.nancykeane.com/rl/406.htm
Annual list of books selected by the students themselves.
www.reading.org/Resources/Booklists/ChildrenChoices.aspx

For readers who struggle, choose books and reading materials that are likely to ensure high-success reading experiences. Search for books and reading materials at a wide range of difficulty levels that help support the theme, topic, or unit being taught.

Section **2.2** INSTRUCTIONAL STRATEGY 10

Classroom Libraries

"A critical factor in literacy engagement is access to books" (Verhoeven & Snow, 2001, p. 4). A well-designed, functional classroom library can contribute to the overall quality of students' learning experiences. Unfortunately, a study conducted by Fractor, Woodruff, Martinez, and Teale (1993) revealed that the percentage of classrooms with a library decreased rather dramatically from kindergarten (72% had libraries) to fifth grade (about 26% had libraries). In middle and high schools, there are many classrooms without libraries. While *school* libraries certainly exist, they do not provide the ready access of a classroom library. Morrow (2003) reported that students read 50–60% more when classrooms have libraries. Ivey (1999) notes that, by middle school, students who struggle in reading can be inspired by getting the right books into their hands. In addition, Langer (2001) contends that "literature can play a central role in students' intellectual, social, and personal development" (p. 177). Content area teachers often have favorite materials that relate to a particular theme or unit. Making them part of a classroom library can increase their accessibility to and use by students. Mercurio (2005) found that students with access to a wide range of books increased the time they spent reading outside the classroom and gained more positive attitudes toward reading. Kasten and Wilfong (2005) found that creating a bistro setting to discuss self-selected reading helped promote reading and interactions among adolescents.

Directions

1. Survey your classroom(s) and identify locations that might function as a library. Strive to be both creative and realistic as you allocate space.

2. Identify materials you have that would be appropriate for the library. A science teacher might have a series of small books that are biographies of scientists. There might also be some science fiction titles and books on easy-to-do experiments.

3. Enlist the assistance of colleagues and your students to identify additional materials and ways to obtain them. Realize that establishing a library takes time and that a library can evolve over the years.

4. Develop a system for how materials are checked out and maintained.

5. Try to secure materials that students like to read. Not every piece of material in the library needs to relate to your content area. Ivey and Broaddus (2001) surveyed over 1,700 middle school students with an interest checklist and found the following types of materials to be of interest. Students could check more than one item. The following types of books and related materials are listed from high (77%) to low (20%). It seems clear that even the lowest rated item is of interest to a fair percentage of students.

- Magazines
- Adventure books
- Mysteries
- Scary stories
- Joke books
- Animals (informational books)
- Comic books
- Series books
- Fantasy
- Science fiction
- Newspapers
- Poetry books
- Biographies
- Picture books
- History (novels/chapter books)
- Science books

- Sports (informational books)
- Books about people their age
- History (informational books)
- Other specific topics

6. Consult other research studies that may offer insights for your library but rely on your observations of students as your primary source of information.

7. Consider establishing a time for free reading as part of your class time. Over 60% of students in the Ivey and Broaddus (2001) study responded positively to free reading as part of class time.

SURF THE WEB

TEENS READ AND WRITE BOOK REVIEWS
Find a Favorite Teenage Angst page where students can read book reviews and write comments at:
www.grouchy.com

Find interviews with authors, book reviews, a newsletter, and message boards where teens can post comments on books, related school issues, and original poetry and short stories at:
www.teenreads.com

SUPPORTING INDEPENDENT READING
Explore a lesson designed to help students analyze their past readings and complete a list of books they hope to read in the future at:
www.readwritethink.org/lessons/lesson_view.asp? id=836

BOOKS FOR ADOLESCENTS
Annual lists (1998–2009) of books that will encourage adolescents to read. The books are selected by the readers themselves. Find approximately 30 books for each year at:
www.reading.org/Resources/Booklists/YoungAdultChoices.aspx

Find more than 15 young adult book sites at:
www.wested.org/stratlit/research/booklinks.shtml

Book awards and selected lists for adolescents:
http://www.ala.org./ala/mgrps/divs/yalsa/booklistsawards/booklistsbook.cfm

---

Assessing Student Learning

Write an Opinionnaire/Questionnaire

Goal: *To help students develop positive attitudes toward content area topics.* Encouraging students to have positive attitudes toward content area topics is essential for learning. Teachers can provide activities that ensure successful learning experiences and acknowledge their feelings and opinions. To build favorable attitudes and foster student success, invite students to write their own Opinionnaire/Questionnaire (Reasoner, 1976). Have students work in pairs or triads to develop an Opinionnaire/Questionnaire about a specific topic in your content area. Ask them to write three to five questions that focus on their attitudes or opinions about the topic as well as their prior experiences with the topic. After the groups of students have written an Opinionnaire/ Questionnaire, allow the groups to survey students in one or more of the groups using their Opinionnaire/Questionnaire. Collect and review the student-designed Opinionnaire/Questionnaires and the gathered responses to assess how students are feeling and what they already know about the content area topic.

Arousing Curiosity for Topics

GOAL

To help students become curious about content area topics

BACKGROUND

After you have determined the important concepts in the text that you are asking your students to read, ask yourself *why* they would want to read it. You want to spark your students' curiosity about the subject matter. When your students' curiosity about a topic is aroused, they will naturally become interested in the topic and begin to consider adding new information to what they already know. Building a bridge between new and known material is a necessary element for comprehension.

Teachers need to provide students with a wide array of material to read if they want to arouse their curiosity. Wolk (2010) noted that youth read a range of different texts in various media outside of school; however, they are given a narrow and predictable set of texts to read in school. As a result, students can become turned off to reading in school. If teachers want students to be turned on to reading, Wolk suggests surrounding students with high-quality text they want to read including books, magazines, newspapers, graphic novels, lyrics, and the like. He concluded, "By making substantive changes to what students read, we can bring immediacy and spontaneity to their learning" (p. 16). As a content area teacher, you can select and use a variety of texts that are interesting and relevant to your students' lives.

Additionally, the texts that you ask your students to read must be manageable, not too difficult and not too easy. Arousing your students' curiosity will help them develop questions about the topic and seek answers to their questions as they read. When students actively seek information, they naturally use cognitive strategies, one of the hallmarks of an engaged reader. The following strategies are designed to arouse your students' curiosity about a topic as they become interested in the topic.

Section **2.3** INSTRUCTIONAL STRATEGY 11

Creating Sentences

Creating Sentences is a strategy that uses some of the vocabulary words that will be encountered in the text to arouse students' curiosity. Students will become curious about the text when they make predictions about the text's contents. In addition to motivating students to read the upcoming text and to determine the accuracy of their predictions, Creating Sentences encourages students to think about the relationships among a variety of words from the assigned selection.

Directions

1. List the important vocabulary words for the text selection where they can be seen by the entire class. Pronounce each word. These words should be core words from the selection and should be able to be defined by their use in the selection. The following example is based on a biology text.

| heart | circulates | arteries | oxygen |
| pumps | blood vessels | cells | veins |

2. Ask students to select pairs of words from the list and, for each pair, to create a sentence that they think might appear in the text.

3. Pick several students to write their sentences where they can be seen by the entire class. Ask them to underline the words that they have included from the list. Some examples follow.

   1. The <u>heart</u> is a muscle that <u>pumps</u> blood.
   2. Blood <u>circulates</u> through our <u>blood vessels</u>.
   3. <u>Arteries</u> carry blood toward the heart, and <u>veins</u> carry blood away from the heart.
   4. <u>Cells</u> in the body store <u>oxygen</u>.

4. Ask students if anyone disagrees with any of the sentences. Encourage discussion about these sentences.

5. Have students read their textbook selection to verify the accuracy of their sentences. Then have students revisit each sentence through class discussion and, if there are any incorrect sentences, invite a student to offer a corrected sentence. In this example, students will find that sentence 3 needs to be modified. The new sentence might read as follows: <u>Arteries</u> carry blood away from the heart, and <u>veins</u> carry blood toward the heart.

6. Invite students to share additional sentences based on the information that has been presented in the text.

SECTION 2.3

CHAPTER 2

web resources

Creating Sentences
Reproducible, 29
Literature Example, 30

Readers Needing Additional Support

Have students work with a partner to create the sentences and read the text. Use small group discussions of the text to maximize student involvement.

Section **2.3** INSTRUCTIONAL STRATEGY 12

Probable Passages

Probable Passages (Wood, 1984) is a strategy that is very similar to Creating Sentences in that it involves students in making predictions about their upcoming reading assignment. However, Probable Passages focuses on larger sections of text. One of the attributes of this strategy is that it lends itself well to both narrative and expository writing. It also can be used effectively for a collaborative effort among small groups of students.

Directions

1. Determine the main concepts in the text selection that you have chosen for your students to read. Then decide if the text has an identifiable organizational pattern such as problem-solution or cause-effect.

2. Identify key words within the selection and categorize them under the text structure labels. The following example is based on a text selection in world history about Africa. The organizational pattern found in the selection is cause-effect.

Cause	Effect
Olaudah Equiano	best
captives	capable
died	healthiest
Africans	disaster
journey	strong
freedom	youngest

3. Write the words where they can be seen by the entire class and explain to your students that you have placed the words in categories according to the text structure.

4. Then provide students with the cause portion of the text selection leaving blanks for the words under the cause label above. Have students fill in the blanks of the first part of the Probable Passage by selecting words from the cause list, as in the following example.

Captured _____ were branded with hot irons and transported as _____ on filthy shelves stacked from floor to ceiling. They were given little food or water on the _____ across the Atlantic. As many as 20 percent of the slaves _____ during the crossing. _____ _____ described this horrible experience in a book he wrote about his life. He proved luckier than most African slaves. In time, he was able to buy his _____.

5. Provide students with the effect portion of the Probable Passage. Write an opening sentence that suggests the contents of the second part of the text passage or the effect. An example follows.

Africa suffered as a result of the practice of slavery.

6. Ask students to select words from the effect list and write a paragraph, such as the following one, about the effects of slavery on Africa.

Africa suffered as a result of the practice of slavery. Although some Africans grew wealthy, the slave trade was a disaster for the continent. The people who were sold as slaves were the youngest and healthiest workers from the region. When a continent loses its most capable and best young people, it is difficult for it to remain strong.

7. Have students read the text selection.

8. Ask students to edit their work in order to correct any contradictory statements or add any missing information.

9. An example of a Probable Passage using a literature text follows. In this example the text structure categories have been grouped according to the elements of the story (setting, characters, problem, and resolution).

SECTION 2.3
CHAPTER 2

web resources

Probable Passages
  Reproducible, 31
Social Studies Example, 32

Literature

Probable Passages

Directions: Place the key words below into the appropriate categories. Then read the incomplete Probable Passage and see if you can write the correct word or words in each blank. After reading the selection, make any necessary changes in your passage.

Key Words

Bellevue Hospital	complicated convalescence	bumbled
operating room	operating jitters	surgery
Dr. George Walters	guilt	appendectomy
Mr. Polansky	responsibility	

Categories

Setting	*Characters*	*Problem*
Bellevue Hospital	Dr. George Walters	operating jitters
operating room	Mr. Polansky	surgery
		appendectomy
		bumbled

Resolution
complicated convalescence
guilt and responsibility

Incomplete Probable Passage

This story takes place in the _____ at _____. Two doctors, _____ and the narrator are about to perform an _____ on _____. Suddenly the narrator, who is the chief surgeon, develops a bad case of _____.

Although the _____ is _____, the operation is completed. As a result, however, the patient endures a _____ and the surgeon is left with feelings of _____.

EXAMPLE

Section **2.3** INSTRUCTIONAL STRATEGY 13

Content Predict-O-Gram

A Content Predict-O-Gram (McLaughlin & Allen, 2002) is an adaptation of a Predict-O-Gram (Blachowicz, 1986). Instead of using words from a narrative text, a Content Predict-O-Gram uses words from an informational text and invites students to assign the words to established categories. The strategy introduces vocabulary that will be important in the text selection and encourages students to think about the topic and make predictions about the content that will be presented in the selection.

Directions

1. Determine categories that would be appropriate for the section, chapter, or unit of text that will be studied. Select vocabulary from the text that will stimulate predictions and curiosity for the topic. In this example, the vocabulary relates to a social studies chapter on ancient Egypt. The vocabulary words selected for the Content Predict-O-Gram and the categories are listed below.

Vocabulary Words

Nile River Valley	irrigation
silt	"Next World"
pharaohs	pyramid
delta	empire
New Stone Age	slavery
hieroglyphics	scribes

Categories

Political Systems	Economy	Social Systems
History	Geography	

2. Write the vocabulary words on the Content Predict-O-Gram found on the website, duplicate it, and distribute a copy to each student.

3. Read the list of words to the students. Then have students read the categories (e.g., social systems, political systems, economy) in the Content Predict-O-Gram and invite volunteers to describe what is meant by each of the categories.

4. Tell students that each of the vocabulary words should be written in one of the five categories based on where students think it would fit. Following is a student's predictions for Social Systems.

Social Systems
scribes
slavery
"Next World"

5. Once students have written in their initial predictions for each of the categories, have them discuss their ideas with partners, in small groups, or with the entire class.

6. Then have students read and study the text selection, making changes in their initial predictions based on the content of the selection.

7. Take time to discuss each of the categories to reach consensus on the most appropriate categories for the words. Have students make additional changes as needed on their Content Predict-O-Grams using arrows to move words to the proper category.

8. Students can use their Content Predict-O-Grams to summarize major content from the text in each of the major areas. The summaries could be done orally or in writing.

9. Additional Content Predict-O-Grams can be created for other content areas. A blank Content Predict-O-Gram for this purpose can be found on the website. Below are some possible categories for middle school content areas.

- Science (astronomy): Earth, moon, stars, solar system
- Math (geometry): lines, angles, polygons, circles
- Science (introduction to lab equipment): equipment for measuring, equipment for observing, equipment for changing materials, equipment for recording data
- English (nouns): common nouns, proper nouns, collective nouns, concrete nouns, abstract nouns
- Reading (poetry): metaphor, simile, onomatopoeia, alliteration, assonance
- Foods (food pyramid): fats/oils/sweets; milk/yogurt/cheese; meat/poultry/fish/beans/eggs/nuts; vegetables; fruit; bread/cereal/pasta/rice

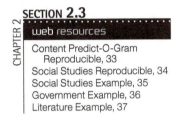

SECTION 2.3

CHAPTER 2

web resources

Content Predict-O-Gram
  Reproducible, 33
Social Studies Reproducible, 34
Social Studies Example, 35
Government Example, 36
Literature Example, 37

Readers Needing Additional Support

Students who struggle with reading or with English can be assigned to work with students who are more proficient in these areas. Provide plenty of opportunities for students to work with a helpful partner or in small groups. If written summaries for each of the categories are to be prepared, it would be helpful to encourage oral summaries first. Key words and phrases could be written on the chalkboard to help students write their summaries.

Section **2.3** INSTRUCTIONAL STRATEGY 14

Poetry Prowess

Sometimes using a different resource in your content area can help arouse curiosity for a particular subject. Poetry and literature have the capability of helping students look at a content area with new vision. Depending on the poem or literature selected, students might be introduced to the humor in a content area or learn a new viewpoint. The work of contemporary poets makes the power of verse useful to other disciplines because of their playful, nontraditional forms (Sandmann, 2005).

Directions

1. Locate a poem that has the potential to gain the interest of your students. The poem may have a unique form, be humorous, or possess some other characteristics that makes it potentially useful. For example, "Pythagorean Theorem," "What's The Point," or Fibonacci Sequence" from the following website (with more than 40 poems and songs) might add some humor to a math class.

    http://www.pleacher.com/mp/mpfrome.html

2. Pick out a poem that deals with the subject you are introducing. For example, the above website contains poems dealing with ratio, pi, circumference, area, sequencing DNA, and many other terms as well as famous names like Euclid, Newton, and Einstein.

3. Poetry can provide insights into a new concept in a way that may be different from the text. In social studies or history, for example, "Paul Revere's Ride" by Henry Wadsworth Longfellow or "Concord Hymn" by Ralph Waldo Emerson could be used to introduce the Revolutionary War. Invite students to look for different viewpoints as you share the poems. Revisit the poems at the conclusion of the unit of study.

4. Poetry could also be used to review material already taught. Leave out key words in the poem to see if students can supply the correct terminology.

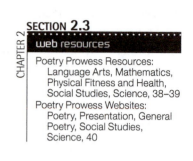

SECTION 2.3

web resources

Poetry Prowess Resources:
  Language Arts, Mathematics,
  Physical Fitness and Health,
  Social Studies, Science, 38–39
Poetry Prowess Websites:
  Poetry, Presentation, General
  Poetry, Social Studies,
  Science, 40

Assessing Student Learning	Think-Pair-Share

Goal: *To help students become curious about content area topics.* Sparking students' curiosity about a content area topic can be enjoyable and informative. Once students' curiosity in a topic is ignited, they become more interested and are open to learning more about it. Students also need to build connections between what they know to the new content to be learned. To determine the extent to which students are curious about a topic, teachers can use an informal cooperative learning activity: Think-Pair-Share. After introducing a new topic to the class, ask students to think individually about the topic for a few minutes. Then, have the students talk about the topic with a partner. While they are talking, have the pairs write down their thoughts in a list or brief summary. Next, invite the pairs to share their thinking about the topic with the whole class. During the sharing, listen carefully to the students' thoughts. After the pairs have shared, collect and review their written notes to gain additional insight into students' musings. Use the collected information to build on students' interests and prior knowledge.

Fostering Motivation

GOAL

To help students become motivated to learn

BACKGROUND

Motivation is a key component of reading engagement. It is enhanced by challenge, choice, and collaboration. When teachers can motivate students to learn, they increase the chances that students will view academic achievement as a worthy pursuit. In a recent study, Pitcher and colleagues (2007) investigated adolescents' motivation to read using the *Adolescent Motivation to Read Profile*, an adaptation of the *Motivation to Read Profile* (Gambrell, Palmer, Codling, & Mazzoni, 1996). They found that adolescent girls had higher perceptions of themselves as readers and valued reading more than adolescent boys. To gain a better understanding of students' reading experiences and motivations, they interviewed about 100 adolescents. Adolescents reported significant use of multiliteracies (e.g., magazines, newspapers, e-mails, instant messages, and the Internet), preferred learning modes (e.g., collaborative groups), and the importance of choice. Pitcher and colleagues concluded, "Using adolescents' preferred reading materials and modes of instruction will lead to increased motivation" (p. 378).

Increasing students' motivation to read is important because it relates to reading engagement. "Engaged reading is the primary pathway toward the competencies and expertise needed for achievement" (Guthrie, 2004, p. 4). To foster engaged reading among adolescents, O'Brien and Dillon (2008) relied on the "Six C's" of motivation (Turner & Paris, 1995): choice, challenge, control, collaboration, constructing meaning, and consequences.

- Choice: Provide students with authentic choices and purposes for literacy.
- Challenge: Allow students to modify tasks so that the difficulty and interest levels are challenging.
- Control: Show students how they can control their learning.
- Collaboration: Emphasize the positive aspects of giving and seeking help.
- Constructing meaning: Emphasize strategies and metacognition for constructing meaning.
- Consequences: Use the consequences of task to build responsibility, ownership, and self-regulation. (O'Brien & Dillon, 2008, pp. 93–94)

Consider using these guidelines to motivate adolescent learners when planning activities for your content area.

The strategies in this section are designed to help motivate students to engage in reading and participate actively in their own learning.

Section **2.4** INSTRUCTIONAL STRATEGY 15

K–W–L

K-W-L (Ogle, 1986) is designed to engage students in becoming active learners and to motivate them to purposefully seek information from their texts and other sources. It can be used effectively as a prereading strategy because it activates students' prior knowledge about a subject and also helps them organize their thoughts and questions before they begin to read. K-W-L involves three basic steps: determining what students already **K**now about a topic; determining what they **W**ant to learn about a topic; and, after reading, assessing what they have **L**earned about the topic. This strategy lends itself well to follow-up activities such as the construction of graphic organizers and summary writing. Blachowicz and Ogle (2001) also present some variations of K-W-L that extend and expand the original strategy.

Directions

1. Introduce the K-W-L strategy prior to assigning a reading selection with a new unit of study. Explain to students that, when they begin to study new material, it is important to determine prior knowledge or what they already know about the material. Use an example from your content area or use the following example. In this example, the new topic is the country of Cuba from a geography text.

2. Ask students to brainstorm what they know about the topic as you record the information under **K**. The following list is an example of sentences describing what students know about Cuba.

Cuba

K	*W*	*L*
Cuba is 90 miles from Miami. Castro is the dictator. The government is communist. They grow sugar.		

3. Ask students what they would like to know about the topic. Some of their questions will arise from curiosity and others from a real desire to know more about the country. Record their questions under the **W** portion of the chart. The following list is an example of questions students asked about Cuba.

Cuba

K	*W*	*L*
Cuba is 90 miles from Miami. Castro is the dictator. The government is communist. They grow sugar.	What language do Cubans speak? What is Cuba's major industry? What is the capital of Cuba? Why are so many Cubans leaving Cuba?	

4. Direct students to read the selection. When they have completed their reading, they are ready to return to the chart and record the answers to their questions in the column labeled **L** as in the following example. For unanswered questions, students should place question marks on the chart.

Cuba

K	*W*	*L*
Cuba is 90 miles from Miami. Castro is the dictator. The government is communist. They grow sugar.	What language do Cubans speak? What is Cuba's major industry? What is the capital of Cuba? Why are so many Cubans leaving Cuba?	Spanish sugar cane Havana ?

5. Involve students in follow-up activities designed to extend their learning. Questions that were not answered in the **W**ant to know column provide opportunities for further reading and research.

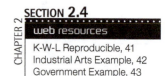

SECTION 2.4

web resources

K-W-L Reproducible, 41
Industrial Arts Example, 42
Government Example, 43

CHAPTER 2

Readers Needing Additional Support

Students who have difficulty with reading or who are English learners can be the first students invited to share for each part of the K-W-L. If necessary, provide clarification or ask clarifying questions.

USING RESEARCH SKILLS
Provide multiday lesson on issues of copyright, fair use, and plagiarism.
http://www.readwritethink.org/classroom-resources/lesson-plans/exploring-plagiarism-copyright-paraphrasing-1062.html

Section **2.4** INSTRUCTIONAL STRATEGY 16

The Imposter

The Imposter (Curran & Smith, 2005) strategy uses text where a contradictory statement, idea, or number is embedded "into a reading passage or mathematical problem" (p. 186). Students are encouraged to read deeply to discover the subtle or bold contradiction. This strategy requires considerable preparation time but can be "a fun way to explore and comprehend challenging reading" (p. 189).

Directions

1. Introduce students to The Imposter by inviting them to share ideas about the meaning of *imposter*. Help students generate words like *fake, quack, deception, charlatan*, and *deceive*.

2. Tell students that you will ask them to read a few simple statements and try to figure out what's wrong with the statement. Begin with statements that are based on generally accepted common knowledge related to topics taught in your curriculum. Some possible "imposter" statements from different content areas are listed below.

Math

- The square of 4 is 8. (8 should be 16)
- If equal quantities are multiplied by equal quantities, the products are unequal. (unequal should be equal)
- Quadrilaterals are open figures with four straight sides. (open should be closed)
- Two-thirds is greater than 7/8. (greater should be less)
- The use of geometry dates back to the 1700s. (1700s should be the dawn of history)

Social Studies

- The capital of the United States is in Washington state. (state should be DC)
- The last state to join the Union was Delaware. (last should be first)
- Delaware is the smallest of the 50 states in area. (smallest should be second smallest)
- To be elected as President, a candidate needs at least a majority of the 538 electoral votes which is at least 260. (260 should be 270)

Physical Science

- There are two classes of solutions. (two should be three)
- A solution is a heterogeneous mixture in which the particles of the mixing substances are evenly distributed throughout. (heterogeneous should be homogeneous)
- The substance being dissolved is the solvent. (solvent should be solute)
- The substance present in the smallest amount is considered to be the solvent. (smallest should be largest or solvent should be solute)

3. Invite students to prepare some statements or brief paragraphs that contain one or more errors. After students have completed the task, have volunteers share their statements with the class to see if other students can discover the error. Students can also share with partners or in small groups.

4. Prepare a selection from your instructional materials with one or more errors or contradictions, duplicate it, and invite students to read, discover, and justify or explain the contradiction(s) or error(s). Begin with smaller segments of text and gradually increase the length of the text segment. Curran and Smith (2005) suggest the following guidelines.

   - "Proof of the error should be found in the text.
   - The errors should be scattered throughout the text, not just at the end.
   - The errors must be evident from the body of the text.
   - A background should be well established before the introduction of the error(s)." (p. 187)

5. Ultimately, several paragraphs can be presented to students. As the passages become longer, students may prefer to work with a partner.

6. A partial example from math, adapted from Curran and Smith (p. 187), along with the explanation of the error is presented below.

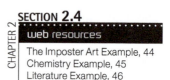

SECTION 2.4
web resources
The Imposter Art Example, 44
Chemistry Example, 45
Literature Example, 46

7. Once students become adept at The Imposter strategy with teacher-developed imposter statements, have the students catch real errors in authentic texts (e.g., newspapers, fiction, and information books) (Kane, 2007).

Math

The Text

If one were converting 11.2 centimeters to millimeters, one would realize that there are 10 millimeters in 1 centimeter and 1.12 millimeters is 11.2 centimeters. Likewise, if one were converting 11.2 centimeters to decimeters, one would realize that there are 10 centimeters in a decimeter and 1.12 decimeters in 11.2 centimeters.

The Error

There are 112 millimeters in 11.2 centimeters, not 1.12. A millimeter is only one tenth of a centimeter. The decimal point moves one place to the right, not one place to the left.

EXAMPLE

WHY FILES
Every two weeks an article is posted that focuses on current science topics in the news. You can use these articles with students to generate discussions in the classroom.
www.whyfiles.org

Section **2.4** INSTRUCTIONAL STRATEGY 17

Draw, Read, Attend, Write (DRAW)

DRAW (Agnew, 2000) is a motivational comprehension strategy based on teacher-prepared questions related to some text (an article, selection, or chapter). A variety of questions are typed on a sheet of paper, duplicated, and distributed to students. The questions on one sheet are cut apart and used for the strategy. An overview of DRAW is presented below.

   D: Draw—Different students or groups draw questions from the master sheet that was cut apart.
   R: Read—Students read the material upon which the questions are based and write their answers on the sheet containing all the questions.

A: Attend—The teacher asks the student (or group) who drew the first question to read the question, answer it, and explain how the answer was determined. Class members then discuss the answer and arrive at a consensus. Students are encouraged to make notes on their sheets that contain all the questions.

W: Write—When all the questions have been asked, answered, and discussed, students put away their question sheets and the teacher collects the individual question slips. Several questions are drawn to make a quiz. Each question is then read aloud, and the students write their answers on a clean sheet of paper. Students may then hand in the quiz to be graded.

Agnew (2000) mentions numerous benefits of using the DRAW strategy. Among them are helping readers who struggle understand the content, encouraging full class participation, encouraging thinking on various levels, and involving students in learning from each other.

Directions

1. Select the text from which to construct the questions. Create literal (factual), inferential (implicit), and application questions to reflect the main ideas, themes, and information in the text. Type the questions and reproduce sufficient copies for students. The following example is from a middle school unit on the Holocaust.

2. Take one sheet of questions and cut it into strips so each question is on a separate strip of paper. Have students form small groups or work with a partner. In this example, the class contained 22 students and the sheet contained 11 questions; therefore, the teacher decided to use partner grouping.

3. Hold up the strips of paper containing the questions and say something like the following. (Adapt what you say to the particular situation.)

   - Before you begin reading the section in your text that deals with the Holocaust, I will have each group draw one question and answer it. You should write out your answer and be prepared to share and discuss it with the entire class.

Social Studies

Directions: You or your partner will be asked to answer one of the following questions. When the questions are discussed in class, you should take notes on all the responses. After our discussion is concluded, some of these questions will be used for a quiz. You will not be able to refer to this sheet during the quiz, so pay attention to the answers and discussion.

1. What group of people was the central focus of the Holocaust?
2. In what country did the Holocaust mostly take place?
3. What does *Holocaust* mean?
4. Why were people persecuted during the Holocaust?
5. How were the people persecuted during the Holocaust?
6. What is the name of the person generally associated with the Holocaust?
7. During which war did the Holocaust occur?
8. How would you feel if this happened to you and your family?
9. Do you think something like this could ever happen to you in the United States?
10. What happened to a particular ethnic group in the United States in the 1940s? Why were these people treated this way?
11. Do you think certain groups of people in the United States are persecuted today because of their ethnic origins? Who are they? Why does this happen?

EXAMPLE

4. After the questions have been drawn, have students read the assigned portion of text (silently or orally with their partners) and answer the question. When students finish, ask the group that drew the first question to read and answer it. Have students explain their answers and possibly refer to the text to support their answers. The factual questions are among the easiest to link with a specific part of the text. Once a consensus is reached through discussion, the other students should write the answers on their sheets containing all the questions.

5. Proceed through the remaining questions in a similar manner. Some of the higher-level questions may promote discussion and debate. The final question in the example may lead to considerable discussion, as more than one group may be identified. The responses to the "why" part of the question may also vary, depending on the particular group identified.

6. When all the questions have been answered and discussed, collect the question strips, have students put away their sheets containing all the questions, and ask students to prepare a clean sheet of paper for a quiz.

7. Decide how many questions to use for the quiz. You or students could draw the number of questions needed. You or a student should read each question aloud as many times as necessary, and students should write their answers. The completed quizzes may be handed in for a grade.

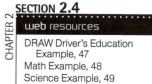

SECTION 2.4

CHAPTER 2

web resources

DRAW Driver's Education Example, 47
Math Example, 48
Science Example, 49

8. Variations of this strategy include dividing the class into two teams and having future quizzes include questions containing important information from earlier material.

Readers Needing Additional Support

When you ask the higher-level questions after reading, invite initial responses from those students who are sometimes reluctant to participate. Their ideas will be the first ones shared and should help get the discussion started.

Section **2.4** INSTRUCTIONAL STRATEGY 18

Information and Communication Technologies (ICTs)

Increasingly, students use information and communication technologies (ICTs) such as the Internet to learn about topics that interest them and to complete school-based assignments. Traditional textbooks, nevertheless, dominate their reading assignments in schools (Wolk, 2010). "If students are prepared only for the foundational literacies of book, paper, and pencil technologies, they will be unprepared for a future in which the new literacies are required by new information and communication technologies" (Leu, Mallette, Karchmer, & Kara-Soteriou, 2005, p. 1). Some of these new literacies include the Internet, search engines, e-mail, wikis, and blogs. For example, when searching and locating information on the Internet, Coiro and Dobler (2007) found evidence of "students using a recursive pattern of four self-regulatory comprehension strategies including mental planning, predicting, monitoring, and evaluating" (p. 228). They noted that reading on the Internet shares some similarities with reading printed text; however, reading on the Internet "is uniquely more complex" (p. 229). The use of ICTs requires students to critically evaluate information on the Internet, use search engines effectively, and master a range of word processing functions. Additionally, students may need to communicate their understandings in threaded discussions, contribute information to wikis, and post ideas to blogs.

Electronic texts "are moving closer to the mainstream of reading and writing" (Reinking, 2001, p. 198). Such texts can be thought of as "a unique configuration of symbol systems, technologies, contents, and situations of use" (Reinking, p. 200) that can help teachers promote engagement, motivation, and enjoyment in reading. There is some evidence (Tobias, 1988) that using digital texts can help students learn expository content. The Internet, websites, e-mail, CD-ROM encyclopedias, blogs and a wide variety of DVDs are now available to help teachers support their teaching. A problem may be that some teachers are challenged to address an area with which they themselves are not fully comfortable. The reality, however, is that ICTs will continue to grow and influence how reading and learning are accomplished. Think about how the Internet and digital texts might be used to enrich your instruction.

Directions

1. Take stock of your current knowledge about ICTs in general. How would you rate your knowledge and use on the following continuum?

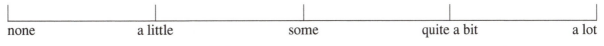

none	a little	some	quite a bit	a lot

2. If you have at least a little knowledge of ICTs, think about how you use them as a teacher. Rate your overall instructional use on the following continuum.

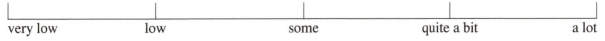

very low	low	some	quite a bit	a lot

3. Select at least one area where you would like to gain additional knowledge to strengthen instruction in your content area using the Internet or other ICTs. Be realistic and begin within your comfort zone.

4. Talk with colleagues or technology specialists in your school or school district to gain insights and to help achieve your objectives. These objectives may include special classes, small group assistance, or one-on-one instruction. Printed resources may also be available. Be willing to devote sufficient time to your objectives and expect some frustrating moments. Several resources are provided for you to explore.

Selected Content Area Websites

Content Area	Website	
English	English Companion Ning	http://englishcompanion.ning.com
	Web English Teacher	http://www.webenglishteacher.comlabout.html
Reading/Literature	SCORE Cyberguides to Literature	http://www.sdcoe.K12.ca.us/SCORE/ cyberguide.html
	The Literacy Web	http://www.literacy.uconn.edu
Science/Math	Science Learning Network	http://www.sln.org
	The Annenberg/CPB Math and Science Project	http://www.learner.org/teacherslab
	Science Spot (science lessons, puzzles, trivia, links)	http://www.sciencespot.net
	ENC Learning Inc.	http://www.goenc.com
	The Math Forum	http://mathforum.com/
	Illuminations (resources for teaching math)	http://illuminations.nctm.org
Social Studies	The United States Geological Survey (resources for teachers)	http://education.usgs.gov
	Atlapedia (physical maps, political maps, facts, and statistics)	http://www.atlapedia.com
	Animated Atlas—U.S. History timeline	http://www.animatedatlas.com/timeline.html
	American Memory	http://memory.loc.gov/ammemlindex.html
	National Archives	http://www.archives.gov/education/

Lesson Plans

Lesson Plans Page
   http://www.lessonplanspage.com/

To find lesson plans that match your criteria, simply begin by selecting a subject or search for specific topics.

The Gateway to 21st Century Skills
http://www.thegateway.org

Search by grade level (K–College) and subject. You can also browse keywords and subject.

Read-Write-Think
http://www.readwritethink.org

Lesson plans in many content areas
http://school.discovery.com/lessonplans/9-12.html

Art lesson plans
http://www.princetonol.com/groups/iad/lessons/high/highlessons.html

General high school lessons at Lesson Plans 4 Teachers
http://www.lessonplans4teachers.com/highschool.php

High school teacher's page for mathematics
http://mathforum.org/teachers/high/lessons-collections.html

Lesson plans for dance, music, theater, and the visual arts
http://artsedge.kennedy-center.org/teach/les.cfm

Lesson plans for the humanities
http://edsitement.neh.gov/

Lesson plans by teachers for teachers
http://teachersnetwork.org/LessonPlans

Lesson plans and resources for teaching with primary sources
http://www.loc.gov/teachers/

Standards-based lesson plans
http://www.thinkfinity.org/

Lesson plans for geography
http://www.nationalgeographic.com/xpeditions/lessons/matrix.html

---

Assessing Student Learning

Simple Concept Map

Goal: *To help students become motivated to learn.* Fostering student motivation is a key factor of reading engagement. When content area teachers motivate students to learn, they provide a pathway for engaged reading which in turn improves academic achievement. To motivate students to learn a specific topic, prompt students to share their experiences and thoughts within a simple concept map. Prior to instruction, have students brainstorm ideas and feelings about the topic in small groups (three to four students). Ask the groups of students to map (list) their ideas and feelings about the topic on a large sheet of paper. Then have the groups share their maps with the whole class. After the groups have presented their maps, post them in the classroom where they can be viewed by the entire class. When possible during instruction, incorporate the ideas and feelings displayed on the maps. After instruction, invite the groups to retrieve their maps, revisit their ideas and feelings, and craft revised maps based on new information.

Activities *and* Journal Entries *for* Teacher Educators

Activities

1. Ask students to think about a time when they were motivated to learn something new. In pairs, have the students share their experiences and tell what motivated them to learn. Once students have shared their experiences with one another, call on students to share what motivated them and write a list that can be viewed by the entire class. Lead a discussion that guides students to: (a) identify which of the listed motivators are extrinsic or intrinsic, and (b) consider which motivators could be a match for their content area.

2. In small disciplinary groups, have students brainstorm types of reading materials they can use in their classrooms (e.g., journals, lab reports, novels). Direct each group to record their ideas on chart paper and post their charts where they can be viewed by the entire class. Distribute a pad of sticky notes to each group and have them tour the posted charts. At each poster, the groups should note additional ideas on a sticky note and affix it to the chart. Once the groups have completed the tour, ask the disciplinary groups to return to their original poster, discuss the additional ideas, and decide which ideas to add to their charts.

3. Arrange the classroom chairs in a circle. Using a Socratic Seminar format, ask students to respond to the following questions.
   a. How can teachers promote reading engagement in their content areas? How do you intend to promote reading engagement in your classroom?
   b. How can teachers personalize disciplinary content for their students? What ideas do you have for personalizing the content for students in your discipline?
   c. How can teachers capitalize on peer interactions when they have students read content area texts? How do you plan to use peer interactions with assigned reading in your discipline?

Journal Entries

1. How will you create learning opportunities that motivate students to search for meaning, satisfy a curiosity, or explore their own interests in your discipline?

2. In what ways can you make literacy experiences in your discipline more relevant to your students?

3. How can you help build students' confidence in their ability to comprehend content area texts?

3 Building Vocabulary

IRA Standards: 1.1, 1.2, 1.3, 2.1, 2.2, 2.3, 3.1, 3.2, 4.2, 4.3, 5.1, 5.3, 6.2

Learning Goals

The reader of this chapter will:

- Understand the foundational theories underpinning vocabulary acquisition
- Understand the use of instructional approaches that develop word recognition, language comprehension, and reading/writing connections
- Develop and use formative assessments to analyze instructional effectiveness and student needs
- Use a variety of classroom configurations to differentiate instruction
- Provide instructional formats that encourage students to assume responsibility for their own vocabulary development

Questions to Consider

1. What are the foundational theories of vocabulary acquisition that can be applied to your discipline?
2. How will the application of the strategies within this chapter enhance your students' understanding of content material?
3. Why is formative assessment usually more beneficial than summative assessment?
4. Why is it important to encourage students to take responsibility for enhancing their own vocabulary development?

OVERVIEW

Most content area teachers recognize, and research confirms, the strong relationship between vocabulary knowledge and comprehension of text (Baumann, Kame'enui, & Ash, 2003). Teachers know that if their students have a well-developed content vocabulary, they will understand written materials within their content area more easily. Conversely, if students do not understand the meanings of content-specific words, they will have difficulty understanding and learning the text material.

Existing literature on vocabulary development emphasizes three main approaches for enhancing students' vocabulary: wide reading, explicit instruction of words and word-learning strategies, and the development of a classroom environment that encourages word consciousness (Yopp & Yopp, 2007). Many authorities in the field of vocabulary acquisition believe that the majority of new words incorporated into our vocabulary throughout our lifetimes are learned incidentally through conversation and wide reading (Cunningham, 2005). Reading theorists have surmised that the more exposure learners have to written texts, both at home and at school through self-selected, independent reading, the greater their vocabulary acquisition (Krashen, 2004).

Vocabulary knowledge involves understanding the meanings of words. It is however, more complex than this as words come to us in two forms: orally and in print. Oral vocabulary includes words that we use and understand in conversation, and printed vocabulary involves reading and writing. Class discussion of new words should always be conducted in order to help students process the meanings of the new words more deeply. As you teach new words, it is important that you teach not only the definitional or general meanings of the words, but also contextual definitions. Contextual definitions are the range of meanings a word may have, determined by the specific context in which it occurs (Readence, Bean, & Baldwin, 2008).

With the knowledge that students' success in school depends to a large extent upon their ability to read and comprehend text, it is mandatory that teachers provide instruction that enhances development in these areas. Because different methods of teaching words are appropriate in different circumstances, teachers need to use a variety of instructional formats. A basic premise of effective instruction is that students must develop a personal tie to the words by interacting with them in individual and meaningful ways. Relating new words or concepts to those already within the learner's schema or background knowledge allows the learner to develop a personal connection. Strategies in this chapter such as Semantic Feature Analysis (Johnson & Pearson, 1984) focus on activities that require students to think deeply about words and endeavor to relate them to their existing schema.

Formative assessment is a major part of an effective classroom. Its purpose is to provide feedback for both teachers and students. Results from formative assessments inform the teacher of what has been well taught and inform the students of what has been well learned. Summative assessment, on the other hand, is designed to judge student performance and determine grades, while the basic purpose of formative assessment is to guide instruction and to improve learning.

Several strategies within this chapter will provide both teachers and students with information about vocabulary acquisition through formative assessment activities.

The National Reading Panel (2006) provided several basic premises for effective vocabulary instruction. The following points are based on the panel's research.

1. Vocabulary should be taught both directly and indirectly.
2. Multiple and repeated exposure to vocabulary words are important.
3. Learning words in rich context is valuable for vocabulary learning. Words selected for instruction should be those that will be encountered multiple times in content texts.
4. In selecting words for instruction, be sure that students understand how the words relate to the context in which they are presented.
5. Vocabulary learning is most effective when it involves active engagement in learning tasks.
6. Computer activities can be used effectively for teaching new vocabulary.
7. Many new vocabulary words are acquired through incidental learning such as through conversation and independent reading.
8. A variety of methods should be used for vocabulary instruction. Dependence on one method will not result in optimal success.

Today's teachers are increasingly presented with diversity among their students. This diversity includes not only ethnicity but also the extent of their students' word knowledge, their linguistic backgrounds, their learning styles, and their literary abilities. Spanish speakers make up an increasing proportion of our schools' population. A report compiled by the Illinois State Board of Education, for example, determined that 81.25% of ELLs in Illinois speak Spanish (ISBE, 2010).

The English language is complicated for many ELLs—particularly words that are abstract such as *justice*, *intention*, or *transition* (Garcia, 1991). Poverty, too, plays a role in vocabulary acquisition as vocabulary competence is influenced by socio-demographic circumstances. It is estimated that by high school completion a student should know about 40,000 words (Nagy & Herman, 1987). But often that isn't the case with students from low-income families. The growing brain needs coherent, novel, challenging input. Frequently the demands of day-to-day survival take precedence over meaningful and productive conversations and word-building experiences (Jensen, 2009). It is, however, the teacher's responsibility and challenge to make word learning enjoyable, meaningful, and effective for all students (Blachowicz & Fisher, 2004).

Linking Vocabulary to Background Knowledge

To help students link vocabulary to their background knowledge

BACKGROUND

Effective vocabulary instruction involves assisting students in relating new vocabulary to what they already know. Helping students make ties to new vocabulary words that are personally meaningful aids in long-term retention of the words. Additionally, relating new vocabulary to previous experiences frequently leads to increased retention and usage (Blachowicz & Fisher, 2000). A variety of simple strategies can be used in your classroom to help students make these personal ties. One such strategy, developed by Gipe (1979), guides students as they read a short passage that uses an unknown word in a defined context. After reading the passage, students are asked to respond in writing to a question or statement with information from their personal experience that further develops the meaning of the unknown word. For example, if the new word is *barbarian*, you might ask students to write about something a barbarian might do if he or she came to their home for dinner. Making this personal connection enhances students' ability to remember the meaning of a new vocabulary word.

Students should be active participants in creating semantic connections between their prior knowledge and new vocabulary. Asking themselves "What do I already know about these words?" should be their first strategic step when new vocabulary is introduced. As they preview an upcoming reading selection, they can also ask themselves "What do I see in this selection that gives me a clue to what these words might mean?" Encourage your students to make preliminary predictions about the relationship between the new words and the topic of their content reading selection. These predictions demonstrate for students the semantic relatedness of words and concepts and underscore the fact that vocabulary learning is a crucial element in understanding textbook material (Blachowicz & Fisher, 2000).

Readers Needing Additional Support

Assist students who need additional support in linking new vocabulary to their existing vocabularies by encouraging them to engage in conversation about personal experiences with other students. Pair a more proficient English speaker with one who needs practice.

- Schema Theory
- Freewriting
- Conversation

Freewriting

Goal: *To help students link vocabulary to their background knowledge.* Assisting students in relating new vocabulary to what they already know provides a pathway to the long-term retention of words. Additionally, relating new vocabulary to previous experiences enhances students' ability to learn the meanings of new words.

An activity known as Word Explorations (Vacca, Vacca, & Mraz, 2011) is a vocabulary exercise that asks students to make connections between a selected term and their prior knowledge. This strategy will demonstrate for your students the importance of activating prior knowledge and discovering what is already known about a topic.

Select a topic related to a content area, such as *capitalism* from a World History class, and invite your students to write spontaneously for five minutes everything they know about this subject. Ask them to do so without regard for spelling, punctuation, grammar, or neatness.

This technique will jog their long-term memories and allow them to amass their thoughts about the topic. Frequently students are surprised to realize how much they already know and to see how many words they can use related to the subject.

Following the Freewriting exercise, conduct a discussion with your students to gauge their understanding of the importance and effect of activating background knowledge before encountering new vocabulary in a text selection.

Section **3.1** INSTRUCTIONAL STRATEGY 1

Knowledge Rating Scale

The Knowledge Rating Scale (Blachowicz, 1986) is a prereading activity designed to introduce a list of potentially unknown content words to your students. The Knowledge Rating Scale uses a survey format to have students determine their knowledge of a word or concept. As students complete the survey and participate in class discussions, they become aware of how much they already know about the subject to which the words are related. Additionally, using a Knowledge Rating Scale activates students' existing background knowledge and helps them begin to forge links with the new vocabulary concepts. As their teacher, you will be able to gauge the depth of your students' existing knowledge and note what areas need special attention during your instruction.

Directions

1. Select a list of important vocabulary words from a new unit or a chapter of text. Prepare a handout for each of your students that lists the vocabulary words followed by three columns labeled *Know It Well, Have Heard/Seen It,* and *No Clue.*

2. Divide the class into mixed ability groups of three or four students to provide students with opportunities to share their background knowledge.

3. Have students consider each word on the Knowledge Rating Scale and place an X in the appropriate column next to the word. Ask students to look carefully at each word. Tell them if they think that they can define the word they should place an X in the first column under *Know It Well.* If they have heard of the word or have seen it, but are unsure of its meaning, they should place an X in the second column under *Have Heard/Seen It.* If the word is totally unfamiliar, they should place an X in the third column labeled *No Clue.*

4. After students have completed the Knowledge Rating Scale, ask them to write sentences using the words they have marked in the *Know It Well* column.

5. Lead the class in a discussion about the words with which students have composed sentences. As students read the chapter in the following days, direct them to add definitions for unknown words and confirm or, if appropriate, change the sentences they have for known words.

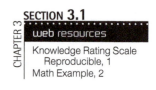

SECTION **3.1**
web resources
Knowledge Rating Scale
    Reproducible, 1
Math Example, 2

CHAPTER 3

Government

Write sentences for words they don't know

Knowledge Rating Scale	*Know It Well*	*Have Heard/Seen It*	*No Clue*
interdependence		X	
refugee	X		
nuclear proliferation		X	
international laws		X	
ethnic intolerance	X		
religious intolerance	X		
chemical weapons			X
biological weapons			X
United Nations	X		
human rights		X	

EXAMPLE

Section 3.1 INSTRUCTIONAL STRATEGY 2

Exclusion Brainstorming

Exclusion Brainstorming (Blachowicz, 1986) is a strategy designed to guide students as they think about what they already know about concept words related to a particular topic. It is a user-friendly technique, easy to implement, and easy for students to understand. Additionally, it accommodates reluctant readers and those students who may be unfamiliar with the topic.

Directions

1. Write the title of a selection or a topic so it can be seen by all students. Use an example from your content area or use the following example from a world history text.
2. Underneath the topic or title, list a mixture of words or phrases—five that are related to the topic, five that are not related to the topic, and five that are ambiguous. List the words in random order. An example follows.

Topic: Chernobyl
Mixture of Words and Phrases

Kiev	rain forests	radiation
illness	energy	exposure
greenhouse effect	death	accident
meltdown	global warming	world climate
nuclear power	thyroid cancer	conservation

3. Ask students to eliminate those words and phrases that they think are not related to the topic or would not be included in a selection about the topic. Ask students to explain their decisions. In this example, students should eliminate the following words and phrases.

Words Unrelated to the Topic

greenhouse effect	conservation
global warming	rain forests
world climate	

4. Next, ask students to choose the words and phrases that they think are most likely to appear in the selection and that are related to the topic. Once again, be sure to ask students to explain their decisions. An essential component of any brainstorming activity is for students to explain why they think the way they do (Blachowicz, 1986). In this example, the words and phrases related to the topic are listed below.

Words Related to the Topic

Kiev	accident
nuclear power	radiation
meltdown	

5. Have students choose those words and phrases that are somewhat ambiguous. The words and phrases that are ambiguous are listed below.

Ambiguous Words

thyroid cancer	death
illness	energy
exposure	

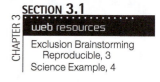

SECTION 3.1
web resources
Exclusion Brainstorming
Reproducible, 3
Science Example, 4

6. Assign the related reading selection and ask students to look for the vocabulary words as they read. Direct students to make particular note of the ambiguous words and phrases to see if they can determine how they are used in the selection.

7. After students have completed the reading assignment, discuss the meanings of the ambiguous vocabulary words and how they relate to the selection. Encourage students to share their knowledge about the meanings of the words. For any words that are still unknown, ask students to determine their meanings by using their dictionaries and the contexts in which the words are presented.

 SAT VOCABULARY WORDS
Visit the interactive site for learning advanced English vocabulary words for the SAT.
www.vocabulary.com

PUZZLES AND GAMES
This is an excellent site for vocabulary puzzles and games.
www.vocabulary.com

Section **3.1** INSTRUCTIONAL STRATEGY 3

Imagine That!

Imagine That! is a strategy designed to encourage students to consider words and situations from a more personal viewpoint (Courtney, 2003). As students read each scenario, they assume an identity, which is impacted by the underlined word or words in the sentence. Students are asked to answer the questions following the sentences, using their new identity as a framework for their responses. By considering situations from a personal viewpoint, students are aided in retaining information and in learning important vocabulary terms.

Directions

1. Pre-select several words or concepts from your text which lend themselves to asking students to assume an alternate identity.

SECTION 3.1
web resources
Imagine That! Reproducible, 5

2. Prepare questions using the word or concept.

3. Ask students to respond to the questions by writing in the first person.

4. Use whole class or small group discussions to share responses.

History

1. It's 1920, you are a female and you're fighting to gain <u>ratification</u> of the Nineteenth Amendment. Why do you care?

   _____

2. It is early in the 1800s. You are an American at sea. The British have captured your ship and you have experienced <u>impressment</u>. What has happened to you?

   _____

3. You are a follower of Ralph Waldo Emerson's philosophy of <u>transcendentalism</u>. What do you believe?

   _____

4. You are Nat Turner and you have organized a <u>rebellion</u>. What are you rebelling against?

   _____

5. Your neighbor just called you an <u>abolitionist</u>. Has he or she insulted you?

   _____

6. Your name is Abraham Lincoln and you've just given the Gettysburg Address. Before your speech people said "<u>The United States are</u>." Afterwards they said, "<u>The United States is</u>." Why have they changed the verb?

   _____

7. You are a former slave now involved in <u>sharecropping</u>. Why are you sharing your crop?

   _____

8. You are a <u>conductor</u> in the Underground Railroad. What is your job?

   _____

9. Your father lives in Rome and is known in the community as a <u>plebeian</u>. Your uncle, on the other hand, is a <u>patrician</u>. What's the difference?

   _____

10. Your name is Galileo and you are a professor in Pisa, Italy. You are about to challenge Aristotle's <u>theory of gravity</u>. What have you discovered?

    _____

Based on Courtney, G. (2003). *Vocabulary acquisition.* St. Charles, IL: Author.

EXAMPLE

AUDIO-PICTURE ENGLISH
This site offers interactive audio-picture English lessons designed for the ELL student.
www.web-books.com/Language

Defining Words

GOAL
To help students
learn the meanings
of words

BACKGROUND

When teachers give their students a list of seemingly unknown words and ask them to find the words in dictionaries, write down definitions for them, and use the words in sentences, they are not involving their students in a meaningful instructional activity. Too often, students will comply with the instructions, complete the exercise, and immediately forget the definitions for which they have arduously searched. No personal connection to the new words is being forged through participation in this activity.

Teachers need to help students define and categorize new words and assist students in making personal connections. Every content area has vocabulary that is unique to its subject matter. These special and technical vocabulary terms provide the framework for learning the information specific to a particular subject.

It is impossible for teachers to predict all of the words that their students will need to know in order for them to gain meaning from a text selection. Stahl (1986) has developed three guidelines for determining which words may need special instruction.

First, decide how important each word is to understanding the text. If the word is one that probably will not be encountered again, that word can be ignored. For example, in a high school art book, the following sentence appears: "This work was done with quick drying *duco* paint." Although the word *duco* may not be in the students' vocabulary, it is not a word that is necessary to teach because it does not affect the meaning of the passage. If, however, comprehension of the material hinges on understanding a particular word, it is important to select this word for special instruction. In the sentence "When applied thickly, oil paint is *opaque*," it might be necessary to teach the word *opaque* because it is important for understanding the meaning of the sentence.

Second, try to decide if students can figure out the meaning of the word through the context in which it is presented. If the word is well defined in context, it is not imperative that you teach it. The following example from a biology text defines *theory*: "If an hypothesis continues to generate successful predictions, it may be promoted to the status of a *theory*. A theory is any hypothesis that is supported by many observations." If, however, the text does not clearly define the word, you may wish to select the word for teaching.

Third, decide how much time you need to spend teaching a particular word. If the word represents a concept that is not within students' understanding but is closely related to a known word, it can be taught relatively easily by providing examples that establish the connection. For example, the word *parsimonious* may be an unfamiliar word to many of your students. However, the word *stingy* is one that most of them will recognize. Making the connection between the two words for your students will assist them in learning and remembering the meaning of *parsimonious*. Discussion may motivate them to pursue further vocabulary exploration as they become more conscious of new words (Stahl, 1986).

Readers Needing Additional Support

Help students define and categorize new words by making a personal connection to them. Allow students to discuss their connections to new vocabulary by conversing with peers. Pre-teach any concepts for which students may not have a cultural reference. Define abstract terms with concrete examples.

Using Context, Word Structure, and Dictionary Definitions

Goal: *To help students learn the meanings of words.* To determine the meanings of new vocabulary words, students may use a combination of three elements: context, word structure, and the dictionary, as they continually endeavor to relate the words to their existing background knowledge. In order to assess Goal 3.2, provide your students with an esoteric paragraph from a book of your choice. Ask students to identify the words within a paragraph or selected sentences whose meanings are unclear. Direct them to determine the meanings of the unknown words using any of the three aforementioned strategies and to write a short paragraph "translating" the sentences or selection.

You may choose to use the following sentences from *Insult to Intelligence* (Smith, 1986).

"Our intellectual tests are abysmal at predicting success. Interests, preferences, and family background are much better predictors of professional achievement than the IQ" (Smith, 1986, p. 49).

"The methodology of systems analysis similarly involves reducing large and complex activities to sequences of small tasks, or objectives, each of which has to be accomplished before there is progress to the next task" (Smith, 1986, p. 65).

"And the teachers whom the writers mentioned were not necessarily tender and permissive. Some of these teachers were difficult and demanding curmudgeons" (Smith, 1986, p. 170).

Section **3.2** **INSTRUCTIONAL STRATEGY 4**

Magic Squares

— Fun prediction activity!

The purpose of Magic Squares (Vacca, Vacca, & Mraz, 2011) is for students to match a content term with its definition. Magic Squares provide a challenging yet enjoyable way for students to think about word definitions as they solve a simple math puzzle based on a particular number combination. Magic Squares can be used as an opportunity for students to predict the meanings of new words by seeing the words in context or as a review for important definitions from a chapter of text.

Directions

1. Construct an activity sheet that has two sections, one for content area terms and one for definitions. See the example on the next page.

2. Direct students to match each term with its definition. As they do this, students consider the numbers denoting the terms as well as the letters denoting the definitions.

3. Instruct students to put the number of a word in the proper space of the Magic Square that is marked by the letter of its definition. For example, the definition of Dali (word 2) is B, a Spanish Surrealist painter, so the number 2 goes in the box labeled B. If student's answers are correct, they will complete a Magic Square. The numerical total will be the same for each row across and each column down in the square. In the following example from an art text, the magic number is 18.

CHAPTER 3

SECTION 3.2
web resources

Magic Square
Reproducible, 6
Statistics Example, 7

Magic Square

Definitions

A. turning something familiar into something strange
B. Spanish Surrealist painter
C. joining images in impossible combinations
D. Belgian Surrealist
E. art movement based on radical ideas and dream-like images
F. the range from light to dark
G. use of space
H. things are not where they naturally belong
I. surface quality

A	B	C
D	E	F
G	H	I

Content Terms (Answers)

1. Scale
2. Dali
3. Texture
4. Magritte
5. Composition
6. Surrealism
7. Juxtaposing
8. Value
9. Transformation
10. Dislocation

Answers

A	B	C
9	2	7
D	E	F
4	6	8
G	H	I
5	10	3

EXAMPLE

4. Vacca, Vacca, and Mraz (2011) offer these and additional patterns for Magic Square compositions (p. 265).

A.

7	3	5
2	4	9
6	8	1

0*   5**

B.

9	7	5
1	8	12
11	6	4

3*   21**

C.

7	11	8
10	12	4
9	3	14

5*   26**

* extra terms needed in answer column   ** magic number

5. The single asterisks above refer to the necessity of adding extra terms to the answer column in order to establish a consecutive order of numbers as in examples B and C. However only 9 of the choices will be used.

Section **3.2** **INSTRUCTIONAL STRATEGY 5**

Graphic Organizers

A Graphic Organizer is an effective framework for organizing content vocabulary. The selected words are those that you consider important for student understanding of the content of the reading. The purpose of the Graphic Organizer is to show the concepts of the reading in relation to each other. There are several forms of Graphic

Organizers but a common one is called a network tree. Vacca, Vacca, and Mraz (2011) suggest the following steps for developing a network tree Graphic Organizer.

In this example, the steps are applied to a section of a reading on the Roman civilization in a high school history book.

Directions

1. Analyze the vocabulary in the reading and select the words important for understanding the content. The following words were selected.

Roman gods	King of the gods	Minerva
realm	Goddess of wisdom	owl
Jupiter	symbol	spear
God of the sea	Neptune	god
eagle		

2. Select a word or phrase from the list that represents the most inclusive concept as the heading and choose words that are subordinate to this concept.

Roman Gods

| God | Realm | Symbol |

3. Review the list and place the appropriate words under each heading.

Roman Gods

God	Realm	Symbol
Jupiter	King of the gods	eagle
Neptune	God of the sea	spear
Minerva	Goddess of wisdom	owl

4. Evaluate the Graphic Organizer and the vocabulary arrangement.
5. Present the Graphic Organizer with the vocabulary relationships to the class and conduct a discussion of the concepts to further your students' understanding.
6. After the discussion, urge students to use the Graphic Organizer as a study guide and to add additional words or phrases as they complete their reading assignment.

CHAPTER 3
SECTION 3.2
web resources
Graphic Organizer
Reproducible, 8

Section **3.2** INSTRUCTIONAL STRATEGY 6

Four Square

Four Square (Eeds & Cockrum, 1985) is an effective strategy that is easy to implement and helps students learn the definitions of new words. In Four Square students make personal connections to new words, thus increasing the likelihood that the words will be retained in their long-term memories.

Directions

1. Draw a square with four quadrants where it can be seen by the entire class.
2. Ask students to select a word from their content text that they consider important or select a word that you want students to learn. Write the vocabulary word in the upper-left quadrant.
3. Guide students in developing an appropriate definition for the selected word. Write the definition in the upper-right quadrant.

4. Ask students to suggest words or phrases that they personally associate with the vocabulary word. Write one of the personal associations suggested by students in the lower-left quadrant.

5. Next, ask students to suggest a word or phrase that does *not* define the vocabulary word. Write this word or phrase in the lower-right quadrant. The following example is from an American government text.

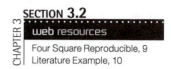
SECTION **3.2**
web resources
Four Square Reproducible, 9
Literature Example, 10

Four Square	
Vocabulary Word détente	**Definition** decrease in tension between countries
Personal Association French for relaxation	**Opposite** strained relations

6. Invite students to develop several Four Square vocabulary examples using words from their text that are important for understanding content material.

Word Storm

Word Storm (Klemp, 1994) combines the use of content area vocabulary with the students' predictions about how the words will be used in context. It is effective as a preteaching activity and will enhance your students' connections with the technical or specialized vocabulary of content area material. Students may work in pairs or in small groups. Encourage students to discuss their responses as they work. Students can determine their answers by drawing on their background knowledge, or they may use a dictionary, glossary, or thesaurus.

Directions

1. Give each of your students a Word Storm sheet from the website with a word in the top space. Assign the words you have selected from your content area so that no more than two groups of students have the same word. Duplication of some words is important to provide insights into the uses of the words during the discussion phase of the activity. For this example the Word Storm word is *combustion*.

2. Next, ask students to write the sentence from the text that contains the word *combustion*. In this case, the sentence is: *Combustion includes many chemical reactions.*

3. For number three, ask students to write some words that they think of when they see the word *combustion*. For this example, the words are *explosion, fire*, and *heat*.

4. Some of the directives on the Word Storm sheet are intentionally ambiguous and may encourage diverse responses from students. In question four, students are asked to think of some different forms of the word given at the top of the page. Students may write down variations of the word. Other forms of the word *combustion* are *combustible, combustibility*, and *combustive*.

5. For question number five, students are to name three people who would likely use this word. Possible responses are *firefighter, chemist*, and *rocket builder*.

6. Students may not be able to answer some of the questions if the word does not fit neatly into the given prompt. For example, if the word were a noun such as *alphabet*, it would be difficult to answer question six. For this question, students are to think of other words that mean the same thing as

SECTION **3.2**
web resources
Word Storm Reproducible, 11
English Example, 12

the word at the top of the page. A nonanswer is also valuable because it encourages students to think about the various forms of words. In this case, other words that mean the same thing as *combustion* are *flaming, burning*, and *visible oxidation*.

7. For the last directive, students should write a sentence using the chosen word (*combustion*) appropriately. A sentence might be: *Combustion is a chemical reaction that gives off heat and light*.

Science

Word Storm

1. What is the word?   <u>combustion</u>

2. Write the sentence from the text in which the word is used.
   <u>Combustion includes many chemical reactions</u>.

3. What are some words that you think of when you see this word?
   <u>explosion</u>   <u>fire</u>   <u>heat</u>

4. Do you know any other forms of this word? If so, what are they?
   <u>combustible</u>   <u>combustibility</u>   <u>combustive</u>

5. Name three people who would be likely to use this word.
   <u>firefighter</u>   <u>chemist</u>   <u>rocket builder</u>

6. Can you think of any other words that mean the same thing?
   <u>flaming</u>   <u>burning</u>   <u>visible oxidation</u>

7. Write a sentence using this word appropriately. Make sure your sentence tells us what the word means!
   <u>Combustion is a chemical reaction that gives off heat and light</u>.

Based on Klemp, R.M. (1994). Word storm: Connecting vocabulary to the student's database. *The Reading Teacher, 48*, 282.

EXAMPLE

SURF THE WEB

DIRECTORY OF RESOURCES
This site, designed to help students learn English, provides a directory of resources organized by media type, including television, radio, films, newspapers, magazines, and music.
        http://englisheverywhere.homestead.com/

WORD-A-DAY
Improve your vocabulary by checking out this Word-A-Day site. Don't be caught verbally unaware!
        www.wordsmith.org

Section **3.2** INSTRUCTIONAL STRATEGY 8

Word Web

A Word Web (Rosenbaum, 2001) is designed to facilitate students' vocabulary development by clarifying and enriching the meanings of known words and introducing students to unknown words. This strategy is designed to integrate the components of effective vocabulary instruction. These components include activating and extending prior knowledge and using context, using a dictionary for clarification, and analyzing the structure of the word in order to establish a personal connection (Rosenbaum, 2001). Urge your students to seek out new and interesting words during independent or assigned reading and record them in a journal or notebook. This will encourage students to assume some responsibility for their own vocabulary development.

Directions

1. Ask students to select an unfamiliar word from their text or vocabulary journal and write it and the page number where it is located in Bubble 1. The example below uses the word *heroine* from page 17 in a history text.

2. In Bubble 2, direct students to record the essential part of the sentence from their text containing the word. The text says, "Rosa Parks is recognized as a national *heroine*."

3. In Bubble 3, ask students to write the dictionary definition of the new word, using the definition that most appropriately supports the context in which the word is used. The dictionary defines *heroine* as "a female who is endowed with courage and strength."

4. Ask students to use a dictionary or thesaurus to select and record both a synonym and an antonym for the new word and to place them in Bubbles 5 and 7. Rosenbaum (2001) suggests that students may choose to substitute a nonexample for their word rather than an antonym, because some words do not have antonyms. For a synonym of *heroine*, the word *champion* was chosen. The antonym in this example is *coward*.

5. Have students record another form of the new word in Bubble 6. Another form of the word *heroine* is *heroic*.

CHAPTER 3

SECTION 3.2

web resources

Word Web Reproducible, 13
English Example, 14

6. In Bubble 8, ask students to write a phrase, a category, an example, or some personal clue to the word they have selected. The personal clue in this example is another heroine, Joan of Arc.

7. The last step in the Word Web is for students to write an original sentence using the word correctly. This sentence will be in Bubble 4. The example sentence is: To become a *heroine*, you have to be a girl and have a lot of courage.

History

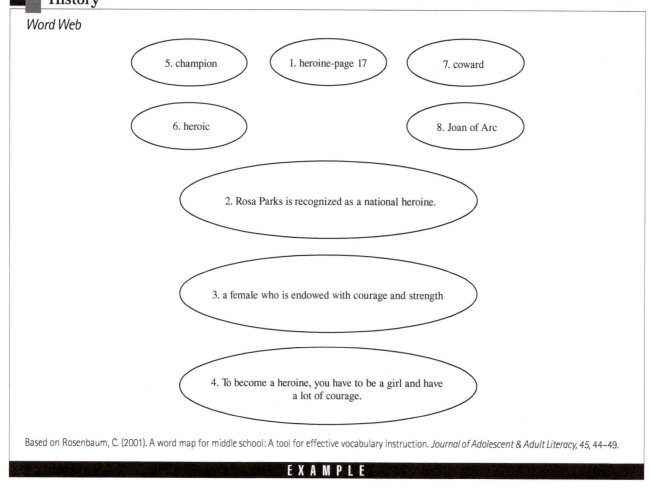

Word Web

- 5. champion
- 1. heroine-page 17
- 7. coward
- 6. heroic
- 8. Joan of Arc
- 2. Rosa Parks is recognized as a national heroine.
- 3. a female who is endowed with courage and strength
- 4. To become a heroine, you have to be a girl and have a lot of courage.

Based on Rosenbaum, C. (2001). A word map for middle school: A tool for effective vocabulary instruction. *Journal of Adolescent & Adult Literacy, 45,* 44–49.

EXAMPLE

Understanding Relationships among Words

GOAL
To help students understand the relationships among words

BACKGROUND

The complexity of learning new words is compounded by the variety of word-level knowledge that students bring with them to the classroom. Beck, McKeown, and Kucan (2002) describe three tiers of vocabulary. These tiers can serve as a guide for teachers in determining which words need to be taught before students begin to read a text assignment. The tiers are as follows.

Tier 1—Basic high-frequency words common to everyday language. Typically, students don't need instruction to understand these words. Examples: *house, family, friend*.

Tier 2—High-frequency and high-utility words but less commonly used in everyday language. Many of these words may require some attention for text understanding. Examples: *antipathy, repulsive, eminence*.

Tier 3—Low-frequency words or phrases but necesary for understanding the content area selection. These words are specific to the subject matter and frequently require pre-teaching. Examples: *political disunity, vassals, polygon*.

Flanigan and Greenwood (2007) added another tier which includes words that appear in the text but are not critical to understanding its content. These are words that the students probably already know and are common in their daily vocabulary. The authors mention, however, that teachers should not assume that all English-Language Learners are familiar with these words and, in some cases, may need to spend time reviewing them.

Another category of words that do not need to be pre-taught are words that do not relate to the teacher's instructional goals or serve the purpose of the lesson. Sometimes textbooks highlight words that may not be pertinent to the teacher's instructional goals. Teachers should not feel obligated to pre-teach these words.

A third category in this tier is words for which the students can infer the meaning from the surrounding text. The authors cite the word *antebellum* from a U.S. History book which was briefly defined as, "before the Civil War." Flanigan and Greenwood believe that this "was all the reader needed to know in order to understand the sentence and the larger concepts in the passage" (p. 231).

A common thread runs through all content area subjects. Students need assistance in developing the ability to construct meanings for unknown words based on their conceptual knowledge of the subject matter and their prior knowledge. They need to develop a repertorie of techniques and strategies in order to determine word meaning and understand content area material. The strategies in this section are designed to provide opportunities for students to use new words in meaningful contexts as they develop a deeper understanding of the relationships among words.

Readers Needing Additional Support

Use brainstorming and discussion probes to determine how familiar students are with the content of the selection you are going to teach. Have students work in pairs or groups to share information. Allow for variation in instruction to accommodate different learning styles. Present new vocabulary in meaningful contexts to assist students in developing relationships among words.

Goal: *To help students understand the relationships among words.* As you complete Section 3.3, you will want to assess your students to determine whether the goal, learning about the relationships among words, has been achieved. One of the strategies in this section (Magnet Words Instructional Strategy 11) is perfect for this endeavor.

After students have completed reading a selected text from a content area of your choice, ask them to identify key vocabulary terms (Magnet Words) from the selection. Write the words offered by your students where they can be seen by the entire class.

Distribute four note cards to each student and ask them to write one Magnet Word from the selection on each card. Ask students to record additional details from the passage related to each of the Magnet Words. Finally, ask your students to write a short paragraph using a Magnet Word and its related words in a short paragraph.

Collect the paragraphs and assess them to see if your students have used the relationship among the words to construct a meaningful paragraph.

Section **3.3** INSTRUCTIONAL STRATEGY 9

Semantic Feature Analysis

A Semantic Feature Analysis (Johnson & Pearson, 1984) is an effective strategy for helping students visualize the relationships among concepts. This activity helps students as they build bridges between new concepts and known concepts that are already part of their background knowledge. As students complete a Semantic Feature Analysis, they establish conceptual frameworks that help them understand the meanings of the words in new contexts. When students participate in this activity, they analyze words and concepts by identifying and comparing their various properties. Through the use of a matrix or a grid, students will be involved in developing their categorization skills as they determine the similarities and differences between related words. A Semantic Feature Analysis is designed to provide a systematic procedure for establishing categories and developing significant relationships among new words and concepts.

Directions

1. Select a topic or category from your text that you want your students to analyze in some depth. The example on the next page focuses on the topic of the art media used by different artists.
2. List terms related to the topic down the left side of the grid. In this example, the names of the artists are listed.
3. List features or properties related to the topic across the top of the grid. In this example, types of art media are listed.

Art

Semantic Feature Analysis

Artists	Art Media					
	Print Making	Watercolor	Acrylic	Oil	Sculpture	Charcoal
Mary Cassatt						
Henri de Toulouse-Lautrec						
Wassily Kandinsky						
Henri-Charles Manguin						
Georgia O'Keeffe						

EXAMPLE

4. Discuss each topic word as you read it aloud. Remind students of the definitions of the feature words written across the top of the grid, briefly discussing each one.

5. Guide students through the matrix. Ask them to decide how each topic word relates to each feature on the top of the matrix. In this particular example, students are to decide if a listed artist used a particular medium. Ask students to place a plus (+) on the grid if the feature relates to a topic word, a minus (–) if it does not, and a question mark (?) if they are unsure.

6. After you have completed this initial phase of the Semantic Feature Analysis, direct students to read the appropriate chapter in their textbooks. Students can also be encouraged to look for the names of additional artists and art media to expand their vocabulary.

7. Discuss the selection with the class and add students' suggestions to the appropriate areas of the grid. Below is an example of a Semantic Feature Analysis based on a mathematics text.

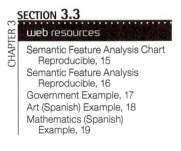

SECTION 3.3

web resources

Semantic Feature Analysis Chart
Reproducible, 15
Semantic Feature Analysis
Reproducible, 16
Government Example, 17
Art (Spanish) Example, 18
Mathematics (Spanish)
Example, 19

Mathematics

Semantic Feature Analysis

Geometric Figures	Features			
	Convex	Exactly 4-Sided	Contains Right Angle	Contains Straight Line Segments
parallelogram	–	+	?	+
circle	+	–	–	–
obtuse triangle	+	–	–	+
polygon	?	?	?	+
quadrilateral	?	+	?	+
nonagon	?	–	?	+
acute triangle	+	–	–	+
right triangle	+	–	+	+

EXAMPLE

Word Sort

A Word Sort (Gillet & Kita, 1979) requires students to organize and classify words based on their prior knowledge about the words. It is a simple activity that lends itself well to small group collaboration. The object of a Word Sort is to group words into categories according to some shared feature. Word Sorts can be conducted in two ways: closed and open. In a Closed Word Sort, the teacher predetermines the categories for students and thus establishes the criterion that the words must have in common in order to form a group or category. In an Open Word Sort, there are no predetermined categories and thus no shared characteristics have been decided in advance. Students are asked to decide for themselves what the words have in common and to group them accordingly. Word Sorts can be used before reading as a predictive exercise or after reading as a way of extending understanding of the concepts (Vacca, Vacca, & Mraz, 2011).

Directions

1. Select 12 to 15 interesting words from a chapter in your content textbook. The words should be ones that you have determined are related to some of the important concepts in the chapter. Write the words on sets of note cards, or where they can be seen by the entire class.

2. Divide the class into groups of three or four students. Tell the students that they are going to participate in a Closed Word Sort and are to sort the words according to the categories you have established. If using cards, distribute a set to each group. The following example is from a biology text.

Biology

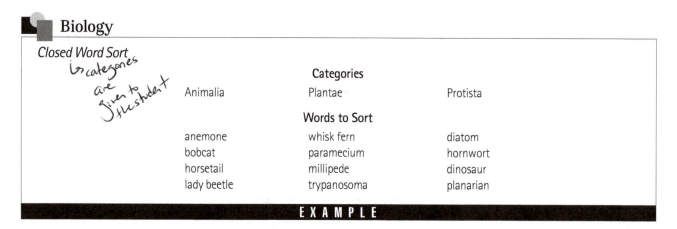

Closed Word Sort
↳ categories are given to the student

	Categories	
Animalia	Plantae	Protista

Words to Sort

anemone	whisk fern	diatom
bobcat	paramecium	hornwort
horsetail	millipede	dinosaur
lady beetle	trypanosoma	planarian

EXAMPLE

3. Allow about 10 minutes for students to sort the words. Ask a student from each group to share one of their group's categories. Continue until all categories have been discussed. Invite students to explain why they sorted the words as they did.

4. To conduct an Open Word Sort, tell students to group the selected words into categories by looking for shared traits among them. The former example would be an Open Word Sort if the categories were omitted. In this case, students would need to establish their own categories for the words.

5. An example of words for an Open Word Sort using terms selected from an accounting text appears on the next page.

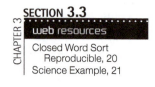

SECTION 3.3
web resources
CHAPTER 3

Closed Word Sort
    Reproducible, 20
Science Example, 21

Words to Sort

accountant	charter	manufacturing business
accounting clerk	corporation	merchandising business
accounting system	fiscal period	partnership
business entity	general bookkeeper	profit
capital	going concern	service business
certified public accountant	loss	sole proprietorship

6. After students have completed the Word Sort, invite a student to share one of the categories and the words placed in that category. An example follows.

Types of Businesses Operated for Profit

manufacturing business	partnership
merchandising business	sole proprietorship
service business	corporation

Section **3.3** INSTRUCTIONAL STRATEGY 11

Magnet Words

Magnet Words, adapted from Magnet Summaries (Buehl, 2009), has students identify key vocabulary terms from a text selection. As students select their words, they are focusing on the main concepts presented in the chapter. Thus, students are provided with opportunities for enhancing two important skills: their understanding of key vocabulary terms and the relationship of the words to each other. Students work in small groups to identify the Magnet Words, which provides them with the chance to work collaboratively.

Directions

1. Use the idea of magnets as you introduce the concept of Magnet Words to your students. For example, make the following comments.

    Magnets attract metal objects and magnet words attract information or details to them. Look over your text assignment and see if you can identify some Magnet Words that the details in the passage "stick to." Most of the information in each section of your text will be connected to the Magnet Words in that section.

2. After students have completed reading a short selection of the text, ask them to suggest possible Magnet Words from the selection. Initially, students may need you to model selecting the Magnet Words from a selection.

3. Write the Magnet Words offered by your students where they can be seen by the entire class. The following words were taken from a world history text.

    Nile River   pharaohs   society   religion

4. Distribute four note cards to each student and ask students to write one Magnet Word on each card.

5. Ask students to recall some important details from the passage related to each Magnet Word. Write these details beneath the appropriate Magnet Word. As you write them, ask students to follow the same procedure on the appropriate note card.

Nile River	Pharaohs	Society	Religion
shaped Egyptian life	Egyptian kings	nobles	maat
linked diverse lands	immortal	peasants	Osiris
fertile farming	pyramids	slaves	Akhenaton
	first illness		
	middle kingdom		
	second illness		

6. Divide the class into groups of three or four students of mixed ability. Ask students to record additional details from the passage related to each of the Magnet Words.

7. Model writing a short paragraph that incorporates a Magnet Word. An example follows.

> The Nile River shaped Egyptian life. It linked diverse lands from the highlands of eastern Africa to the Mediterranean Sea. The river brought water to Egypt from the distant mountains, plateaus, and lakes of central Africa. When the river receded each year in October, it left behind a rich, wet deposit of fertile black mud perfect for farming.

CHAPTER 3

SECTION 3.3
web resources
Magnet Words Reproducible, 22
Science Example, 23

8. Ask each group of students to share a paragraph using a Magnet Word. Encourage class members to offer suggestions for effectively incorporating other words relating to the Magnet Word into the paragraph.

Section **3.3** INSTRUCTIONAL STRATEGY 12

Classifying Challenge

Classifying words is a thinking skill that supports students' use and exploration of word meanings (Graves, 1986).

Directions

1. Find one, two, or three words from your text that may be new to your students. For this example, the word *perpetuity* is used.

2. On small cards, print up to 10 synonyms or associations for each of the new words. Synonyms for *perpetuity* might include *everlastingness, constancy, eternity, infinity, time without end, deathlessness, immortality,* and *continuity*.

3. Introduce the new words to students by writing them where they can be seen by the entire class. A sentence using *perpetuity* could be: The *perpetuity* of public education is based on our country's belief that everyone has the right to be educated.

4. Using the context provided, encourage students to discuss the meanings of the new words. After the discussion has been completed, provide students with an explicit definition of the new words. The explicit definition of *perpetuity* is time without end or the quality, state, or condition of being perpetual.

5. After the new words have been introduced in this fashion, write each of them as category headings.

6. Distribute the note cards containing the synonyms or phrases to the students. Ask them to discuss with a partner or in a small group the word category to which their synonym belongs. Invite students to come forward and write their synonym under the appropriate word category heading.

7. When all of the synonyms are placed in the appropriate categories, ask students to select one of the new words and write a short descriptive paragraph using as many of the synonyms under their chosen category word as they can.

Developing Independence in Vocabulary Acquisition

GOAL

To help students develop independence in acquiring and refining their vocabulary

BACKGROUND

Nearly 400,000 graphically distinct words are used in school texts. This figure does not include proper names, of which there are approximately 100,000 (Nagy & Anderson, 1984). It is estimated that students learn close to 3,000 new words per year during their school years, and a high school senior's vocabulary contains approximately 40,000 words (Nagy & Herman, 1987). Clearly, the vocabulary learning challenge for students is extensive.

A goal in teaching any subject is to assist students in becoming independent learners so that they eventually will assume responsibility for their own learning. However, this will not happen automatically. Teachers must scaffold instruction to help students learn independently from texts and other sources. Scaffolding instruction involves supporting students as they develop the confidence to learn on their own. It is essential that students develop the use of strategies that will provide them with the tools they need to develop this independence.

One way in which students learn new words is through using the context in which the word appears. Artley (1975) wrote that it is context, not the dictionary meaning, that gives each word its unique flavor. Knowing that words have denotative meanings as well as connotative definitions is an important aspect of developing vocabulary knowledge. By teaching students to consider the context as they determine word meanings, you will help them to further develop independence in building their vocabularies.

For students to develop independence as they increase their vocabularies, they should sometimes be allowed to select the words they wish to learn, define the words in their own terms, and engage in word play so that they gain an appreciation for a versatile vocabulary (Moore, Moore, Cunningham, & Cunningham, 2006). For a student for whom English is a second language, self-selection is critical as well as empowering (Jiminez, 1997). This section will present several strategies designed to help students to develop independence in extending their word knowledge.

Assessing Student Learning

Vocabulary Journals

Goal: *To help students develop independence in acquiring and refining their vocabulary.* As a teacher, your goal is to assist students in becoming independent learners with the idea of their ultimately being responsible for their own learning. In order for students to develop independence in word acquisition as they increase their vocabularies, they should be encouraged throughout the year to select words they wish to learn and to record them in a personal vocabulary journal.

A worthy goal throughout this chapter is for your students to increase their vocabularies through a variety of strategies. To assess their efforts in this direction, select a date during the semester when you will collect their vocabulary journals as described in Instructional Strategy 13, Vocabulary Self-Collection.

Develop benchmarks and a point scale with your students for self-evaluation. It may resemble the following.

Benchmarks and Points

I have selected at least 10 new words for my journal. (1 point per word)

I have selected words for my journal that have connections to topics discussed in this class. (5 points)

I have written clear definitions of the words. (5 points)

I have used the words correctly in sentences. (5 points)

I have made personal connections to the words. (5 points)

As you evaluate students' journals you may wish to include comments such as *Exceeds Expectations, Meets Expectations,* or *Needs Improvement.*

Allow students to select the words they wish to learn and to define the words in their own terms. When appropriate, assist students in using cultural or native language references in order to help commit definitions to long-term memory.

Section **3.4** INSTRUCTIONAL STRATEGY 13

Vocabulary Self-Collection ⟶ consider student population

Vocabulary Self-Collection (Haggard, 1986) is designed to promote growth in both the students' general vocabulary and content area vocabulary. This strategy facilitates long-term retention of words that are used in a variety of academic disciplines. Students work in teams to choose the vocabulary words they believe are important to the meaning of a text selection, thus expanding their vocabulary as they assume responsibility for their own learning.

Directions

1. After students have completed reading and discussing an assigned text selection, divide the class into groups of three or four students. Ask students to go through the text selection and identify one word that they think should be studied further by the class. Model the procedure by selecting a word and presenting it to the class.

2. Explain that each group is to choose an individual to present the selected word and its definition.

3. Write the word you selected and those selected by the students where they can be seen by the entire class. As you record each word, invite students to present its definition from its original context. Use the following example from a history text or an example from your textbook.

    conquistadors: Spanish explorers who claimed new colonies for Spain during the 16th century.

4. Discuss each word's meaning and add whatever information is necessary to clarify the definitions. Use the following example as a guide.

    conquistadors: Spanish explorers crossed the Atlantic to claim new colonies for Spain during the 16th century. They traveled first into the Caribbean islands and along the coasts of Central America and South America. Then they swept through Mexico and south to the tip of South America.

5. Complete the discussion and instruct students to review the list and eliminate words that are duplicates, words they already know, and words that they do not think are important to the comprehension of the text selection.

6. Ask students to define the remaining words and record them in their vocabulary journals or notebooks.

SECTION 3.4
CHAPTER 3
web resources
Vocabulary Self-Collection
Reproducible, 24

TOAST

= study strategy

Dana and Rodriguez (1992) developed TOAST to provide students with a system for studying vocabulary independently. TOAST is an acronym for *Test*, *Organize*, *Anchor*, *Say*, and *Test*. This strategy provides students with the opportunity to learn at their own rate and to choose words to study that seem particularly difficult for them.

Directions

1. **TEST.** After students have completed reading a text selection, choose some words or phrases that you would like them to learn in order to facilitate their understanding of the material. Ask students to make up a set of vocabulary cards that will contain the vocabulary word on one side and the definition and a sentence using the word on the other side. For example, a word from a math text that is important for understanding might be *probability*. It is defined as the likelihood of the occurrence of a specific event. A sentence follows: In all *probability*, we will have a math quiz on Friday. As a test, students are to examine each word, attempt to define it, and use it in a sentence. They can check for understanding by reading the other side of the card.

2. **ORGANIZE.** Direct students to organize their vocabulary words into categories that will enhance their ability to remember the words and their meanings. For example, students might choose to organize their words semantically or place them into categories based on structural similarities. *Probability*, the example word, might be placed with other words ending in *-ility*, such as *reliability*.

3. **ANCHOR.** At this point, it is necessary for students to devise some strategy for anchoring the vocabulary words and their meanings into their long-term memories. There are a variety of ways to achieve this goal. Students might choose to work with a partner to teach and test each other, or they might use a tape recorder to tape, listen to, and recite definitions. Another effective tool is to try to find a word that will act as a mnemonic link to the vocabulary word. Perhaps linking the word *probability* to the word *probably* would provide a mnemonic link for this word.

4. **SAY.** A periodic review of the words is necessary for students not to forget them. Dana and Rodriguez (1992) suggest that students review the words (say them) and their definitions 5 to 10 minutes after learning the words, a week later, and once again at a later date.

5. **TEST.** Students should conduct a posttest when they have completed each review, in order to determine their success in learning the words. It can be done in the same way as was the initial test.

6. Encourage students to become familiar with this strategy so that they will use it independently to strengthen their vocabulary knowledge.

Using Words Effectively

GOAL

To help students use words effectively in speaking and writing

BACKGROUND

When writers use literal language, they convey the ordinary, everyday meanings of words. In order to communicate ideas beyond the literal meanings of particular words, and to use words effectively, writers may use figurative language. The purpose of using figurative language is to describe things in ways that allow the reader to visualize or feel the author's intended meaning in a more colorful and interesting fashion. Consider the following example.

Literal: The sun went behind the clouds.

Figurative: "Like blurred lenses, winter clouds cast a shade over the sun." (From "Marian" by Truman Capote)

Although the literal statement makes sense, nothing about it encourages the reader to visualize the darkening day and to feel the drabness of the moment.

Three of the most common and effective kinds of figurative language are simile, metaphor, and personification. The following chart describes each of them and gives examples.

Simile	A comparison, using *like* or *as*.	The sun was as bright as a shiny penny.
Metaphor	A direct comparison that does not contain *like* or *as*.	The summer night is a dark blue hammock.
Personification	Giving human qualities to an object, animal, or idea.	The daisies bowed and curtsied in the field.

Using figurative language to communicate ideas beyond the literal level adds interest and color to ordinary writing. Authors who use figurative language such as similes, metaphors, and personification give their readers the opportunity to see everyday objects and situations in more colorful ways. Encouraging students to use figurative language in their writing will add a new dimension of interest to their compositions. In order to understand how to use figurative language, students must first understand that words have both denotations and connotations.

The dictionary definition of a word is that word's denotation. Many words have more than one denotation or dictionary definition. For example the word *pawn* has several denotations including 1) something given as security for a loan, 2) a person serving as security: hostage, 3) a chessman of lowest value, and 4) a person used to further the purposes of another.

Writers must consider their word choices carefully because many words have multiple associations attached to them. These added associations are called connotations. Connotations refer to the implied feelings or ideas associated with a word. They suggest a meaning beyond the literal, explicit definition. For example, the denotation or dictionary definition of the word *proud* is feeling satisfaction over an attribute or act while the word *conceited*, a connotation of the word *proud*, means holding too high an opinion of oneself.

This section will provide strategies to help students identify and use three kinds of figurative language and to become aware of both the denotative and connotative meanings of words.

Changing Bland to Beautiful!

Goal: *To help students use words effectively in speaking and writing.* Figurative language is used by writers to enhance a reader's interest in a subject. Authors frequently use similes and metaphors to make their writing more colorful and more interesting, thus enabling their readers to visualize the intended meaning. After completing Section 3.5, present your students with the following sentences and invite them to complete the suggested tasks in order to see if they grasp the meanings of similes and metaphors.

In the following sentences, identify the metaphor and write a brief explanation of its meanings.

1. This class is a three-ring circus!

   Meaning: _____

2. She is the apple of my eye.

   Meaning: _____

3. Mom's answer was music to my ears.

   Meaning: _____

4. I needed a couple of days to digest the information.

   Meaning: _____

5. Jim is an airhead in math class.

   Meaning: _____

Complete the following sentences with a simile.

1. The night sky looked as dark as _____.

2. The little girl is as pretty as a _____.

3. Our classroom was as quiet as _____.

4. Bill's mood is as sour as _____.

Readers Needing Additional Support

When working with ELL students, figurative language can be difficult because it is not literal. Whenever possible, present concrete examples to aid students in making connections between literal and figurative expressions.

Section **3.5** INSTRUCTIONAL STRATEGY 15

Identifying Figurative Language

Figurative language allows writers to communicate ideas beyond the literal meanings of words. When authors use figurative language, they help their readers develop more vivid pictures or concepts in their minds. Teaching students to identify figurative language in literature will have the added benefit of encouraging them to use similes, metaphors, and personification elements in their own writing.

In order to expand your students' ability to identify figurative language, you might ask them to identify particular aspects of it in literature selections you are currently studying. The following sentences, some taken from literature, contain examples of similes, metaphors, and personification.

Directions

1. Ask students to read each of the following sentences.

   The man is a snake!

   Simile _____ Metaphor _____ Personification _____

   Literal meaning _____

   Intended meaning _____

"There is no frigate like a book
To take us lands away." (Emily Dickinson)

Simile _____   Metaphor _____   Personification _____

Literal meaning _____

Intended meaning _____

2. Direct students to place a check mark indicating the type of figurative language used.

3. Ask them to explain their choices by writing a few words stating what they believe to be the literal meaning of the sentence and the intended meaning.

4. After completing the sentences, students might enjoy writing their own sentences using the figurative language you have taught.

SECTION 3.5
web resources
Identifying Figurative Language
Reproducible, 25
Language Arts Examples, 26

Section **3.5** INSTRUCTIONAL STRATEGY 16

Sensing Similes and Metaphors

This strategy invites students to use their five senses as they write similes and metaphors. For this activity, Portopopescu (2003) suggests putting together a small display in the classroom including objects of fruit, flowers, and food in order to stimulate students' thinking as they write. For example, the display might include an orange, a rose, and Oreo cookies.

Directions

1. Hold a brief discussion with students about the appearance of the objects, encouraging them to use descriptive words as they talk.

2. Encourage their comments by asking questions such as, "What does the Oreo cookie remind you of?" or "How does the orange feel when you hold it in your hand?"

3. After a brief discussion, write the five senses (seeing, hearing, tasting, smelling, and feeling) where they can be seen by the entire class.

4. Encourage students to touch, taste, smell, and feel the fruit, flower, and food as they begin to think about similes and metaphors.

5. Begin the simile and metaphor writing with a few sentence starters as students become comfortable with the process. Write the sentence starters where they can be seen by the entire class. Sentence starters and possible responses could include the following examples.

     As orange looks as round as _____. (a globe)

     The rose smells as fresh as _____. (a bar of soap)

     The Oreo cookie tastes like _____. (a chocolate sundae)

6. Encourage students to write similes or metaphors for each of the objects using their five senses.

7. Tell students to work in pairs or alone as they write.

8. When the class has completed writing their similes and metaphors, invite them to share their responses.

SECTION 3.5
web resources
Sensing Similes and Metaphors
Reproducible, 27

Choosing Stronger Connotations

Some words are neutral and carry no special connotation. The word *noise*, for example, is a neutral word. The word *cacophony*, however, suggests sound that is jarring or discordant. Writers frequently choose certain words because of their connotations or implied meanings. Before beginning this strategy, be sure students understand that words have both denotations (specific meanings) and connotations (implied meanings).

Directions

1. Ask students to look up the word *evil* in their dictionaries.
2. Initiate a discussion with the entire class as to what the word *evil* means to them.
3. Write their responses where they can be seen by the entire class and encourage students to move beyond the dictionary definition to connotative meanings of the word.
4. When students seem comfortable with the differences between the denotative and connotative meanings, write the following sentences where they can be seen by the entire class as examples.

   My mother said <u>overeating</u> is a sin. (gluttony, feasting)
   There is a strong <u>disagreement</u> between the two countries. (argument, conflict)

5. Tell students the sentences are followed by two connotations of the under-lined word. One of the words in parentheses will give a stronger meaning to the sentence.

SECTION 3.5
CHAPTER 3
web resources
Choosing Stronger Connotations
Reproducible, 28
Language Arts Examples, 29

6. Guide students in determining which of the two words they think strength-ens the meaning of the sentence.
7. Divide the class into pairs or small groups. Print and distribute copies of the additional sentences found on the website.

8. Tell students to underline the word in parentheses that gives the sentence a stronger meaning.
9. When students have completed the sentences, invite them to share their responses. Be sure students explain their choices.

Positive or Negative Connotations?

In order to give added meaning to the words they choose, writers consider several connotations as they write. Some connotations have a positive impact on meaning (using the word *delightful* instead of *nice*), some have a negative impact (using *depressed* instead of *unhappy*), and some have a neutral impact (using the word *sound* instead of *noise*). The following strategy will give students practice in selecting connotations of words and in de-termining whether their choices are positive, negative, or neutral.

Directions

1. Write the following pairs of words where they can be seen by the entire class.
   - clandestine or private
   - happy or joyous
   - cloudy or overcast

2. Ask students to look at each pair of words and to choose the word with the *stronger* connotation. For example in item number one, students are asked to decide which word, *clandestine* or *private*, has the stronger connotation and to decide whether their chosen word is positive, negative, or neutral.

3. A student might respond by saying that *private* means secluded or hidden from sight, but *clandestine* means concealed for some secret purpose. Thus *clandestine* is a stronger connotation and is negative.

4. Encourage students to use dictionaries to determine the denotation, or specific definition of any word for which the meaning is uncertain.

5. When students have completed their choices, invite them to share their responses in small groups and talk about the associations they have for each word.

6. This strategy will be especially helpful for ELL students who are becoming familiar with the nuances of the English language.

SECTION **3.5**

CHAPTER 3

web resources

Positive or Negative Connotations?
Reproducible, 30
Example, 31

 SURF THE **WEB**   Access this website for a variety of useful ESL resources.
http://www.utexas.edu/student/esl/computer/vocab.html

Activities *and* Journal Entries *for* Teacher Educators

Activities

1. Ask students to select a chapter from a content area textbook. Direct them to make a list of all of the words within the chapter they think will be important to the meaning of the chapter and those words which might be unfamiliar to students. Have them analyze the words in order to determine which ones they will teach to their students before asking them to read the chapter. Ask them to select two strategies from Chapter 3 that they can use to teach the selected words and to explain the steps they will use in implementing the strategy.

2. Invite students to develop a Graphic Organizer (Instructional Strategy 5) for a text chapter in the discipline of their choice. Show how the Graphic Organizer can be used as a study guide to relate new information during class discussion of the material.

3. Organize the class into several small groups. Ask each group to examine the following list of vocabulary words used in this chapter.

prior knowledge	predictions	word sorts
comprehension	definitions	ELL
context	wide reading	semantic feature analysis
brainstorming	strategies	magnet words
technical vocabulary	word consciousness	

Using these words, direct students to create two of the following.

Word Sort	Possible Sentences
Concept Map	Magic Square

Following completion of the activity, conduct a discussion with the class about the plusses and minuses of each strategy.

4. Prepare Exit Slips for your students at the close of a class. Give students small pieces of paper with space for writing. Ask students two questions.

What is the most important thing you learned today?
What did you find confusing and would like to revisit during our next class?

Collect the exit slips and analyze them for promoting discussion and indentifying areas of weakness or confusion that you can clarify with further teaching.

Journal Entries

1. The more we know about a concept, the more words we can bring to our understanding of the concept. In your journal, reflect on how you can help students link new vocabulary words in a text chapter to their existing background knowledge. Also include ideas for helping students think of words in their existing vocabulary related to the chapter subject.

2. Write a paragraph supporting the position that knowing about word structure can help students understand word meanings. Support your ideas with examples.

3. Discuss the difference between formative assessment and summative assessment as they relate to vocabulary instruction. Include the effectiveness of each type of assessment in your response.

4 Word Study

IRA Standards: 1.1, 1.2, 1.3, 2.1, 2.2, 2.3, 3.3, 4.1, 4.2, 5.1, 5.3, 5.4, 6.2

Learning Goals

The reader of this chapter will:

- Understand the foundational basis related to word study and its instruction
- Gain knowledge in how to approach word study from an instructional perspective
- Learn instructional strategies that promote, monitor, and assess word learning

Questions to Consider

1. What are word study strategies?
2. What word study strategies do you use as you read?
3. Why is it important for students to learn and integrate a flexible approach to word study?
4. Which instructional strategies would be especially helpful to students in your discipline?

OVERVIEW

The progression to expertise in reading and learning from texts through accumulated skills and strategies is evident in numerous information processing theories (Paris, 2009). One such theory was proposed many years ago by LaBerge and Samuels (1974). Their theory, in very broad terms, posited that helping students develop automaticity with word recognition would enhance reading. Automaticity, the ability to pronounce words quickly and accurately, would free students to concentrate their attention on the essence of reading—constructing meaning. Samuels (2006) notes that when he is reading an important article that is difficult to understand, his attentional resources are focused on the words in the text and for constructing meaning. The more attention he needs for words, the less attention he has for comprehension.

Importance of Word Study

Words are important in reading. They stimulate the student's background knowledge and experiences so meaning can be constructed. Unfortunately, many texts used in the content areas of middle and high schools contain specialized vocabulary representing concepts that are challenging and overwhelming for many students. As one content area teacher noted, "It's tough for students to comprehend the text if they don't know the words." A decade ago, Ivey and Broaddus (2001) observed that middle school students with limited word analysis skills rarely get the help they need. We believe that their observation also applies to high school students. The unfortunate consequences of failing to help students with word study can result in their frustration with texts, decreased motivation, and lowered achievement. The National Assessment of Educational Progress (NAEP), a barometer of student achievement in the United States, has found that a significant number of students (approximately 35%) are unable to read at basic level (http://nces.ed.gov/nationsreportcard/).

Most professional texts for teachers and perspective teachers devoted to reading and learning in middle and high schools give scant attention to word study. There is attention to vocabulary development with minimal attention to word study. Even the articles in recent issues of professional journals seldom have an article related to word study. In a similar vein, the Report of the National Reading Panel (2000) included chapters on vocabulary and comprehension but nothing focused on word study related to students in middle and high schools.

Areas for Word Study

We believe that word study is important. This chapter will provide some valuable strategies for teachers. For the strategies to be successful, teachers will need to take the time to teach them to their students. Graves (2006) has identified four areas of word study strategies that are effective and worthwhile to teach. They are listed below.

- Using context
- Using prefixes
- Using the dictionary and related reference resources
- Knowing Greek and Latin roots

Graves (2006) is emphatic in stressing the importance of helping students become "more proficient independent word learners" (p. 91). Such word learning will enable students to "more than double the number of words they learn" (Graves, 2006, p. 91).

Instructional Models to Guide Word Learning

The model suggested for teaching word learning has been built on substantial theory and research for the last several decades. Graves (2006) cites eight studies (e.g., Duffy, 2002; Sweet & Snow, 2003) that support the direct-explanation approach and five studies (e.g., Pressley, 2002; Reutzel, Fawson, & Smith, 2003) in support of transactional strategies instruction.

The direct-explanation approach, supported by numerous research studies, "is a powerful, effective, and efficient way to teach a strategy" (Graves, 2006, p. 92). There are five basic components in the approach. First, the teacher provides an explicit description of the strategy and indicates how and when it should be used. Second, teacher and/or student modeling of the strategy takes place. Third, there is a collaborative use of the strategy in action. Fourth, students practice using the strategy with teacher guidance as necessary, and gradually responsibility is released to the student. This step is often called gradual release of responsibility. Finally, students use the strategy independently (Duke & Pearson, 2002). In this approach, the teacher does most of the work initially, but subsequent instruction is modified so that students assume primary responsibility.

To help ensure that students actually use the taught strategies when reading in and out of school, transactional strategies instruction (Sales & Graves, 2005) can be used. It has some features in common with the direct-explanation approach, but the major difference is less structure and time. Basically, teachers use a teachable moment to highlight a particular strategy within the context of an ongoing lesson. Such instruction is not pre-planned, so many teachers find it difficult to do. Our advice is to focus on the direct-explanation approach within the context of the lesson and/or unit. An overview of that type of instruction is described below.

A Recommended Approach for Word Study

Effective instruction in word study should be based on the following general approach. First, create an awareness of the strategy and help students understand how learning and using the strategy will make them better readers. For example, help students understand that context is, in a broad sense, our surroundings, and then make the link to context as it applies to reading texts. Using context clues while reading will lead to "more effective processing and overall accuracy in deriving the meaning of unfamiliar words" (Bean, Readence, & Baldwin, 2008, p. 147).

Second, define the strategy and model its use. Be alert for how you can use your content area texts and related resources to show students how the strategy can be implemented. You might also be on the lookout for examples in your daily reading where you can demonstrate the application of the strategy for students. It is important to help students understand that the strategies are useful in a variety of reading situations. Another effective modeling strategy is to think aloud as you work out the pronunciation of a word or use context to try to determine its meaning.

Third, provide guided practice in the use of the strategy, preferably by using materials from your content area, and be sure students are aware of the value of their investing in the knowledge of the strategy you are teaching. For example, if word parts are being presented (e.g., prefixes), tell students that there are 20 prefixes used in nearly 3,000 words and knowing these prefixes will provide them with a valuable resource to aid in word identification (Bean, Readence, & Baldwin, 2008).

Finally, invite students to apply the strategy in an authentic reading situation. You might alert students by saying something like the following. "When you read pages 243–248 in your text, there are at least 22 words containing prefixes. Remember what you have been learning about prefixes and use that knowledge to help you pronounce those words and predict their meanings." As you gradually release responsibility, encourage students to apply what has been taught when reading in school and outside of school. Take time for students to share successes and failures of taught strategies.

Rarely are effective lessons on word study one-shot approaches. Instruction may not be particularly lengthy, but it could take place one or two days a week over the course of several weeks, a semester, or the entire school year. Although word study is a foundation for effective reading, developing the strategic behavior necessary for students to generalize and apply what was taught is a major challenge. Students need to develop a flexible plan for what they will do when they encounter unknown words in their reading. Graves (2006) suggests that students incorporate the following six-step plan into their reading behavior.

1. Recognize when an unknown word occurs.
2. Decide whether you need to identify the word in order to understand the passage.
3. Try to figure out the meaning of the word by using context clues.
4. Try to figure out the meaning of the word by looking at the word parts.
5. Try to sound out the word and see if you can come up with a word that makes sense in the sentence.
6. If you are still stymied, consult a dictionary, glossary, or another person for the meaning.

Teachers who integrate the strategies presented in this chapter into their curriculum will help students become better readers. The essential ingredient is to prioritize the class period so instruction of this sort can become a reality.

Using Context

GOAL

To help students use context to anticipate known words and to predict meanings of unknown words

BACKGROUND

There are two major uses of context in reading. One is using the words in a sentence to predict the next _____ (word). By the middle grades, this strategy may be understood and used by students. Use of this strategy while reading often enables students to predict the next word, sometimes before they turn the page in a text. The second major use of context is to predict meanings of words. There are times when the words near an unfamiliar word will provide clues to the unfamiliar word's meaning. The strategies in this section will help students learn to apply these two major uses of context.

As you teach the uses of context, keep the following guidelines in mind (Edwards, Font, Baumann, & Boland, 2004). First, actually provide instruction in how contextual analysis works. Use the strategies that follow to create lessons that take full advantage of using examples and making connections to your discipline. Second, help students monitor their ability to predict words and verify word meanings. This ability is sometimes referred to as metacognition, or the ability to think about one's thinking. Finally, be sure students grasp the idea that they will often find "context-lean" text when it comes to predicting meanings for unknown words. In some instances, the words around or near the unknown word are not enlightening as to the meaning of the word.

Section **4.1** INSTRUCTIONAL STRATEGY 1

Anticipating Known Words

The student can sometimes use the other words in a sentence to predict an upcoming word. The process may be very natural for some students and unfamiliar to others. Using cues within the text to read fluently and anticipate words is a hallmark of efficient and effective readers. The following strategy represents one way to sensitize students to this important cueing system.

Directions

1. Begin a discussion with students about the meaning of context. Explore students' perceptions of the word. One student might say that context refers to the circumstances or situations within which something happens. Invite students to suggest some of these situations and list them where they can be seen by the entire class. Some possible areas follow.

football game	movie
pep rally	assembly
field trip	eating out

2. Select one of the areas and have students describe the context. A football game, for example, would take place on the school grounds and would involve players, officials, spectators, refreshment stands, a band, cheerleaders, and a playing field. Discuss the context in some detail.

3. Use the discussion to present some oral sentences to students and see if they can use their knowledge to fill in missing words. Some possible oral sentences follow.

- The football players on the opposing team were dressed in blue and white _____. (uniforms)
- My friends and I sat in the _____. (stands, bleachers, stadium)
- At halftime, the _____ played. (band)
- My friend Cote plays a _____ in the band. (any of several musical instruments)
- When our team scored a touchdown, the crowd _____. (cheered, yelled, screamed, etc.)

4. Take time to discuss the words suggested by students. When more than one word is suggested, discuss whether the words make sense in the context. Help students understand that they are using their knowledge and background experiences to predict words that would make sense in the context of the sentence.

5. Shift the discussion to text and help students understand that they can also use the context of the sentence to predict words that make sense. Stress that good readers make use of context in this way. Several examples from different content areas are provided below.

- The Bedouins live in the Middle _____. (East)
- Life in the village revolves around the care of the cattle and other _____. (animals)
- The countries of Kenya and Tanzania are located in eastern _____. (Africa)
- The animal kingdom can be divided into approximately 20 major _____. (groups)
- Roberto Clemente was the first Hispanic player to be elected to the Baseball Hall of _____. (Fame)
- Modern society has _____ greatly affected these proud and noble people. (not)
- There are three types of _____ vessels in the human circulatory system. (blood)
- With each contraction or _____, the heart moves blood throughout the body. (beat)
- In a normal adult, the _____ beats about 70 times a minute. (heart)

SURF THE WEB

WORD CONNECTIONS
Use this list of connections to find various links to word sources on the Internet.
www.lexfiles.com/index-connections

Section **4.1** INSTRUCTIONAL STRATEGY 2

Predicting Words

Predicting Words builds upon the previous strategy and focuses more specifically on texts used in the various content areas. This strategy makes use of modeling and helps students realize the importance of their previous experiences in making predictions about words in text.

Directions

1. Use this strategy after your students have a general understanding of context developed in Instructional Strategy 1, Anticipating Known Words.

2. Tell students that you want to help them understand how to use context cues in their reading to predict words that they already know. Briefly review the students' general understanding of context and how it relates to their lives. Then focus on context as it applies to reading. You might use a personal example or say something like the following.

- Context refers to the environment in which a word is found. For example, the word *STOP* can appear on a sign near a traffic intersection. You can also use context to predict the word missing from this traffic sign: *DO NOT ____ (PASS)*. When reading a book or words from a computer screen, the words appear in context. The context is the other words around a particular word.

- When I read, I can sometimes use the context to predict a word. For example, just the other day, I was reading about federal taxes. One of the sentences I began reading was that the federal government sends an income tax (and then I had to turn the page to continue with the text). But before I turned the page, I had already predicted the next word would probably be *form*. I turned the page and, sure enough, I was right. What I saw was the word I had predicted.
- I can also use the other words in a sentence to help me predict words. In that same article about taxes, a sentence began, *Send in any payments due no later than.* . . . I was able to predict that *April 15* would complete the sentence. I was correct. Although I may not always be right, I can use context to help me predict words that make sense. The words I predicted in these cases are words I know and understand.

3. Invite students to share instances where they have used context to predict a word. One student might share how she used the context to figure out a word in a handwritten note from a friend. Another student might share how he was able to predict a word before turning the page in a novel he was reading.

4. Shift the discussion to your content area and provide written examples. Invite students to predict the covered word in each sentence. Write students' predictions where they can be seen by the entire class. Discuss the predictions and the reasons supporting them. Then uncover the word and have students compare their predictions to the word used in the text. Take time for students to discuss their predictions, especially those that differ from the text. In the first example below, *employment* could also be a suitable word—even though the author did not use it. The discussion should lead to an understanding that some words make sense even if they do not match the word used by the author. Other words suggested by students may be off target. It is important that students share their thinking. Stress that predictions may not always be accurate, but the more that is known about a topic, the greater the likelihood of more accurate predictions. Some possible sentences from different content areas appear below.

   - The United States' labor force refers to the number of people over 16 who are employed or who are actively seeking _____. (work) [Employment is another word that makes sense.]
   - Careers in the life sciences can be divided into two professions: _____ and _____. (biology, health) [Only these two words fit in the text consulted.]
   - Probability is the _____ that something will happen or not happen. (chance) [Possibility and likelihood are other words that make sense.]
   - How the Gray Panthers started is an _____ story. (interesting) [Entertaining is another word that makes sense.]
   - A French word that means "summary" of your job qualifications is _____. (résumé) [No other word fits this context.]
   - Ray gazed down the long _____ towards his locker. (corridor) [Hall and hallway also make sense.]

5. Extend students' understanding by sharing actual examples from your own reading to help them realize that good readers use this strategy. Encourage students to write down examples from their reading and share them with classmates at a designated time. Encourage discussion.

Predicting Words

Goal: *To help students use context to anticipate known words and to predict meanings of unknown words.* Assessing whether students can use context is largely dependent upon their background knowledge as it relates to the topic of their reading. Students with good background knowledge of a topic will have an easier time using context to predict words. Some students will be able to predict the word on the next page before they turn the page. Other students may predict a word or phrase on the next line before they make the return sweep to that line with their eyes. Still other students will be able to predict an upcoming word because of the content of the passage.

One way to informally assess student learning is to have them keep a record for several days noting how well they were able to anticipate and predict words. A partial sample sheet you can develop is shown below.

Book/Chapter Title	Page	Word Predicted	Were You Correct? Explain.

After students have recorded their ability to predict words, collect their sheets and sort them into three piles: 1) five or more examples, 2) two to four examples, and 3) none or one example. For those students who experienced the most difficulty, you could reteach the strategies using several examples where students are likely to experience success. English Language Learners and other students with limited background knowledge on the topic may need to be given materials that relate more closely to their knowledge base.

Section **4.1** INSTRUCTIONAL STRATEGY 3

Cloze

Cloze refers to sentences or passages containing word deletions in which lines are substituted for words. Students are asked to supply the missing words using context and syntactic clues. Baker and Brown (1984) note that better readers perform at higher levels on Cloze tasks than younger and poorer readers (including students in middle and high schools). Cloze can be used in at least three ways as a teaching technique: 1) a line of standard length is used for each word deleted, 2) lines of various lengths are used to reflect the length of the actual word, and 3) one or more letters of the word are included to provide information about the specific word deleted.

Directions

1. Decide which of the Cloze strategies or combination of strategies you will use with students. You might initially select easier deletion patterns using your text or the example below.

    Most reptiles are covered with hard _____ or plates. Some live on land, and some live in _____. All breathe by means of _____. The loggerhead turtle, _____ example, can spend long periods under w_____ before coming _____ for _____.

2. Write the example where it can be seen by the entire class with the text enlarged. Invite students to read the text selection silently and try to predict the missing words.

3. After students have read the selection, proceed with one sentence at a time. For the first sentence, invite students to share their predictions. Write their predictions so they can be seen by the entire class. Be sure to have students share reasons for their predictions. You might ask questions like the following ones.

    - Why did you choose that word?
    - Did any other words in the sentence help you?

- What did you already know about the topic that may have been useful?
- Were there any other words you considered initially? What caused you to abandon those words?

4. After several predictions have been shared, have students predict which of the words was probably used in the first sentence by the author. Then share the actual word (*scales*) and have students reflect on their predictions. Guide students in evaluating their words, so they can determine whether their words were close to the author's word in meaning. Point out any word that is the wrong part of speech or doesn't make sense.

5. Continue with the remaining sentences, using a similar approach. The author's words are *water, lungs, for, up,* and *air.* If there is full agreement on a particular word, have a volunteer explain how the context, the length of the line, or a letter helped to predict that particular word.

6. Make the point that good readers use the context, the length of the word, the sense of the sentence, the cues offered by letters, and their background knowledge to help predict and pronounce words.

7. Invite students to make a short Cloze activity from their text and share it with a partner who makes predictions for the missing words. After discussion, have the students switch roles and repeat the process.

8. Use Cloze from time to time with texts to sharpen students' ability to use context for prediction. Another sample passage is provided below.

> The class Mammalia includes hairy, intelligent, _____-blooded vertebrates. The females have mammary glands that produce m_____ for their y_____g.
> Mammals _____ two pairs of l_____ and breathe by means of _____.
> [The author's words are *warm, milk, young, have, limbs,* and *lungs.*]

SURF THE WEB

CREATING CLOZE EXERCISES
Learn how to make Cloze activities.
www.auburn.edu/~mitrege/knowlege/cloze.html

Section **4.1** INSTRUCTIONAL STRATEGY 4

Predicting Meanings

Predicting Meanings refers to using context to determine the meaning of a word whose meaning is unknown. It is commonly agreed that context determines the meaning of a specific word. But how often does context reveal the meaning of an unknown word to the reader? The answer is that "context reveals meaning far less frequently than has commonly been supposed" (Deighton, 1959, p. 2). The box that follows (based on Deighton) contains some guidelines to keep in mind as you develop this strategy with students.

Guidelines for Using Context to Reveal Meaning

1. Context reveals meanings of unfamiliar words less often than is commonly supposed.
2. The experience of the student impacts how well the context is used.
3. Vocabulary growth through context takes place over time.

The above guidelines suggest that you will need to help students learn the common patterns for how context operates (see bulleted list on the following page) and demonstrate to students their use in text materials. Such efforts should help students become more perceptive readers who are able to use this strategy on their own.

Directions

1. Context can reveal meaning in a variety of ways. We recommend that you develop separate or unified lessons for each of the following ways that context can reveal meanings of unknown words.

- Definition: an outright definition is provided.

  Lincoln used the word *score* in the Gettysburg Address. *Score* refers to a time period of 20 years.

- Example: examples are cited. The examples often use signal words such as the following ones: *such as, such, like, especially, for example, other, this* or *these* (followed by a synonym), *the way,* or *in that way that* (Deighton, 1959, p. 7).

  Do you take your hands and arms for granted? If so, you probably never considered just how much these [signal word] *organs* make you different from the typical animal.

- Modifiers: phrases, clauses, or single words. Sometimes the modifier "appears after a linking verb in the position of a predicate adjective" (Deighton, 1959, p. 7).

  She was *consolidating* her gains, making secure her position before moving ahead.

- Restatement: signal words (*that is,* or with a synonym, *in other words, to put it another way, what this means, which is to say*) or mechanical devices (a dash, i.e., parenthetical expressions).

  It is not uncommon for scientists to make a *hypothesis* (a sort of guess) about how to explain an unusual occurrence.

- Appositive: "the unfamiliar word is separated only by commas from the word or phrase which illuminates it" (Deighton, 1959, p. 8).

  A majority of the committee was against the bill so it was pigeonholed, *put aside to be forgotten,* as the committee moved on to another bill.

- Inference: the student must make connections that are not specifically stated. This ability requires an attentive reader who has been taught to look for clues not specifically stated, such as "a sentence that restates a thought or provides an example without use of signal words" (Deighton, 1959, pp. 10–11). In such instances, the student must become a detective of sorts who gathers details, perceives relationships, and makes connections to construct the meaning of a particular word.

2. Tell students that they will be learning how context can be used to help determine meanings of unfamiliar words. You might begin with a straightforward example from your content area or use the following example.

   - Context refers to the words around a particular word. If the meaning of a particular word is unknown to you, sometimes the context can help you predict, or guess, the meaning of the word. Context won't work every time, but it is one strategy that you can try. Let's see what you can do with this example.

     In the kitchen there were quarts of almonds, dozens of oranges, pounds of raisins, stacks of biffins, and soup plates full of nuts.

3. Write the above sentence so students can view it. Have students read the sentence to themselves. Then ask if any words are unfamiliar. It is likely that the word *biffins* will be identified as an unfamiliar word. You might then make the following comments.

   - Who can pronounce the word I've underlined? [Call on a volunteer to pronounce the word.] Can you use any of the other words around the word to make a prediction or guess about the meaning of the word?

4. Invite students to work briefly with a partner to share their ideas. Then have the entire class share. Possible typical comments from students are presented below.

   Sophia: I think the word means some type of food.

   Teacher: What makes you think so?

   Sophia: Well, there are other foods mentioned in the sentence, and it seems like biffins would also be a food.

   Zack: I agree and I think biffins are biscuits.

   Teacher: Does the context make the meaning of biffins clear?

   Zack: I don't think so, but I think biffins are like biscuits.

   Teacher: What do some of the rest of you think? [Other students name various foods. Then the teacher may comment as follows.]

   Teacher: We all agree that the word biffins likely refers to something that can be eaten. That knowledge may be sufficient for now but suppose we wanted to be sure?

   Josh: You could tell us or we could look up the word in a dictionary.

5. In subsequent lessons, present some of the other ways context can be used to help determine the meanings of unfamiliar words. A few sentences from various content areas are presented below for possible use in such lessons.

    - "Here I am, sir!" shouted Mark, suddenly replying from the edge of the quay and leaping with a bound on board the ship.
    - The group was very loquacious; they talked incessantly.
    - The pocket-handkerchief was taken in and out of the flat reticule at least a dozen times. The woman seemed very nervous.
    - Most computers are digital computers, which means that before information goes into the computer it is changed into a code in which groups of digits stand for letters, symbols, and numbers.
    - The main component of a computer is a CPU, or central processing unit. It is in the CPU that information and instructions are stored and processed.
    - An atlas contains many different kinds of maps.
    - In the submarine view port, I could make out the seabed, a rough terrain of deep cracks and giant boulders.
    - The submarine edged out of the fissure. (probably no help or limited help from context)
    - A bunch of freshly picked kingcups was put in a vase on the dining room table.

Assessing Student Learning	**Predicting Meanings**

Goal: *To help students use context to anticipate known words and to predict meanings of unknown words.* Provide students with a sheet where they can write unknown words they encounter in their reading for several days. In the example below, students would write the page and sentence containing the unknown word and then assess the degree to which context helped them.

Book/Page	Sentence Containing Unknown Word (Underlined Word)	Did Context Help With Meaning? (Yes!, No, I Don't Know) Explain.

Collect the students' papers and look for instances where students did not find context helpful, but the sentence offered helpful clues to the word's meaning. Use these examples for instruction. Think aloud to demonstrate how the context may have offered clues that were missed by the student.

Section **4.1** INSTRUCTIONAL STRATEGY 5

Predictions, Definitions, and Connections

Predictions, Definitions, and Connections invites students to identify an unfamiliar word, place it in context, predict one or more possible definitions of the word, determine the actual definition, and then connect the word to content areas and personal experiences. The strategy encourages students to work actively among themselves to arrive at a definition and make connections.

Directions

1. Identify an important term or concept from your text or unit of study that is likely to be unfamiliar to students. You could also use the example from social studies that follows.

2. Tell students that you will share a strategy to help them learn the meanings of unfamiliar words and link them to their experiences. Distribute copies of the Predictions, Definitions, and Connections reproducible from the website. You might make the following comments.

> I have selected a word from our text that may be unfamiliar to you. I'll write the word first and then you write it on your sheet in the proper place. Now turn to page 184 in your text and find the section titled "Statehood at Last" in bold print. Go to the second paragraph in that section and you will find the word. Please write the sentence containing the word in the second box on your sheet. When you have finished, work with two classmates sitting near you and write some possible definitions of the word based on the context of the sentence or your experiences. Your predictions may be right or wrong—what's important is that you make predictions.

3. Give students a few minutes to share their ideas and to write possible definitions. Then have students share some of their ideas with the entire class. As ideas are shared, write predicted definitions so students can see them. Encourage students to look for commonalities among the definitions. It is possible that an actual definition might emerge from the discussion. It might also be necessary to look up the word in a dictionary or glossary. Through discussion and reference sources, help students arrive at the actual meaning of the word in that context. Students should write the definition in the appropriate box on their sheets. Be sure that students understand how the word is pronounced.

4. Ask students to complete the remaining two parts by making connections to other content areas and to their lives. Then give students an opportunity to share their connections in small groups or with the entire class. Be sure you help make connections to other content areas when appropriate.

5. Have students add the completed sheet to their word study folder. Use the Predictions, Definitions, and Connections reproducible from time to time with guidance. You can also provide blank copies of the sheet for students to complete independently while reading a text selection. Remember to provide time for students to discuss and share their work.

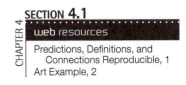

CHAPTER 4 **SECTION 4.1**
web resources

Predictions, Definitions, and Connections Reproducible, 1
Art Example, 2

▊◗ Social Studies

Predictions, Definitions, and Connections

Unfamiliar Word: *repudiated*

Sentence Containing Unfamiliar Word
Congress repudiated the Alaska Statehood Bill several times during the period between 1916 and 1957.

Predicted Definitions Based on Sentence Context/Experiences
1. *refused*
2. *failed to act on*
3. *did not pass*

Actual Definition/Meaning
to reject or refuse to recognize

Connections to Content Areas
1. *In a novel one character repudiated another.*
2. _____

Personal Connections
Sometimes my parents repudiate my behavior.

EXAMPLE

Contextual Redefinition

Contextual Redefinition (Bean, Readence, & Baldwin, 2008) is a strategy designed to assist students as they use context to determine the meanings of unknown words. Contextual Redefinition stresses the necessity for using syntax or word order in predicting word meanings and making informed decisions about an author's intent. When using this strategy, students have another method for developing independence in their reading.

Directions

1. Identify several words in conjunction with a reading assignment. Select words that students must understand to adequately comprehend the text selection. Use an example from your content area or the following example. The following words have been selected from a world history text.

utopia	Huguenot
Reformation	theocracy
predestination	geocentric theory

2. Present the words in isolation, pronounce them, and ask students to provide a definition for each word.

3. As students present their definitions, they should try to provide a rationale for their thinking. Although trying to determine meaning without context seems to be counterproductive in teaching the strategy, this particular activity demonstrates the difficulty in determining the meanings of words presented in isolation. Record the definitions given by students.

4. After all of the definitions have been recorded, present the words in the sentences taken from the textbook or in the sentences you have constructed. Use the textbook sentences if they present the words in a manner that provides information for determining their meanings. Otherwise, create your own sentences. An example follows.
   - *Utopia* was an imaginary perfect society.
   - The *Reformation*, a religious crisis in the Roman Catholic Church, was started by Martin Luther.
   - John Calvin's *predestination* doctrine stated that God has known since the beginning of time who will be saved.
   - Calvin hoped for a *theocracy*, a government controlled by church leaders.
   - *Geocentric theory*, or earth-centered theory, was defended by Aristotle.

5. Once again, ask students to provide definitions for the selected words. As students determine the words' meanings, they should use the context in which the words are presented. Students should provide a rationale for their definitions. A possible explanation follows.

   Predestination means that your path in life is set at the time you're born. That would fit Calvin's beliefs about everything being set since the beginning of time.

6. Have students use their dictionaries to evaluate the definitions constructed using context clues. Students should share the dictionary meanings with the entire class and compare them with their own definitions. Point out to students that the quality of their definitions should increase from their initial encounter with the words in isolation to their use of context in determining their meanings.

Word Questioning

Word Questioning (Allen, 1999) provides students with questions that require them to interact with vocabulary words at the levels represented by Bloom's (1956) classic taxonomy: knowledge, comprehension, application, analysis, synthesis, and evaluation. Students first record a word as it appears in context. Then students respond to the questions that prompt them to develop a deeper understanding of the targeted word.

Directions

1. Make copies of the Word Questioning reproducible found on the website and distribute them to students.

2. Select a sentence from your content area that contains an important vocabulary word or use the example from a health text that is the basis for this lesson.

3. Direct students to the sentence in the text containing the word and have students copy the sentence in the center box of the Word Questioning reproducible as you model the process. Have students underline the word in the sentence.

4. Systematically complete the sheet, beginning with the analysis box in the upper left. Be sure students can pronounce the word. Word parts can help students pronounce the word *impair*; however, there is little help for the meaning of the word.

5. Proceed to the comprehension box in the center top and invite students to share their ideas for the word's meaning. Students can use their background knowledge, the context of the sentence, and a dictionary or glossary to determine the word's meaning. Write their ideas where they can be seen by the entire class and then try to arrive at a consensus definition. Have students write the definition in the appropriate box.

6. Continue completing the remaining boxes in a similar manner. An alternative approach is to have students form small groups and brainstorm ideas for each of the questions as they complete their own sheets.

7. Once the sheets are completed, encourage whole class sharing, stressing the importance of making the responses personal so it is easier to remember the word. A completed Word Questioning sheet for health follows.

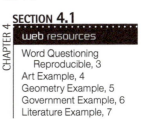

CHAPTER 4

SECTION 4.1

web resources

Word Questioning
  Reproducible, 3
Art Example, 4
Geometry Example, 5
Government Example, 6
Literature Example, 7

*Word Questioning**

What are the parts of the word I recognize?

"im-" can be a prefix that means <u>not</u>

analysis

What does the word mean?

to lessen the quality, strength, or value of; damage; weaken

comprehension

What is an example for the word?

alcohol can impair

application

What is not an example for the word?

water does not impair

application

Sentence using word

So if you don't drink sufficient water, you can <u>impair</u> every aspect of how your body works.

How does this word go with other words or concepts I know?

• read a story about kids with impairments
• health teacher said alcohol impairs a person's thinking

synthesis

Why is this word important for me to know?

understand what we read and discuss in health

evaluation

What might I be reading about when I find this word?

• things about the human body
• handicaps

knowledge

*Adapted from Allen (1999)

EXAMPLE

8. Completed sheets can become part of a student's vocabulary notebook.

Readers Needing Additional Support

Be sure that the meaning of the word is clear and understood. Use defining words that are familiar to students. Make the definition student friendly. Stress the synthesis aspect of Word Questioning, guiding students as needed to make connections with other words or concepts. Such connections can help aid recall. Some students may prefer to sketch or draw illustrations and/or use pictures for the knowledge, application, or synthesis parts of Word Questioning.

Decoding and Meaning

GOAL

To aid students in decoding words and using word parts to help construct meaning

BACKGROUND

Lewkowicz (2000) notes that the lack of decoding skills can be a serious handicap for older students and that teachers need to assume greater responsibility for identifying students who have decoding problems. Words are the catalysts that stimulate students' backgrounds so they can construct meaning from texts. The heavy vocabulary and concept load in the content areas means that teachers must devote special attention to the intentional and systematic learning of strategies that help students pronounce words and use word parts, when possible, to help them understand what the words mean. Johns and Lenski (2010) have provided a variety of foundational strategies to build essential phonics skills for readers who lack the most basic word identification skills. In this section, attention will be focused on promoting fluency and working with longer words. The intent is to help students acquire strategies for decoding longer words and using word parts (such as prefixes and suffixes) to help construct meaning. Attention is also given to some foreign words and phrases that appear in selected content area texts.

Section **4.2** INSTRUCTIONAL STRATEGY 8

Repeated Readings

Repeated Readings is a strategy designed to help students develop fluency in word identification. Since its development (Samuels, 1979), this strategy has helped middle-grade students as well as second graders through college freshmen in regular, "remedial," and special education settings. Improvements in word accuracy, speed of word recognition, and comprehension have been documented, and the improvements appear to transfer from practiced passages to reading of new material (Dowhower, 1989). The version described here was initially developed for use with seventh- and eighth-grade students working in pairs (Ferroli, Beaver, Hagan, & Moriarty, 2000).

Directions

1. Explain to students that they will be reading and rereading some portions of their books in a timed manner. This timed reading will help them increase their word accuracy, speed, and comprehension. (Note: Although increasing rate is a by-product of word accuracy and not the primary goal of repeated readings, students, especially readers who struggle, enjoy the idea of speed reading.)

2. Make copies of the Repeated Readings Record Sheet (Ferroli, Beaver, Hagan, & Moriarty, 2000) found on the website and distribute to the students.

3. Explain the Repeated Readings Record Sheet (Ferroli, Beaver, Hagan, & Moriarty, 2000) to students. The numbered steps enable the students to independently complete the activities, after just a brief explanation and demonstration.

4. Show students that they will be timing one another in steps 2, 3, 5, 6, 8, and 9. The timing works well when the partner who is to read declares "ready," and the listening partner is taught to say "go" when the second hand of a wall clock or watch reaches the 12. Stopwatches, of course, make this step even easier.

5. Explain that in steps 4 and 7 listeners will write about what their partners have read. The explanation might go as follows.

  - The sentences you write might be a simple summary of what you heard. This step helps you to follow your partner's reading.

6. Point out that in step 10 students read to themselves for the first time. No timer is used here. This final writing in step 10 is about their own passage. Some students are tempted to write step 10 without first doing the silent reading as they have read the passage three times already. Encourage students to enjoy the speed and ease of the fourth reading and to see completing the Repeated Readings Record Sheet as involving four readings and three writings.

7. Help students understand that the optional lines for vocabulary at the end of step 10 are intended to encourage readers to be alert for challenging words.

8. Assist students with text selections for the Repeated Readings activity. They should choose materials of personal interest. The ideal selections are books they are reading for other purposes (e.g., the class novel, their own recreational reading, even content area texts). It is important that partners do not read the same passages for Repeated Readings so that there is no direct comparison. Competing with another student rather than trying to increase one's own rate and accuracy misses the point of self-improvement.

9. Teach students to count passages of 200 to 250 words for step one. (Counting two words at a time helps.) The segments should begin and end with whole paragraphs. Students become adept at estimating 200 words after a few cycles through the Repeated Readings Record Sheet. This estimation procedure is acceptable so long as students understand that they can only compare themselves on a single passage and not across passages of different lengths. Four readings of passages of this length will normally take about 30 minutes.

CHAPTER 4

SECTION 4.2

web resources

Repeated Readings Record Sheet Reproducible, 8–9

Section **4.2** **INSTRUCTIONAL STRATEGY 9**

Two Questions

Two Questions (Cunningham, 2000a) helps sensitize students to pronouncing words, spelling words, and seeing possible relationships between the key word in the lesson and other words in their listening vocabularies. Cunningham notes that the two questions "could be used by any teacher in any subject area" (p. 288) from fourth grade through high school. The two basic questions follow.

Do I know any other words that look and sound like this word?
Are any of these look-alike/sound-alike words related to each other?

Directions

1. Write the first question so students can see it. Then write the key word that is being introduced. Use an example from your content area or the following example, adapted from Cunningham (2000a), from a mathematics text.

    equation

2. Direct students' attention to the word *equation* and use examples to build meaning for the concept. You might explain as follows.

    An equation is divided into two parts. One part is to the left of the equal sign. The other part is to the right of the equal sign. If the equation is correct, both sides are equal. A simple equation is $2 + 3 = 5$. Ask students to give some other examples of equations.

3. After students have provided several examples, have students pronounce *equation*. Then invite students to share any words they know that look and sound like *equation*. Write the words where they can be seen by the entire class as students share them. Be sure to underline the word parts that are the same. Have students pronounce the words, emphasizing the part that is pronounced the same as *equation*. Several examples are provided below.

<u>equa</u>te	addi<u>tion</u>
<u>equa</u>l	vaca<u>tion</u>
<u>equa</u>tor	multiplica<u>tion</u>
<u>equa</u>lize	subtrac<u>tion</u>
constitu<u>tion</u>	sensa<u>tion</u>
na<u>tion</u>	

4. Refer to the question you wrote and ask: Do I know any other words that look and sound like this word? Have a student read the question. Then help students understand that thinking of words that look and sound the same as a new word may aid in pronouncing and spelling the new word. Model as necessary, using appropriate words shared by students. Add additional words as needed. The *equa* and *tion* from the other known words are clues that can be used to help pronounce *equation*.

5. Direct students' attention to the second question: Are any of these look-alike/sound-alike words related to each other? Cunningham (2000a) suggests taking sufficient time to help students understand that "words, like people, sometimes look and sound alike but are not related." Other people look alike and are related. The analogy to people in families may be useful. In Cunningham's words:

> Not all people who look alike are related but some are. This is how words work. Words are related if there is something about their meaning that is the same. After we find look-alike/sound-alike words that will help us spell and pronounce new words, we try to think of any way these words might be related in the same meaning family. (p. 289)

6. Guide students to understand that the words in the first column are related because of the meaning of *equa* in each of the words. You might explain in the following manner.

> *Equate* means to make equal. *Equator*, an imaginary line, divides our earth into two equal halves: the Northern Hemisphere and the Southern Hemisphere (demonstrate with a globe). *Equalize* means to make equal, like when we balance teams so there are the same number of players on each side. An *equation* is also balanced on each side of the equal sign. When words are related to each other, we get clues as to what they mean.

7. You might also present students with *sequel*. Explain that the word looks like it is related in meaning to the other words but it is not. If necessary, share the definition of *sequel* (something that follows; a continuation of an earlier movie or literary work). Note that linking *equal* to *sequel* is an answer to the first question and that realization can help with the pronunciation of *sequel*.

8. Display the two questions on a chart in the classroom, so students can use the questions to help them decode new words. Use the Two Questions strategy in an intentional manner to help students internalize the power of patterns and chunking to pronounce words and get possible clues to their meanings.

SECTION **4.2**
web resources
Two Questions Reproducible, 10

CHAPTER 4

Section **4.2** INSTRUCTIONAL STRATEGY 10

Compare-Contrast Procedure

Teachers of upper-grade readers necessarily concern themselves with helping students to improve vocabulary, comprehension, reading rate, literary appreciation, and study strategies. Some students, however, still need assistance in developing proficiency in word analysis—the ability to work out the pronunciation of longer words.

The Compare-Contrast Procedure provides students with a strategy for figuring out multisyllabic words by searching for letter patterns that are easily recognizable. It uses neither "rules" nor syllabication jargon; moreover, it is based on an understanding of what proficient readers really do when they encounter words that require some degree of word analysis. Originally used in a small group setting, this adaptation was developed for use with seventh and eighth graders in a whole class setting (Ferroli, Cooper, & Zimmerman, 2001).

Directions

1. Select 8 to 12 longer words from reading material in your existing curriculum. The Compare-Contrast Procedure requires no special materials or set of words.

2. Allocate about 10 minutes for a Compare-Contrast session. Students will begin to adopt and apply the strategy when they receive regular instruction—about twice a week for four to six weeks. The lesson can be a prereading activity to prepare students for reading chapters of a class novel, selections from an anthology, or content area texts.

3. Explain to students that when they encounter longer words that are not immediately recognizable, they can employ the Compare-Contrast Procedure. They compare these new words to other words they know that have similar letter patterns. These are called "match" words.

4. Present a word to students without pronouncing it. Model the process by writing the word *quiddich* where it can be seen by the entire class or use a longer vocabulary word from your content area. You might think aloud in the following manner.

   If I can't immediately recognize this word, I make matches for each part. Looking at the first part, I make a match with *hid*. Looking at the second part I make a match with *itch*. I say the match words then the target word: "*hid . . . itch . . . quidditch.*"

5. Encourage the students to refrain from pronouncing the target word until the matches have been made. This is important because, even if the target word is known, the activity causes them to search through their mental "word stores" for words that look like the target word. It can sometimes be more helpful to make matches for longer words that they already recognize than it is to make matches for words that are initially perplexing.

6. Provide additional examples, remembering to present each word in writing without pronouncing it. Two additional examples are shown below.

   mattress—Looking at the first part I make a match with *cat*. Looking at the second part I make a match with *less*. I say the match words and then the target word: "*cat . . . less . . . mattress.*"

   suppose—Looking at the first part I make a match with *cup*. Looking at the second part I make a match with *nose*. I say the match words and then the target word: "*cup . . . nose . . . suppose.*"

7. Continue to model more examples. Invite students to contribute and discuss their own matches. Remember that there are no certain matches that are the right ones. The only condition that must be met is that the match words must **look like** the target word. The words must share a spelling pattern.

8. Demonstrate, as opportunities arise, that partial matches occur and are resolved by remembering that the objective is to arrive at a close approximation of the target word so that it becomes recognizable. Presented with the target word *brilliant*, students might match it with *hill* and *giant*, resulting in something like: "*brill – I – ant.*" Having students say the resulting word a few times: "*brill – I – ant,*" "*brill – I – ant,*" or even "*hill . . . giant . . . brill – I – ant*" often results in identification of the real word as the approximate pronunciation is close enough to trigger recognition of the actual word. Likewise, a word like *conjure* can be matched with *on* and *sure* and result in a pronunciation slightly removed from the actual target word. Once again, saying the resulting approximate pronunciation a few times usually triggers recognition.

9. Demonstrate a similar solution for mismatches. Presented with *defrosting*, common matches are *he, most,* and *sing*. (Actually, students often don't bother to make a match for a simple word ending like *ing*, choosing to add that part after other matches are made.) The mismatch of *most* for *frost* still might result in identifying the actual word, but even if it doesn't, the student should be praised for the match that is accurate in terms of

its spelling pattern. The following chart shows how nine words might be matched with easy examples, partial matches, and mismatches.

Target Word	Easy Matches	Partial Matches	Mismatches
Quidditch	hid . . . witch		
mattress	cat . . . less		
accident	tack . . . hid . . . went		
conjure		on . . . sure	won . . . pure
Hagrid	bag . . . hid; lag . . . bid		
defrosting	me . . . cost . . . ring		he . . . most . . . sing
suppose	cup . . . nose		
brilliant		will . . . ant	hill . . . giant
bandages		and . . . cages	

10. Increase the amount of practice by having students make individual matches. For the target word *Hagrid*, students might write *bag . . . hid, sag . . . did, lag . . . bid*, or any combination. Have students pronounce the target word and discuss their match words. Emphasize that students can have different match words because readers have different words stored in their memories, or they simply retrieve different words from their memories.

11. Direct students to make written matches in a notebook. Writing increases the amount of individual practice, but it can slow down the activity. Students need only write match words, not the target word. One student's entries for the words *unimportant, chimpanzee, passenger, independent,* and *engagement* looked like this example.

unimportant	*sun, him or ant*
chimpanzee	*him pan me*
passenger	*pass end her*
independent	*in he pen went*
engagement	*men age went*

12. Tell students that when they read on their own and encounter words they do not immediately recognize, they should search for matches. Some students replace the idea of "sound it out" with "match it out."

Section **4.2** **INSTRUCTIONAL STRATEGY 11**

Making Big Words

Cunningham (2000a) developed Making Big Words to help students learn how to create words by manipulating a series of letters. Each lesson begins with a strip of paper containing certain letters. The letters on the strip are cut or torn apart. These letters are then used by students to make words, as directed by the teacher. All lessons contain a big word or secret word that uses all the letters. As words are made, they are placed in a pocket chart. Later words are sorted into patterns of various types. The lessons help students learn about parts of words and how this knowledge can be used to make new words. Such knowledge can transfer to students' reading and spelling of new words. This strategy is easy for teachers to use because Cunningham and Hall (1994, 1997) have prepared books of lessons. The lessons follow the steps in the box on the following page.

(Cunningham, 2000a)

1. Give students strips of paper on which they write the letters that will be used for the Making Big Words lesson. Write the vowels first and then the consonants. Students should then cut or tear the strips so they can manipulate the individual letters. The teacher writes the same letters on large note cards and places them in a pocket chart or on the ledge of the chalkboard.

2. Know the order in which the words will be made. Tell students to make the first word and then have one student use the large letter cards to make the word. If necessary, use the word in a sentence. In addition, tell students when they should just change the order of the letters, add a letter, or remove a particular letter and add another letter.

3. Invite students to compare their words with the word made with the large letter cards. Students should correct any misspellings but be sure to maintain a brisk pace to the lesson. The student who makes the word with the large letter cards could begin shortly after other students in the class start making the word.

4. Every lesson has a secret word that uses all of the letters. After all words for the lesson have been made, invite students to make the secret word. If no one is able to figure out the secret word, say it and have students make the word.

5. Prepare large cards with all the words that were made. Then have students sort the words. Some patterns include the same prefix, root or base word, and ending. Students should spell a few words with the same part.

6. Sort the words into rhymes. Tell students that rhyming words can help them read and spell words. Write two new rhyming words on cards and have students "place these words under the rhyming words and use the rhymes to decode them. Finally, say two rhyming words and help them see how the rhyming words help them spell them. If possible, use some longer rhyming words" (Cunningham, 2001a, p. 287).

Directions

1. Select the secret word (a word that can be made with all the letters) and other words that can be made using some of the letters. Choose some words that are easy to make, some that are harder, some that rhyme, and some that are morphologically (meaning) related. Prepare large index cards with each of the individual letters and words that will be used in the lesson. Place the large letter cards in the pocket chart or along the chalkboard ledge.

2. Give students strips of paper containing the letters arranged with vowels first. Arrange the consonants in alphabetical order. Have students cut or tear the letters from the strips of paper. On the following page are letters for a lesson.

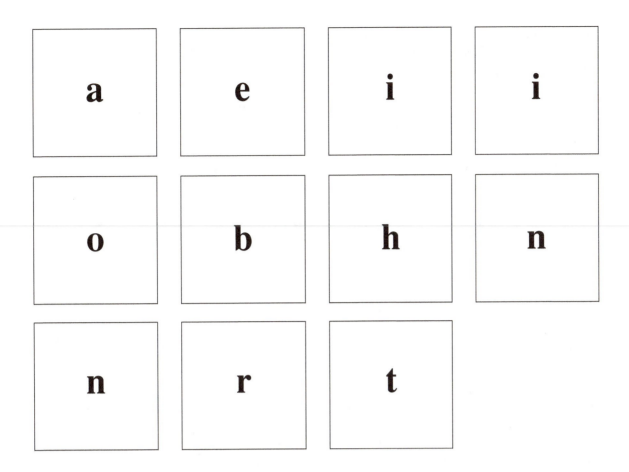

3. Begin the lesson by giving students directions for making words. As students make each word, have one student come to the pocket chart or chalkboard ledge and use the letters on large cards to make the word. Below are typical directions you can use for making words.

- Take three letters and make *hit*.
  The basketball player hit the final basket just as time expired.
- Take away a letter, add two letters, and make *hire*.
  I must hire someone to help me.
- Change the first letter in *hire* to make *tire*.
  The tire on the car is flat.
- Let's spell another four-letter word you know—*neat*.
  Your desk is very neat.
- Now, just change the first letter and spell *beat*.
- Using four letters, spell *hero*.
  He was called a hero for saving the child.
- Now, let's make some five-letter words. Spell *orbit*.
  The planets orbit around the sun.
- Take away the *i* and the *b* and then spell *other*.
  She is my other sister.
- Let's spell some six-letter words. Take six letters and spell *nation*.
  The United States is a nation that is made up of 50 states.
- Change just the first letter and *nation* becomes *ration*.
  They had to ration water because of the drought.
- Let's spell another six-letter word—*intern*.
  The intern worked at the hospital.

- Now, it's time for a seven-letter word—*inhabit*.
  I watched the birds inhabit the dense bush.
- Make this seven-letter word—*another*.
  I have another chore to do.
- I have only one word left on my list. See if you can figure out the secret word that can be spelled by using all of your letters. I am coming around to see if any of you have made the secret word (*hibernation*).

4. Once all the words are made, sort for various items (e.g., same prefix, root, ending, rhyming words, and -tion words). In this lesson, words can be sorted for -tion and rhyming words. Below are the words made in this lesson.

hit	neat	nation
hire	beat	ration
tire	hero	intern
	orbit	inhabit
	other	another
		hibernation

5. Engage students in a variety of sorting activities using all the words created. The words are placed in the pocket chart or along the ledge of the chalkboard. First, have students sort for patterns and related words. Two examples are shown below.
   - Students may see that *other* and *another* are related. Use the word cards created prior to the lesson and place the words so that the relationship can be seen more easily. Help students see *other* in *another*. Then ask students how they might use *other* to spell *mother*.
   - The words *ration*, *nation*, and *hibernation* are related because of the *tion*. Ask students how they would spell *motion, mention, conviction, contribution*, and *generation*.

6. Sort for rhyming words. As the rhyming words are sorted, help students see that rhyming words can help them read and spell words. Some examples are shown below.
   - *Hire* and *tire* rhyme. How would these words help you spell *fire* and *wire*? You can also place the new words on cards and place these words under the rhyming words and have students use the rhymes to decode them.
   - *Neat* and *beat* rhyme. How would these words help you spell *heat, retreat, wheat*, and *seat*?

7. Remember that books by Cunningham and Hall (1994, 1997) have many lessons that make this strategy easy to use. Some of the lessons focus on the following words and may be appropriate in various content areas. Below are the big words from Cunningham and Hall that might be incorporated in themes or units in the content areas. For example, science teachers may be able to use words such as atmosphere, chimpanzee, circulation, computers, earthquakes, earthworms, experiments, and so on. A business teacher may use words such as advertisements, commercials, computers, headquarters, information, international, leadership, responsibility, and resourceful. In *Making More Big Words*, Cunningham and Hall (1997) assign the words to 13 themes or units to aid teachers in making curriculum connections.

advertisement	arguments	atmosphere
breakfast	championship	chimpanzee
circulation	commercials	communities
computers	constitution	construction
conversation	democratic	dictionary
disagreements	disappearance	earthquakes
earthworms	encyclopedia	entertainment
experiments	explosions	expressions
generations	grasshopper	headquarters
hospitals	hurricanes	imagination
information	instruments	intermission

international	introduction	investigator
jellyfish	languages	leadership
measurements	microphones	microscopes
mountains	operation	performances
personality	population	porcupines
president	rattlesnake	responsibility
resourceful	revolution	satellites
snowflakes	spaghetti	strawberries
submarines	subtraction	telephones
television	temperature	thermometers
thunderstorm	transportation	traveling
underground	unforgettable	vegetables
videotapes	Washington	weightlessness

Section **4.2** INSTRUCTIONAL STRATEGY 12

Foreign Words and Phrases

English contains a number of foreign words and phrases. Some words (for example, *essay* and *mesa*) may seem as though they have always been a part of our language. Other words (for example, *tête-à-tête* and *coup d'état*) contain accents and a form that suggest an etymology from another language. Many languages have influenced the words in the English language, and the resulting English word may have the same meaning as or a different meaning from the word in the original language. Students who learn the meanings of key words and phrases in your content area will better understand the material.

Directions

1. Ask students if they are aware of any foreign words or phrases. List them where they can be seen by the entire class and have students predict their meanings. Then have students look up the words in their dictionaries to verify meanings. You could also suggest some words: *fiancé, fiancée, chic, passé, coup,* and *khaki.* Help students determine the origins of the words. Then tell students that some of the words in their text are foreign words and phrases that are important to know in order to understand the passages in which they occur. A list of foreign abbreviations, words, and phrases for reference and possible use can be found on the website.

2. Survey your content area to identify key foreign words and phrases. Teach them in the context of the unit or passage in which they occur. The example below uses words from a social studies text: *coup d'état, faux pas,* and *laissez faire.*

3. Direct students to the passages in the text containing the words or phrases or print the sentences where they can be seen by the entire class.

   Several extreme groups in the country debated the government's *laissez faire* policy.
   Within a year, a *coup d'état* occurred.

   Historians agree that the major *faux pas* was the government's inability to reach a workable solution with the extremist groups.

4. Ask for a volunteer to read the first sentence. Have students identify the foreign phrase and invite students to use their experiences or the context as a possible clue to the meaning of the phrase. If necessary, use the glossary or a dictionary to help determine the meaning and pronunciation of the phrase. Then help students understand the meaning of the words or phrase in the context of the sentence. Stress that the meaning is more important than the pronunciation.

5. Proceed to the next two sentences and engage students in a similar manner as described in step 4. It might be helpful to have students keep a list of useful foreign words and phrases relevant to your content area. A reproducible that can be used for that purpose can be found on the website.

6. Students could also be encouraged to bring to class any foreign words or phrases they encounter in their general reading for sharing and discussion. Be sure that attention is devoted to the meanings of the words or phrases.

CHAPTER 4

SECTION **4.2**

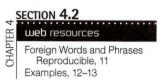
web resources

Foreign Words and Phrases
Reproducible, 11
Examples, 12–13

Using Reference Sources

GOAL

To help students use various source materials to pronounce and understand words

BACKGROUND

Strategic readers learn and use various ways to decode words and determine their meanings. Some of those ways have already been described in earlier sections of this chapter. In this section, attention is focused on resources that may be available in the text and the dictionary. Within a text are footnotes, pronunciations of technical or unusual words, and definitions of words in a glossary. The dictionary is also a valuable tool that can be used for pronouncing words and determining meanings of words. The use of these resources can help students achieve greater independence as readers.

Section **4.3** INSTRUCTIONAL STRATEGY 13

Right on the Page

Many content area texts have key words in bold or italic type, definitions in the text, and a pronunciation key in parentheses for selected words. A precalculus book, for example, may have important words highlighted for emphasis and easy reference. It is important that you guide students in understanding how to use the particulars of your content area text or resource materials to help them pronounce and understand words.

Directions

1. Invite students to share a page of their content area text that helps them pronounce words or understand what the words mean. Write their ideas where they can be seen by the entire class. Some key ideas follow.

    The especially important words are in bold type.
    The definition may be near the word in bold type.
    Sometimes there are pronunciation symbols in parentheses to aid in pronouncing the word.

2. Select a page from materials used in your content area that contains one or more features that may help students understand or pronounce a word. Then guide students through the particular items that relate to your text or materials, as shown in the following examples from different content areas.

3. For words highlighted with bold type, you might make the following comments.

    Take a look at page 2 in your precalculus book. How many words do you see that are in bold type? Let's look at each of those six words in context. The first term is **real numbers**. It is in bold type. As I read the sentence, I see that real numbers describe quantities such as miles per gallon, age, and population. Then there are some examples of symbols to represent real numbers. I get 25.5 miles per gallon with my car, so that would be an example of a real number. Your age would also be another real number. Notice that the symbol for *pi* is also an example of a real number. What might be some other examples of real numbers? Note that the term **real numbers** was defined by using examples rather than an actual definition. Now let's look at the word **rational**. [Use a similar procedure and contrast *rational* with *irrational*.]

4. For words defined explicitly in the text, you might make the following remarks.

On page 110 of your math text, there are two words in bold type: **perimeter** and **area**. Look where it says that the distance around a figure is called its perimeter. The word is defined right there. Then the next sentence says, "The amount of space a figure covers is called its **area**." Once again, the word is defined in the sentence. Sometimes words are defined directly in your text. Because they are also in bold type, they are likely to be important.

5. When the pronunciation of a word is given in parentheses, you might display the following sentence and say something like what follows.

A **scalene** (skay LEEN) triangle is a triangle in which no two sides have the same length.

Read this sentence to yourself. You can see that the word is defined in the sentence. But how is the word pronounced? If you look inside the parentheses, you will be given an idea of how to pronounce the word. There are two syllables as indicated by the space between the two parts. The part in all capital letters means that the second syllable is given more stress or emphasis. I'd like someone who doesn't know how to pronounce the word to give it a try. Look at the actual word and refer to the information in parentheses. [Invite a few students to offer their pronunciations. Pronunciations may differ, but praise their efforts. Then have a student who knows the word pronounce it.] As you can see, your efforts using the pronunciation guide may or may not result in the correct pronunciation, and you may need to verify your attempt with someone who already knows how to pronounce the word.

6. Provide other examples of words and pronunciation hints. Invite students to share their ideas about how the words are pronounced. You may need to teach the sounds commonly associated with certain symbols (for example, ə). Emphasize that, in most cases, the meanings are more important than the pronunciations. Some examples of words to use for pronunciation from mathematics practice follow.

pentagon (PEN tə gon)	parallelogram (par ə LEL ə gram)
hexagon (HEK sə gon)	equilateral (ee qw ə LAT ər əl)
trapezoid (TRAP ə zoyd)	quadrilateral (kwod rə LAT ər əl)

Section **4.3** INSTRUCTIONAL STRATEGY 14

Footnotes

Footnotes may be used to assist with word meanings and pronunciations or to provide helpful information. Although students may frequently skip this in-text aid, a short lesson can help students realize the value of footnotes.

Directions

1. Select an example from your content text or use the following example about the Nile.
2. Tell students that footnotes may provide information and possibly help with the pronunciation and/or meaning of a word. Write the following sentence so students can see it.

We love you, O Nile![1]

3. Tell students that the raised numeral is a signal to look at the bottom of the page to find a footnote with the same numeral. Present the following information to students.

[1]A river that runs through Egypt up to the Mediterranean Sea. The Nile is one of the world's longest rivers.

4. Have a student explain how the footnote helps with the word *Nile*. Clarify and expand the response if necessary. Then have students consider the following sentence.

The flooding Nile nourished the orchards created by Ra.[2]

Ask if anyone knows what the word *Ra* means. After students have made their predictions, refer them to the footnote.

[2]Ra is the Egyptian god of the sun.

5. Provide other sentences and footnotes. Have students assess the degree to which the footnotes help with the pronunciations and/or meanings of the words. Several examples are provided below.

> Sentence: You are the greatest treasure of Seb.
> Footnote: Seb is the Egyptian name for Earth.
> Sentence: The water flowed through the royal city.
> Footnote: Cairo is the royal city being referred to.
> Sentence: The gazelles roamed near the Nile.
> Footnote: gazelles (g ZELZ): small antelopes

6. As students read their texts, have them share instances when footnotes helped them pronounce words or understand their meanings.

Section **4.3** **INSTRUCTIONAL STRATEGY 15**

Glossary

A number of content area texts contain a glossary. A glossary might be thought of as a specific dictionary for the important words in that particular content area. Generally, most glossaries will assist students with the meanings of words, and many of these words are in bold print in the text. Informal conversations with students in high school reveal that the glossary is a helpful resource, especially when key vocabulary is used in study guides, quizzes, and tests.

Directions

1. Review your content area texts to determine whether a glossary is included. If so, introduce it early in the course of study. Adapt the following information, if appropriate, to the texts and materials used for instruction.

> Today, I want to share an important part of your geometry text. Turn to page 705 where you will find a glossary. A glossary is like a dictionary because it contains the meanings of many words.

2. Point out the features contained in the glossary. In the geometry book, there are definitions of words and a number of illustrations. A unique feature of the glossary is a page number in parentheses that refers to the location in the text where the word is found.

3. Choose one of the words in the glossary that students probably already know, discuss the word and definition, and relate the word to the text. You could make the following comments.

> Let's find the word *compass* on page 707 in the glossary. Follow along as I read. "A compass is an instrument used to draw circles and arcs of circles." You probably already understand this word. Now look at the end of the definition. You will see the number 25 in parentheses. That tells you where the word can be found in your text. Turn to page 25 and find *compass*.

4. When students have found the word, point out that the word is not in bold type. You might remark as follows.

> When you are reading this text, there will be times when you come across an unknown word. You could check the glossary to see if the word is defined. Note that this word is not in bold type, but it is in the glossary. The word *straightedge*, on the same line as *compass*, is not in bold type. Check to see if *straightedge* is in the glossary. [Verify the definition and discuss it.]

5. Direct students to page 8 and have them locate the first word in bold type. Have them check for the word in the glossary. Lead students to the understanding that most words in bold type will be found in the glossary. Make the point that the glossary can be a useful resource.

6. Refer to the glossary when appropriate and encourage students to use this source to review important terms and clarify the meanings of words.

Section **4.3** INSTRUCTIONAL STRATEGY 16

Dictionary Orientation

Dictionaries, in existence for over 4,000 years, were originally used as bilingual aids for travelers to translate one language into another. Just think of using a clay tablet produced in Mesopotamia (Greenwood, 2004; Johnson, 2001). Today's dictionaries are many in number and are available in printed and electronic formats.

A dictionary can be used to help students with both the pronunciation and meaning of a word. Being able to locate a word in an efficient manner by knowing the general organization of the dictionary and how to use guide words is critical. Johns and Lenski (2010) have developed foundational lessons to help students understand alphabetical order and how to use guide words. Refer to these lessons if needed. The following lesson serves as a general orientation to the dictionary.

Directions

1. Hold up a dictionary and invite students to share what they know about this reference source. Write their ideas where they can be seen by the entire class. Tell students that most dictionaries contain over 50,000 words.

2. As students share, highlight or introduce the following items into the discussion. Use an example from your dictionary or use the reproducible on the website. Be sure to highlight the definition and the pronunciation symbols or respelling.

   - **Entry word**—This is the name given to each word, abbreviation, prefix, suffix, or group of words that a dictionary explains.
   - **Guide words**—These are two words printed in boldface type at the top of each dictionary page. The left guide word shows the first full entry word; the right guide word shows the last full entry word.
   - **Syllables**—The centered dots in the entry word show where the word is divided. Syllables can help you pronounce the word or show you where to divide a word when you cannot write it all on one line.
   - **Pronunciation symbols** or **respelling**—The information appearing in parentheses following the entry word can help you pronounce the word.
   - **Etymology**—The origin and history of the word are shown in brackets, using symbols and abbreviations. Some examples are shown below.

     < means derived from
     OE means Old English
     L means Latin
   - **Definitions**—Meanings of the entry word are listed together, according to their parts of speech. Parts of speech are usually abbreviated as follows: *n.* for noun, *adj.* for adjective, *v.* for verb, *interj.* for interjection, *prep.* for preposition, and so on.
   - **Idioms**—An idiom is a group of words that has a meaning different from the meaning of the words by themselves. Idioms, if included, are at the end of the entry for the key word.
   - **Illustrations**—Some entry words contain an illustration to exemplify or clarify the entry word.
   - **Synonyms**—This is a word that means about the same as the entry word. Look for **syn.**
   - **Example sentence**—Sometimes the entry word is used in a sentence to help clarify the meaning or to show how the word is used.

3. Have students use their dictionaries to look up some words you identify or conduct activities such as the following ones. Questions could also be asked about word origins and parts of speech.

- Compare and contrast the meaning of *plane* in your geometry text to the meanings in your dictionary.
- Is *bitumen* a food source people eat? (No, it's coal.)
  How is *bitumen* pronounced? (bi too mən)
- What color is *bisque*? (red-yellow)
- Where is a *bivalve* found? (on a mussel or clam)
- What is a *dobbin*? (horse)
- What is a common word for *calyx*? (leaves)
- What use might a *divining rod* have? (to help locate water below the surface)
- Could you put something on a *docket*? (yes)

CHAPTER 4

SECTION 4.3
web resources
Dictionary Challenge
Reproducible, 14

Section **4.3** INSTRUCTIONAL STRATEGY 17

Pronouncing Words

The pronunciation symbols found at the bottom of a dictionary page may be used to help pronounce unknown words. There are several points to keep in mind. First, most pronunciation symbols show how words are pronounced by those who speak Standard English. Some of the pronunciation symbols may not be appropriate for where you teach. Second, it is difficult for anyone who uses the pronunciation symbols to be sure that the word is pronounced correctly if it is not in the person's listening vocabulary. Often, however, someone who already knows how to say the word can verify its pronunciation. Third, the meaning of the word may be more important for students to understand than the pronunciation. Finally, this lesson represents an introduction to using pronunciation symbols. Remember to provide multiple opportunities for students to strengthen their use of pronunciation symbols.

Directions

1. If you have already used pronunciation symbols in the glossary of your content area text, make the connection from this source to the dictionary (or *vice versa*). Help students to also understand that they may know words similar to the words they are unable to pronounce, and they can use this knowledge to help decode or pronounce words.

2. Have students locate the pronunciation symbols at the bottom of their dictionary pages. Keep in mind that not all dictionaries use exactly the same symbols or example words. Tell students that the pronunciation symbols at the bottom of the page can be related to the pronunciation symbols or respellings in parentheses beside each entry word.

3. Choose several entry words that most students can probably pronounce and have students establish the connection between selected symbols in words at the bottom of the page and the entry words. Some possible words to look up for this activity follow.

right	bittersweet	bison
coveralls	cower	crab
change	characteristic	collector
collarbone	erupt	modulate

4. From these and other examples, help students realize that no marks over a vowel indicate a "short" sound, and the macron (a "long" marking) indicates the "long" sound. You may also want to teach some of the other special marks that signify certain sounds. Several of these pronunciation symbols and examples are provided below. If you have a classroom set of dictionaries, be sure to verify that the pronunciation symbols are used in the same manner. Some dictionaries use a ˘ for the "short" sound (păt).

Some Dictionary Pronunciation Symbols

Symbol	Name	Example Word
ä	Umlaut over a	Fär
ô	Circumflex o	tôrn
ū̃	Tilde u	fūr
ə	Schwa	a in ago

5. Model how you would use the pronunciation symbols to pronounce an unknown word. Select a word of your choice or use the example below.

   ● Suppose I come across a word I can't pronounce, and I decide to look it up in a dictionary. Here are the pronunciation symbols for the word. [Write the following symbols on the chalkboard: mō-dăl' ə-tē.]

6. Think aloud as you use the pronunciation symbols to try different pronunciations and link the symbols to specific sounds. For example, you might begin by making the following observation.

   ● I notice that the mark over the *o* represents the long sound like the *o* in *toe*.

7. Continue with the remaining sounds and then blend the sounds together to form an incorrect pronunciation of *modality*. Try another pronunciation and ultimately say the word correctly.

8. Invite students to use the pronunciation symbols and key words from their dictionaries to try to pronounce the following respellings to make real words. Consider using related words to help students become more familiar with the pronunciation symbols. The words should also be in students' listening vocabularies (i.e., words they are likely to have heard before). Be sure to remind students to try different pronunciations, especially for the vowels, until they say a word that they have heard before.

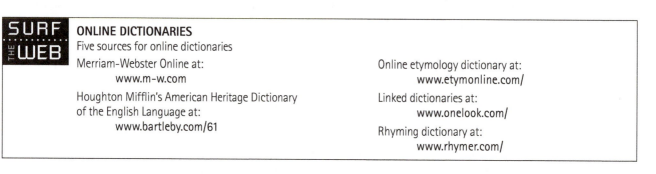

Pronunciation Symbols or Respellings*	Word
kwit	quit
rōd	road
rō′ stər	roaster
shôr′ sīd′	shoreside
skwûr′ əl	squirrel
skwosh	squash
taz mā′ nē ə	Tasmania
tō′ ga	toga
un′ kan fôr′ mit ē	unconformity
ves′ ta byoōl′	vestibule
wûrth′ lis	worthless

*From the unabridged version of *The Random House Dictionary of the English Language* (2nd ed.)

SURF THE WEB

ONLINE DICTIONARIES
Five sources for online dictionaries
Merriam-Webster Online at:
   www.m-w.com

Houghton Mifflin's American Heritage Dictionary
of the English Language at:
   www.bartleby.com/61

Online etymology dictionary at:
   www.etymonline.com/

Linked dictionaries at:
   www.onelook.com/

Rhyming dictionary at:
   www.rhymer.com/

Choosing a Dictionary Meaning to Fit the Context

A dictionary or glossary can be a useful resource to help determine the meaning of an unknown word in the text. Context may also be used (see Instructional Strategy 4, Predicting Meanings).

Directions

1. Begin with a word whose meaning in a sentence is likely to be unknown. Choose a sentence from your content area text or use the following example.

   A *bittern* was seen in the distance.

2. Invite students to share their thoughts about the word. Students might note that the word is likely to be a noun, because of its position in the sentence. Other students may make some predictions about the meaning of the word. Write students' ideas on the chalkboard. Then have students look up the word in their dictionaries. Have students read the definitions and choose the best definition for the word. Then have a student share why that particular definition was selected.

   bit•tern[1] (bĭt'ərn) *n.* Any of several wading birds of the heron family
   having molted, brownish plumage and a deep, resonant call.
   [ME biture<OFr. butor]

   bit•tern[2] (bĭt'ərn) *n.* The solution of bromides, magnesium, and calcium
   salts remaining when sodium chloride is crystallized out of seawater.
   [< BITTER]

3. Ask students to name some words that have more than one meaning or definition. Write the words where they can be seen by the entire class and then select a few words to look up in the dictionary. Explore the various meanings of the words. You might also use a few words from your content area or choose from the following words.

case	base	compass	bisque
angle	bit	element	sum
colony	plain	mask	elevator

4. Then provide a sentence with a word that has more than one meaning (e.g., *element*). Have students look up the word and determine which meaning fits the context. Two possible sentences and brief definitions of *element* follow.

   The symbol Kr signifies an element.
   Setting is a story element.

   element
   1. a fundamental or essential part of something
   2. a number of a set
   3. a substance composed of atoms
   4. one of four substances (earth, air, fire, water) formerly regarded as a fundamental part of the universe

5. Think aloud about how you choose the definition that best fits the context of the first sentence. You might say the following.

   I'll read the definitions quickly to see if there is one that seems to make sense in the sentence. [Read the definitions aloud.] I think that the second definition is more related to math, so I will rule that out. The third definition seems like it might work, because I know that there are elements that are identified by symbols. The fourth definition seems like it doesn't fit this context, unless Kr stands for fire, water, earth, or air. I don't think Kr would stand for any of those elements. The first definition does not seem like it fits as well as the third definition, so I think the third definition works best.

6. Use examples and definitions for words with multiple meanings. Have students select the best meaning for the context and then share their thinking. Select both common words and more difficult words. Some possible words to use follow. Be sure to use them in sentences.

elevate	erupt	eradicate	flow
flock	grate	granule	hire
mobilize	mixture	pannier	powwow

Section **4.3** INSTRUCTIONAL STRATEGY 19

Using a Thesaurus for Word Mapping

A thesaurus or thesaurus dictionary (Wittels & Greisman, 1996) provides students with an easy means to expand and enrich their vocabularies. These reference books can be especially helpful when students are seeking synonyms rather than definitions while they are reading or writing; however, Beck, McKeown, and Kucan (2002) warn that using the synonym approach alone doesn't help students build a deep understanding of words. Students should also examine the complex dimensions of the words which form the basis for a more precise usage in different contexts.

Directions

1. Establish the context for the vocabulary words. In this example, students have read their science text and a variety of other resources in order to gather information on the planets of our solar system. From the notes they have taken, they will complete a writing assignment based on the facts they have recorded about the planets. In this example, the words will relate to the planets of the solar system. Use this example or create one based on your content area.

2. Direct the students to choose a graphic organizer for recording their words. One example is shown on the right.

3. Anticipate words that the students might be using in their writing. In this example, it is likely that students would use words like *big* or *small* to describe the size of the planets, *hot* or *cold* to describe the temperatures, or *rough*

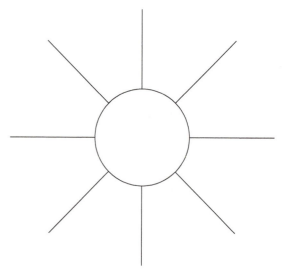

to describe the surface. These words provide the basis for the lesson. As an alternative approach, encourage students to suggest words that could make their writing about a topic more specific and descriptive.

4. Present students with the words *big* and *little* and ask them to list words from their background knowledge that would be more descriptive. After a period of time, write the words suggested by the students. At this point, a graphic organizer for the selected word might resemble what is shown on the right.

5. After students have completed their suggestions, have them consult a thesaurus or thesaurus dictionary, the latter being easier for students to use. With this reference source, students should be able to add more words to their graphic organizers. These words can be shared with the class as you write the additional words.

6. At this time in the lesson, facilitate a discussion about the selection or elimination of some word choices. Help students focus on the context of the text (planets) and draw their attention to the different dimensions of the words' meanings. In addition, help students use the thesaurus more effectively in order to locate even more descriptive words.

> Yes, *important* is listed for *big*, but would it be used when describing the size of a planet? Why? When might you use the word *important*?

> The only words for *big* that seem to relate to size are *large, great,* or *grand.* Let's see what you find when you look up *large.*

> Now you have even more words that relate to size. Which words can you add to your graphic organizer?

> By looking up *large*, students could add words such as *mammoth, colossal,* and *massive.* The graphic organizer is shown on the right.

7. Ask students to choose a synonym from their Word Map and to write a sentence using the more interesting word.

8. By using the thesaurus or thesaurus dictionary in conjunction with a content area and a related writing assignment, students should be able to incorporate more descriptive vocabulary words into their writing, thereby encouraging their understanding and continued use of these words.

SECTION 4.3

web resources

Word Map Reproducible, 15
Literature Example, 16

Readers Needing Additional Support

English Language Learners may find other words in the thesaurus that will help them with word meanings. Be sure to help them understand the context for some synonyms. Use numerous examples and have them relate the words to their lives.

Using Greek and Latin Roots

GOAL

To help students use Greek and Latin roots to pronounce and understand words

BACKGROUND

Numerous professionals in reading identify Greek and Latin derivatives (roots) as a helpful and powerful way to help students strengthen their reading (Blachowicz & Fisher, 2006; Newton & Newton, 2005). The reason is simple: "Well over half of English words—nearly 75% according to some estimates—are derived from Greek and Latin roots" (Padak, Newton, Rasinski, & Newton, 2008, p. 6). Students who have knowledge of the distinctive semantic features and consistent orthographic patterns of Greek and Latin prefixes, bases, and suffixes will be able to pronounce more words and also construct meanings for many words, including some they may be encountering for the first time. Knowing that *uni-* can mean one, students who read about a *unilateral* agreement between countries in a social studies text may be able to infer that the agreement pertains to, or affects, only one of the countries.

A thoughtful and careful approach to Greek and Latin derivatives should have a powerful effect on many groups of learners. One group is English Language Learners (ELLs) whose first languages are semantically embedded in the Latin lexicon. Spanish speakers, the largest growing population in schools in the United States, represent one example of such learners. A second group, students who struggle in reading, is an all-too-common occurrence in many classrooms. Research by Harmon, Hedrick, and Wood (2005) demonstrated the positive outcomes of teaching Greek and Latin derivatives to students who struggle in reading. A third group might be referred to as typical students who meet many new words as they continue their schooling. The magnitude of new words encountered is staggering. Nagy and Anderson (1984) estimate that texts used in grades three through nine contain over 88,000 word families; moreover, "most of the new words will be of Greek and Latin origin" (Padak, Newton, Rasinski, & Newton, 2008, p. 7).

Concerted attention to Greek and Latin roots should be a hallmark of effective content area teachers. Texts used in the content areas have a large number of words derived from Greek and Latin roots. Science and technology represent two areas, but all content areas have their share of prefixes, suffixes, and roots that are based in the classical languages of Greek and Latin. Do not neglect this key area of instruction.

Section **4.4** INSTRUCTIONAL STRATEGY 20

50 Essential Big Words

Cunningham (2000a), with thorough and careful study, created a list of 50 essential words that contain "all the most useful prefixes, suffixes, and spelling changes" (p. 290) that can be used as transferable chunks for decoding, reading, and spelling many new words. The basic idea is to help students learn these words, their meanings, and how to spell the words. This knowledge can then be used to decode, read, and spell new words.

Directions

1. The 50 words, along with their prefixes and suffixes or endings, can be found on page 112. We have also assigned these words to some major curriculum areas in middle and high schools. This list is presented on the following page and may be used as a beginning point for teaching the words and showing how they can be used to help decode or identify words in your content area.

Social Studies	Literature/ General	Speech/ Business	Science	Arts
communities	beautiful	conversation	antifreeze	beautiful
community	different	employee	classify	composer
continuous	encouragement	expensive	deodorize	discovery
discovery	forgotten	illegal	discovery	musician
dishonest	happiness	impossible	electricity	performance
forecast	hopeless	impression	forecast	unfinished
governor	impression	misunderstood	impossible	valuable
illegal	irresponsible	performance	international	
impossible	midnight	rearrange	misunderstood	
independence	misunderstand	replacement	nonliving	
international	prettier	richest	prehistoric	
invasion	rearrange	semifinal	rearrange	
misunderstand	richest	signature	swimming	
overpower	semifinal	supermarkets	underweight	
prehistoric	signature	transportation	valuable	
rearrange	supermarkets	unfinished		
replacement	swimming	valuable		
signature	unfinished			
submarine	unfriendly			
transportation	unpleasant			
unfriendly	valuable			

2. Choose one of the words for teaching. For example, *prehistoric* might be a part of a science or history unit. Print the word where students can see it. Then have students say or chant the word several times. The word might also be placed on a Word Wall along with other big words from the list.

3. Talk about the word and the part or parts that could be applied to other words. If you use *prehistoric*, talk about the prefix *pre* and the root or base word (*history, historic*). Cunningham suggests that students try to think of other words that look and sound like *prehistoric* and then decide if the *pre* parts of those words have anything to do with the notion of *before* or *prior to*. Have students suggest words that begin with *pre* and then categorize the words, perhaps along the lines shown in the example below.

Possibly means *before* or *prior to*	Probably doesn't mean *before* or *prior to*
preapprove	premier
prepay	preppy
predetermine	precision
precast	prefer
precancerous	premise
prefab	prepare
precook	predator
preheat	predict
preflight	present
precondition	president

4. Take time to have students realize that the *pre* may help with the meanings and pronunciations of the words in the first column. Equally important, however, is to help students realize that not all words that begin with *pre* will help with a word's meaning or pronunciation. Have students examine the words in the second column.

5. Guide students to the answers to questions like the following ones.
   - For which words might the *pre* be helpful in determining the pronunciation? (premier, precision, prefer)
   - What problems exist if you try to use *pre* in pronouncing *preppy* and *premise*?

50 Essential Big Words

Word	Prefix	Suffix or Ending
antifreeze	anti	
beautiful		ful (y-i)
classify		ify
communities	com	es (y-i)
community	com	
composer	com	er
continuous	con	ous
conversation	con	tion
deodorize	de	ize
different		ent
discovery	dis	y
dishonest	dis	
electricity		ity
employee	em	ee
encouragement	en	ment
expensive	ex	ive
forecast	fore	
forgotten		en (double t)
governor		or
happiness		ness (y-i)
hopeless		less
illegal	il	
impossible	im	
impression	im	sion
independence	in	ence
international	inter	al
invasion	in	sion
irresponsible	ir	ible
midnight	mid	
misunderstand	mis	
musician		ian
nonliving	non	ing (drop e)
overpower	over	
performance	per	ance
prehistoric	pre	ic
prettier		er (y-i)
rearrange	re	
replacement	re	ment
richest		est
semifinal	semi	
signature		ture
submarine	sub	
supermarkets	super	s
swimming		ing (double m)
transportation	trans	tion
underweight	under	
unfinished	un	ed
unfriendly	un	ly
unpleasant	un	ant
valuable		able (drop e)

From *Phonics They Use*. 3rd ed. by Patricia M. Cunningham. Copyright © 2000 by Addison-Wesley Educational Publishers, Inc.

Take time to help students realize that it is important to be flexible in using word parts or chunks to arrive at the correct pronunciation of a word. The goal should be to try a particular chunk and, if it doesn't result in a word the student has heard before, to try other pronunciations. Sometimes the word will not be one the student has heard before, so it may be impossible for the student to know if it is pronounced correctly. In such cases, the dictionary or an expert source (e.g., another student or the teacher) is essential.

6. Help students learn how to spell and pronounce the 50 words over time and use patterns to help students see connections. For example, you might extend the lesson by using the following examples.

    ● You know how to spell *prepare*. How would you spell *prejudge*? What about *predigest*?
    ● Who knows the base or root word of *historic*? Yes, *history* is the base or root word and it often refers to events in the past. What do you think *historic* might refer to? Now, use what you know about the spelling of *historic* to spell *heroic*.

7. Help students understand that the suffixes or endings on the list of 50 words change how the word can be used in a sentence. Look for opportunities in daily lessons to help students use the 50 words to become more proficient in decoding words and using word chunks for assisting with meaning and spelling.

FOCUS ON LATIN AND GREEK ELEMENTS OF ENGLISH
Students can experience the wonder of words by viewing the Latin and Greek elements of English by logging on to Focusing on Words.
www.wordfocus.com

Section **4.4** **INSTRUCTIONAL STRATEGY 21**

Word Spines

Word Spines is a strategy adapted from the work of Rasinski and colleagues (2007). This strategy illustrates the interconnectedness of vocabulary among a variety of content areas and can be used as a reinforcement of 50 Essential Big Words (Strategy 20 in this section). It can be used by individuals, partners, small groups, or whole groups to build and expand student knowledge of root words.

Directions

1. Introduce Word Spines by discussing how a spine's function is to communicate messages from the brain to the rest of the body. You might make the following comments.

    If your brain sent an impulse to kick with your right leg, but instead your left hand scratched your head, it would be obvious that your brain's message was misunderstood. In like manner, words stimulate your background knowledge so the author's message can be understood. To understand, you need to know the meanings of words or think of a way you can analyze the word to help determine its meaning. One way to analyze word meaning is to look for roots used in the word. Roots are word parts that have set meanings. As you learn the meanings of roots, you can use this knowledge to decode and understand new words.

2. Display the Word Spine so students can see it. Write the root word *act* on the spine. Elicit from students what this root word means (*do*) and write the meaning on the spine in parentheses. As you model for students how you decode a new word by looking for recognizable word parts, you might say something like the following.

    When I see the root *act,* I try to remember that it means *do*. This can help me understand new words with the root *act*.

Ask students to think of and suggest words that include the root *act*. As students volunteer words, write each word on a nerve. Reinforce how each word contains the meaning of *do*. Some examples are *action, actor,* and *enact*. Try to elicit enough words to fill the nerves. Explain that prefixes and suffixes are other word parts that are considered roots in Greek and Latin.

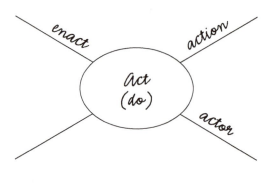

3. Select another root from the list on pages 115–116 and guide students through a second example. Try to select a root that has a connection to your content area. See the website for a reproducible to use with Word Spines.

4. Encourage students to fill in Word Spines with either assigned or self-selected roots. Students should be encouraged to use classroom resources such as textbooks, glossaries, dictionaries, and word walls to develop their Word Spines. Point out that the same root can be used in a variety of ways within words. Discuss with students the meanings of the roots and the words. Emphasize the connections between roots and words made from those roots. Give students extended opportunities to discuss their roots and words to help reinforce the concept and to integrate new words in their vocabularies.

5. Encourage students to keep their Word Spines with them throughout the school day. Ask them to keep track of roots and words using roots as they learn new words in other classes. During a future class session, display Word Spines of different roots around the room. Ask students to read the Word Spines and add words to the nerves after confirming the root is used correctly. Let students add Word Spines for additional roots. Another example of a Word Spine is shown below.

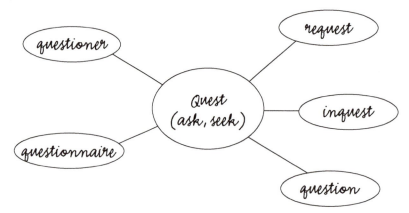

6. Another way to use this strategy is to draw Word Trees instead of Word Spines. Have students draw their own tree. The roots of the tree represent the word meaning, the tree trunk represents the word root, and the branches are different words that can be formed from the word root.

CHAPTER 4

SECTION 4.4
. . . .
web resources

Word Spine Reproducible, 17
Word Tree Reproducible, 18
Science Example, 19

Selected List of Greek and Latin Roots

Word Part/Origin	Meaning(s)	Examples
a, abs, ab (L)	away	abstract, absent
act (L)	do	action, actor, enact
aero (G)	air	aerobics, aerodynamics, aeronautics
agri (L)	field	agriculture, agrarian
alt (L)	high	altitude, alto
ambul (L)	walk	ambulance, amble, somnambulant
andr (G)	man	androgynous, android
art (L)	skill	artisan, artist, artifact
belli (L)	war	belligerent, bellicose, rebellion
biblio (G)	book	bibliography, bible
brev (L)	short	abbreviation, brevity
cal (L)	hot	calorie, caldron, scald
cap (L)	head	caption, capital, decapitate
cardi (G)	heart	cardiologist, cardiac, cardiogram
centr (L)	center	eccentric, egocentric, centrifugal
chron (F)	time	chronological, anachronism
cline (L)	to lean	incline, decline, disinclination
cred (L)	believe	credit, incredible, incredulous
cycl (G)	circle, ring	bicycle, tricycle, cycle, cyclone
dent (L)	tooth	dentist, trident, indent
dict (L)	say, speak	contradict, dictaton
dox (G)	belief	orthodox, unorthodox
duc (L)	lead	duct, induct, conduct
fac (L)	do, make	manufacture, facsimile
fer (L)	carry	reference, transfer
fid (L)	faith	fidelity, infidelity, confidence
flex (L)	bend	reflex, flexible, flexor
funct (G)	perform	function, malfunction, dysfunctional
gen (G)	birth, race	generate, genocide, progeny
gram (G)	letter, written	telegram, diagram, grammar
graph (G)	write	autograph, telegraph, phonograph
homo (L)	man	homicide, homage, hombre
hum (L)	ground	exhume, inhume
hydr (G)	water	hydrant, dehydrated
init (L)	beginning	initiate, initiative, initial
ject (L)	throw	project, inject, trajectory
kine (L)	movement	kinetic, hyperkinesis
laps (L)	slip	elapse, collapse, relapse
loc (L)	place	locate, location, dislocate
loqu (L)	speak	eloquence, eloquent
luc (L)	light	lucid, translucent
lust (L)	shine	luster, lackluster, illustrious
man (L)	hand	manacle, manual, manuscript
mania (G)	madness	maniac, maniacal, pyromania
migr (L)	change, move	migrate, immigrate, migratory
morph (G)	shape	amorphous, polymorphous
mort (L)	death	mortal, immortal, mortgage
narr (L)	tell	narrator, narrative
neg (L)	no	negative, renege
neuro (G)	nerve	neurology, neurosurgery
numer (L)	number	numeral, numerous, enumerate

(continued)

Selected List of Greek and Latin Roots *(continued)*

Word Part/Origin	Meaning(s)	Examples
onym (G)	name	pseudonym, homonym, synonym
ortho (G)	straight, right	orthodox, orthodontist
path (G)	to feel, hurt	pathetic, pathology
ped (L)	foot	pedal, pedestrian, pseudopod
phil (G)	love	philosophy, philanthropy, Philadelphia
port (L)	carry	portage, import, transport
psych (G)	mind, soul	psyche, psychology, psychopath
quest (L)	ask, seek	request, inquest, quest
reg (L)	guide, rule	regal, regulate, regime
rupt (L)	break	interrupt, rupture, erupt
san (L)	health	sanitary, insane, sanguine
sanct (G)	holy	sanctify, sanctuary
soph (G)	wise	sophisticated, philosopher
struct (L)	build	construct, construction, structure
tain (L)	hold	retain, pertain, retainer
therm (G)	heat	thermometer, thermal, thermostat
trans (L)	across, beyond	transport, transatlantic, transact
trib (L)	give	contribute, attribute
urb (L)	city	urban, urbane, suburb
vac (L)	empty	vacate, vacuum, vacation
vict (L)	conquer	victory, victim, conviction
vid (L)	see	video, provide, evidence
xen (G)	foreign	xenophobic, xenophobia

From *The Power of Words* by Scott C. Greenwood. Copyright © 2010 by Scott C. Greenwood. Reprinted by permission of Rowman & Littlefield Education.

Assessing Student Learning

Greek and Latin Roots

Goal: *To help students use Greek and Latin roots to pronounce and understand words.* As you teach the three strategies that comprise this section, be on the lookout for students who seem to be experiencing difficulty with the various activities. One way to be more systematic in your observations is to develop a grid with your students' names on the left side of a sheet of paper and the following categories across the top.

Student	Getting It Engaged Doing Fine	Some Learning Partial Engagement Good Effort	Minimal Learning Limited Engagement Limited Effort

Use tally marks and brief comments to help evaluate students' progress in learning and using Greek and Latin roots. Look for students who respond during lessons as well as those who seem passive. During group and partner activities, observe and make notes as appropriate. Consider using some of the Word Spines as an independent activity to help evaluate learning.

For those students who may need extra assistance to achieve at higher levels, offer targeted small group instruction. You could also partner a student who is experiencing difficulty with another student who is farther along in learning. In some cases, providing easier practice activities and examples that relate more closely to students' interests may be helpful. Finally, remember that lots of appropriate practice spread out over the course of several weeks is likely to produce better learning than too much information presented too quickly.

Slash Dash

Identifying Greek and Latin roots in English words can be exciting and fun for students. One method of rapidly expanding students' recognition of roots and English vocabulary is a strategy called Slash Dash. Slash Dash is an adaptation of strategies described by Newton and Newton (2005) and Rasinski and colleagues (2007). Twenty of the most frequent prefixes are used in 2,859 words (Graves, 2006; White, Sowell, & Yanagihara, 1989). Helping students learn 2,859 words by rote would be boring. Teaching students how to play Slash Dash with 20 prefixes and various roots to make more than 2,859 words is engaging and can result in students' ability to both identify and understand some of the unknown words they encounter during reading.

Directions

1. Introduce Slash Dash by asking students to name as many roots as possible. Students can use Word Spines (Strategy 21 in this section), their texts, word walls, or other references to aid their recall. Write roots where students can see them. Lead students in a word search using the roots they shared. You might say something like the following.

   > Can we put some of these roots together to make words? Here we have the prefix *re* and the root *act*. Can those two parts be put together to make a word? What do these word parts mean? What does that tell us about the word *react*?

   > Now, let's consider the root *gram*. The root *gram* means *letter* or *written*. Can we put it with any word parts we've already written? Is *telegram* a word? Can we use what we know about these two word parts to get an idea of the word's meaning?

   Build student knowledge and competence of roots by providing them with a list of roots and meanings from Strategy 21 in this section (see pages 115–116) and a list of the 20 most frequent prefixes (see page 118). Have students use these lists to create a set of cards. Each root should be printed on one card, and the meaning(s) should be printed on another card (see examples below). Display the cards face up and have students in small groups take turns matching a root with the appropriate meaning(s). You can also have partners play to build their dexterity with roots. If students are just beginning to build their roots vocabulary, break the list into chunks of five prefixes and five bases. Have students add additional roots and prefixes as they demonstrate mastery.

2. Tell students that identifying words starting from the roots is similar to building compound words. You might describe the process by saying something like the following.

   > Compound words are made from two single words that combine to form one word with a specific meaning. *Football* is a single word using *foot* and *ball* combined to describe something different from both feet and balls. Using roots is a little like compound words. Knowing that *quadru-* means four and *ped* means feet can help you pronounce a new word like *quadruped* and possibly understand its meaning.

3. Using 10 of the words from the list developed in Step #1, ask students to identify the roots in each of the words and what the word means. As they discuss each word, explain how the second word part usually describes the main idea, while the first word part details or supports the main idea. After the 10 example words have been discussed, introduce students to Slash Dash.

4. Choose one of the roots from Step #1. Write it where students can see it. Have students identify three or four words using that root. One example might be *gen (birth, race)* which can be used to build these words: *genesis, generate, generation, genocide*. Ask students to identify what each word means and how it relates to the root *gen*. Guide students as necessary.

5. Have students break into pairs to play Slash Dash. Using the cards developed in Step #1, player 1 shows player 2 a card. Player 2 must identify the card as a root or a meaning. If it is a meaning, player 2 shows a card to player 1. If it is a root, then both players quickly write down as many words as possible using that root. When they exhaust their vocabularies, or 20 seconds have passed, they compare lists. Same words counteract each other, so players only count the unique words that the other player doesn't have. Each unique word is a point. Play continues by having the other player show the next card in their deck. Play for 10 minutes. The student with the most points at the end wins. Larger Slash Dash decks can be created by introducing more roots to the students. Slash Dash can also be played by teams.

6. A variation using the Slash Dash cards is a twist on Bingo. Separate the deck into roots and meanings. Students place the root cards randomly arranged into a 5 x 5 square in front of them. One student is selected to say the meanings. If a student has a root with that meaning, he or she turns that card over. Play continues until someone has five cards in a line turned over. That student reads the roots and says the meaning of the roots to check for accuracy. Alternatively, the roots can be called and the meanings can be turned over.

Twenty Most Frequent Prefixes in Rank Order

Prefix	Meaning(s)	Example
un-	opposite	uncover
re-	back	return
in-, im-, ir-, il-	not	impossible
dis-	opposite of, not	disappear
en-, em-	in	encompass
non-	opposite	nondirective
in-, im-	in, into, within	inborn
over-	too much	overachieve
mis-	bad, wrong	misapply
sub-	under, beneath, subordinate	submerge
pre-	before in place, time, rank, order	predawn
inter-	between	intercept
fore-	in front of, before	foreground
de-	remove	defog
trans-	across	transcontinental
super-	above, over, beyond	supercharge
semi-	half	semicircle
anti-	against	antisocial
mid-	middle	midday
under-	below	understudy

Adapted from White, T., Sowell, J., & Yanagihara, A. (1989). Teaching elementary students to use word-part clues. *The Reading Teacher, 42*, 302–308.

Activities *and* Journal Entries *for* Teacher Educators

Activities

1. Select a content area text in your discipline. Review one or more of the chapters to determine the aids (e.g., glossary, words in bold, embedded textual definitions) for important vocabulary and concepts that will help students pronounce and understand key words. Compare your findings with classmates who reviewed a different book in the same discipline.

2. Choose two different strategies from different sections of this chapter that are likely to be especially useful in your discipline. Adapt the strategies to your discipline, relating them to a specific chapter of the text or unit of study.

3. Instructional Strategy 4 (Predicting Meanings) in Section 4.1 lists six ways context can be used to help reveal a word's meaning. Evaluate a chapter from a text in your discipline and determine the most common way context is used. Realistically and critically assess how helpful students are likely to find this use of context. Then share ideas as to how you can stimulate students to use this aid to get more from their reading.

Journal Entries

1. Think about your own reading of technical texts in other courses you have taken or are taking. How did you deal with words that you couldn't pronounce or whose meanings were vague or unknown? List strategies you used or didn't use and how their use or non-use impacted your understanding. To what extent might your behavior be similar to middle and/or high school students who are asked to read a section of text in your discipline?

2. Reflect on the need to balance the teaching of selected strategies in this chapter with the need to teach the content in a particular chapter or unit. What seems to be a realistic way to integrate the two (strategies and content) to benefit students?

3. Discuss how you can justify teaching strategies for word study in your discipline when there is so much content to be acquired by students.

4. What would likely result if all the content area teachers in a school devoted five or 10 minutes each day to word study that is specific to their discipline? How might such an idea be implemented across disciplines?

5 Comprehending Literary Texts

IRA Standards: 1.1, 1.2, 1.3, 2.1, 2.2, 2.3, 3.1, 3.2, 4.1, 4.2, 5.1, 5.2, 5.3, 5.4, 6.2

Learning Goals

The reader of this chapter will:

- Learn a number of instructional strategies that will enhance student comprehension and enjoyment of literary texts
- Understand the process of differentiating instruction to meet the needs of all students
- Learn how to implement curriculum that activates students' background knowledge and world experiences
- Understand and recognize various types of text structures to increase text comprehension

Questions to Consider

1. Why does understanding and appreciating literature involve more than reading the words on a page?
2. How does accessing background knowledge help create a framework for reading assignments?
3. Why are pre-reading strategies important?
4. What are some elements of character development?
5. How does knowledge of text structure enhance comprehension?
6. What strategies can students employ to monitor their comprehension of literary texts?

OVERVIEW

To achieve success in curricular areas, students need to develop "strategic comprehension behaviors" as they construct text understanding (Buehl, 2009, p. 4). Effective comprehension instruction comprises activities that provide students with strategies that facilitate their leaving a reading experience with "fresh perspectives, vital information, and new ideas" (Block & Pressley, 2003, p. 220). Some students may not be able to understand and enjoy the texts they are assigned due to limited background knowledge and an inability to apply effective strategies to enhance their understanding. As a content area teacher, you will have an important role to play in helping your students learn literacy-enhancing strategies.

Some authors (Bean, Readence, & Baldwin, 2008; Vacca & Vacca, 2002) have employed the term "content literacy" to describe the process of reading strategically. It has been defined as "the ability to use reading and writing to learn subject matter in a given discipline" (Vacca & Vacca, 2002, p. 15). A key component of reading strategically is to be metacognitively aware or to "systemically apply strategies and monitor comprehension" (Ruddell, 2002, p. 42). Strategic readers ask themselves questions while they are reading, and they consider whether what they are reading makes sense. They view reading as an active process that requires them to think, monitor their understanding, and apply strategies to "fix-up" their comprehension when they encounter comprehension problems.

Strategic readers create mental images as they read. They use visual and sensory images to imagine details, draw conclusions, interpret text, and synthesize information. Using mental imagery is particularly valuable when reading literature because it enhances the sensory aspects authors create with their selection of words.

Successful readers also know how texts are organized, and they use this information to enhance their comprehension. Novels and fictional stories, for example, are organized according to story grammars that include components such as setting, characters, goal, problem, and resolution. If students become aware of these structures, they will have a framework for approaching and comprehending literary texts more effectively.

"Teaching students to use comprehension strategies is sensible because self-regulated use of comprehension strategies is prominent in the reading of exceptionally skilled adult readers" (Pressley, 2000, p. 554). Additionally, through strategic reading, students are afforded the privileges, responsibilities, and advantages of skillful readers. To read actively and strategically means that students have the right to question the beliefs and statements of others rather than to passively submit to their ideas.

Learning does not end when students have finished reading their texts. Literacy is, in fact, a phenomenon that permeates life well beyond the classroom. Understanding key ideas, reacting to what was read, and extending learning are important aspects of the reading process. By providing opportunities for students to discuss, write, and engage in meaningful activities after reading, you enable students to react to their reading by connecting it to personal responses. In addition, students can deepen their understanding of what they read by putting ideas into their own words, applying what they have learned, and making judgments about ideas and concepts from their reading.

The instructional strategies in this chapter promote comprehension and provide multiple opportunities for students to apply these strategies in meaningful contexts so that they will begin to internalize and use them while reading independently. While it may not be easy for students to accomplish this goal, you will begin to notice improved comprehension as a result of teaching students strategies for preparing to read, using text structure and monitoring understanding during reading, and extending meaning beyond the classroom after reading.

Accessing Prior Knowledge

GOAL

To help students use prior knowledge to comprehend literary texts

BACKGROUND

Researchers have determined that a reader's prior knowledge, including experiences and attitudes, determines the ways in which new information is processed and understood (McCormack & Pasquarelli, 2010). New information is assimilated more easily when it can be related to a reader's background. The term schema is used to describe how people use world or prior knowledge to organize and store information in their heads. Paris and Lindauer (1976) found that some readers may not activate prior knowledge on their own and may need a teacher's assistance to do this before reading a text selection.

Students who are able to access their prior knowledge before reading are more likely to make useful predictions about the text and set purposes for their reading (Oczkus, 2010). These predictions can become hypotheses to test during reading (Neufeld, 2005). Not only do readers need to activate prior knowledge as a prereading activity, they also can use prior knowledge during and after reading to infer meaning and elaborate on the content (Vacca, Vacca, & Mraz, 2011).

The strategies in this section are designed to help students access their prior knowledge and to prepare them for reading literature. By engaging students in these activities, you will help build a foundation for their comprehension of literary texts.

Assessing Student Learning	Drawing Inferences

Goal: *To help students use prior knowledge to comprehend literary texts.* Readers need to activate their prior knowledge in order to fully comprehend and enjoy literary texts. Frequently, you will need to assist your students in this endeavor prior to their reading a text selection. The strategies in this section are designed for that purpose and will help your students realize what already exists in their schema that relates to the selected literature selection.

Brozo and Simpson (1995) suggest that prior knowledge allows readers to draw inferences, or read between the lines, and to focus on the big ideas in the text rather than getting caught up in the details. As a way of determining whether your students are able to infer a character's feelings in a story, select a text the class is familiar with, and choose an incident in the story where a character's feelings are displayed through actions. Read the selection aloud and ask your class what they can infer about the character's feelings. Invite them to find other selections that require the reader to draw inferences. The following statement can be used as a clarifier to connect the inference and their prior knowledge.

"I inferred that the character felt _____ and I know from experience that
_____." (Based on Oczkus, 2010).

Readers Needing Additional Support

Before beginning a selection, students should read the title and look at the pictures. Tell them to skim through the pages and stop periodically to read some of the words. As they do so, they can make predictions about the content of the story.

Story Impressions

Story Impressions (Denner & McGinley, 1987) is a prereading strategy designed to create interest in an upcoming narrative text. By connecting words or phrases and using prior knowledge, students can form impressions about the story before they actually read it. In addition to creating interest, this strategy helps students develop anticipatory outlooks that will be confirmed or modified as they read the text.

Directions

1. Preview a story or text selection and select several words or short phrases related to plot events or characters.

2. Explain to students that the purpose of this activity is to look at the series of selected words and phrases in order to predict how the author will use them in the selection they are about to read.

3. Write the list so it can be seen by the entire class. The following words and phrases have been taken from the picture book *Piggybook* by Anthony Browne (1986).

Simon and Patrick	cooking
nice house	nowhere to be found
important job	pigsty
Mom	Dad
ironing	"you are pigs"

4. Direct students to write their own stories incorporating words from the Story Impressions list in Step #3. Ask them to underline all of the words their Story Impressions include. After completing their stories, students might enjoy sharing their written passages in small groups. The following is a Story Impressions example.

   > I think this is a story about a family with two boys, <u>Simon and Patrick</u>, and a <u>Mom</u> and a <u>Dad</u>. Dad probably is the one with the very <u>important job</u> and the Mom does the <u>cooking</u> and <u>ironing</u>. Someone goes missing and is <u>nowhere to be found</u>.

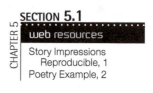

CHAPTER 5

SECTION 5.1

web resources

Story Impressions
    Reproducible, 1
Poetry Example, 2

5. Have students read the author's version and compare their Story Impressions with the actual story.

Anticipation Guide

An Anticipation Guide (Herber, 1978) consists of a series of statements that forecast the content of the upcoming text. Although it is primarily used with informational text, Anticipation Guides are also effective with literature selections. "Anticipation Guides may vary in format but not in purpose. In each case the readers' expectations about reading are raised before they read the text" (Vacca, Vacca, & Mraz, 2011, p. 182). The greatest value of an Anticipation Guide lies in the discussion that ensues after students have completed the guide.

Directions

1. Analyze the text to be read. Determine the major ideas students will need to consider.
2. Write those ideas in three to five short, declarative sentences. Try to focus the statements on experiences and beliefs that relate to students' lives.
3. Arrange the statements in an order and format that will elicit predictions and invite students' participation in a discussion.
4. Present the Anticipation Guide reproducible from the website by providing a copy for each student or by displaying it where it can be seen by the entire class. Use the following example or create one from a literature selection.

Literature

Anticipation Guide

"The Dinner Party" by Mona Gardner

Read the following statements about the story.
Put a check mark next to the statements with which you agree.

_____ 1. A woman always screams when she is badly frightened.

_____ 2. In India, a bowl of milk may be bait for a snake.

_____ 3. A man who is frightened usually exhibits perfect control.

_____ 4. Cobras are a common sight in India.

EXAMPLE

5. Give students a few minutes to respond to each of the statements and to consider how they will explain and support their responses.
6. Discuss the students' responses before they read the selection.
7. Explain to students that as they read the text they should consider their ideas from the Anticipation Guide and whether their views have stayed the same or have changed after reading the text.
8. Following the reading, engage students in a follow-up discussion to contrast their predictions with the author's ideas.

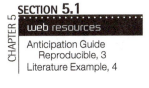

CHAPTER 5

SECTION 5.1

web resources

Anticipation Guide
Reproducible, 3
Literature Example, 4

Section **5.1** INSTRUCTIONAL STRATEGY 3

Character Quotes

Character Quotes (Buehl, 2009) is a strategy that motivates students to analyze the personality traits of characters in a literature selection and sparks their curiosity about the selection. Students draw on their prior knowledge about people as they form generalizations about a character.

Directions

1. Preview a story or novel to identify several quotations by a character that illustrate different elements of his or her personality. Select quotations that will encourage students to develop varying descriptions of what kind of person this character might be. Write each quotation on a separate slip of paper or note card as in the following example from a short story, "After You My Dear Alfonz" by Shirley Jackson (1943).

I guess all of you want to make just as much of yourselves as you can.

Now eat as much as you want, Boyd. I want to see you get filled up.

Boyd, Johnny has some suits that are a little too small for him and a winter coat. The coat's not new, of course, but there's lots of wear in it still. And I have a few dresses that your mother or sister could probably use. Your mother can make them over into lots of things for all of you.

There are many little boys like you, Boyd, who would be very grateful for the clothes someone was kind enough to give them.

Don't think I'm angry, Boyd. I'm just disappointed in you, that's all. Now let's not say anything more about it.

I'll bet he's strong though. Does he . . . work?

2. Organize students into cooperative groups with three or four students in each group. Give each group a different quotation to consider. Each group then has the responsibility to generate as many words as possible that might describe this character. For example, students might use some of the following words to describe the character: condescending, prejudiced, generous, curious, and self-serving.

3. Ask a member from each group to read a quotation to the entire class and share the list of qualities and traits that he or she associated with the character. Write these qualities where they can be seen by the entire class as they are presented. Then tell students that all of the quotations were uttered by the same individual.

4. Assist the students in making some generalizations about this character or individual. Have the students work again in their cooperative groups to write a preliminary "personality profile" of this character by using the qualities and traits listed by the entire class. The summary should contain four or five statements that integrate important qualities from the list. An example of a personality profile for a character from this short story is presented here.

Personality Profile

The character whose words we analyzed seems to mean well, but she sounds very self-serving and smug. She speaks to Boyd in a condescending manner and seems to assume that he needs her help. We get the impression that she doesn't really know him but is making judgments about him, perhaps because of the way he is dressed or the color of his skin. We think she probably believes that she is doing the "right thing" when, in fact, her comments are very insulting.

5. Direct students to begin reading the story, novel, or other text assignment. After completing their reading, they can return to their "personality profiles" to discuss what new qualities or traits they might add. Students can also discuss how they would change their profiles to make them better match the true nature of the character.

SECTION **5.1**

CHAPTER 5

web resources

Character Quotes
    Reproducible, 5
Literature Example, 6

Studying Aspects of Characterization

GOAL

To help students identify traits of characterization

BACKGROUND

Each person, animal, or imaginary creature in a piece of literature is called a character. An author's method of developing a character in a story may be through the dialogue the character uses. Writers use dialogue to bring out the personalities of their characters and to set the tone of a story. Another method of character development is through physical description and the character's interactions with other characters.

Adequate character development is essential to a reader's understanding of and appreciation for a literature selection.

A writer uses words to create precise images so that readers can visualize characters, events, and surroundings. Characters who are described vividly and realistically become alive and unforgettable. Who can forget, for example, Tom Sawyer, Anne Frank, or Jane Eyre? The descriptive words an author chooses have a major impact on a reader's understanding of and feeling for the characters in a story.

When your students begin to read a literature selection, alert them to be aware of the aspects of character development. Tell them to listen closely to what the characters say, to notice how the characters relate to each other, and to be aware of their actions within the story.

Readers Needing Additional Support

Tell students to pay close attention to what the characters say and do as a way of visualizing the characters and making the events of the story clearer. Explain to them that authors use precise language as a way of helping them "see" the events in the story.

Section **5.2** INSTRUCTIONAL STRATEGY 4

Biopoems

Biopoems (Gere, 1985) follow a pattern that encourages students to reflect on the personality traits of a character in a story or poem and to synthesize what they have learned. It is a valuable tool for helping students focus on the important aspects of a character's personality and enables students to analyze how the character's traits may have influenced his or her actions within the story.

Directions

1. Ask students to write down the name of a character in a book or a television personality whom they find compelling.
2. Have them make a list of the person's characteristics. They should include their subject's physical characteristics, family members, likes and dislikes, hopes and aspirations, his or her attitude toward and interactions with other people, and any other information about the person that they consider important.
3. Tell students they are going to write a Biopoem about this person, using the ideas on their lists.

4. Make copies of the Biopoem reproducible from the website and distribute one to each student.

5. Ask students to complete a Biopoem using information from their lists.

6. Invite students to share their Biopoems with a small group or with the entire class.

7. An example of a Biopoem follows.

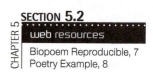
■ Literature

Biopoem

Subject: *Bode*

Four traits that describe the subject: *brazen, unintimidated, athletic, confident*

Relative of: *Two sisters who snowboard*

Lover of: *rap music, raisin bran, turkey subs*

Who feels: *driven, anxious, competitive*

Who needs: *good snow, his Atomic skis, boots*

Who fears: *very little*

Who gives: *interviews to the media*

Who would like to see: *several Olympic gold medals*

Resident of: *Franconia, New Hampshire*

Last name: *Miller*

Susan Lenski, Mary Ann Wham, Jerry Johns, & Micki Caskey. *Reading and Learning Strategies: Middle Grades through High School* (4th ed.). Copyright © 2011 by Kendall Hunt Publishing Company (1-800-247-3458, ext. 4). May be reproduced for noncommercial educational purposes within the guidelines on the copyright page. www.kendallhunt.com/readingresources

EXAMPLE

Section **5.2** INSTRUCTIONAL STRATEGY 5

Missing Person's Report

The words a writer uses have a direct impact on a reader's understanding of and feelings for a character in a story. The way a writer develops a character's personality is called *characterization*. Through a character's words, actions, and descriptions of his or her appearance, the reader can infer a great deal about the character's personality and lifestyle. For example, in "The Secret of the Wall" by Elizabeth Borton de Trevino (1989), a laborer walking home at the end of the day is described as wearing "plaster-covered shoes" and a "dusty shirt and trousers." By contrast, another character in the same story is said to be wearing "a clean freshly ironed cotton work shirt." The reader can infer from the writer's words that the two individuals have contrasting lifestyles and occupations.

Poetry writers also create images through word choice. Poet Mary Oliver, for example, describes a swan as "slim and delicate with a poppy-colored beak." Attention to detail and choice of words enable readers to visualize the characters in a story or poem and to draw inferences about them.

Directions

1. Skim through a story or poem, pointing out to students the descriptive words and phrases the author uses to create images and impressions of the characters.

2. Tell students that one of the characters in the story has gone missing and it is their job to write a Missing Person's Report for the local police department as in the following example for Sir Walter Scott's (1995) "Lochinvar."

Missing Person's Report

Lochinvar is a brave young man in his early twenties. He was last seen in Scotland at Netherby Hall where he boldly interrupted a wedding celebration. His intent was to halt the wedding of Ellen, his beloved, whose father had forbidden Lochinvar to woo his daughter.

Lochinvar is described by his contemporaries as a dashing young man who is faithful in love and dauntless in war. He is an excellent swimmer and an accomplished dancer as well as being an expert horseman. Lochinvar is believed to be armed with only a broadsword.

When found, he may be charged with kidnapping due to the fact that Ellen, who is also missing, is believed to be with him. It appeared to observers, however, that Ellen left willingly with Lochinvar. Any person with information leading to the whereabouts of Lochinvar and Ellen is asked to contact their local police department.

3. Remind students to include details about the missing person's height, weight, distinguishing features, clothing, and where he or she was last seen and by whom.

4. Suggest to students that they can enhance their Missing Person's Report by including details of the person's personality when they describe him or her.

5. Students might enjoy sharing their descriptions of the missing persons with the class or a small group to see if other students can identify the missing person.

CHAPTER 5

SECTION 5.2

web resources

Missing Person's Report
Reproducible, 9
Literature Example, 10

Section **5.2** INSTRUCTIONAL STRATEGY 6

Attribute Web

An Attribute Web involves constructing a visual representation of a character from a text selection. It is, in fact, a form of character analysis. By completing an Attribute Web, students are able to visualize a character's distinguishing traits and to summarize their impressions of him or her. Students may complete the web as a way to recap information about a character, or it may be completed gradually as events in the story unfold that reveal the character's personality. Several divisions of the web are suggested, including the following ones.

- How a character looks
- How a character acts
- How a character feels
- How other characters feel about him or her
- Examples of what the character says

Directions

1. Review with students the importance of analyzing a character's actions and words as a way of understanding and appreciating a story.

2. Remind students that an author develops the theme of a story through the actions and words of the characters.

3. Make copies of a blank Attribute Web from the website and distribute them so that each student has a copy.

4. Select a character from a familiar story and direct students to write the character's name in the center circle.

5. Guide students as they complete the Attribute Web and address each of the categories.

6. After completing the Attribute Web as a class, distribute additional blank copies of the Attribute Web and ask students to pick a character from another story with which they are familiar.

7. Tell students to complete the Attribute Web using words and phrases to express their impressions of the selected character.

8. After completing the Attribute Web, students may enjoy sharing their webs in small groups.

SECTION **5.2**

CHAPTER 5

web resources

Attribute Web
  Reproducible, 11
Literature Example #1, 12
Literature Example #2, 13

| Assessing Student Learning | My name is... |

Goal: *To help students identify traits of characterization.* Character development plays a major role in a reader's understanding and enjoyment of a story. Authors use dialogue, physical description, and character interaction to set the tone of a story and to assist readers in visualizing the characters about whom the story is written. The words an author uses to describe the character are as much a part of character development as are the dialogue and story events.

From a literature textbook, select a short story that has multiple characters, and read it to your class or invite your students to read it independently. Ask each student to select a character from the story whom they find compelling and to visualize this character's appearance, mannerisms, and interactions with other people.

After your students have had several minutes to study a character, tell them that they are to assume the character's identity for a role playing experience. Choose several students to come to the front of the class to be interviewed by their classmates. The selected students are to "become" the characters through their mannerisms, dialogue, and reactions to questions.

Question starters such as the following can be used to get the role playing underway, but students will soon be off and running with their own questions.

1. Why did you . . .
2. How did you feel when . . .
3. If you could have . . .
4. What would you have done differently instead . . .
5. When did you realize . . .

This activity will assess your students' understanding of character development and focus their attention on the importance of developing character attributes.

Recognizing Story Structure Features

GOAL

To help students use text structure to comprehend fictional texts

BACKGROUND

Text structures are the ways in which texts or chapters are organized and are another feature that impacts a reader's comprehension. Effective readers are aware of text structures and are able to use this information to help them anticipate, monitor, and comprehend what they are reading (McCormack & Pasquarelli, 2010).

Literary and informational texts are structured differently. Basic literary texts are organized around the concept of a story grammar that includes setting, characters, goal, conflict, and resolution. Many students may already be familiar with the organization of fiction, because during their elementary years, they read a great deal of literature. They may need assistance, however, with developing a clear understanding of the more complex, fictional stories and novels they will be reading during their middle and high school years.

At these levels, fictional stories may include the following elements.

- Theme: the main idea of the story.
- Setting: the time and place in which the action of the story takes place.
- Characters: the people, animals, or imaginary characters that are part of the action in the story.
- Conflict (problem): a struggle involving two or more opposing forces.
- Resolution (solution): the conflict is resolved or solved.
- Events: occurrences or incidents that are of some significance to the plot.

By helping your students develop an awareness of the fictional text organizational patterns and literary elements, you will provide them with an important tool for comprehension and enhance their enjoyment of reading.

Assessing Student Learning	Strategies as Assessment

Goal: *To help students use text structure to comprehend fictional texts.* Various types of texts are structured differently. During the middle school and high school years, fictional texts frequently have a more complex organizational pattern than those students encounter during elementary school. If your students can identify and understand fictional text structures, they will be more likely to understand the ideas they encounter while reading.

Ask your students to partner up. Assign each group a story from a fictional collection and ask them to identify the following elements within the story.

Theme:

Setting:

Characters:

Conflict (problem):

Resolution (solution):

Events of significance:

Perspective from which the story is told:

After they have identified these story elements, ask them to consider how the story would be changed if it were told from a different perspective than that chosen by the author.

Invite students to write a short summary of their work. You may wish to call on various groups to share their findings with the entire class.

Section **5.3** | INSTRUCTIONAL STRATEGY 7

Story Maps

Story Maps are graphic organizers for fictional texts. Fictional texts have a different text structure than informational texts. Fictional texts are organized around the elements of fiction: setting, characters, theme, and events in the plot.

Directions

1. Remind students that as they read they should identify the elements of fiction to help them understand the story.

2. Write the elements of fiction where they can be seen by the entire class. Include blank spaces after each term as listed below.

    Setting (time and place) _____

    Major characters _____

    Minor characters _____

    Problem _____

    Events _____

    Solution _____

    Theme (main point of story) _____

3. Review the elements of fiction using a story or book that students have read. Tell students that the setting is the time and place the story took place. If students are reading "The Ransom of Red Chief" by O. Henry, for example, tell them that the setting is in western Illinois during the westward expansion. Have students complete the blank next to the term *setting*. Then have students identify the major and minor characters in the story. After that, have students identify the problem in the story, the events in sequence, and the solution. Finally, have students identify the theme of the story.

4. Tell students that they should use what they know about the way fiction is organized to help them understand the story. Invite students to explain how the Story Map can enhance their understanding. Encourage students to use Story Maps to identify and record a story's elements during reading.

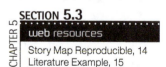

CHAPTER 5 | **SECTION 5.3**
web resources
Story Map Reproducible, 14
Literature Example, 15

TEACHING COMPREHENSION
This site contains lesson plans that promote comprehension.
www.lessonplanspage.com

Conflict-Resolution Paradigm

In literary texts, authors generally build their plot around a problem-solution paradigm, also called conflict and resolution. A conflict or problem usually involves a character's struggle with an external force, such as another character or perhaps with an element of nature. An internal struggle or conflict may occur within a character's mind when he or she has to deal with conflicting feelings or a difficult decision. Resolution or solution occurs when the main conflict in the plot has been resolved. However, in some stories, not all of the conflicts are resolved. At this point, the story usually ends.

Directions

1. Ask students to read a story that centers around a conflict such as "Aaron's Gift," by Myron Levoy (1997). A brief synopsis of the story follows.

    In the story "Aaron's Gift," a young boy finds a pigeon with a broken wing and brings it home as a gift for his aged grandmother. His grandmother loves Aaron's gift. Some neighborhood toughs hear about the pigeon and tell Aaron that he can join their gang if he gives them the pigeon as their mascot. Aaron wants very much to be accepted by the bigger, stronger boys. He meets with the gang members and knows that he has to give up the pigeon if he wants to be accepted by the gang. He becomes involved in a physical struggle to save the pigeon when the gang members decide to sacrifice the pigeon as a rite of passage. In the midst of the turmoil, the pigeon flies away to freedom, and Aaron runs for home bruised and battered to tell his family of the events that have transpired.

2. Divide the class into small groups and tell them to identify the conflicts that exist in this or the story you have assigned. An example for "Aaron's Gift" is provided below.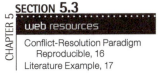

3. Ask them to decide whether the conflict is external, internal, or both.

4. After students have identified the conflicts in this scenario or in a story you have selected, ask them to determine the way in which the conflict was resolved.

    SECTION 5.3
    web resources
    Conflict-Resolution Paradigm
    Reproducible, 16
    Literature Example, 17

5. When students have completed their discussion, ask one student in each group to present the group's ideas to the class as in the example that follows.

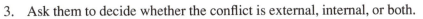

Conflict-Resolution Paradigm

Title: "Aaron's Gift"
Author: Myron Levoy

Conflict

Aaron had a pet pigeon that he was planning on giving to his grandmother for her birthday. However, Aaron had a chance to become a member of a neighborhood gang if he would give the gang members his pigeon as a mascot. He wanted very much to be accepted by the members of the gang. Aaron met with the gang members but decided at the last minute that he didn't want to sacrifice the pigeon and ran away. In the midst of the chaos, the pigeon flew to freedom.

Resolution

Aaron ran home in tears and told his family and his grandmother what had transpired. Rather than being upset with him, his grandmother kissed him and thanked him for a present which she said was far better than the pigeon. He had made an appropriate and important decision.

What's Your Perspective?

The point of view of a story or poem is the perspective from which it is told. The author decides who will tell the story. An omniscient point of view is that of the narrator who is relating the events in the story to the reader. It's an eyewitness account of the events. A first person point of view is a personal account, such as in an autobiography. In first person writing, the pronouns *I, we, me*, and *us* are used. A third person point of view is from the perspective of one or more of the characters who are part of the plot.

Strategies such as "What's Your Perspective?" will increase students' ability to read with a greater depth of comprehension and appreciation, as they will be guided in understanding the story from an alternative point of view or a different perspective.

Directions

1. Ask students to read through a story, article, or other selection.
2. Following the completion of the reading, ask students to identify the perspective from which the events are told.
3. Invite them to consider an alternate perspective. For example, if students have read a selection about Buffalo Bill and the expansion of the railroad in the West, they might view the expansion from the viewpoint of a Native American, a fur trader, a homesteader, or perhaps even a buffalo.
4. Make copies of the What's Your Perspective? reproducible from the website and distribute them to the class.
5. Divide the class into small groups and assign each group a different perspective from the selection.
6. Refer to the following completed What's Your Perspective? diagram examining the railroad expansion from the buffalo's perspective (based on Buehl, 2001).

CHAPTER 5

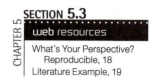

SECTION 5.3
web resources

What's Your Perspective?
Reproducible, 18
Literature Example, 19

Social Studies

What's Your Perspective? (Buehl, 2001)

Your name _Buffalo_

Title of the story in which you appear _"Building the Railroad"_

What are your needs?

grazing land   safety from predators

water   space to roam

What are your concerns?

being killed   not enough space to live in

lack of food   being made into a tepee

What events have impacted your life?

Buffalo Bill and other hunters have shot thousands of buffalo.

The railroad is taking 20 square miles of grazing land for each mile of track!

The farmers are following the railroad and are plowing up the land.

How do you feel about this?

This is murder! What kinds of beasts are these humans?

I don't have any space left to roam.

There goes my food supply!

Summarize Your Situation

The railroad has destroyed our way of life on the prairie. It has taken up lots of land and brought people who have plowed up the grasses we eat. It also brought out the white men who have murdered us by the thousands—not like the Native Americans who only killed a few of us for food and supplies. In my opinion, progress is not what its cracked up to be.

EXAMPLE

Enhancing Learning with Literature

BACKGROUND

Understanding and appreciating literature involves more than reading the words on a page. By drawing inferences through reading between the lines and making connections to their own lives, students can discover a world of ideas and experiences far beyond the classroom. Once students are comfortable with the strategies for thinking about and interacting with literary text, they will see that the same strategies can apply and be effective across the curriculum.

Encourage students to predict what they think will happen, ask questions about the text as they read, make personal connections with the story, and develop opinions about the information presented by the author. All of these endeavors will strengthen their comprehension of text, both in their literature experiences and in their other curricula areas.

The strategies in this section are designed to enhance students' comprehension of both fiction and non-fiction. Students will see how the techniques they use for comprehension of literary text can be applied across the curriculum.

Section **5.4** INSTRUCTIONAL STRATEGY 10

Locating Literary Devices

Locating Literary Devices can be effectively implemented as a prereading, during reading, or postreading strategy. Students enjoy it because it incorporates three key motivational elements: challenge, choice, and collaboration (Wang & Han, 2001). You may use this strategy to determine students' background knowledge about literary elements, to measure their ability to identify literary elements in a reading selection, or to review elements in a literature assignment.

Locating Literary Devices is challenging because students need to be familiar with the meanings of literary elements or terms in order to complete the assignment. Choice is involved as students choose examples to demonstrate their knowledge of the terms, and collaboration can occur if you assign students to complete the assignment in pairs or in small groups.

Directions

1. Teach the following literary elements or devices to students or select some from your current literature curriculum.

    Irony—used to convey meaning by saying the direct opposite of what is really meant. In "Julius Caesar," Anthony uses irony during his funeral oration when he says, "Brutus is an honorable man."

    Metaphor—a comparison of two unlike things without using a connective word such as *like, as*, or *than*. "Fear was a heavy fog in the lungs of all of us." (From "A Shipment of Mute Fate")

    Onomatopoeia—Use of a word whose sound imitates its meaning (thwack, whirr, squeak, and meow).

Personification—An animal or object described as if it were human or had human qualities. Poet William Wordsworth describes daffodils as "tossing their heads in sprightly dance."

Alliteration—Repetition of the same or similar initial consonant sounds of two or more words that are close together. A common example from playground verbiage is "Peter Piper picked a peck of pickled peppers."

Hyperbole—An exaggeration or extravagant statement used as a figure of speech. Emily Dickinson used a form of hyperbole when she wrote, "I'm nobody! Who are you?"

2. Provide each student with a copy of the Locating Literary Devices reproducible from the website. An abbreviated example is shown below.

3. Tell students to find examples of each of the literary elements listed in column one in literature selections or poetry you have read in class.

4. Direct students to write the name of the selection in which they find the element on the appropriate line in the second column.

5. In the third column, students should write the page number where the example is located.

6. In the fourth column, students should write a phrase, sentence, or example that illustrates the literary element they have identified.

7. This strategy may also be implemented by writing the name of a literary element on the front of a three-by-five note card and asking students to write the requested information on the back of the card.

SECTION 5.4

CHAPTER 5

web resources

Locating Literary Devices
Reproducible, 20
Literature Example, 21

Literature

Literary Device	Location	Page Number	Example
Alliteration	Beowulf	46	"Now Beowulf bode in burg of the Scyldings."
Personification	Daffodils	490	"I wandered lonely as a cloud." (Wordsworth)
Irony	Oedipus Rex	87	King Oedipus, who has unknowingly killed his father, says he will banish his father's killer when he finds him.

E X A M P L E

SURF THE WEB

AMERICAN AND ENGLISH LITERATURE RESOURCES
This site offers an extensive bibliography of resources pertaining to American and English literature available on the Web. It includes information for finding electronic versions of classic texts and the home pages of various authors. Sites are organized first by American literature and then by English literature. These main categories are further divided by genre.
http://library.scsu.ctstateu.edu/litbib.html

Section **5.4** INSTRUCTIONAL STRATEGY 11

Connecting Fact and Historical Fiction

Relating the factual information of social studies texts to historical fiction allows students to experience important events in history through the eyes of people who were actually there. Connecting Fact and Historical Fiction is designed to enhance students' learning by engaging them in interacting with accurately portrayed fictional texts and connecting the information to the parallel textbook account.

In this strategy, students read novels that have an important historical informational dimension and connect them to material in their social studies textbooks. By experiencing factual information in interesting fictional accounts, students are provided with a foundation upon which to make connections with the informational texts. A list of historical literature, compiled by Dr. Pamela Nelson from Northern Illinois University, can be found on the website.

Directions

1. Select an historical informational novel or short story appropriate to your social studies curriculum. For this example, a story called, "The Dog of Pompeii" by Louis Untermeyer (1997) will be used.

2. If you are using this story, preview the events that occurred with the eruption of Mt. Vesuvius and the resulting destruction of Pompeii. Otherwise, preview the historical events that will occur in the novel or story you have selected.

3. For this example, tell students that they are going to read a fictional account of a blind boy, Tito, and his dog, Bimbo, who lived in Pompeii at the time of the eruption. Allow students time to read the selection.

4. Make copies of the Connecting Fact and Historical Fiction reproducible from the website. Give each student a copy of the reproducible.

5. Locate a factual account of the events at Pompeii in a social studies text.

6. Guide students as they examine their textbooks for facts that are related in the fictional account and have them record the information on the Connecting Fact and Historical Fiction reproducible.

7. Occasionally, a fact will appear in the fictional account that may not be verified in the textbook account, or it may be refuted in some way. In this instance, students should place a check mark in the fourth column titled "Requires Further Research."

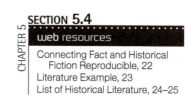

SECTION **5.4**

CHAPTER 5

web resources

Connecting Fact and Historical
    Fiction Reproducible, 22
Literature Example, 23
List of Historical Literature, 24–25

Literature

Title and Author: "The Dog of Pompeii" by Louis Untermeyer

Story Information	Textbook Verification	Page Number	Requires Further Research
Mt. Vesuvius suddenly erupted.	The blast occurred in A.D. 79.	87	_____
The ground trembled and the air was filled with ash.	The blast was as strong as a nuclear blast.		✓
Tito followed people to the sea and escaped.	Many people died in their homes, and others were trapped at the sea gate.	89	_____
Bimbo was unable to escape and died.	The remains of the city have been excavated, and many bodies were preserved by the ashes.	90	_____

E X A M P L E

Assessing Student Learning

Recognizing Figurative Language

Goal: *To help students learn through reading literature.* Writers who use figurative language do so to help their readers visualize ordinary things in more interesting ways. Similes, metaphors, onomatopoeia, personification, alliteration, hyperbole, and irony are all literary devices that can transform a piece of text from unremarkable to engaging.

The following verses are taken from Lewis Carroll's poem, "The Walrus and the Carpenter" (1871). Invite your students to identify some of the literary devices Carroll used in this engaging poem.

The Walrus and the Carpenter

(1) The sun was shining on the sea,
Shining with all his might:
He did his very best to make
The billows smooth and bright
And this was odd, because it was
The middle of the night.

(2) The moon was shining sulkily,
Because she thought the sun
Had got no business to be there
After the day was done
"It's very rude of him," she said,

(5) "If seven maids with seven mops
Swept for a half a year,
Do you suppose," the Walrus said.
"That they could get it clear?"
"I doubt it," said the Carpenter.
And shed a bitter tear.

(11) "The time has come," the Walrus said,
"To talk of many things:
Of shoes and ships and sealing wax
Of cabbages and kings
And why the sea is boiling hot
And whether pigs have wings."

Activities *and* Journal Entries *for* Teacher Educators

Activities

1. After reading several literature selections with your class, ask students to select a character from one of the selections and write a Biopoem or Missing Person's Report about that person. Invite them to read their poem or report to classmates and challenge their classmates to identify the character about whom the piece is written.

2. Direct students to select an historical novel or a fictional short story based on an historical event. Ask them to locate a factual account of the selected event and to complete the Connecting Fact and Historical Fiction reproducible (Section 5.4, page 22) located on the website. Suggest that they share their findings with a small group of their fellow students.

3. As a way of beginning class discussion, prepare Admit Slips for your students, and distribute them to students as they enter the classroom. A reproducible form is on the website. Ask students to respond **anonymously** to the following: 1) What questions do you have about this week's reading assignment? 2) Which strategy do you find most challenging? 3) Is there a strategy you would like to revisit for further clarification? 4) Which strategy do you find most useful? Read their anonymous responses and lead an open discussion about classroom content and procedures.

4. Discuss with your students the rationale for the explicit teaching of comprehension instruction for reading a literary text. Elicit responses from them to the question, "How can comprehension be improved by teaching students to use specific cognitive strategies as they read?" Ask students if there are particular strategies that they find most effective for this purpose.

Journal Entries

1. Do you find that your knowledge of text structure is helpful when approaching a reading assignment? Please explain your answer.

2. Select a short story from http://www.bibliomania.com. As you read the story, see if you can identify some of the literary devices described in Instructional Strategy 10, Locating Literary Devices. Make a list of the examples in your journal.

3. How do the words an author chooses for his or her story help to construct a visual representation of a character? From a selection that you have read and enjoyed, select a character and explain how the author's words created a visual picture of that character for you. Cite some examples.

6 Understanding Informational Texts

IRA Standards: 1.1, 1.2, 1.3, 2.1, 2.2, 2.3, 3.3, 4.1, 4.2, 4.3, 5.2, 5.3, 5.4, 6.2, 6.4

Learning Goals

The reader of this chapter will:

- Understand the foundational theory underpinning the way in which readers comprehend informational texts
- Learn a number of instructional strategies that promote comprehending informational texts and ways to assess comprehension
- Understand why informational text structure is unfamiliar to many students, especially ELLs
- Understand how students should flexibly apply reading strategies

Questions to Consider

1. How can you encourage students to adopt a reading stance in different places along the efferent-aesthetic continuum?
2. Which instructional strategies are the best fit for students in your discipline?
3. What kind of text structures does your discipline most often use, and how can you teach these patterns to ELLs?
4. How do you flexibly use strategies as you read?

OVERVIEW

Many students, even good students, have difficulty comprehending informational texts. The Nation's Report Card, the National Assessment of Educational Progress (NAEP), indicates that the majority of secondary readers (60%) are able to read at a basic level, but only 5% are able to read and interpret complex texts. These results have remained stable over the past 20 years (see http://nces.ed.gov/nationsreportcard/). There are a number of reasons why secondary students have difficulty reading disciplinary texts, such as social studies, science, and math textbooks. One reason is that elementary students have limited experiences with such texts (Duke, 2000). Jeong, Gaffney, and Choi (2010) confirmed this finding a decade after Duke's results were published. Not a lot has changed in elementary schools; students still spend little time reading informational texts. Another reason why students have difficulty reading disciplinary texts is that content area teachers generally do not teach the strategies that students need when reading textbooks (National Reading Panel, 2000). In a study in which the researchers interviewed high school students, Pitcher and colleagues (2010) found that students knew they had trouble reading course materials, but they did not believe that they were getting help with strategies that would aid in understanding those materials. This may be because many secondary teachers do not know which strategies will help their students comprehend the texts in their disciplines so they do not provide students with reading assistance (Denti & Guerin, 2004).

Comprehending Informational Texts in the Disciplines

Informational texts are a type of academic writing (Gipe, 2010). These texts reflect specialized information about a topic using vocabulary that is often new to students. The language of the passages is often abstract, the concept load is high, and the grammatical structures can be unfamiliar to students. Informational texts, for example, use a more passive voice than do other types of rhetorical structures. Therefore, informational texts are typically more challenging for students to comprehend than literary texts (Gee, 2004).

Informational texts may take many forms. Traditionally, texts have been defined as communication in print, such as a textbook chapter in a book. A current view, however, suggests that the term *text* has a broader interpretation. Texts do not have to be print sources; they can be any source that communicates meaning. Texts, therefore, can include trade books, textbooks, news articles, feature articles, encyclopedia entries, book reviews, historical documents, essays, research reports, and literary analyses. These traditional texts are a subset of all of the informational texts students read. In addition to the kinds of texts stated above, students might also read print and nonprint sources such as websites, music, drama, video, art, and gesture. According to the International Reading Association and National Council of Teachers of English (1996), texts are anything that can be stored in a reader's memory and from which the reader constructs meaning.

When teachers want students to learn a concept in their discipline (e.g., How did the 1920s change America?), they often use a multimodal method of instruction (Boyd & Ikpeze, 2007). This means that the teacher might use excerpts from the textbook, websites, art, music, and other forms of texts to illustrate the main concept. Lenski and colleagues (2007) call these units multigenre text sets. Informational texts come in a variety of forms, and "teachers need to focus on developing multiliterate students who are comfortable reading a range of texts and technologies including paper, electronic, and live texts" (Lenski et al., 2007, p. 19). Using a variety of texts is also beneficial for English learners. According to Ajayi (2009), "Multimodal/multiliteracies pedagogy has the potential to provide students in culturally plural classrooms with a more representative platform for meaning-making" (p. 586).

Reader's Stance

Readers should approach informational texts with a different approach than they do literary texts. Louise Rosenblatt (1978) theorized that readers could approach a text from an efferent stance, in which they are taking something from the text, or an aesthetic stance, in which they bring their personal experiences to the text. Some educators believe that readers of informational texts approach from a more efferent stance and use an aesthetic stance when reading literary texts. Paulson and Armstrong (2010), however, suggest that the aesthetic-efferent stance description should be thought of as a continuum. There are times when teachers want students to read informational texts from more of a personal (i.e., aesthetic) stance, such as when teachers want students to read a textbook passage and make personal connections to it. It is important for teachers to consider how they want students to approach a selection of reading, because students will use different processes, depending on their purposes for reading and the stance they need to take.

Processing Informational Texts

This chapter contains 21 strategies that teachers can use to support students who are reading informational texts. According to Beach and O'Brien (2007), strategies are thoughtful plans about how to process texts. The strategies in this chapter (and in the entire book) are representations of ways good readers process texts. The current thinking in content area reading is that secondary teachers should make sure they are not teaching strategies out of context, but use them to help students learn the content that is being taught and to help students become strategic readers. Good readers do not merely apply reading strategies at random; they apply strategies flexibly and with reason. According to Cartwright (2009), a reader's knowledge of his or her own cognitive processes can influence reading comprehension. Good readers use cognitive flexibility; they simultaneously reflect on how well they are comprehending while attending to constructing meaning. As they read, good readers apply the strategies that they need to make meaning. Many students are able to become flexible readers on their own. Others, however, need teachers to demonstrate and teach how good readers process texts.

Addressing Diversity

Many ELLs will face an additional obstacle in learning how to process informational texts. Academic writing is culture specific. According to Herrera, Perez, and Escamilla (2010), the discourse pattern of academic English is extremely linear. Much of academic writing is organized in a main idea-detail pattern with few extraneous details and a minor amount of transition. In fact, academic English is much more linear than Semitic, Asian, Romance, Russian, and Navajo languages. Therefore, the text structures taught in school are probably different from the ways texts are organized in the ELL's native country. Most ELLs, therefore, will need explicit instruction in the discourse patterns of academic writing.

Not only are the text structures of informational texts new for ELLs, the way that academic sentences are organized is also different. The transition and function words used in informational texts will be new for many ELLs, even those who are proficient in conversational English. For example, consider the following sentence: *Shortly after the bombing of Pearl Harbor on December 7, 1941, Japanese Americans became viewed as a threat to national security.* To understand this cause-effect sentence, readers need to know that the term *shortly after* indicates that the facts in the first part of the sentence depend on the facts in the second part. This type of sentence could be difficult for many ELLs. Teachers, therefore, need to show students how to make meaning from academic sentences.

Challenging but Worth It

Informational texts are challenging for students to read, but they have great potential as a learning tool. Saul and Dieckman (2005) emphasize the need for teaching informational texts in middle and high schools. They note that informational texts can draw students into learning by expanding their knowledge of the world. Teachers can explicitly teach students how to construct meaning from all types of informational texts (print and nonprint alike) as they teach the content in their disciplines. The instructional strategies in this chapter can help teachers develop lessons to teach the critical strategies students need to learn in order to construct meaning as they read informational texts.

Demonstrating General Understanding

GOAL

To help students develop a general understanding of informational texts

BACKGROUND

When students read, they develop an initial interpretation of meaning which can be deepened as they reflect on the texts (Mackey, 1997). Developing a general understanding of informational text, however, can be difficult for many students. Good readers think about the text before reading, make predictions as they read, look for main ideas, and summarize after reading (see Donovan & Bransford, 2005).

As students read, they develop a general understanding. This includes identifying key ideas and details to determine what the text says explicitly and to make logical inferences from the text. Readers also need to determine central ideas or themes, analyze their development, and summarize the key ideas and supporting details. Students do not just identify facts from the passages; they also need to analyze how the ideas develop and interact over the course of the text (see *Common Core Standards* from the National Governors Association, 2010).

As students develop a general understanding of the text, they need to identify the facts and determine how the facts fit into the larger picture. Strategies such as the ones in this section can help students to achieve this goal.

SECTION **6.1**
web resources
Idea Web Assessment Health/ Science Example, 1

CHAPTER 6

| Assessing Student Learning | Idea Web Assessment |

Goal: *To help students develop a general understanding of informational texts.* Assessing whether students can develop a general understanding of informational texts is contingent on student, text, and contextual factors as noted in Chapter 1. Students who have a strong background or interest in the topic will tend to have an easier time understanding the text. Students will also have an easier time understanding the text if the text difficulty is matched to student ability. Furthermore, on some days students will do better, depending on how their attention is focused and what's happening in the classroom. All of these reasons make it difficult to determine whether students can actually comprehend informational texts at a basic level.

You can, however, make some general evaluations of student learning of this goal. Ogle (2011) suggests using an Idea Web Assessment to determine whether students are able to understand a specific text. If you do several of these assessments in the course of a year, you will have a good idea about which students are able to read informational texts.

To administer an Idea Web Assessment, select a passage that you believe students will be able to read and whose topic is familiar. An example is given on the website. You might need to give ELLs and struggling readers a different passage from the proficient readers in your classroom. Have students read the passage independently. Then ask them to develop a web with the topic in the center, main ideas in each of the radiating spokes, and details listed below them.

To score the Idea Web Assessment, develop your own web and count the number of ideas you found in the passage. This number is the total students could get correct. Then count the number of correct ideas students produced and compare that number to yours. If students are able to score 80% of the total, you can consider them to have met the goal for that text. Remember, however, that students may have more difficulty comprehending texts for which they have little background knowledge.

> Readers who need additional support in middle and high schools may need to use a strategy that helps them develop meaning at the sentence level as well as the text level. Flood, Lapp, and Fisher (2002) suggest that struggling readers parse sentences before trying to develop a general understanding of complete text. To parse sentences, students would think about the subject, the verb, and the object or descriptor. In other words, students would first think through the structure of each sentence and then combine the meaning of the sentences to develop overall comprehension.

Section **6.1** INSTRUCTIONAL STRATEGY 1

Prereading Plan (PreP)

The Prereading Plan, called PreP for short, was developed by Langer (1981) to generate students' interest in content area reading and to access and determine the level of background knowledge that students bring to a reading assignment. PreP guides students to make associations with a topic, reflect on their associations, and reformulate their knowledge. You will probably find that students have differing levels of background knowledge about the topic to be studied. Based on this information about students' background knowledge, you can develop appropriate instruction to meet the needs of students, thus increasing the likelihood that students will comprehend the texts they are asked to read.

Directions

1. Select a passage of text students will be reading. Examine the text for key words and concepts students will need to understand from the reading. Determine a central concept that will be the main focus of the strategy.

2. Once the central concept is identified, introduce PreP to students. Explain to students that the strategy will help them activate their background knowledge and better understand their reading. Model PreP by using an example from your content area or the following example from a biology text.

3. Identify the main topic of the reading selection. Tell students that they will be reading a new chapter from their textbook. Explain that before reading students should access their prior knowledge so that they will better understand the text. Tell students that they can access their prior knowledge before they read by thinking of words and phrases that they associate with the topic.

4. Divide the class into groups of three or four students. Have students list ideas and concepts about the central theme, focusing on any ideas that come to mind when they hear the key concept. Give students five minutes to list ideas; then have students share their initial lists with other members of the class.

5. As students share their ideas, write them so they can be seen by the entire class. Try to organize or group the ideas as students share them. Group ideas by making lists or by constructing a semantic map to show how ideas are connected. Consult the following example to see the types of responses students may generate at this stage of the strategy.

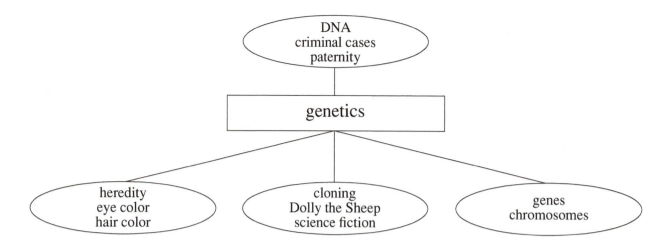

6. Assist students as they reflect on their initial associations with the topic. Ask students to explain their reasons for the associations they suggested for the semantic map. Explain to students that, by listening to ideas that other students share, they will develop an awareness of the networks of associations possible for the term. As students discuss the main concept, add new ideas to the semantic map. Encourage students to explain their thinking by asking them the following questions.

What made you think of _____?
How is _____ related to _____?
What do you know about _____ and _____?

7. Next, guide students to reformulate their knowledge about the topic. The following questions can be used at this stage of the strategy.

Based on our discussion about _____, what new ideas do you now have about _____?
Is there anything we need to delete or change from our earlier list of ideas about _____?

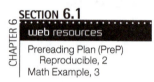

SECTION **6.1**
web resources
Prereading Plan (PreP)
Reproducible, 2
Math Example, 3

8. Have students write their answers in paragraph form.

9. Explain to students that when they use the PreP strategy they access their prior knowledge. Tell them to use the PreP activity to help them construct meaning as they read.

Section **6.1** INSTRUCTIONAL STRATEGY 2

Anticipation/Reaction Guide

An Anticipation/Reaction Guide (Herber, 1978) enhances students' comprehension by activating their background knowledge, focusing their attention on key concepts to be addressed in the text reading, and inviting them to react to ideas in the text. An Anticipation/Reaction Guide is composed of a series of statements that support students' opinions or challenge their beliefs about the topic of the text. The statements invite multiple responses based on students' experiences and opinions. Students mark whether they agree or disagree with a specific statement prior to reading about the topic. The real impact of this activity lies in the discussion that occurs after students have marked their responses. During this discussion, the teacher activates and agitates students' thoughts by asking open-ended questions such as "Why do you feel that way?" or "What ideas help to support your view?" Students then read the text to see if their responses change after reading or if their responses agree or disagree with the author's ideas. Another discussion occurs after reading to encourage students to discuss how and why their ideas and opinions changed after reading the text.

Directions

1. Analyze the text to be read. Determine the major ideas students will need to consider.
2. Write those ideas in short, declarative sentences. Try to focus the statements on experiences that relate to students' lives. Limit the number of statements from four to six so ample time can be devoted to thinking about and discussing each statement fully.
3. Arrange the statements in an order and format that will elicit predictions and invite students' participation.
4. Present the Anticipation Guide to students by duplicating and distributing the Anticipation Guide that follows, on the website, or by using an example from your context area.

Science

Anticipation/Reaction Guide

Directions: Before reading the selection, respond to the following statements. Write "yes" in the blank preceding the statement if you agree or "no" in the blank if you disagree. Be prepared to discuss the rationale for your responses. After you read the selection, write "yes" in the blank after the statement if you agree or "no" in the blank if you disagree. Be prepared to discuss your responses.

Before Reading		After Reading
_____	1. Water belongs to everyone.	_____
_____	2. There is plenty of water for people to use around the world.	_____
_____	3. Animals can migrate if there is not enough water.	_____
_____	4. Droughts mainly affect people and animals in desert climates.	_____
_____	5. The availability of water impacts the lifestyles of humans.	_____
_____	6. Pollution is the greatest threat to the availability of water.	_____

EXAMPLE

5. Give students a few minutes to respond to each of the statements and to consider how they will explain and support their responses.
6. Discuss each statement. Ask students to support their responses.
7. Explain to students that as they read the text they should consider their ideas from the Anticipation/Reaction Guide and whether their views have stayed the same or have changed after reading the text.
8. After students complete the reading, engage them in a follow-up discussion to determine whether their responses have changed and why.
9. Have students write a persuasive paragraph using evidence from the text to support their opinion.

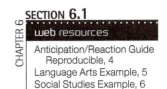

CHAPTER 6

SECTION 6.1

web resources

Anticipation/Reaction Guide
Reproducible, 4
Language Arts Example, 5
Social Studies Example, 6

USING AN ANTICIPATION GUIDE
This site provides a detailed lesson on ways to use an Anticipation Guide before reading.
http://www.adlit.org/strategies/19712

Section **6.1** INSTRUCTIONAL STRATEGY 3

Think, Predict, Read, Connect (TPRC)

Think, **P**redict, **R**ead, **C**onnect (TPRC) (Ruddell, 2005) is a strategy that helps students develop their general knowledge before, during, and after reading. When students use this strategy, they think about the topic, predict what will be in the text, read the text, and then make connections to their own lives. TPRC is a strategy that students can use with all informational texts.

Directions

1. Identify an informational text selection that students can read to learn about a particular topic.

2. Duplicate and distribute the TPRC reproducible found on the website. Tell students that they will be learning a strategy that will help them focus on the information in the text.

3. Tell students the topic of the lesson. For example, you might be teaching about the super nutrients in health class. Have students write the name of the topic on the topic line.

4. Divide the class into groups of three or four students. Have students think (T) about what they know about these super nutrients and write the information in the "think" column.

5. Tell students that they will be reading about the vitamins and minerals that are crucial for optimum health. Have students reread what they wrote in the "think" column and place a check mark by any of the ideas that they predict (P) will be found in the text.

6. After students have made predictions, have them read (R) the selection. Encourage students to underline or highlight the predicted ideas that they actually found in the text.

7. Tell students that as they read they also make connections (C). Provide a few connections between the topic and your own knowledge about the content. Then have students write several more connections in the space provided.

 Topic: Super Nutrients

Think	Predict
I know that people need calcium for strong bones so that might be a super nutrient.	
Vitamin C is really good for you.	
Everybody needs protein.	

Read   Article on Super Nutrients: pp. 52–58

Connect   I've always taken a vitamin pill, and I also take calcium. My brother eats lots of protein but that's not a super nutrient. I didn't realize that Vitamin B is so important, but I know that it's part of my multivitamin pill.

CHAPTER 6   **SECTION 6.1**
web resources
Think, Predict, Read, Connect
(TPRC) Reproducible, 7
Social Studies Example, 8

8. Remind students to use the TPRC strategy as they read informational texts independently.

Section **6.1**   **INSTRUCTIONAL STRATEGY 4**

GIST

GIST (Cunningham, 1982) is a strategy designed to improve students' comprehension of text material and to enhance their ability to write a summary paragraph. The acronym **GIST** stands for **G**enerating **I**nteractions between **S**chemata and **T**ext. While practicing this strategy, students will have the added benefit of "honing their ability to analyze and synthesize content area readings" (Sejnost & Thiese, 2001, p. 160).

Directions

1. Choose a three to five paragraph passage from your content area text. Reproduce it and display it so it can be seen by the entire class. You may use an example from your content area or use the following example from a history text about the emergence of capitalism during the Middle Ages.

The modern economic system of capitalism has its roots in the Middle Ages. Capitalism, also known as free enterprise, is defined as an economic system based on private ownership for the purpose of producing goods and services. Capitalism involves competition and profit.

During the Middle Ages, as towns grew and manors declined, an economy based on land began to be replaced by an economy based on money. Thus the quantity and quality of goods and services being sold began to have an impact on prices.

Because of the change in the economy, serfdom began to disappear. Although serfs were not slaves, they could not leave the land and were still obligated to a lord. By the end of the fourteenth century, many serfs were paying rent. The serfs' obligations to their lords became a money payment as a reflection of the new capitalistic society.

Adapted from *The Pageant of World History*. (1994). Needham, MA: Prentice-Hall.

2. Divide your class into small groups of four to six students. Show the students only the first paragraph of the passage.

3. Ask students to read the first paragraph silently and to independently write a summary of the paragraph in 25 words or fewer. Tell students that it is important for them to use as many of their own words as possible.

4. After approximately 10 minutes, ask students to share their summary paragraphs with their groups. Direct them to pool their ideas and write one summary paragraph based on their group's ideas.

5. Using your students' suggestions as a basis for discussion, write a class summary of the first paragraph. It may look something like the following.

   Capitalism had its beginning in the Middle Ages and is an economic system based on private ownership. It involves competition and profit.

6. Show students the second paragraph and again have students independently write a summary of 25 words or fewer. This time, however, their summary paragraphs are to encompass the information from **both** paragraphs. Once again, ask students to share their paragraphs in their small groups and write one summary paragraph based on their group's ideas. Their paragraph may look something like the one that follows.

   Capitalism is based on private ownership and involves competition and profit. It developed during the Middle Ages when towns grew and manors declined.

7. Continue this process until all three paragraphs are incorporated into a GIST summary. The final summary could look like the following one.

   Capitalism, based on competition and profit, developed during the Middle Ages. As manors declined, serfs were still obligated to their lords but started to pay rent.

8. As students become more proficient at generating GIST summaries, encourage them to practice the strategy on their own. This will help them learn to delete trivial information, focus on main ideas, and use their own words to make generalizations.

SECTION **6.1**

CHAPTER 6

web resources

GIST Reproducible, 9
Music Example, 10

Using Text Structure

GOAL

To help students use text structure to comprehend informational texts

BACKGROUND

Various types of texts are structured differently. Effective readers are aware of the structures of texts, and they can use this information to help them anticipate, monitor, and comprehend what they are reading (Taylor & Beach, 1984). Authors use a structure, or organization of ideas, to present their writing in a way that communicates with the reader (Ruddell, 2002). By helping your students develop an awareness of the common text organizational patterns, you will provide them with an important tool for comprehension. If your students understand and can identify text structures, they will be more likely to understand, remember, and apply the ideas they encounter in their reading (Weaver & Kintsch, 1991).

Literary and informational texts are structured differently. Informational texts are often more difficult for students to comprehend because they may not understand how these texts are organized. Informational texts are generally organized around five common text patterns: description, sequence, compare-contrast, cause-effect, and problem-solution. Authors often use signal or flag words to help readers identify the text structure being used. For example, an author may use words such as *because, since, therefore, consequently*, and *as a result* to signal that the cause-effect text structure is being used. Most informational writing is complex, including content area textbooks, and several text structures may be used in a section of text. If you are aware of the text structures used in a specific text, you will be more able to help your students become aware of signal words and text structures. Helping your students to identify and understand common text structures could enhance their comprehension (Saul & Dieckman, 2005).

Few students have much experience with informational text structure outside of school reading. All students have many experiences with narrative texts from television, stories they hear from friends, and listening to teachers read aloud. The language from informational text is heard much less often, and is more removed from daily experiences (Fang, 2008).

Most students, especially ELLs, need explicit instruction in how informational texts are organized. Text structure, both narrative and informational, is culture specific. The kinds of organizational patterns in this section describe the way informational texts are organized in English. Therefore, the text structures taught in school are likely different from the ways texts are organized in the ELL's country of origin, and need to be described and modeled using strategies such as those in this section.

Readers Needing Additional Support

Students who have difficulty with reading often need more explicit instruction in how to make meaning from text. Fisher, Schumaker, and Deshler (2002) suggest that teachers should use more "strategy systems" in their instruction so that students are able to follow cognitive processes. Many students who struggle with reading, whatever the reason, respond well to heuristics, or graphic steps that help them learn how to think. Examples of these strategies are graphic organizers, main idea-maps, and so on. Teachers should demonstrate the use of graphic organizers frequently so that all students learn how to use them.

Retelling

Goal: *To help students use text structure to comprehend informational texts.* It is relatively easy to assess whether students are able to use the graphic organizers, idea-maps, and signal words described in this section. The purpose of using these strategies, however, is for students to use text structure as an aid in comprehending informational texts. To do this, you need to determine how well students comprehend both the text structure and the meaning of the text. Retelling is one way to do this. Although retelling is often used for narrative text, it can also be used to assess this goal.

Select a short piece of text that has a clear text structure that you can identify. You will notice that many of your textbook passages are written in main idea-detail structure and that many others are combinations of structures. Read the selected text and count the number of ideas that are presented. Then have students read the text using a graphic organizer or idea-map and have them tell you what they learned. Give students 1 point if they identify the text structure and 1 point for each idea they remember. Compare the number of ideas the student identified with your answer. If students were able to identify the text structure and the ideas in the passage, they were successful in using text structure to comprehend texts. If students were unable to identify the text structure, they need more instruction and experience with that particular structure. If students were unable to retell the ideas from the text, they need more instruction in demonstrating general understanding.

Section **6.2** INSTRUCTIONAL STRATEGY 5

Graphic Organizers

Graphic Organizers are pictorial representations of how ideas in a text are connected and organized. They help students understand main ideas in what they read, how ideas are related, and how important details support main ideas. According to Fisher and Frey (2008), students rated Graphic Organizers as one of the most helpful strategies they learned. Graphic Organizers serve purposes similar to outlining, but they provide more flexibility and capitalize on students' interests and facility with visual representations (Burke, 2002b).

Directions

1. Tell students that, when they understand the ways texts are organized, they will be able to organize the information and understand it better. Explain to students that by using Graphic Organizers they can organize information more readily.

2. Select a passage that you want students to read. Explain to students that you will be modeling the use of Graphic Organizers to help them understand how the information is organized, thus promoting better comprehension.

3. Explain that there are five main patterns for organizing content texts: description, sequence, compare-contrast, cause-effect, and problem-solution. Write these words where students can see them.

4. Present the Compare-Contrast Graphic Organizer by displaying it so that it can be seen by the entire class. Explain that one item being compared goes in each circle, and the overlapping area contains information that the concepts have in common as in the following example.

Compare-Contrast Graphic Organizer

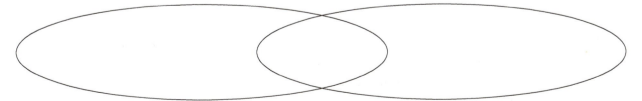

5. Model for students how to read the text and identify important information to include in the Compare-Contrast Graphic Organizer. Continue to use examples from your content area or use the following example.

**Compare-Contrast Graphic Organizer for
North and South Positions on Slavery Issues**

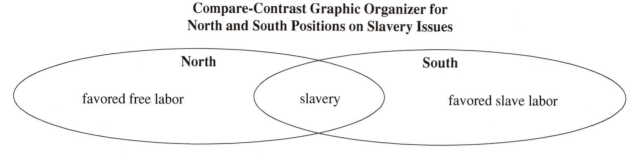

North   favored free labor   slavery   South   favored slave labor

6. Ask students to read the remaining parts of the section and fill in important comparisons and contrasts between the North and the South on their Graphic Organizers. Then have students, in small groups, discuss their compare-contrast charts to clarify and expand on their comparisons. Students may also include some comparisons that are not important. Such comparisons should be deleted.

7. In future lessons, introduce other Graphic Organizers to help students learn how to use them for other text organizational patterns. (Several Graphic Organizers are provided on the website.) Provide modeling and practice so students can learn how to use Graphic Organizers to understand text organizational patterns and improve their comprehension of texts.

CHAPTER 6

SECTION 6.2

web resources

Compare-Contrast Graphic Organizer Reproducible, 11
Physical Education Example, 12
Description Graphic Organizer Reproducible, 13
Math Example, 14
Sequence Graphic Organizer Reproducible, 15
Science Example, 16
Cause and Effect Graphic Organizer Reproducible, 17
Social Studies Example, 18
Problem and Solution Graphic Organizer Reproducible, 19
Consumer Education Example, 20

SURF THE WEB

GRAPHIC ORGANIZERS
This site contains good quality downloadable graphic organizers.
http://www.edhelper.com/teachers/graphic_organizers.htm

Section **6.2** INSTRUCTIONAL STRATEGY 6

Idea-Maps

An Idea-Map is a strategy that helps readers see how information in an expository text is organized (Armbruster, 1986). The visual nature of the Idea-Map strategy helps students see and understand the organizational pattern of a text and how the various components fit together. Depending on the text to be studied, different forms of Idea-Maps can be used. For example, Idea-Maps can be designed for use with description, sequence, compare-contrast, cause-effect, and problem-solution patterns (Johns & Lenski, 2010). A type of graphic organizer, Idea-Maps help students organize thoughts and are especially useful for story problems in mathematics (Zollman, 2009).

Directions

1. Select a passage that you want students to read and learn. Determine the organizational pattern of the text. Select the appropriate Idea-Map for the text. Several types of Idea-Maps are included on the website.

2. Tell students that you will be demonstrating how to use a strategy called Idea-Maps to help them understand how their content textbooks are organized.

3. Explain that there are five main patterns for organizing content texts: description, sequence, compare-contrast, cause-effect, and problem-solution. Write these words so they can be seen by the entire class.

4. Model the Idea-Map strategy using examples from your content area or use the following science example. Tell students that the first step in using an Idea-Map is to identify the text's organizational pattern. Model how to determine the text's pattern as in the following example.

> We will be reading section 11-2 from our science textbook. This section focuses on how the digestive system works. Skim through the section. You'll notice that there are a series of steps that occur in the digestive system. This is a good clue that the text is using the organizational pattern of sequence.

5. Present the Idea-Map for sequential text patterns by displaying it as in the example that follows.

Sequence Idea-Map

Topic: Digestion is a process that breaks down carbohydrates, fats, and proteins for use in the body.

Digestion begins in the mouth with the teeth, saliva, and enzymes breaking down the food.
↓

Next, the food moves from the mouth down the esophagus to the stomach. This process is called peristalsis.
↓

6. Tell students that they can use the same techniques that you modeled to fill out the rest of the Idea-Map. Provide time for students to read the rest of the section and fill out the remainder of the Idea-Map.

7. Ask students to share and refine their Idea-Maps. Remind students that the Idea-Map is a helpful tool that uses text structure to improve their comprehension.

8. In future lessons, introduce other Idea-Maps that are appropriate for your texts. Provide sufficient modeling and practice opportunities so students can learn how to use the Idea-Maps to improve their understanding of text structures and content texts.

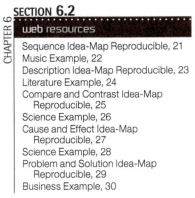

CHAPTER 6

SECTION 6.2

web resources

Sequence Idea-Map Reproducible, 21
Music Example, 22
Description Idea-Map Reproducible, 23
Literature Example, 24
Compare and Contrast Idea-Map
  Reproducible, 25
Science Example, 26
Cause and Effect Idea-Map
  Reproducible, 27
Science Example, 28
Problem and Solution Idea-Map
  Reproducible, 29
Business Example, 30

Section **6.2** INSTRUCTIONAL STRATEGY 7

Signal Words

Signal Words help students identify text patterns and understand what they are reading. Teaching students common Signal Words and the signals they provide help students become more skilled readers of content area texts. Tomlinson (1995) suggests teaching Signal Words through modeling and application activities. Teaching specific Signal Words helps students understand how text is organized and enhances their comprehension of the internal paragraph structure (Montelongo, Herter, Ansaldo, & Hatter, 2010).

Directions

1. Select a section of content text and identify its main organizational pattern. Develop a list of common Signal Words for this organizational pattern.

2. Make photocopies of the text section so students can write on the text.

3. Explain to students that authors use Signal Words to give readers clues about how the text is organized and what information is important. Use examples from your content area or use the following example to model this strategy for students.

Signal Words can help you understand our geography text. We will be reading a section called "Population Issues." This part of the text is mainly organized using a problem-solution pattern. We have a list of Signal Words that we will use to help you better understand how the text is organized and what ideas are important. A list of Signal Words follows.

because	as a result of	accordingly
since	this led to	if . . . then
therefore	so that	thus
consequently	nevertheless	subsequently

4. Model the process of identifying Signal Words and then annotating the text to focus on important ideas. Continue to use examples from your content area or use the example provided below.

> As I begin to read the section, I am looking for Signal Words from the list. I see the word *therefore* in a sentence. It says, "One of the most basic needs threatened by overpopulation is food; therefore, many countries have programs for population control" (p. 119).
>
> I will highlight the word *therefore*, and in the margin I will write a brief note called an annotation to remind myself of this important idea. I will write "overpopulation and limited food = problem; population control = solution." I can continue to use this same technique as I work through the text section.

5. Distribute the photocopies of the text section to students. Provide them with highlighter markers or colored pens to identify Signal Words and to write brief annotations in the margins.

6. Provide time for students to read the section and highlight and annotate the text.

7. Ask students to share the Signal Words they identified and the annotations they wrote. Discuss how this strategy is helpful when they are reading and studying.

8. In future lessons, introduce and model Signal Words for other text patterns. (See the table below for Signal Words.)

9. After multiple experiences with various text patterns and their common Signal Words, students will begin to identify text patterns and Signal Words on their own. A list of sample Signal Words is provided in the table.

Signal Words for Text Patterns

Description	Sequence	Compare-Contrast	Cause-Effect Problem-Solution
for instance	on (date)	however	because
to begin with	not long after	but	since
also	now	as well as	therefore
in fact	as	on the other hand	consequently
for example	before	not only . . . but also	as a result of
in addition	after	either . . . or	this led to
characteristics of	when	same as	so that
	first	in contrast	nevertheless
	second	while	accordingly
	next	although	if . . . then
	then	more than	thus
	last	less than	subsequently
	finally	unless	
		similarly	
		yet	
		likewise	
		on the contrary	

10. Have students find Signal Words as they read and write informational texts.

CHAPTER 6

SECTION 6.2

web resources

Signal Words Reproducible, 31

Developing an Interpretation

GOAL

To help students develop an interpretation of a text

BACKGROUND

According to the Reading Framework for the 2009 National Assessment of Educational Progress (American Institutes for Research, 2005), students who read informational texts need to have a general understanding of the texts and also to be able to develop an interpretation of the texts. That means that when students read they need to do more than comprehend; they need to infer an author's meaning and draw conclusions about the texts by developing a point of view, a position, or a central idea. When students read informational texts, they need to think about the texts and actually make the meaning personal and real. To help students develop an interpretation from informational texts, Beers (2003) suggests that students learn how to create inferences by developing conclusions from facts presented in the texts. This section includes a variety of strategies to help students think about texts and to develop interpretations.

Readers Needing Additional Support

Students who have difficulty with reading or who are ELLs often need to experience the content of text in more than one modality. Chapman and King (2003) suggest that teachers use creative dramatics to help students develop an interpretation after reading. When students can watch or participate in acting out a scene from history, for example, they are more likely to be able to express the meanings of the texts that they read.

Section **6.3** INSTRUCTIONAL STRATEGY 8

It Says—I Say—And So

When students develop an interpretation from text, they need to think about what the text says, what they think, and what it means. Beers (2003) suggests that students think about text using the graphic organizer It Says—I Say—And So. This strategy is similar to a dialectical journal in which students write about the text in the left-hand column and write their responses in the right-hand column. The difference between the two strategies is that It Says—I Say—And So includes a column for students to think about the intersections between the meaning of the text and their own personal experiences. When students develop this thinking process, they learn how to build inferences from text and form interpretations.

Directions

1. Tell students they can develop interpretations from text by thinking about what the text says, what they think, and what they think the text means. Remind students that applying their own knowledge to text is an important way to develop interpretations.

2. Duplicate and distribute the It Says—I Say—And So reproducible found on the website. Tell students that when they read they need to think about the words from the text and develop a general understanding of what the text says.

3. Demonstrate It Says—I Say—And So by using the language arts example that follows or create one for your content area to use as an example.

It Says	I Say	And So
Proper nouns are the names of unique entities and are capitalized.	Names that are specific such as my name, the name of my school, and the name of my city are all proper nouns.	I need to capitalize words that specifically name people, places, or things.
Concrete nouns refer to definite objects. Abstract nouns refer to ideas.	Nouns that name something that uses one of my senses, such as seeing, hearing, smelling, tasting, or feeling are really concrete nouns.	When I am writing, I need to be aware of whether I want to name something that is concrete or whether I should use an abstract term. If I'm aware of the difference, I can make better choices in my writing.

4. Tell students that as they read they should be aware of what the text says and how they incorporate their own experiences with the text's information to develop an interpretation.

5. Use this strategy as the basis for academic writing. It uses both textual information and personal experiences for evidence.

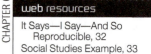

SECTION 6.3

CHAPTER 6

web resources

It Says—I Say—And So Reproducible, 32
Social Studies Example, 33

Assessing Student Learning

Strategy as Assessment

Goal: *To help students develop an interpretation of a text.* Many of the strategies in this book can be used for a variety of purposes. They can make your instruction more lively and interesting, they can help students learn what good readers do, and they can serve as assessments of learning goals. It Says—I Say—And So is one of these strategies.

When you use It Says—I Say—And So as an instructional strategy, students learn how to develop an interpretation of a passage using evidence from the text and their own personal experiences. When you use this strategy in your teaching, you are furthering students' reading ability. If, however, you want to assess the literacy goal of this section, you can use this strategy for that purpose as well.

After you have taught It Says—I Say—And So as an instructional strategy, and students are comfortable using it, you can use it for assessment. Select a passage that students can read independently. (Refer to Chapter 1 for information on text complexity.) You might need to give ELLs and struggling readers an easier text. Write your interpretations of the text to use as a scoring sheet.

Have students read the passage and respond using the It Says—I Say—And So format. Collect the papers and score the And So section. You want to know whether students are able to make the interpretations of the text, and the And So section answers that question. The sections It Says and I Say are the evidence the students have used. Compare the students' answers to your answer, remembering that there should be allowances for some differences. Give the students 3 points if their answer is very close to yours. Give them 2 points if they are missing some ideas or if some of their ideas do not represent the meaning of the text. Give them 1 point if they have a couple of ideas but their answer is incomplete. Give them 0 points if the students did not write any of the ideas from the passage.

To evaluate whether students are able to develop an interpretation, consider scores of 2 and 3 as acceptable. Remember, however, that even students who are able to construct an interpretation of this text need to continue working on this learning goal with more difficult texts through their schooling.

ReQuest

ReQuest (Manzo, 1969) enhances students' comprehension by teaching them to ask their own questions about what they are reading. When students ask themselves questions while reading, they have a greater likelihood of monitoring their understanding of the text and of having better comprehension. ReQuest was originally designed for use with individual students; however, it can easily be adapted for use with a group of students.

Directions

1. Select a content text your students will be reading. Choose a section that contains many new ideas that may be challenging to students.

2. Introduce the ReQuest strategy to students by modeling its use. Use examples from your content area or use the following example from a science text. Tell students that they will be using a strategy called ReQuest to help them read, monitor, and understand the textbook passage. Begin reading the first paragraph of the text aloud. Ask and answer questions about the contents of the passage in the following manner.

    Question: What is heat?
    Answer: Heat is the transfer of energy from something with a higher temperature to something with a lower temperature. For example, if you touch a hot surface like a stove, you feel the heat on your hand.

    Question: What is temperature?
    Answer: Temperature is a measurement of how much heat or thermal energy there is in an object. Temperature is used to measure the weather, or how much heat there is outside. It is also used to measure the heat in a stove or the amount of heat in our bodies.

    Question: Are heat and temperature the same or different?
    Answer: Heat and temperature are related, but they are not the same. Heat is the amount of thermal energy in an object, and temperature is the way we measure heat.

3. Ask students to read the next section of text. Limit this section to no more than a paragraph or two. Tell students that they will be taking turns asking you questions about what they read, and you will answer their questions, just like you modeled for them.

4. Ask students to read the next section of text. Inform them that you will be asking them questions about the section and they will be answering your questions.

5. Continue to alternate between student-generated questions and teacher-generated questions until the entire passage has been read.

6. Remind students to ask themselves questions as they read, because such questions will help them monitor and understand what they are reading.

CHAPTER 6

SECTION 6.3
web resources
ReQuest Reproducible, 34
Driver's Education Example, 35

Inference Chart

An Inference Chart is a helpful way for students to make inferences by connecting clues or details they read in narrative text to their own experiences. Making inferences is a strategy readers use to "read between the lines." Writers do not always specify the links between details and events in stories; they expect readers to do that. Some students, though, need explicit instruction and practice in learning how to make inferences. An Inference Chart can help students with this strategy.

Directions

1. Tell students that as they read they make inferences; they read between the lines. Provide examples from your teaching when you have made inferences.

2. Ask students why they think that inferences are made, not merely known. Reinforce the idea that inferences are personal and that they can vary with each individual and in each reading situation. There can also be inferences that we agree on like the one in the example that follows. Remind students that inferences should be built using text information.

3. Duplicate and distribute the Inference Chart from the website or use the example that follows. Point out the areas on the chart that students will use: the details or clues from the text, their experiences, and inferences.

Clues from Text	My Experiences	My Inference
Deserts have less than 10 inches of rain per year. One third of the world is covered by deserts. Deserts can be semiarid, arid, or extremely arid.	I expected to see huge sand dunes when I went through the deserts in the Southwest, but instead I saw lots of scrub grass and cactus. I have seen many movies with deserts, but I guess they were the Saharan Desert in Africa.	Even though all deserts have little precipitation, there is a great variety of deserts. The deserts in most of the movies are extremely arid deserts.

4. Have students select ideas from the text to write in the first column of the Inference Chart. Ask students to write one of their personal experiences in the next column that relates to the text. Illustrate how to connect text details with personal experiences to build inferences in the science example above.

CHAPTER 6

SECTION 6.3
⟶ web resources
Inference Chart Reproducible, 36
Art Example, 37

5. Write other details from the text on the Inference Chart. Have students generate their own experiences that build on the ideas from the text. Discuss the students' experiences and talk about the inferences they can draw from their experiences.

6. Ask students to list two or three additional ideas from the text to write on their Inference Chart, write their own experiences, and make inferences. Reassure students that each person's experiences and inferences could be different.

7. Remind students to use textual clues to aid them in making inferences as they read independently.

Section **6.3** INSTRUCTIONAL STRATEGY 11

Three-Level Guide

Three-Level Guides help students think about texts on the literal, interpretive, and applied levels. Three-Level Guides facilitate students' comprehension by moving from lower to higher levels of comprehension and are useful in helping students understand how to use facts to develop an interpretation (Herber, 1978).

Directions

1. Select a text that students will be reading. Identify literal information that students should know after reading the text. This information should focus on explicit ideas that are clearly presented in the text.

2. Identify interpretive information you want students to understand after reading the text. Include inferences or other examples of "reading between the lines."

3. Identify applied level information that you want students to consider. These ideas go beyond what is written in the text and require students to use information, express opinions, and create new ideas.

4. Develop a Three-Level Guide that presents three to six statements for each of the three levels: literal, interpretive, and applied. These statements should be written clearly and simply. An example follows.

Social Studies

Three-Level Guide for Southern Colonies

I. Literal Level

Check the items that specifically show what the author wrote in the chapter. Be prepared to support your choices.

_____ 1.   Lord Baltimore founded the colony of Maryland to provide a place for Catholics to worship freely.

_____ 2.   The Act of Toleration in 1649 provided religious freedom to all people.

_____ 3.   The Carolinas had large estates that were worked by slaves.

II. Interpretive Level

Check the items that show what the author meant in the chapter. Be prepared to discuss supporting evidence from the chapter.

_____ 1.   Wealthy tobacco planters controlled the best lands in Virginia because they arrived in the colony first.

_____ 2.   Bacon's Rebellion was organized to show the colonists' lack of support for the Virginia governor.

_____ 3.   Georgia was started as a place for freed debtors to get a fair, new start in life.

_____ 4.   The colonies of North Carolina and South Carolina had more similarities than differences.

III. Applied Level

Check the items that you agree with and be ready to share examples from the text and your own knowledge to support your responses.

_____ 1.   Religious freedom was the most important reason for starting the Southern colonies.

_____ 2.   The settlers believed that they had the right to take land from the Native Americans.

_____ 3.   The Southern farmers worked mainly for survival.

_____ 4.   England wanted military men to lead colonies because they were good leaders.

EXAMPLE

5. Have students read the assigned text selection that will be addressed by the Three-Level Guide and then check the items that apply to each section.

CHAPTER 6   SECTION 6.3

web resources

Three-Level Guide Reproducible, 38
Literature Example, 39

SURF THE WEB

THREE-LEVEL GUIDES
This site presents additional directions for writing three-level guides and provides several examples.
http://www.tki.org.nz/r/esol/esolonline/classroom/teach_strats/3levels/home_e.php

Questioning Texts

GOAL

To help students question texts during reading

BACKGROUND

According to Trabasso and Bouchard (2002), "there is strong evidence that question generation instruction during reading benefits reading comprehension" (p. 181). Expert readers ask questions of the text to clarify meaning, change misconceptions, and improve memory. This process of questioning is often subconscious, so teachers sometimes forget that novice readers are not aware of the benefits of asking questions while reading. Question generating can also be motivational (Ciardiello, 2007). The strategies in this section raise the visibility of questioning and give teachers some vocabulary to discuss the important cognitive strategy of questioning text.

Assessing Student Learning

Performance Assessment

Goal: *To help students question texts during reading.* Performance assessments are designed to help students use what they have learned. The goal of this section is to teach students to question texts during reading. The three strategies in this section were developed for students to learn different ways to ask questions as they read. We suggest that you teach all three strategies over the course of several months. After students are familiar with the different ways to question texts, assess whether they have achieved the goal by giving them a performance assessment.

Select a passage that you know students are able to read independently. (See Chapter 1 for ways to assess text complexity.) Tell students that they can use any of the three strategies to question the text as they read: Questioning the Author, Question-Answer Relationships, or Inquiry Questions. Have students take out a blank sheet of paper. Tell them that they should write questions on the sheet as they read the text, similar to what they would do when reading on their own. To determine whether the students have achieved the goal of questioning during reading, rate their answers by deciding whether the question is appropriate. Put a plus next to each good question. Students who are able to question during texts should have generated several good questions.

Readers Needing Additional Support

Students who struggle with reading in middle and high schools need instruction to be differentiated (King-Shaver & Hunter, 2003). One way to design differentiated instruction for students is to have them focus on different questions at different times. If students are reading difficult texts, for example, you might have some students develop literal-level questions so that you are sure that they have a general understanding of the texts before they move on to higher-level questions. (Students who read texts easily can often skip the literal questions.) Once students have an understanding of texts, however, they need to be guided in thinking along more abstract lines with higher-order questions.

Questioning the Author (QtA)

Questioning the Author (QtA) (Beck, McKeown, Hamilton, & Kucan, 1997) is a comprehension strategy designed to increase students' active understanding of texts. When using the QtA strategy, students step back from the text and ask pertinent questions to help them understand what the authors are expressing. These questions should be used as prompts to facilitate class discussion (Beck & McKeown, 2006).

Directions

1. Tell students that they will be reading their source texts using a strategy that is different from the usual strategies they use. Explain that as they read they need to think that authors are real people who may or may not have been successful in communicating their ideas. Help students realize that they need to actively discern what the authors are trying to communicate and how texts answer students' research questions.

2. Tell students that you will be demonstrating a strategy that promotes active thinking about texts during reading. Begin modeling the QtA strategy by choosing a text from your content area or by using the following example.

   We have been reading about fungi in biology class and are answering the following research question: In what ways do we encounter fungi in everyday life? I will use the QtA strategy using material from Chapter 20 in our biology text.

3. Duplicate and distribute the QtA questions that follow. A QtA reproducible can be found on the website.

   1. What are the authors trying to say here?
   2. What are the authors' messages?
   3. What are the authors talking about?
   4. Did the authors explain this clearly?
   5. Is this passage consistent with other passages?
   6. How does this passage connect with previous passages?
   7. Do the authors adequately explain things?
   8. Why are the authors telling us this now?

CHAPTER 6   **SECTION 6.4**
web resources
Questioning the Author (QtA)
Reproducible, 40

4. Segment the text by finding places that would lend themselves to good discussions.

5. Stop at these points and use the questions as prompts to facilitate discussion. For the biology example above, you might use the questions that follow.

   What do the authors mean when they write "fungi are important?" Does that mean they are an important part of everyday life? What do you think the authors meant and why do you think they included that sentence in the text?

6. Model ways to use the QtA strategy for your students so that they become comfortable asking questions as they read.

Question Answer Relationship (QAR)

The questions that students should ask as they read texts have been identified by Raphael (1982) and developed into the Question Answer Relationship (QAR). Raphael and Au (2005) write that "the vocabulary of QAR—In the Book, In My Head, Right There, Think & Search, Author & Me, and On My Own—gives teachers and students a language for talking about the largely invisible processes that constitute listening and reading comprehension across grades and subject areas" (p. 208). Students reading informational texts can use the QAR strategy to ask questions of texts and to deepen their comprehension while asking and answering questions.

Directions

1. Identify an informational text that you want students to read carefully. Tell students that they will be reading the text but also generating different types of questions about the text.

2. Duplicate and distribute the QAR reproducible found on the website. Tell students that they will be generating each kind of question as they read.

3. Instruct students to read a short portion of the text. Then have students develop one or more In the Book questions. Tell students that In the Book questions are those in which students can find the answers to the questions in the words on the pages. Explain to students that there are two types of In the Book questions. The first is Right There, a question that has the answer in a sentence similar to the question. The second type of In the Book question is a Think & Search question. To find the answer to Think & Search, students will have to look through different parts of the text to answer the questions. Demonstrate In the Book questions by using the following example.

   In the Book: Right There
   - What crop helped the Virginia colony become prosperous? [tobacco]

   In the Book: Think & Search
   - Who worked in the tobacco fields in the Virginia colony? [slaves from Africa]

4. Tell students that the answers to some questions are not in the book; they are In My Head. Explain to students that to answer some questions they need to think about what they have read and draw conclusions. Remind students that In My Head questions will not be stated explicitly in the text. Tell students that there are two kinds of In My Head questions. One is Author & Me in which students need to think about what the author writes and combine that knowledge with their background to form an opinion. The second type of In My Head question is On My Own. This type of question has students reflect on their learning and think for themselves about the topic. Demonstrate these types of questions using the following examples.

   In My Head: Author & Me
   - How did the expansion of tobacco crops facilitate slavery as an entrenched institution?
     [Because the tobacco growers did not want to do fieldwork and the Indians would not work, the growers turned to kidnapping Africans to do the heavy work. The Africans could not escape from the fields as easily as the Indians because they were in a new country and were unfamiliar with the language and geography.]

   In My Head: On My Own
   - What would have happened to Virginia if they had not begun growing tobacco?

SECTION 6.4

CHAPTER 6 **web resources**

Question Answer Relationship (QAR) Reproducible, 41

5. Divide the class into groups of three or four students. Have them develop additional QAR questions for the text. Have students share their questions and guide students to understand how their questions differ.

6. Tell students that one of the purposes of QAR is for them to think of the different types of questions as they read independently. Use the vocabulary from QAR as you discuss texts in the class so that students become accustomed to the terms.

Inquiry Questions (IQs)

Inquiry Questions (IQs), as described by Unrau (2004), are questions that readers ask themselves as they read. IQs are based on Bloom's taxonomy (1956), specifically knowledge, comprehension, application, analysis, synthesis, and evaluation. When students ask IQs as they read, they can begin to understand the depth of learning that can take place while reading.

Directions

1. Tell students that there are many types of questions that they can ask themselves as they read. Tell students that QAR (Instructional Strategy 13) is one way to think about questions, but they can also frame their questions in a different way called Inquiry Questions (IQs).

2. Duplicate and distribute the IQs reproducible found on the website. Point out the categories of questions, definitions, and question starters. Then have students practice developing questions for each of the IQs categories.

Category	Definition	Question Starters
Knowledge	Recall data or information.	define, describe, identify, label, list, match, name, outline, recall, retell, state, select, who, what, when, where
Comprehension	Understand the meaning, translation, interpolation, and interpretation of instructions and problems. State a problem in one's own words.	conclude, defend, distinguish, estimate, explain, extend, generalize, give examples, illustrate, infer, interpret, paraphrase, predict, rephrase, rewrite, summarize, translate
Application	Uses a concept in a new situation or unprompted use of an abstraction. Apply what was learned in the classroom in new situations.	apply, change, compute, construct, demonstrate, discover, manipulate, modify, operate, predict, prepare, produce, relate, show, solve, use
Analysis	Separate material or concepts into component parts so that the organizational structure may be understood. Distinguish between facts and inferences.	analyze, break down, categorize, classify, compare, contrast, deconstruct, diagram, differentiate, discriminate, distinguish, identify, illustrate, infer, outline, relate, select, separate
Synthesis	Build a structure or pattern from diverse elements. Put parts together to form a whole, with emphasis on creating a new meaning or structure.	categorize, combine, compile, compose, create, design, devise, explain, generate, modify, organize, plan, rearrange, reconstruct, relate, reorganize, revise, rewrite, summarize, tell, write
Evaluation	Make judgments about the value of ideas or materials.	appraise, compare, conclude, contrast, criticize, critique, defend, describe, discriminate, evaluate, explain, interpret, justify, relate, summarize, support

3. Develop questions for your content area or use the following examples to help students understand the different types of questions. Tell students that many people find the first three types of questions—knowledge, comprehension, and application—to be easier than the last three—analysis, synthesis, and evaluation. Tell students that these last three types of questions are commonly called higher-order thinking questions.

Knowledge	Can you describe "dribbling" in basketball?
Comprehension	Can you give examples of the kinds of behavior that would result in a "traveling" violation?
Application	Can you construct a diagram that shows man-to-man defense?
Analysis	Can you compare the fouls in basketball to the rules in soccer?
Synthesis	Can you summarize the keys to effective shooting?
Evaluation	Can you defend the placement of neighborhood basketball courts?

4. Explain to students that they can begin with higher-level thinking questions, especially with primary source material where they need to evaluate the reasons the text was created before they can understand the main points (Wineburg & Schneider, 2009).

CHAPTER 6

SECTION **6.4**

web resources

Inquiry Questions (IQs)
Reproducible, 42

5. Remind students to ask themselves different types of questions as they read.

BLOOM'S TAXONOMY
This site includes background about Bloom's Taxonomy, sample questions, and other links.
http://www.officeport.com/edu/blooms.htm

Making Connections

GOAL

To help students make connections from current texts to past texts, life experiences, and the world

BACKGROUND

When students read texts, they construct meaning using the texts they are reading, their prior experiences, and other texts. For example, middle school students learning about Impressionism may remember previous experiences with texts on the subject. One student may recall a trip to the Art Institute in Chicago. Another student may remember watching the movie *Pollock*. Yet another student may think about an Internet tour of the Louvre. A fourth student may remember reading Irving Stone's *Lust for Life* and discussing it with friends. A student's understanding of any passage, therefore, is shaped by prior experiences with texts and with life.

Students bring experiences with past texts to each reading event in your class. This process, called intertextuality, is a natural process. All of us are natural synthesizers. We learn new information by connecting it to what we already know, creating an evolving web of meaning. As readers construct meaning, they "transpose texts into other texts, absorb one text into another, and build a mosaic of intersecting texts" (Hartman, 1995, p. 526).

Making connections is an important skill for students who are reading informational and narrative texts. As stated in the Chapter 6 Overview, readers approach texts along a continuum of stances from efferent to aesthetic. When reading from an efferent stance, students are connecting to facts or information. When reading from an aesthetic stance, students make personal connections. According to Hansen (2009), students who make emotional and personal connections to a subject, such as history, become more interested in the topic and learn more. Students make connections during discussions and in their writing by supporting their statements with facts and experiences (Kamil et al., 2008). Teaching students when to use facts and when to use personal experiences are important ways to make connections.

To be good readers, students need to make connections. Although making connections is natural, students need to be encouraged to integrate knowledge they have from outside school with school learning. When students are guided to make connections, they generally do so. The strategies in this section were designed or adapted so that you can guide students, while they are reading new texts, to use texts they have already experienced.

Readers Needing Additional Support

Personal connections are the easiest type for most students. If students have difficulty with these strategies, teach one type of connection at a time, beginning with the text-to-self connections.

SURF THE WEB

READING STRATEGY OF THE MONTH: MAKING CONNECTIONS
This site provides additional information about the need for making connections while reading. Includes graphic organizers.
        http://www.itrc.ucf.edu/forpd/strategies/stratText.html

---

Connections Chart

A Connections Chart helps students make connections during and after reading to prior experiences, other texts, and the world at large. Making connections is an internal reading process that good readers use and that can be taught directly (Hartman, 1995). Students who make connections during reading are more easily able to understand the overlapping ideas of different content areas (Lenski, 2001).

Directions

1. Tell students that when they read they should make connections to their lives, other books they have read, and the world. Explain that these connections are typically called text-to-self, text-to-text, and text-to-world. Provide an example of a book you've read and the connections that came to your mind as in the example that follows. The book *Flight to Freedom* by Ana Veciana-Suarez (2002) is about a young girl who emigrates to the United Stated from Cuba.

Text-to-Self	Text-to-Text	Text-to-World
My grandfather came to the U.S. from Italy on a ship.	*Friends from the Other Side: Amigos del otro lado*	Cuba is a small island south of Florida.
I've got friends from Cuba.	*A Movie in my Pillow: Una pelicula en mi almohada*	There are many people from Cuba who live in our area.
I know lots of immigrants.	*My Diary from Here to There: Mi diario de aquí hasta allá*	Children who immigrate to a new culture need extra support in learning procedures and rules.
I did a research project on the Cuban influence in Miami last year.	*Mama does the Mambo*	Learning a new language can take many months or even years.

2. Explain to students that when they read they make connections to things they know, but that these connections can be made so quickly that they may not remember all of them. Tell students that using a Connections Chart can help them remember the connections that they make.

3. Encourage students to share the connections they have made with other students in the class. Explain to students that when they hear about connections others have made they can also expand their knowledge.

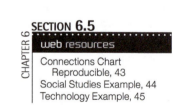

CHAPTER 6

SECTION 6.5

web resources

Connections Chart
Reproducible, 43
Social Studies Example, 44
Technology Example, 45

Using a Connections Chart as Assessment

Goal: *To help students make connections from current texts to past texts, life experiences, and the world.* A Connections Chart is an excellent way to assess whether students are able to make both informational and personal connections. To assess this goal, have students complete a Connections Chart after they have read or heard a piece of informational text. Tell students you want them to make as many connections as they can and to try and have equal numbers of connections in each column: text-to-self, text-to-text, and text-to-world. Evaluate their Connections Chart by giving 1 point for each reasonable connection, and compare the number of connections in each column. Then compare the results from all of the students. For some texts, students will have an easier time making text-to-self connections, but for other texts, students will be able to generate more text-to-text or text-to-world connections. Look for areas that show strengths and weaknesses. For some classes, students will be strong in making text-to-self connections. In that case, they will need no further instruction on that skill. The same may be true for the other types of connections. Look for areas that you need to teach more explicitly to the entire class; also determine which students need extra instruction in any of the three areas of connections.

Section **6.5** INSTRUCTIONAL STRATEGY 16

Share What You Know (SWYK)

Students make connections to their lives as they read content area texts and learn about new ideas from content area classes. When students share their connections with others, they give credence to the knowledge that they already have. The sharing of connections also helps students think more broadly about the topic they are learning. Share What You Know (SWYK) helps students formalize the connections they make in two ways: through words and through pictures. This strategy is useful in all content areas.

Directions

1. Tell students that they are continually making connections to their lives as they read and learn but that these connections are often fleeting. Explain to students that the connections they make are important to adding new knowledge to what they already know. Tell students that the strategy Share What You Know (SWYK) will help them record and remember some of the connections they make while reading.

2. Duplicate and distribute the SWYK reproducible found on the website so that students can use the strategy as they read.

3. Demonstrate the SWYK strategy using an example from your content area or by using the science example that follows.

4. Tell students that as they read they will probably think of other things they've learned about the topic. Have students record what the text reminded them of in the first section of the SWYK reproducible.

   This reminds me of . . .

   As I read about tornadoes in this section of the science book, I was reminded of a couple of books I read in middle school. One of them talked about a tornado that hit a small town not once but twice. I remember that the main character described the sucking sound of the drains as the tornado went by. I wonder why this happened. I think it has something to do with the low pressure but I'm not sure. I also remembered a tornado I saw from a distance. The tornado was sweeping through a cornfield and hitting a barn. It was really scary.

5. After you have demonstrated what the text reminds you of, have students draw a picture of an idea from the text. Tell students that connections from reading could be in words but they can also be in pictures. An example follows.

This is how I picture it . . .

6. Have students use the SWYK strategy as they read a selection of text or as they learn something new. Then have them share their connections in small groups. After students have shared their connections, tell them that they should choose some of the items from their conversations to help them remember the new information.

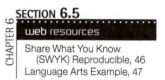

SECTION 6.5
web resources
Share What You Know
(SWYK) Reproducible, 46
Language Arts Example, 47

7. Encourage students to make connections independently as they read or learn area concepts.

Section **6.5** **INSTRUCTIONAL STRATEGY 17**

Intra-Act

Intra-Act (Hoffman, 1979) is a strategy that can be adapted to encourage students to use intertextual links to reach a personal decision about a topic. The Intra-Act procedure has four phases. First, students construct meaning from a text selection. Second, they connect what they have learned about the topic with other texts. Third, students express their personal values and feelings about the topic. Fourth, they reflect on the values they have formed.

Directions

1. Choose a topic or ask students to choose a topic that would be of special interest to them. The topic should be one about which students can form a personal opinion. Describe the differences between topics that lend themselves to opinions and topics that are explanatory. Provide a sample topic about which an opinion can be formed as in the following example.

> Read about the history and status of Puerto Rico. Think about whether Puerto Rico should remain a commonwealth, become the 51st state, or become an independent nation.

2. Use comprehension strategies, such as K-W-L, to teach the reading selection.

3. Ask students to use the contents of the text to write opinion statements that could be answered *yes* or *no*. Model examples of opinion statements that could be deduced from the text. Explain why a statement such as "Puerto Rico should become the 51st state" is an opinion and a statement such as "Puerto Rico primarily has an agricultural economy" is not an opinion.

4. List on a grid four or five of the most controversial statements students generated. Distribute copies to students.

5. Divide the class into groups of four to six students. Students should be of mixed abilities. Assign one student from each group as the discussion leader. Then ask each student leader to conduct a discussion by summarizing the text selection. The members of each group can add details that clarify the leader's summary.

6. Ask the group leaders to brainstorm additional texts that supplement the summary of the text selection. You might list categories of texts so that students think of both print and nonprint texts. Encourage students to add categories as they think of other types of texts. List the remembered texts on a large piece of paper.

7. After the members of each group have shared texts that relate to the topic, ask them to participate in the valuation phase of the discussion. Each group leader should distribute a paper with a set of four declarative statements based on the selection's content. These value statements should reflect opinions that could be inferred from the text.

8. Have students write the names of the group's members on the top line. Then ask students to agree or disagree with the statements independently. Direct them to write *yes* or *no* under their names for each statement. Finally, ask them to predict what they think other members of the group would answer by writing *yes* or *no* in the spaces under their classmates' names as shown in the following example.

Puerto Rico at a Crossroads

Statements	Shelly	Teresa	Juan	Aaron
Since the people of Puerto Rico are already United States citizens, Puerto Rico should become the 51st state if its people vote for statehood.	yes	yes	yes	yes
Operation Bootstrap is an illustration of the way the Puerto Ricans can maintain themselves as an independent nation.	no	yes	yes	no
Because Puerto Rico primarily has an agricultural economy with limited natural resources, it cannot stand on its own as a nation and either should remain a commonwealth or become a state.	yes	yes	no	yes
Spanish is the basic language of Puerto Rico and, although many people speak English, the language barrier should prevent Puerto Rico from becoming a state.	no	no	no	yes

9. Begin reflection by asking the members of each group to reveal how they responded to the four statements. As students discuss their answers, others should check to see whether their predictions about their classmates' responses were correct.

10. Conduct a class discussion allowing students to discuss, challenge, support, and question one another's responses. Discuss how the roles of the central text and the texts from the students' memories influenced final opinions.

11. Have students write an essay incorporating their classmates' ideas.

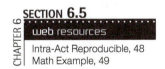

CHAPTER 6

SECTION 6.5

web resources

Intra-Act Reproducible, 48
Math Example, 49

Using Text Features

BACKGROUND

To achieve content literacy, students need to be able to use text features to improve their comprehension. These visual aids have a specific function, which is to summarize and condense written information into a visual form and to make it easier for readers to understand the meaning of the written material. For students to gain meaning from visual aids such as graphs, charts, and maps, they must be able to make connections between the graphic aid, the text, and their background knowledge (Sejnost & Thiese, 2001).

For many students, it is difficult to interpret and understand the graphics in their content area textbooks. The strategies in this section are designed to help students understand the information that is presented in a visual aid form within their texts. Many students will focus on the literal information found in the graphic aid. It is the responsibility of the teacher, however, to ask inferential and applied questions to help students make the link among the graphic elements, relevant parts of the text, and their background knowledge in order to reach a supported conclusion.

According to Saul and Dieckman (2005), "the importance of graphic elements can hardly be overstated. Layout, visual organization, and the integration of text and illustration create what is variously called attractiveness, format, design, or 'kid-appeal' " (p. 502). Text features, such as titles, subheadings, italics, captions, sidebars, photos, illustrations, charts, and tables, alert students to information to learn; moreover, they are functional. Text features add information to the texts that help readers interpret the content and reach reasoned conclusions.

Assessing Student Learning	Pre-Assessment

Goal: *To help students use text features to reach a supported conclusion.* To assess whether students are learning how to use text features, you should consider individually pre-assessing each of the components of the goal. Because each of the components is different, students who are successful with one may not be able to use another text feature to construct meaning from the text. For example, a student who can read a timeline may not be as successful in reading a bar graph. Each component needs specific, explicit instruction, but, before instruction, it is useful to know whether the skill is new to many of the students. In some cases, you will only need to provide a brief review; in others you'll need to provide in-depth instruction as illustrated in Instructional Strategy 18.

Before asking students to read a sample of text that has a specific text feature, show students another example of the feature, and ask them questions to show you how well they can read it. For example, if students will need to read a timeline in a selection, draw a short timeline on the board with important dates listed in chronological order. Ask students to individually answer three questions on note cards using the timeline. Collect and grade the cards. Put the cards into three piles: those with all three correct answers, those with two correct answers, and those with one or no correct answers. If most of the cards are in the pile with all three answers correct, you might only review timelines, but if many of the students were able to get only one or two answers correct, you should take time to teach the skill. If only a small group of struggling readers or ELLs had difficulty with the skill, and they have teaching assistants, you could have the assistants teach the skill in a small group. The pre-assessment should be used to help you tailor your instruction to the needs of your students so that you can spend time teaching the skills that students need to learn.

Section **6.6** INSTRUCTIONAL STRATEGY 18

Text Preview

Students who preview a text before reading are in a strategic position to take control of their learning and comprehension. Using the Text Preview strategy before reading helps students consider what they already know about a topic they will be studying. By helping students activate their prior knowledge about the topic, the Text Preview prepares students to understand what they will be reading.

Directions

1. Identify a section of text that may be challenging for students. This strategy works best for texts that contain organizational aids such as headings, subheadings, chapter introductions, summaries, chapter questions, pictures, diagrams, and other graphics. Begin modeling this strategy using a think-aloud procedure with the following example or create one from your content area.

   - Notice that our textbook contains many useful organizational aids. These organizational aids are helpful for preparing to read and while reading the textbook.
   - By using a prereading strategy called the Text Preview, you can figure out the kinds of information the text will contain and how it will be presented. In addition, the Text Preview will help you determine what is important to understand as you read.

2. Guide students through the organization of the chapter, focusing their attention on the important organizational aids in the chapter or section. For example, the textbook will probably contain a title, an introduction, headings, words in bold type, graphics, and chapter questions. Demonstrate this process by saying the following to students.

   - This section has a title, introduction, headings, words in bold type, graphics, and chapter questions. These organizational aids will be very helpful as you get ready to read the textbook. They indicate important information and let you know how key concepts are connected.

3. Direct students to look at the title and make predictions about the subject of the chapter. Provide time for students to share their predictions.

4. Tell students that this textbook also contains an introduction that will provide an overview of what the section will be about. Provide time for students to silently read the introduction. Ask them to list the major ideas that they think will be covered in the section. Provide time for students to share their ideas. Pose questions such as those listed below to help guide students through this step.

   - What seems to be the major focus of the chapter according to the introduction?
   - What are the key ideas mentioned in the introduction?
   - Based on the information in the introduction, what do you think you will learn in this section? Why do you think so?

5. Have students skim the section and look at the headings printed in large, bold type. Ask students to think about the kinds of information that will be contained under each of the headings and why. Guide them through the first section heading to model the process they should use when doing this activity. Use the example below or create one for your own content area.

- First, I will skim the section and look at the headings printed in large, bold type. I will think about what types of information will be contained in each of these sections.
- For example, if I turn to the heading **Population Growth**, I can ask myself questions such as the following ones.
  - What will this section be about and why?
  - What ideas do I already have about population growth?
- I think the section will be about how and why populations grow. I think it might also describe problems of overpopulation in an area. I know that population growth can be a problem for animals, like when too many deer survive the winter and there is not enough food for them in the spring. I also know that population growth can be a problem for humans when they need to expand the roads, increase food supply, and provide water for lots of people.
- I will also look through the paragraphs under this heading to see if there are any words in bold type. Under this heading, there are several words and phrases in bold type. They are **birthrate, death rate, standard of living, life expectancy**, and **population explosion**. I can ask myself the following questions.
  - Do I already know any of these words?
  - Do these words give me any clues about the subject of this part of the section?

6. Instruct students to continue this pattern of looking at headings and words in bold type until they have worked through the remaining headings in the section. Provide time for students to share their findings and ideas.

7. Direct students' attention to graphics in the section and provide time for them to discuss the types of information the graphics provide and why they might be included in the section. Model this process for them using the following example or create an example from your content area.

- On the next page, I see a photograph with a caption. What can I tell about the population of the area in the picture? I wonder why the textbook's authors included this picture in this section of the chapter.
- Figure 6-1 looks important. What types of information does this figure provide? Why might the authors include a figure about actual and projected world population growth in this section of the text? Does this figure give me any additional ideas about what this section might be about? Why?

Ask students to look at any remaining graphics in the section. Encourage students to ask themselves questions such as those that follow.

- What types of information does the graphic provide?
- Why did the authors include it in the section?
- What does the graphic tell me about the types of information that will be in the section?

8. Inform students that the questions at the end of a section are very helpful when preparing to read. Tell students that these questions will help them understand what is important in the section and what they should understand when they finish reading the section. Model this stage of the strategy by using the following example or create an example from your content area.

- At the end of the section, I see the "Content Check" questions. I know these questions are important because we often discuss them in class. Sometimes similar questions are on a test. The first question asks me about some vocabulary words from the section. What important terms should I know and understand after reading this section? I should probably make a list of these words so I can pay attention to them when I read the section.

9. Ask students to look at the remaining questions and have them consider what they will be expected to know after reading the section. Remind students that the Text Preview strategy is an important prereading technique. Encourage them to think about the ideas from the Text Preview strategy as they read.

SECTION 6.6

web resources

Text Preview
Reproducible, 50–51

CHAPTER 6

In the Feature, but Not in the Text

Sometimes text features include information that is not in the text. Smolkin and Donovan (2005) suggest that students use the strategy In the Feature, but Not in the Text as they read maps, charts, and other graphic features along with their texts to develop comprehension. Sometimes students ignore graphic features rather than realizing that features can add information that the text does not have. In the Feature, but Not in the Text is a strategy that focuses on comprehending texts using both graphics and texts.

Directions

1. Identify a text in which students will find graphic features like maps, charts, diagrams, and graphs that add to the text information.

2. Tell students that when they read text they need to also glean information from the text features. Remind students that text features are titles, subheadings, italics, captions, sidebars, photos, illustrations, charts, tables, and so on.

3. Duplicate and distribute the In the Feature, but Not in the Text reproducible found on the website.

4. Demonstrate how to use the strategy by using an example from your content area or the technology example that follows.

5. Ask students to read the text and to write down what they learned from the text in the first column. Discuss what students learned from the text.

6. Explain to students that they can also learn information from text features. Point to a text feature and have students read and interpret the information found in the graphic.

7. Have students then write down what they learned from the graphic in the second column.

8. Divide the class into groups of three or four students. Have students discuss the differences between the two columns. Then have students write in the third column what the text feature added to their learning.

Information in the Text	Information in the Feature	Information in the Feature, but Not in the Text
You can add characters to a Web page that are not on the keyboard.	The feature shows 100 characters that can be inserted.	The feature shows the specific characters that can be added to a Web page.
You can find several paragraph formats on the Format toolbar.	The feature shows what the drop-down list looks like.	The feature shows what it looks like and the specific paragraph format labels.
You can delete sections of the text.	You can right-click selected text to display a context menu for more options.	The feature has added information about options that were not described in the text.

9. Remind students that they should combine knowledge from text features with what they learned from reading the text as they develop an interpretation of the entire text.

CHAPTER 6

SECTION 6.6

web resources

In the Feature, but Not in the Text Reproducible, 52

Reading Bar Graphs and Charts

Graphs represent information visually so that readers can make comparisons between types of information. A bar graph is a drawing that shows a relationship between two sets of numbers. Graphs can take the form of charts, maps, and diagrams. Graphic comprehension, or graphic literacy, refers to the ability to interpret charts, maps, and graphs that are frequently used to supplement textbooks and other nonfictional material.

Directions

1. Many students skip over graphs and charts as they read their texts. However, these visual aids are intended to enhance and clarify comprehension. As you begin a lesson on reading graphs, have students open their texts to a graph. Briefly explain the purpose of the graph and show students how to read it.

2. Display the bar graph on the website and make individual copies of the graph and questions for each of your students. You may choose to construct an example from your content area.

3. Introduce the graph to your students. You might say, "This graph was constructed after a survey was given to students in a local high school." Ask students to look at the graph as you guide them through the following lesson. (The bar graph follows, including answers to questions.)

4. Tell students to look at the title of the graph. Ask them the following questions.

   What is the subject of the graph? (sports participation)
   What data are recorded on the graph? (sports participation among girls and boys)

5. Direct your students' attention to the small boxes at the top of the graph. Ask, "How do we know which numbers on the graph represent girls and which numbers represent boys?" (Code indicates that the white bar is for girls and the black bar is for boys.)

6. Invite students to look at the sports categories on the left-hand side of the graph. Ask students how many categories of sports there are. (six) Ask for a volunteer to read the names of the sports. (golf, track, soccer, tennis, swimming, and volleyball)

7. Focus students' attention on the numbers at the top and at the bottom of the graph. Say something like, "These numbers represent the number of males and females who participated in each of the listed sports. You will notice that the numbers are displayed in increments of five. As an example, who can tell me how many boys participated in volleyball?" (10)

8. After a brief discussion of the graph, distribute copies of the graph and the related questions. Ask students to use the graph information to answer the questions.

9. After students have finished answering the questions, review the information as a class and suggest to students that they develop their own graphs. Students might enjoy polling class members for information regarding favorite TV shows, jobs held to earn money, or ways they spend leisure time.

CHAPTER 6 **SECTION 6.6**
web resources
Bar Graph Physical Education Example, 53

Use the bar graph to answer these questions.

1. How many girls participate in soccer? _____40_____ How many boys? _____30_____

2. How many girls play tennis? _____25_____ How many boys? _____5_____

3. In which three sports do girls outnumber boys? _____*soccer*_____, _____*tennis*_____, and _____*volleyball*_____

4. In which two sports do boys outnumber girls? _____*track*_____ and _____*swimming*_____

5. What is the total number of boys and girls who participate in volleyball? _____35_____

6. Which sport has the *most* female participants? _____*soccer*_____

7. Which sport has the *fewest* male participants? _____*tennis*_____

8. What is the total number of boys who participate in sports? _____145_____

9. What is the total number of girls who participate in sports? _____165_____

10. Which sport has the greatest overall participation? _____*soccer*_____

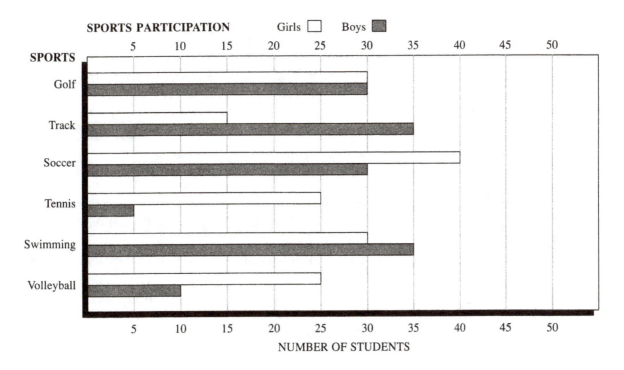

Timeline

A Timeline is a type of chart that shows events in chronological order, the order in which they happened. The bar of a Timeline is usually divided into sections of time, by days, months, years, decades, or centuries. Events are recorded at the selected dates placed on the Timeline.

Directions

1. Tell students that a Timeline is a continuum that graphically delineates events that have occurred in succession from the past through the present and sometimes into the future. Make copies of the Timeline labeled Historical Events from the website for students and display it so it can be seen by the entire class.

2. Tell students that this Timeline illustrates some historical events that occurred in the world between 1929 and 1942. Point out to students that the first event on the Timeline occurred in 1929 when the Stock Market crashed in the United States.

3. You might then say to students, "When I look at the year 1935, I see that the United States was experiencing a Dust Bowl in the Great Plains."

4. Point out the other events included on the Timeline up through 1941 when the United States entered World War II.

5. When you believe that students are able to read and understand the Timeline, ask them the following questions.

    - How many years after the Stock Market crashed was Franklin Roosevelt elected president for the first time? (three years)
    - According to this Timeline, how many times was Franklin Roosevelt elected president? (three times)
    - When did Hitler become the leader of Germany? (1933)
    - When did Germany invade Poland? (1939)
    - When did the United States enter World War II? (1941)

SECTION 6.6

CHAPTER 6

web resources

Timeline Reproducible, 54
Social Studies Example, 55
Timeline School Memories
Reproducible, 56

6. Following a discussion about this Timeline, students might enjoy making their own Timeline depicting some of the events in their school lives starting with their kindergarten or preschool experiences. Invite students to tell the stories of their school experiences by writing one memory for each school year on the appropriate lines. You may choose to duplicate the Timeline from the website for students or have them develop their own Timeline on a sheet of paper.

7. Following completion of their personal Timelines, invite students to share their school histories in small groups.

8. As an additional activity, students might enjoy constructing a Timeline for events in a social studies or history text, or they might like to develop a Timeline for a biography or a literature selection. The following example is based on the book, *Hatchet*, by Gary Paulson.

Literature

Timeline

Directions: Make a Timeline of Brian's adventure into the Canadian wilderness. You should be able to include at least one or two events from each chapter in the book. You may wish to include some illustrations on your Timeline.

Chapter 1	Brian leaves for Canada on a bush plane.
Chapter 2	Brian flies the plane.
Chapter 3	Brian crash lands into a lake and crawls to shore.
Chapter 4	Brian thinks about his mother and sleeps.
Chapter 5	Brian is hungry.
Chapter 6	Brian builds a shelter and eats some berries.
Etc.	
Chapter 19	Brian is rescued.

EXAMPLE

Activities *and* Journal Entries *for* Teacher Educators

Activities

1. In mixed content area teams, develop a list of strategies presented in this chapter that would benefit students' overall literacy development.
2. Select a strategy from this chapter and adapt it to your discipline.
3. Select a piece of text that would be common for students in your discipline. Read it and do a think-aloud about your own reading process. Record your response and identify the strategies you used as you read.
4. Select five passages that have been assigned to students in your discipline. Identify the text structure and develop a lesson plan to teach ELLs how to read these unfamiliar text patterns.

Journal Entries

1. Reflect on your own reading process. Think about how the strategies that you use as an expert reader can be used to help the novice readers in your classroom.
2. Consider how the strategies presented in this chapter can be embedded into your classroom instruction. How can you help students become better readers in your discipline at the same time you are focusing on content?

7

Reading Critically

Learning Goals

The reader of this chapter will:

- Understand the foundational theories underpinning critical literacy
- Understand how critical pedagogy applies to different disciplines
- Understand the importance of reading critically for diverse students
- Recognize the importance of taking social action after reading critically
- Learn a number of instructional strategies and assessments that promote reading critically

Questions to Consider

1. What foundational theories of critical literacy are similar to those that are central to your discipline?
2. How can you incorporate critical literacy practices into your discipline?
3. Why do students from diverse backgrounds need to learn to read critically?
4. Why is it important to include social action when teaching students to read critically?

OVERVIEW

For students to develop a deep understanding of your discipline, they must be able to construct meaning from the texts they read. Constructing meaning is more than merely understanding the message that print conveys; it is reading and thinking critically. According to the Carnegie Council on Advancing Adolescent Literacy (2010), by the time students graduate from high school, they need to be able to judge the credibility of sources, evaluate arguments, understand and convey complex information, and be able to exercise their rights as citizens in a democracy. This document also reports the scores for the most recent National Assessment of Educational Progress (NAEP), which indicates that very few high school students are able to accomplish this kind of reading.

In recent years, there has been a new focus on reading critically. According to Lenski (2008a), critical reading is a way to read, analyze, and evaluate texts while raising students' critical and social consciousness. When teaching students to read critically, they are asked to move from constructing an initial understanding of text to thinking about texts deeply and personally—taking a stance that challenges the text's assumptions. Reading critically means that readers are aware that texts are products of social beings with feelings, biases, and opinions. Texts are never neutral, but are representations of ideas and belief systems of the authors (Wink, 2001). When teaching students to read critically, teachers encourage students to read texts "in such a way as to question assumptions, explore perspectives, and critique underlying social and political values or stances" (International Reading Association & National Council of Teachers of English, 1996, p. 71).

Critical reading was developed from a group of theories called critical literacy. Critical literacy originated with Freire (1970), who criticized education as using a "banking system" where knowledge was deposited into empty accounts. Freire argued that students are not empty vessels who should receive knowledge from a teacher, but they are equal partners in education with their own knowledge and abilities. He wrote that marginalized groups were oppressed, and were not able to change their situations without a strong voice in challenging the knowledge they received in schools. The foundational principles of Friere were combined with other theories, such as reader response theory, linguistics and grammatical analysis of critical linguistics, and feminine, poststructuralist, postcolonial, and critical race theory, along with cultural and media studies to culminate in what we now call critical literacy theory (Luke & Woods, 2009).

Critical Pedagogy

Critical literacy is currently evolving. While critical theorists have been working on theory descriptions, educators have developed what is called critical pedagogy. Proponents of critical pedagogy base schooling on critical literacy theory. They suggest that education is inherently political, and that every dimension of schooling and every form of educational practice is a politically contested space (Kincheloe, 2007). Other educators see critical literacy as a frame through which to view the world. Vasquez (2010) is one such educator who developed a useful set of critical literacy tenets for educators that are the basis for this chapter.

1. Critical literacy involves having a critical perspective.
2. Students' cultural knowledge and multimedia literacy practices should be used.
3. The world is a socially constructed text that can be read.
4. Texts are never neutral.
5. Texts work to position us in particular ways; therefore, we need to interrogate the perspectives of others.
6. We read from a particular position and so our readings of texts are never neutral, and we need to interrogate the position from which we read.
7. What we claim to be true or real is always mediated through discourse (see Gee, 2005). Discourses are ways of being, doing, and acting through which we live our lives.
8. Critical literacy involves understanding the sociopolitical systems in which we live, and we should consider the relationship between language and power.

Critical Literacy in the Disciplines

As you read the tenets of critical literacy, you might wonder how it can be applied to your specific discipline. Moje (2008) writes, "producing knowledge in a discipline requires fluency in making and interrogating knowledge claims, which in turn requires fluency in a wide range of ways of constructing and communicating knowledge" (p. 99). Part of this fluency, Damico and colleagues (2009/2010) assert, should include critical literacy principles, including encouraging students to use their cultural and contextual knowledge to learn how texts are shaped and read.

Most social studies, science, and English teachers find critical literacy an easy fit; they are constantly asking students to comprehend texts analytically, to look for deeper meaning in the texts, and to interpret texts socially, politically, and culturally. According to Stevens and Bean (2007), the goals of critical literacy are to tease out various agendas, purposes, and interests represented in texts. Teachers in English, social studies, and science typically do this in their teaching.

Art, music, and physical education teachers might also find critical literacy easy to apply. When interpreting art and music, performers and listeners are able to recognize how an artist or composer makes decisions about what to express. They recognize that the fine arts are representative of cultural groups. Physical education teachers also understand how the sports we teach in school are culturally determined. For example, why is baseball typically an American sport? Why is hockey central to Canada, and why are Europeans so enthusiastic about soccer? The emphasis on specific sports is culturally determined, and physical education teachers can help their students understand the role sports play in society. This is particularly important for immigrant students who probably use the term "football" for the sport we know as soccer.

Mathematics teachers have their own term for critical literacy, called ethnomathematics. According to Mukhopadhyay, Powell, and Frankenstien (2009), no academic discipline is neutral, including mathematics. The central tenet of ethnomathematics is that there is a wealth of historical and cultural mathematical knowledge and practices of all people that goes beyond academic mathematics. Ethnomathematicians work to break the myths of neutrality and objectivity in mathematics and to look at more complex ways to interpret numbers. For example, as this book was being written, the World Cup was being played. The United States team surprised the soccer community by tying England. One newspaper reported the results with the headline, *U.S. Beats England, 1-1* (*Columbian*, 2010). In this case, the numbers might represent much more than a tie game. The underlying message of the headline might be that a tie was a success for the U.S. team and a loss for England. So, the numbers 1-1 can be contextualized to mean something other than what they represent at face value.

In the classroom, mathematics teachers can challenge and extend students' ideas about mathematics, helping them to understand the context for the numbers, and to add political awareness. One classroom example of applying ethnomathematics is documented when a group of students used mathematics to document, analyze, and confront the overcrowding in their schools (Turner & Strawhun, 2006). Another example is when a math club confronted the mathematical assumptions used by a school board when discussing the closure of a highly diverse school. The board claimed that they used an objective, neutral mathematical procedure for determining which school to close. The math club used an alternative method of analyzing the data and convinced the school board not to close the school (Gutierrez, 2009/2010). In big and small ways, mathematics teachers can apply critical literacy principles to their teaching, as can teachers in all disciplines.

Addressing Diversity

Diversity, as it plays out in American schools, is often a mirror of power relationships that are present in American society. Some cultural groups are perceived as having less status than others. In schools, some students come from backgrounds that are not viewed as mainstream, and often find themselves in these same situations of powerlessness. When teachers approach reading and writing from a critical literacy perspective, however, diverse students are able to question, challenge, and critique the often inherited and oppressive beliefs, values, and ideologies of schooling (Friere & Macedo, 1995). In essence, critical literacy can redefine power structures for students from diverse backgrounds (McLean, Boling, & Rowsell, 2009).

According to Moje (2007), disciplinary literacy should include not only opportunities to learn but opportunities to question, challenge, and even reconstruct knowledge rather than to reproduce the status quo. Daniel and Lenski (2007) wrote, "Engaging ELLs in provocative dialogues sets up a classroom society that is not centered on the majority culture's viewpoint, nor is it centered on the interpretation of words from an author's perspective or the teacher's stance. Students learn that it is safe to question past and present historical events" (p. 34). In a classroom example of teaching critical reading using the graphic novel, *Maus,* to ELLs, Chun (2009) found that students were able to link their personal experiences with socio-historical and institutional power relations. Students were able to critically engage with and reflect on the politics of historical representations. This example shows that when diverse students have the chance to participate in critical literacy activities, their backgrounds and opinions are valued as members of a questioning community.

Not all students will find questioning and challenging the status quo comfortable. Some students may have felt ignored and silenced for years. Soares and Wood (2010) write, "Critical literacy allows young social scientists to critically examine their social studies text to understand how the language of power benefits dominant voices. However, for students who have been marginalized along race and class lines, this is not an easy task, for their voices may have been silenced as well" (p. 489). Other students may fear opening themselves to criticism if they disagree with mainstream thought. Still others, especially some immigrant students from countries that have a form of government other than a democracy, may not have experienced the kinds of open dialogue and free speech that are present in American society. Once they experience critical literacy, however, these students may find that "authors, authority figures, politicians, teachers, parents, and students are joint creators of a democratic society" (Daniel & Lenski, 2007, p. 33).

There are many ways that teachers can help diverse students learn how to read and think critically. Daniel (2006) recommends that teachers consider incorporating the following questions into their teaching routines.

- How will deconstructing this text help my ELLs better understand the world in which they live?
- What stereotypical behaviors are promoted by the author of this text?
- Will reading this text give power and voice to my learners and facilitate adaptation to American society?
- Might the topic of this text serve as a source of conversation for my ELLs with their parents?

As diverse students learn how to read texts critically, they can become empowered by questioning the current state, and by imagining a future in which they will have a stronger voice in improving society and righting injustices.

End with Optimism

Teachers who incorporate critical literacy into their instructional framework sometimes worry that students will become jaded and cynical. Critical literacy was developed to empower readers, not to discourage them. Luke and Dooley (2010) remind us that critical literacy has the potential to give students agency, or the ability to take control over their lives and to relieve them from oppression. When students read from a critical literacy perspective, they think about ways to transform relations of cultural, social, and political power. Texts are viewed as products of real people such as themselves, who have their own agendas and biases. With this in mind, students can feel that they are not powerless; but as readers they can agree or disagree with the author, based on their own informed opinions.

In her most recent book, *Teaching for Joy and Justice* (2009), Linda Christensen reminds teachers to infuse their teaching with joy, not just a critical attitude. We agree. If you are asking students to read texts from a critical literacy framework, also ask students to imagine the kinds of social action that could result from their readings. Don't just stop with railing against the system. Encourage students to develop their own positive responses.

As you teach and assess the learning goals in this chapter, you will be providing your students with the tools to develop a habit of reading critically. As you provoke students toward social action, you will help them see that reading critically can be the basis for making real changes in their world.

Determining Authors' Qualifications, Perspectives, and Purposes

GOAL

To help students determine whether authors are credible sources and to evaluate the perspectives and purposes they bring to texts

BACKGROUND

The texts that you ask your students to read will vary in quality. Texts are written by an author, a team of authors, a committee, or a publisher. Authors bring various levels of expertise to their writing, so students should think about authors' qualifications as they read. Some texts, such as textbooks, may be written by committees. In the case of many textbooks, the authors listed act as consultants but the content of the textbook is determined by the publisher who may be guided by a particular social or political stance. Students, therefore, should consider the authors' qualifications, perspectives, and purposes as they read. Authors, who are fallible and have particular perspectives on issues, write texts. Some of the texts that your students read will be outdated; some will contain biased viewpoints; and others may treat issues superficially. One of the biggest legacies you can leave your students is to teach them to think about the authors of texts—to determine whether the authors are qualified and from what perspectives the authors are approaching the texts.

Writers make deliberate choices of the words, images, and information they use; they leave other information out of their texts. Critical readers become aware of the social context of writing by trying to understand something about the authors (Leonardo, 2004). Readers should "consider the source" by asking questions about the authors, the purposes of the texts, and the conditions under which they were published. The answers to these questions can influence the judgments the reader makes when trying to determine what parts of the texts to use to develop ideas and beliefs.

After students understand something about the authors' qualifications, the publication date, and the authors' word choices, students should think more deeply about the authors' perspectives. Texts are not neutral. Authors indicate or convey their perspectives in many subtle ways. As students analyze texts as critical readers, they try to understand from what perspectives the authors are writing (Luke & Woods, 2009).

Because of the proliferation of literary bias, it is now more important than ever for students to be able to determine an author's qualifications and to understand an author's perspectives and purposes. In your classroom, students will probably read texts that you have previewed and that you consider credible. But when students read on their own, especially online sources, they may view texts that have not been reviewed. The strategies that are described in this section are illustrated using print-based materials, but they can also be used with online sources. As students become familiar with the strategies, encourage them to use them as they read online, and other texts, independently.

Readers Needing Additional Support

When teaching students to think about authors' credibility, you might want to select texts that are easy to read, especially for students who have difficulty reading. The concepts of authors' credibility and perspective can be difficult for many students, so using texts that are easy to read lightens the cognitive load. Once students have experience determining authors' credibility or understanding authors' perspectives, you can move toward the use of grade-appropriate text.

Section **7.1** INSTRUCTIONAL STRATEGY 1

Consider the Source

One of the first things students need to do as they think critically about a text is to make some determination about the credibility of the source. Although most of the texts you will ask your students to read probably have been sanctioned by you, a curriculum committee, or the school board, students still will need to think about the factors in the texts that could influence the texts' credibility. A strategy you can use to initiate critical questioning of the source by your students is called Consider the Source. This strategy is a list of questions with examples for you to model with your students to elicit questions about pertinent aspects of the texts. You may want to use this activity several times during a school year with examples from your content area. Your goal, however, is for students to think independently about the credibility of sources before they read. Consider the Source can be used in various subject areas.

Directions

1. Duplicate and distribute the Consider the Source reproducible that can be found on the website.

2. Ask students to look at the source of the passage you have asked them to read. Ask them to look for the date of publication. Discuss the importance of the copyright date. Tell students that information with a copyright date of 2010 was probably written at least a year earlier and may be considerably older than that. Explain that, even when authors are discussing historical events, dates are important. New information can, at times, influence what is believed about an event. Books that are written in the near or distant past, however, are not necessarily incorrect. The date of the publication is one factor for establishing credibility, but newer is not necessarily better.

3. Use an example such as the following to illustrate the importance of dates of publication. Discuss why the publication date is important in these examples.

    > Today Germany is two separate countries. They are different from each other in a number of ways. One of the most important differences is the form of government. East Germany has a Communist government.

    > Built in 1961, the Berlin Wall separates the city of Berlin into two sections—East Berlin, or the Communist section, and West Berlin.

    > From *Exploring Our World: Eastern Hemisphere*. (1980). Chicago: Follett, p. 135.

4. Discuss the importance of the authors' qualifications. Many of the textbooks used in schools have a list of authors with their credentials stated at the front of the book. Look for the list of authors, read about their backgrounds, and discuss whether they appear qualified to write the book. You can use the following example for class discussion.

    > In a middle school music class using a music text, students can look at the qualifications of the authors at the beginning of the book. Fourteen authors are listed: six middle school teachers of music, five university professors, one composer, and two choral directors.

    > Discuss how the qualifications of a middle school teacher would be different from the qualifications of a composer. Discuss whether the balance among middle school teachers, university professors, and professional musicians is appropriate for the text.

5. Discuss what seem to be the authors' primary purposes in writing the book. Some books are written primarily for information, some are written for instruction, and others are aimed at persuasion. Find examples of each type of text from your content field and discuss how readers can identify the purpose of the authors. The following is an example from a world literature class.

> In a world literature class reading a book on Celtic myths, scan the Table of Contents looking for the topics that are included in the text. The Contents includes introductory chapters with titles such as "The Divine Race of Ireland" and chapters with categories of myths such as "Animals in Cult and Myth." Discuss whether the author's choice of words indicates a particular bias toward the subject.

6. After reading portions of the text, discuss whether the writing was informational, instructional, or persuasive. The book on Celtic myths, for example, seems to be informational, but the author appears to have a heavy bias toward the subject. Discuss whether the author's bias might detract from the informational aspects of the book.

7. Remind students that they should apply the Consider the Source questions before they read most texts.

SECTION **7.1**
web resources
Consider the Source Reproducible, 1
Math Example, 2
Science Example, 3

CHAPTER 7

| Assessing Student Learning | Mini-Fishbowl |

Goal: *To help students determine whether authors are credible sources and to evaluate the perspectives and purposes they bring to texts.* Considering an author's qualifications is not an exact science. Although you can create examples that clearly show that one author is more qualified than another, when students are reading on their own, an author's qualifications may be more ambiguous. The most appropriate way to provide students with feedback might be through an informal type of assessment called Mini-Fishbowl (Tuttle, 2009). Have students work in pairs to complete the Consider the Source reproducible that you can find on the website. Ask a third student to act as an observer and to give feedback. The student who gives feedback should be someone you have observed, through class discussion, to have a good understanding of how to determine an author's qualifications. After the pair of students has completed the Consider the Source strategy, the student giving feedback can provide the pair of students additional ideas about the author's qualifications. After students have been given sufficient feedback, use the reproducible to assess whether students have achieved the goal to determine whether authors are credible sources and to evaluate the perspectives and purposes they bring to texts. If students are having a difficult time with the strategy, model how you think about an author's qualifications using several different examples.

Perspective Guide

After students have considered the credibility of the author, they should think about the perspective the author may be taking. Many of the texts your students read will take a subtle perspective about a subject. Neutral texts would be bland beyond belief. It is important that students are able to identify the perspective the author is taking. A Perspective Guide presents quotations from two or more passages that have a similar theme but different perspectives. When students are able to identify an author's perspective, they are able to use what they know about the author's perspective along with the author's qualifications to make an informed decision about the topic.

Directions

1. Choose two or more texts written around a central theme in which the authors have different perspectives about an issue. You can choose texts from the same medium, such as the two short stories in the example, or you can choose different types of texts. The texts, however, should have a similar theme.

2. Choose four to eight quotations (or ideas) from each passage that relate to the central theme. Write the quotations in random order so that they can be seen by the entire class. List the sources of the quotations at the top of the page.

3. Divide the class into groups of three or four students. Have students read and discuss the quotations, focusing on ideas about the perspectives of the authors. Then have the students match the quotations with the sources as in the example below.

Literature

Perspective Guide

Directions: After reading the two stories "Aging in the Land of the Young" and "Woman Without Fear," match the following quotations with the stories and discuss the view of aging taken by each author. Use A for "Aging in the Land of the Young" and B for "Woman Without Fear."

1. _____ Aging paints every action gray, lies heavy on every movement, imprisons every thought.

2. _____ The world becomes narrower as friends and family die or move away.

3. _____ Although Grace was 64 years old, she was as active as a boy and worked with smooth dexterity.

4. _____ When she saw me, she hurriedly picked up the four-foot rattlesnake who had been sunning himself while his box was being cleaned and poured him into his cage.

5. _____ There is nothing to prepare you for the experience of growing old.

6. _____ I first heard of Grace Wiley when Dr. William Mann handed me a picture of a tiny woman with a gigantic king cobra draped over her shoulders like a garden hose.

7. _____ I am afraid to grow old—we're all afraid. In fact, the fear of growing old is so great that every aged person is an insult and a threat to the society.

8. _____ "Don't trip over an alligator," she added as I came forward. I noticed for the first time in the high grass a dozen or so alligators and crocodiles.

From Curtin, S. (1984). Aging in the land of the young. In *Literature* (pp. 389–391). Evanston, IL: McDougal, Littell. Mannix, D. (1984). Woman without fear. In *Literature* (pp. 325–333). Evanston, IL: McDougal, Littell.

E X A M P L E

4. After students complete the Perspective Guide, ask them to discuss their reasoning for their choices and guide them to identify the different perspectives of the authors. In this example, one of the authors discusses a woman's fear of aging while the other celebrates the life of a courageous older woman. Discuss reasons why perspectives about a topic may differ. Then discuss alternative perspectives on the topic.

5. Ask students to write an essay or short story from a third perspective.

CHAPTER 7

SECTION 7.1

web resources

Perspective Guide Reproducible, 4
Health Example, 5
Social Studies Example, 6

Section **7.1** **INSTRUCTIONAL STRATEGY 3**

Ask the Author

Students who understand an author's perspective can gain a deeper understanding of the text by identifying with the author. Ask the Author is an adaptation of a Creative Reasoning Guide (Jacobson, 1998) that can be tailored to provide students with the opportunity to answer questions from the author's perspective. When students are able to put themselves in the place of the author, they develop a more thorough understanding of the author's perspective.

Directions

1. Identify an event that is not fully explained in the text. For example, suppose your text includes Cicero's speeches for Archias. However, the text does not explain the reasons why Cicero would discuss literature with Archias.

2. Write the event as a scenario so that it can be seen by the entire class. In the scenario, direct a question to the author for reasons that caused the event. See the following example for a sample scenario.

   Earlier in this course you read stories from Pliny and Galleus and speeches from Cicero. This section contains several of Cicero's speeches for Archias, some dealing with the value of literature. With what you know about Roman culture and Cicero's character, what reasons would Cicero have to discuss literature with Archias? Give at least three reasons.

3. Divide the class into groups of three to five students. Give students the Ask the Author scenario. Ask them to brainstorm at least three reasons that would answer the question. The reasons should be logical in light of past knowledge, but creativity should be encouraged. The following is a second example from a Latin class.

Latin Class

Ask the Author

Directions: After reading "The Value of Literature" in your Latin book, read the following scenario and think about answers to the question.

Scenario

In further passages, Cicero discusses his views on poets. Three of the speeches are titled "Poets are Sacred," "No Fame Without Poets," and "Poets Give Immortality." What reasons would Cicero have for revering poets to such an extent? Give at least three reasons.

EXAMPLE

4. In a whole group setting, ask the students to share the reasons listed during the brainstorming activity. List all of the reasons. Discuss the ideas the students have generated and guide the discussion to identify characteristics and perspectives of the author.

CHAPTER 7

SECTION 7.1
web resources
Ask the Author Reproducible, 7
Literature Example, 8
Science Example, 9

Section **7.1** INSTRUCTIONAL STRATEGY 4

Determining the Authors' Purposes

Authors can have many purposes for writing. Their purposes can influence how they present the texts, how students should read, and what students should learn. For example, an author whose purpose is to inform readers might subtly be trying to persuade the reader to believe certain information. Readers, however, cannot always infer an author's purposes easily or accurately. As students read, though, they can try to understand what purposes authors have for writing through some of the authors' word choices. As students look for authors' purposes, they begin to read more deeply and critically.

Directions

1. Identify a text that you could use in your classroom to illustrate the purposes authors have for writing, or use *The Art of Black & White Photography* (Garrett, 2003).

2. Duplicate and distribute the Determining Authors' Purposes reproducible that can be found on the website.

3. Ask students to identify the author or authors of the text and write their names on the first line. In this case the author is J. Garrett.

4. Then have students identify several details from the text that could shed light on the author's purpose for writing the book. Details from *The Art of Black & White Photography* follow.

- The author states that he wants to simplify the art of taking black and white photographs.
- The book shows color photos next to black and white photos.
- The author gives practical suggestions for taking photographs, such as looking for contrasting tones.
- The photographs on the pages are large and the text is small.

5. Tell students that authors have purposes for their writing and that readers can figure out some of the purposes through the details of the text. Discuss the details with students, asking them whether they can infer reasons why the author wrote the book. Have students give some possible purposes for this book. Prompt them, if necessary, with the following ideas.

- Garrett is really passionate about black and white photography and wants it to have more visibility.
- Garrett wants to explain how he takes such outstanding photographs.
- Garrett wants a place to publish his photos.

6. Tell students that they should think about the author's purposes as they read.

SECTION 7.1

web resources

CHAPTER 7

Determining the Authors'
  Purposes Reproducible, 10
Literature Example, 11
Social Studies Example, 12

Considering Alternative Views

GOAL
To help students consider alternative views when reading

BACKGROUND

Critical readers who have determined the authors' qualifications and perspectives and have reached back into their memories for related past texts to connect with new knowledge can expand the meaning they construct by considering alternative views. One of the hallmarks of a thinking person is the ability to acknowledge new ideas and different points of view.

Students who are reading and learning in your content area need to keep their minds open as they read. Often, students who are learning about new concepts have already established ideas about those concepts. Sometimes those ideas are faulty. When students are exposed to counterintuitive concepts, or concepts that don't make inherent sense to them, they tend to resist these new ideas, even after they are proven to them (Stahl, Hynd, Glynn, & Carr, 1996). For example, students often believe that a heavier object will fall faster than a lighter one even though one of the principles of physics is that all objects fall at the same accelerating rate. Because many students resist new information if it is in conflict with previously held beliefs, some textbooks directly refute misconceptions. An example of a refutational warning in an algebra class would be the note that "2 to the third power = 8 is not the same as $2 \times 3 = 6$." Because students bring misconceptions to reading situations, an important skill for critical readers is to take into account new ideas and to try to generate alternative views as they read.

Assessing Student Learning

Exit Cards

Goal: *To help students consider alternative views when reading.*   The strategies in this section will help you teach students how to consider alternative views when reading. You can assess this goal in a number of ways: one of which is by using Exit Cards. After using several of the strategies for instruction, provide students with a new reading passage. Ask students to write two phrases or sentences on cards that show alternative views for the passage. Collect the cards and quickly read them to determine which students were able to formulate two perspectives and which ones were not. Sort the cards into two groups. If the larger of the two groups contains the cards of students who could come up with two reasonable statements, you know that most of your students can use the strategies without much instruction. For those students who had difficulty, you should first determine whether the students had difficulty reading the passage. If reading is not the issue, model for students how you read the passage, highlighting words or phrases that alert you to one view or another. Then model for students how you identify alternative views from the passage. Use the Exit Card assessment strategy later in the year with a more complex passage to determine how well students have learned to "consider alternative views when reading."

Readers Needing Additional Support

If students have difficulty thinking about alternative views, have them draw conversation bubbles (like those used in cartoons or graphic novels) to depict different ways people can think about an issue.

Discussion Web

A Discussion Web (Alvermann, 1991) is an organizational tool for you to use to guide discussions that present an issue and opposing points of view. A Discussion Web is designed so that students can identify and discuss two viewpoints about the question, ponder the views, and come to a conclusion.

Directions

1. After the students have read a passage from your text, introduce a central question. The question should be one that lends itself to opposing viewpoints. Write the question so it can be seen by the entire class. For example, ask students the following question after they read "The Man Without a Country" by Edward Everett Hale.

    Did Philip Nolan receive a just penalty?

2. Divide the class into groups of three or four students. Ask students to brainstorm at least three reasons for answering *yes* to the central question. Then have them generate at least three reasons for answering *no* to the central question. When students have written their reasons for answering the question in the affirmative and the negative, ask them to volunteer some of their ideas. Write the ideas in two separate columns as listed below.

Reasons why the penalty wasn't just	Reasons why the penalty was just
• Nolan had a good background. • He was tricked by Aaron Burr. • His words were impulsive. • He was sorry.	• Nolan broke the law. • He was a traitor to his country. • He was aware of the consequences. • He was part of a rebellion.

3. Discuss both sides of the question as objectively as possible. Then encourage students to take a position either for or against the issue. Some students will want to take both sides. Tell them that, although they understand both sides of the issue, they need to take one position.

4. Ask students to come to conclusions independently, defending the side they have chosen and using the alternative perspective as a counterargument. Have them write their conclusions on note cards. Collect the note cards when the students are finished and use them to learn which conclusions students have reached. An example follows.

CHAPTER 7

SECTION 7.2

web resources

Discussion Web Reproducible, 13
Health Example, 14

> **Conclusion**
> Philip Nolan was a young, fiery man who was used by Aaron Burr. Although he deserved punishment for his wrongs, the punishment he received, banishment, was too severe for the crime.

5. Have students write a persuasive essay defending their position.

READWRITETHINK LESSON PLAN: DISCUSSION WEB
This site provides a lesson plan with the text "Harrison Bergeron" by Kurt Vonnegut, Jr., that uses a discussion web.
http://www.readwritethink.org/lessons/lesson_view.asp?id=819

Discussion Continuum

A Discussion Continuum (Stephens & Brown, 1994) is a visual example of the range of views that are possible on a given topic. It provides students with the opportunity to express their viewpoints, listen to other students' ideas, and amend their own thinking. The ability to state and defend one's views and the capacity to appreciate the views of others is necessary when considering alternative views on a subject.

Directions

1. Give students opposite statements related to your content area that you think would elicit a range of responses such as these examples from a biology class.
   - The government should prohibit all stem cell research.
   - The government should fund and promote stem cell research.

2. Write the statements on the opposite ends of a straight line so they can be seen by the entire class.

3. Have students come up to the Discussion Continuum and write their initials at the points on the line that best represent their positions, as in the following example.

   aF   *WH*   *MC*   *RL*   *BB*
   _____

   The government should prohibit   **The government should fund and**
   all stem cell research.   **promote stem cell research.**

4. After all of the students have had the opportunity to mark their positions on the continuum, have students discuss their positions in small groups using text material to support their views, or have students line up according to their belief.

5. Invite students to share their beliefs with the entire class; then provide students with the chance to change their positions on the Discussion Continuum if they desire.

CHAPTER 7

SECTION 7.2

web resources

Discussion Continuum
   Reproducible, 15
Social Studies Example, 16

Options Guide

Students who are able to identify and consider alternative viewpoints in their reading should begin to think about the range of views that exist about any topic. An Options Guide (Bean, Sorter, Singer, & Frazee, 1986) is a type of study guide that helps students think of predictions and possibilities about an issue from their texts. Students read up to a critical point in the passage and then stop and consider possible options and the results of the different options.

Directions

1. Identify a topic and a portion of a text that would be of interest to your students. Analyze the passage for major concepts that leave events in doubt. The following example illustrates an Options Guide for a parenting class.

2. Develop a brief scenario about the text. Write several questions and a list of options that could result from the scenario. Write the scenario so it can be seen by the entire class.

Parenting

Options Guide

Fifteen-year-old Nina was spending the day with her older sister, Olivia, who was just recovering from the flu, and Olivia's month-old son, Hector. Just before noon, Nina and Olivia decided to drive to a nearby store to get some milk.

As they were getting into the car, Nina asked, "Where's Hector's car seat?"

"Oh, no," sighed Olivia. "I left it in the apartment. Well, it's only a few blocks. You just hold him. This won't take long."

Which option will Nina choose? Why do you think so? What could be the result of each option?

a. Nina will go along with Olivia and ride with the baby in her lap.
b. Nina will stay home with Hector.
c. Nina will drive to the store without a valid driver's license.
d. Nina will persuade Olivia to return to her apartment for the car seat.

EXAMPLE

3. Divide the class into groups of four or five students. Ask students to discuss the possible options and the results of each option. After students have discussed options in small groups, have them share their thinking with the entire group. If necessary, guide the discussion so that students understand the cause-effect relationship for each option.

4. Have students write their options in well-formed paragraphs.

CHAPTER 7

SECTION 7.2

web resources

Options Guide Reproducible, 17
Science Example, 18

Section **7.2** **INSTRUCTIONAL STRATEGY 8**

Questioning Editorial Perspectives

Students need to become aware that, unless they are critical readers, the way a writer presents information can sway them toward a particular opinion. By having students consider multiple viewpoints, rather than a single perspective, you are assisting them in reading critically (Paul, 1993). Newspapers provide an excellent tool for developing students' critical thinking skills and comparative analysis skills (Laffey & Laffey, 1986).

Most newspapers publish editorials written to express a stance on a particular issue. In addition to editorials, newspapers may report news events from their particular perspectives just as authors write textbooks from a variety of perspectives. The following strategy allows students to question a newspaper's editorial stance on a controversial issue.

Directions

1. Explain to students that when they read newspapers they need to be aware of the writer's perspectives. This is particularly true when reading editorials, as editorials provide a forum for newspaper writers to express their opinions on particular issues.

2. Discuss editorials that students may have read in the past. Ask students to share information about particular editorials they have read in which the writers presented obvious opinions. Have copies of a variety of newspaper editorials available to facilitate the discussion.

3. Tell students that they need to ask themselves questions as they read an editorial. Write the following questions (Robinson, 1975) so they can be seen by the entire class.

    Questions for Reading Editorials
    - What is the title of the editorial?
    - What is the issue in this editorial?
    - What stance on the issue is represented?

- What specific evidence is given to support this side of the issue?
- Is there any evidence apparent in this editorial to suggest another viewpoint?
- Does the writer show a bias? Are there any particular words or patterns of writing used to accomplish this? If so, what are they?

4. Provide students with an editorial from a local newspaper. Ask students to read the editorial and answer the questions.

5. Divide the class into groups of three or four students. Ask students to share their responses to the questions as they discuss the writer's viewpoint.

6. Invite each group of students to write a counterargument to the published editorial. Share the students' editorials during a whole class discussion or as part of a class-produced newspaper.

CHAPTER 7

SECTION **7.2**

web resources

Questioning Editorial Perspectives
Reproducible, 19

Developing Informed Opinions

GOAL

To help students evaluate the logic of a text and to develop informed opinions

BACKGROUND

Students are exposed to many different kinds of texts in school, from texts that are written by qualified authors with editorial review boards to texts that are written by someone with a biased viewpoint. For that reason, students need to be able to read texts in their content classes critically and to evaluate independently the logic of a passage and form a reasoned judgment.

Most of the writing that students read in our disciplines has a logical progression of ideas that leads to a conclusion. That conclusion is backed up by supporting claims. These claims can be about what the author thinks is true (knowledge claims), about what causes something (causal claims), about what is likely to happen (predictive claims), about what is good (evaluative claims), about what is right or wrong (moral claims), and about what ought to be done (policy claims). Some claims overlap into two or more categories and can be considered mixed claims (Unrau, 1997).

When students read texts, they need to be able to evaluate the worth of the author's conclusions and to evaluate whether the arguments the author makes support the conclusions without undue bias. Furthermore, students need to be able to examine the author's claims and to be able to determine what they believe about the topic. Merely challenging an author's point can lead to cynicism. Therefore, we want students to evaluate arguments in texts and come to independent conclusions about what they believe about the topic.

To assist your students in evaluating arguments and developing an informed opinion, you can create lessons that mirror the thinking process you use when critically evaluating a text. This section provides four different strategies that help students begin to evaluate arguments and develop opinions. As you use or adapt each of these strategies to your content area, remember that any activity that promotes the effective evaluation of an author's claims can assist students in becoming more critical readers of texts.

Readers Needing Additional Support

Students who have difficulty finding evidence from a text might need an easier text to learn the strategy. You can find short, easy informational articles from children's nature or sport magazines. These magazines have content that is interesting to all ages but is written at an easy level. Reproduce articles for struggling readers so they can highlight evidence from the text before completing the assignment.

Section **7.3** INSTRUCTIONAL STRATEGY 9

State-Question-Read-Conclude (SQRC)

Critical readers draw conclusions as they read, but many students may need help learning how to come to reasoned judgments. State-Question-Read-Conclude (SQRC) (Sakta, 1998/1999) guides students through the thinking processes that occur during reading and helps them draw conclusions from their reading.

Directions

1. Identify a text selection that is conducive to drawing conclusions as in a text on drilling for oil in the arctic. Teach unfamiliar vocabulary before the lesson so that students' comprehension is not hindered by lack of knowledge of text-specific words.

2. Duplicate and distribute copies of the SQRC reproducible from the website.

3. Develop a question from the text that is controversial and write it so it can be seen by the entire class. An example follows.

   Should drilling in the Arctic National Wildlife Refuge be permitted?

4. Tell students that people have a variety of opinions about this issue and that the text they will be reading will present one or more of these opinions. Before students read the text, have them write their own opinions on the first line of the SQRC sheets. Do not share your own opinion about the issue because it could influence some students' thinking.

5. Tell students to reframe their opinions in the form of questions. Explain that the questions will guide their thinking as they read the text. Provide one or more examples of questions for students as in the following examples.

   Statement: Wildlife will be threatened.
   Question: Will wildlife be threatened by drilling?

   Statement: The world has enough oil without additional drilling.
   Question: Does the world have enough oil without additional drilling?

6. Have students read the text. Tell students to look for information to answer their questions as they read. If students find facts that support or refute their position statements during reading, have them write those facts on their SQRC sheets. Some students may not find facts that support or refute their statements in the text. These students might want to research the topic further.

7. After students have read the text and written facts that support or refute their position statements, have them reread their notes and write a brief conclusion in the final spaces of their sheets.

8. Have students share their position statements and conclusions. Tell students that people can reach different conclusions after reading the same material. If that occurs, discuss how students have applied different values or reasoning to the text to reach their conclusions.

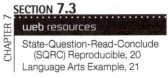

SECTION 7.3

web resources

State-Question-Read-Conclude (SQRC) Reproducible, 20
Language Arts Example, 21

CHAPTER 7

Section **7.3** INSTRUCTIONAL STRATEGY 10

Opinion–Proof

Students will read and be exposed to many opinions during their schooling. Opinions can be found in their textbooks, lectures, conversations with peers, and outside reading. By middle school, students should be able to identify an opinion. Evaluating opinions is much more complex. To help students learn how to evaluate the logic of an opinion, you can use the strategy Opinion-Proof (Santa, Dailey, & Nelson, 1985). Opinion-Proof is a strategy that helps students understand how to evaluate the arguments supporting an opinion and come to a conclusion about that opinion. It takes students through the steps of forming an opinion, supporting the opinion, looking for reasoning fallacies, and writing convincingly about the opinion. A list of common reasoning fallacies that you may want to develop into a chart for classroom use can be found on the next page.

Appealing to authority: Invoking authority as the last word.

Appealing to emotion: Using emotion as proof.

Appealing to force: Using threats to establish the validity of a claim.

Appealing to the people: Justifying a claim based on its popularity.

Arguing from ignorance: Arguing that a claim is justified because its opposite cannot be proved.

Begging the question: Making a claim and producing arguments that do not support the claim.

Contradiction: Presenting information that contradicts a claim.

Evading the issue: Talking around the issue rather than addressing it.

False analogy: Comparing unmatched elements.

False cause: Crediting an effect to a cause without evidence.

Hasty generalization: Drawing a conclusion from too few examples.

Poisoning the well: Committing to one position and explaining everything in light of that position.

Directions

1. Explain, if necessary, the characteristics of an opinion statement. Invite students to generate and share opinion statements.

2. Generate an opinion statement from one or more texts students have read. You may write the opinion statement or have students write one.

    After reading excerpts from Thoreau's book, *Walden*, his essay "Civil Disobedience," and a section on Jeffersonian democracy, present the following opinion statement.

    Opinion statement: Thoreau believed in Jeffersonian democracy.

3. Explain that opinions need to have evidence to support them and that the weight of the evidence will assist the reader in forming a judgment. Discuss the sources from which students can find supporting evidence for the opinion statement. In this case, evidence can be found in their textbooks. Have students find and write supporting evidence for the opinion.

4. Ask students to share the evidence they found in their texts. Write the evidence so it can be seen by the entire class.

    Evidence
    - Jefferson believed that there are no limits to how much the human race can improve.
    - Jefferson believed that free people should follow the dictates of reason.
    - Jefferson believed in minimal government.
    - Jefferson said that those who labor in the earth are the chosen people of God.
    - Thoreau valued his freedom above all else.
    - Thoreau said that people can elevate their lives.
    - Thoreau believed that government should be restricted.
    - Thoreau did not believe in governmental taxation.
    - Thoreau said that government gets in the way of human accomplishments.
    - Thoreau lived by himself for five years at Walden Pond, doing all of the manual labor.

5. Explain that not all evidence will support the opinion. Discuss which evidence supports the opinion and which does not.

    Supporting Evidence
    - Jefferson believed that there are no limits to how much the human race can improve.
    - Jefferson believed that free people should follow the dictates of reason.
    - Jefferson believed in minimal government.
    - Thoreau valued his freedom above all else.

- Thoreau said that people can elevate their lives.
- Thoreau believed that government should be restricted.
- Thoreau did not believe in governmental taxation.
- Thoreau said that government gets in the way of human accomplishments.

Evidence That Does Not Support Topic
- Jefferson said that those who labor in the earth are the chosen people of God.
- Thoreau lived by himself for five years at Walden Pond, doing all of the manual labor.

6. Write an essay as a group or have students write independently using the opinion and the evidence the students have identified. In some instances, you might introduce some reasoning fallacies. For example, the following is a section from an essay.

> The evidence from both Thoreau's *Walden* and his essay "Civil Disobedience" indicates that he was a strong believer in Jeffersonian democracy. Coming from the Age of Enlightenment, Jefferson believed that in a democracy people needed to use reason rather than government to rule themselves. Thoreau also espoused those beliefs. He did not believe that the government should tax people, for example. Instead, he thought that people should go about their own business and take care of themselves.

7. After students have written an essay, have them evaluate the persuasive power of the essay, looking for any reasoning fallacies. You might use or adapt the essay story/guide on the website to evaluate the essays.

SECTION **7.3**

CHAPTER 7

web resources

Opinion-Proof Reproducible, 22
Opinion-Proof Essay Evaluation
   Scoring Guide Reproducible, 23

Section **7.3** INSTRUCTIONAL STRATEGY 11

Support Your Position (SYP)

The Support Your Position (SYP) strategy encourages students to use the text to support the positions they take during reading. When students read, they should take positions about the text from two sources: their personal experience and the text itself. Expert readers know that they need a balance between text-based evidence and experience in order to clarify their positions.

Directions

1. Tell students that when they read they should take positions on their reading based on their personal experience and evidence from the text. Explain to students that they need a balance between their experiences and evidence from the text to support the positions they take.

2. Duplicate and distribute the Support Your Position (SYP) reproducible found on the website.

3. Identify a text for students to read from which they could generate a position. For example, you might have students read a physical education text on training with a heart rate monitor.

4. Have students read the text and develop a position statement from that text. Have students write their position statement as in the example that follows.

5. Tell students that they need evidence to back up their position. Explain to students that their personal experience can count as evidence. Remind students that personal experience can be something they've learned in school, seen on television, read about in books or on the Internet, heard about from others, and so on. Have students list one or more experiences on the SYP sheet that could count as evidence.

6. Ask students to reread their text and look for evidence to support their position. When they find evidence, have them list it on the SYP sheet as shown on the next page.

Position Statement	
The use of heart rate monitors can improve the rate of training.	
Evidence from Personal Experience	**Evidence from the Text**
The best triathletes use heart rate monitors during training sessions.	In clinical trials, heart rate monitors have been found effective for improving the training of runners.

7. Remind students to list several items under each column on the SYP sheet. If students cannot find evidence for their statement, have them revise their position statement.

8. Tell students that looking for evidence to support a position is a strategy that good readers use when forming positions.

SECTION 7.3

CHAPTER 7

web resources

Support Your Position (SYP)
Reproducible, 24
Science Example, 25

Section **7.3** INSTRUCTIONAL STRATEGY 12

SOAPS + Claim

The SOAPS + Claim strategy (Speaker, Occasion, Audience, Purpose, Significance + Claim) allows students to analyze and evaluate a document in a systematic way. The strategy was developed for Advanced Placement history students reading primary sources and political cartoons, but it has since been adapted and used for students at all levels. SOAPS + Claim is currently used for texts that include narrative and expository writing and also visual representations such as art. All texts can be evaluated using the same approach since they all have a Speaker (author), were developed for an Occasion, have an intended Audience, were written for a Purpose, and have some Significance. Furthermore, authors of complex texts also have made a Claim or are trying to prove a certain point. When students are able to understand these textual elements, they can evaluate the passage and develop their own opinion about the text.

Directions

1. Provide a text that is central to your teaching and one that students are able to read. Make copies of the text for students and provide them time to read the text independently or in pairs. An example of the primary source of part of the Truman Doctrine can be found on the website. Remind students of the central question for the unit: How did the Cold War shape the United States in the second half of the 20th century?

2. Download one or more of the reproducibles from the website. Students who are good readers should be given the SOAPS + Claim reproducible, and students who have difficulty reading should be given the SOAPS + Claim sentence frames.

3. Give students time to read the reproducible. Direct them to determine what each section of SOAPS + Claim stands for.

4. Divide the class into groups of three or four students. Ask students who the Speaker of the document is. Then have students talk about who would have drafted the document, which could have been White House policy makers as well as President Truman. Ask students to discuss what they know about Truman's political stance and views.

5. Have students discuss the Occasion of the document. Have students discuss the time and place from which the document was developed. In this case, the document was produced in Washington, DC in 1947. Have students discuss their understanding of the events that led to its publication. Make sure students discuss why the Doctrine was considered the impetus for the Cold War.

6. Invite students to discuss the Audience for the document. There could be many audiences for the Truman document, including the heads of state from Europe, as well as the American Congress and people. Have students discuss the assumptions that they could make about the audience. Then have students look at the specific language of the document to see if they can find anything unusual or different.

7. Have students discuss the Purpose of the document. In this case, the Truman Doctrine was written to express to the world the position of the United States in supporting Turkey and Greece so they wouldn't come under the power of the USSR.

8. Ask students to discuss the Significance of the document. You might ask them why Truman wanted to aid Turkey and Greece, and why he did not like the idea of the USSR interfering with the policies of other countries. Then ask students why this document is important, and why they are reading it more than 60 years after it was written.

9. Finally, have students discuss the Claim of the document by stating what Truman was trying to prove or establish. (The Claim of this document is to change the U.S. policy from being an ally of the USSR to containing Soviet expansion.) Make sure students understand that an author's Claim is different from the document's Significance.

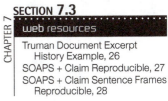

SECTION 7.3

CHAPTER 7

web resources

Truman Document Excerpt History Example, 26
SOAPS + Claim Reproducible, 27
SOAPS + Claim Sentence Frames Reproducible, 28

10. After students have completed the SOAPS + Claim strategy, tell them that they can use the components of this strategy to evaluate the logic of the texts that they read independently.

| **Assessing Student Learning** | **Rating Scale** |

Goal: *To help students evaluate the logic of a text and to develop informed opinions.* If you use SOAPS + Claim regularly, you will be able to assess how well a specific student, or a group of students, is able to evaluate the logic of a text and to develop informed opinions by recording how well students perform on each component of the strategy. Each time you have students read using SOAPS + Claim, record how well they did on each component of the strategy using a 3-point scale. If students answer completely with insight, give them a 3. If they answer with facts, but with no deep understanding, give them a 2. If they have a partial answer, give them a 1, and if they do not answer, give them a 0. Keep track of the number of students who respond each time you use SOAPS + Claim using an assessment grid such as the following.

Score	**3**	**2**	**1**	**0**
Speaker	9 students	11 students	6 students	2 students
Occasion	2 students	8 students	12 students	8 students

The assessment data indicate that for this passage, students have more difficulty identifying the Occasion than they do the Speaker. Since comprehension is contextual, it may be that the time and place from which the passage was written is difficult for students to understand. If you notice similar results the next time you have students read using SOAPS + Claim, you might determine that students are having difficulty with this specific part of reading. If that is the case, model with several different passages how you or another good reader can figure out the Occasion of a passage. Then have students try it again and record the results to see if they are making progress in their learning.

Promoting Critical Literacy

GOAL

To help students identify and respond to social and cultural factors present in texts

BACKGROUND

Critical literacy is an evolving set of beliefs based on Freire's (1985) ideas that readers should read texts critically and then move beyond reading to become agents against oppression and for social justice. An increasing number of teachers are helping students read critically by helping them identify and respond to social and cultural factors present in texts. Reading critically is a way of approaching texts with an understanding of the backgrounds and biases authors bring to texts, the influences texts have on readers, how texts can support or erode existing power bases, and how texts influence culture.

Although reading critically means different things to each discipline, teachers can help students become critical readers by teaching them that no text is neutral; even texts that seem objective. Teachers can also provide strategies for students to identify and challenge texts that position and create social identities, provide opportunities for students to give voice to their positions, and help students better understand how they can draw on their own experiences and cultural backgrounds to make meaning (Giroux & McLaren, 1992). Or, as Soares and Wood (2010) write, reading critically "allows students to bring their own lived experiences into discussions, offering them opportunities for participation, engagement in higher levels of reading and discussion, and to understand the power of language" (p. 487).

The goals of being able to challenge texts and to move toward social action are important skills for all students. As Gilbert (2001) writes, it is a "part of a real attempt to read the social: to make sense of the texts and signs of our culture" (p. 81). These skills are important for students who are from mainstream backgrounds as well as for those who come from other cultural groups. The strategies in this section have been developed to help teachers raise questions and develop discussions about texts as well as to provide students with methods they can use to see the ways texts produce and reproduce existing power structures, so they can ultimately take action against injustices.

Readers Needing Additional Support

Students who are not able to read difficult texts, such as struggling readers and some ELLs, can still participate in critical literacy activities (Lenski & Ehlers-Zavala, 2004). Students who do not have command of printed English are often able to analyze texts in group discussions. Critical literacy is a way of thinking that should be taught with and without texts.

SURF THE WEB

CRITICAL LITERACY
This comprehensive site discusses critical literacy, its importance, questions asked of texts, what critical literacy looks like in the classroom, where to find more ideas to use with students, and much more.
http://www.learnnc.org/lp/pages/4437

Discussion Spreadsheet

Goal: *To help students identify and respond to social and cultural factors present in texts.* Students will have a variety of responses to reading critically. Many students will have no problem making progress on the learning goal to identify and respond to social and cultural factors present in texts, but some will have difficulty thinking in this new way. One way to assess how well students are making progress toward this goal is to record how often students respond successfully in class discussions to Problematizing Text questions.

Develop a spreadsheet with the names of students on the left and dates on the top when you are conducting discussions with the goal of reading and responding critically. As students respond in class with any kind of appropriate comment, place a checkmark next to their names. After three or four class sessions, review the spreadsheet to determine which students are successfully making progress toward the goal.

Student Name	October 1	October 15	October 21
Xavier	✓	✓	✓✓
Melanie	✓✓	✓✓✓	✓✓
Lin		✓	
Jake	✓		✓

In this case, you can see that Xavier and Melanie have contributed consistently in each class, but Lin and Jake have not. Before concluding that Lin and Jake are not making progress toward the learning goal, look at other kinds of work products, such as on the Problematizing Text reproducible. Make sure that these students have completed the reproducible independently to find out whether they are really learning. If neither class discussions nor written products indicate that Lin and Jake are successfully learning, spend additional time modeling how to identify and respond to the social and cultural factors present in texts.

Section **7.4** **INSTRUCTIONAL STRATEGY 13**

Reciprocal Teaching Plus

Reciprocal Teaching Plus was developed by Ash (2005) to add a critical literacy component to the research-supported Reciprocal Teaching strategy (Brown & Palincsar, 1984). Reciprocal Teaching Plus promotes improved reading comprehension through active thinking. In this strategy, students use five thinking strategies as they read: questioning, clarifying, summarizing, predicting, and critiquing. When students use these strategies on an ongoing basis, they are more likely to have deeper comprehension of the material being read (National Reading Panel, 2000).

Directions

1. Select an unfamiliar narrative or informational book or passage for students to read such as "A Sign in the Sky," which is a short chapter in a history book about Halley's Comet.

2. Duplicate and distribute copies of the Reciprocal Teaching Plus reproducible found on the website. Show students the cover of the book and read the title of the chapter. In this case, it would be helpful to tell students that the chapter will be about Halley's Comet because the chapter title is not specific. Ask students to make several predictions about the book based on this information.

3. Have students read the chapter. Tell students that as they read they should monitor their predictions and also look for words, images, or ideas in the text that are confusing. Direct students to write any ideas that are obstacles to their comprehension in the column marked Clarifying. Tell students that they will be discussing these ideas in their groups later.

4. Divide the class into small groups and have students discuss the words, images, and ideas that they have listed in the Clarifying column. Then have students develop questions about the text that will help them understand to what extent their peers have comprehended the selection.

5. Have students lead discussions in their small groups by taking turns asking the questions they have developed and having the group answer them. The group might need to revert to clarifying ideas from the text in order to answer the questions.

6. After students have been given the opportunity to discuss the questions they generated, have each student write a summary of the text in the next column.

7. After students have a good understanding of the text, have them think about the text critically. Ash (2005) suggests that students respond to the following questions:
   - Whose story is being told? What is the perspective of the author or narrator?
   - Does the author believe certain things about the world? How can you tell? Does the author tell us the perspective from which the story is being told?
   - Whose story is not told in this text selection? Why or why not?
   - Do you agree or disagree with the ideas the author is presenting? Why or why not?

SECTION 7.4

CHAPTER 7

web resources

Reciprocal Teaching Plus
Reproducible, 29
Language Arts Example, 30
Math Example, 31

8. Select one or more of the critical text questions to ask the students. Have students respond to the questions individually by writing their thoughts in the column labeled Critiquing. After students have responded, have them discuss their ideas in small groups or with the entire class.

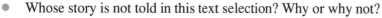

Predicting	Clarifying	Questioning	Summarizing	Critiquing
The people will see the comet but will think it's something mystical.	Modern science	Why was 1607 a pivotal year for Europe?	Halley's Comet occurred at a time when England began to become a world power.	Looking at the event from the vantage point of hindsight so opinion might be skewed.
They wouldn't know what the comet was.	Galileo	How did this change in Europe influence the settlement of new territories?	The religious changes in England precipitated emigration.	There must have been other reasons for the massive emigration. I wonder about issues of poverty.

9. Remind students to use the Reciprocal Teaching Plus strategy as they read independently so they internalize the reading processes exemplified in the strategy.

Critical Literacy Response

A Critical Literacy Response Sheet (Vasquez, 2010) draws on reader response theory by having students make a personal response to the text by using a critical literacy perspective. This strategy can help students learn how to respond critically in a structured way.

Directions

1. Select a text that you think students would be able to read in a critical light. The text can be fictional or informational. For example, *The Outsiders* (Hinton, 1967) would be a good choice for young adolescents.

2. Duplicate and distribute the Critical Literacy Response reproducible from the website. Read the sections with the students, providing explanations when needed.

3. Model the thinking process you would use when answering the questions. As you think-aloud, write your answers so they can be seen by the entire class. An example of answers from *The Outsiders* follows.

Why do you think people should or should not read this book?	What questions would you like to ask the author of this book?
• *Young people might want to think about tensions between social groups.* • *Teachers might want to understand teenagers better.*	• *Why is the poem in the book important for you?* • *What group were you in when you were in high school?*
What surprised you about this book?	**Write an experience from your own life that connects with this book.**
• *That the boys had no parents* • *Ponyboy's interest in school*	• *Our group wanted to fight another group.*
Write a statement about the worldview represented in this book. *Teenagers naturally look for a group of friends with whom to identify.*	**Write a statement from a perspective not represented in this book.** *Parents are important influences in adolescents' lives.*

4. Have students complete a Critical Literacy Response individually or in groups. Provide time in class to discuss the response.

5. Use the Critical Literacy Response Sheet as the basis for journal writing activities.

SECTION 7.4

CHAPTER 7

web resources

Critical Literacy Response
  Reproducible, 32
Physical Education Example, 33
Science Example, 34

Power Graph

Critical literacy includes identifying power relationships of characters in fictional texts and also of power influences in informational texts (Johnson & Freedman, 2005). Students can easily identify how the power of characters waxes and wanes in fiction which helps them identify how power plays out in their own lives and the lives of others.

Directions

1. Select a text that has different characters, countries, or other groups in power during the reading.

2. Duplicate and distribute a Power Graph reproducible found on the website.

3. Discuss how different people or groups can have power in one section of the book or during one time and how that often changes. Illustrate using television programs or personal experiences that are common to your students.

4. Use the text you have selected as a further demonstration of the Power Graph. Have students list the main characters below the graph and use initials to identify each character. Then have students rate how powerful the characters were during the first part of the book. Plot the number that represented their power on the graph, beginning on the left side of the graph.

5. Divide students into groups of three or four. Have each group think about how powerful each character was during five points of the plot and how the power of the characters changed during the book. Tell students to develop a graph line for each character. See the example from *Gone with the Wind* (Mitchell, 1936).

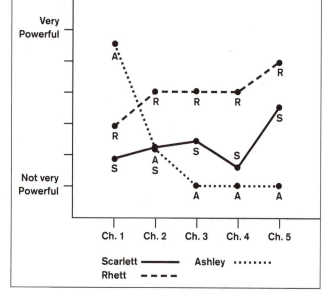

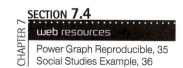

SECTION 7.4
web resources
Power Graph Reproducible, 35
Social Studies Example, 36

CHAPTER 7

Looking at Language

One of the most basic critical thinking skills for readers is to determine how words are used (Gunning, 2008). Consciously or subconsciously, writers select words to express meaning, and the words that are used can influence how readers interpret a passage. For example, consider how the nouns in each of the following sentences are used and how this affects meaning.

- I was kayaking alone and out of reach when I saw a large pod of **orcas** swimming toward me.
- I was kayaking alone and out of reach when I saw a large pod of **killer whales** swimming toward me.

You may have felt a sense of threat when reading the second sentence that you did not feel when reading the first one—all because of a synonym that changed the tone of the sentence. Freire (1970) was one of the first writers to draw our attention to how the language of texts is influenced by social, cultural, political, and historical forces, and how readers need to look closely at how language is used. In classrooms, for example, teachers can help students detect gender bias by looking for ways in which males and females are portrayed—not merely examining the use of personal pronouns but by looking closely at the way language is used. Or teachers can look at how language is used to shape decisions as Hefferman and Lewison (2009) did when they helped sixth grade students critically examine the criteria used for award-winning books. By teaching students to look critically at how an author uses language, students can become aware of power relationships and bias as they read.

Directions

1. Locate a selection from a book or the Internet that applies to your content area. Provide students with copies of the text.
2. Have students read the text looking for references to males and females. Prompt them by saying something like the following example.

   In this article on polar expeditions, you'll find descriptions of the scientists and the crew at the polar outpost. Look for ways the authors have described different characters. For example, notice that they write about Bob's medical training, and they mention that Emily is petite. Pay attention to everything that refers to the people in the article.

3. Ask students to highlight the references to the different genders. Tell students that they are collecting facts and should not be looking for specific biases.
4. Divide the class into groups of two or three students. Have students compile their highlighted lists so that they create group lists of gender references.
5. Collect the groups' lists and develop a class list. Write the list so that it can be seen by the entire class, as in the following example.

Bob	Emily
degree from Harvard	petite
wife and children at home	from the Midwest
former expeditions	only woman in group
athletic	personable

6. Have students read the completed lists and draw generalizations about the use of gender in the text. You might need to provide guidance using a think-aloud as in the example that follows.

   As I read my lists, I noticed that the writers discussed Bob's degrees, while they said nothing about Emily's qualifications.

7. Remind students that gender stereotypes are often reinforced in subtle ways through language and that critical readers are aware of the influence language has on their views of cultural groups.

SECTION 7.4

CHAPTER 7

web resources

Looking at Language
Reproducible, 37
Music Example, 38

Problematizing Texts

Students who read critically also need to explore the ways diverse cultures are represented in literature and problematize texts as they read (Bean & Moni, 2003; Comber, 2001). Problematizing texts means to look at what exists in the texts, what isn't present, and what those authorial choices mean. Writers make choices during the writing process; they choose how to represent gender and cultural groups, what to say, and what not to say. If students read with attention to what is and is not in the texts, they problematize the texts.

Directions

1. Select a picture book to read to students that presents an interesting story. Picture books often contain cultural messages that are appropriate for all students (Lenski, 2008). For example, the book, *Click, Clack, Moo: Cows that Type* (Cronin, 2000) is a picture book about farmyard animals that find a typewriter and make written demands on the farmer. The book illustrates the use of literacy in action.

2. Tell students that you want them to listen for more than the plot as you read aloud. Explain to students that you want them to problematize the text.

3. Duplicate and distribute the list of Problematizing Text Questions from the website. Explain that not all questions will apply to this particular story, but that the questions are representative of a different way of understanding text.

4. Read the book to students and provide time during the reading for students to refer to the list of questions.

5. After reading, have students discuss the book in light of the Problematizing Text Questions that follow.

Problematizing Text Questions

- How does the author represent different groups in the text?
- How are meanings assigned to certain figures?
- How does the author try to convince readers to accept his or her premise?
- How are meanings assigned to events in the text?
- What is the purpose of the text?
- Whose interests are served by the dissemination of this text? Whose interests are not served?
- What view of the world is put forth by the ideas in this text? What views are not?
- What are other possible constructions of the world?
- What is included in this text?
- What is missing from this text?
- What does this text tell us about our culture?
- How might we rewrite this text to deal with the gaps and silences?

---

6. Several sources of ideas for picture books follow.

Carr, K. S., Buchanan, D. L., Wentz, J. B., Weiss, M. L., & Grant, K. J. (2001). Not just for the primary grades: A bibliography of picture books for secondary content teachers. *Journal of Adolescent & Adult Literacy, 45*, 146–153.

Tiedt, I. M. (2000). *Teaching with picture books in the middle school.* Newark, DE: International Reading Association.

Trelease, J. (2001). *The read-aloud handbook* (5th ed.). New York: Penguin.

SECTION 7.4

web resources

Problematizing Texts
Reproducible, 39

CHAPTER 7

7. Once students have had experience problematizing picture books, have them ask the same questions of the texts they use in class.

Taking Social Action

The primary aim of critical literacy is to promote social justice by taking social action (Christiansen, 2000, 2009; Singer & Shagoury, 2005/2006). Literacy can be used as a tool for furthering this aim. One example of taking social action is when students in Kentucky used reading, writing, speaking, and listening skills to influence those in power to responsibly mine the highest peak in the state (Powell, Cantrell, & Adams, 2001). Looking for ways to promote social action is the most effective type of strategy you can use as you promote critical literacy because it gives students power to change their lives.

Directions

1. Encourage students to become aware of local social issues that apply to your subject area, such as the need to clean up vacant yards, the underfunding of schools, and so on. Post newspaper and Internet site listings about these issues in a prominent place in your classroom.

2. After you've collected a number of postings about issues, have students generate a list of the issues that are represented by these texts.

3. Duplicate and distribute the list of issues to students. Ask students to prioritize the list starting with number one and continuing until all issues are included.

4. Collect the prioritized lists and determine which issue is of most interest to the class as a whole. Announce the number one issue.

5. Have students collect print and nonprint information related to the issue. For example, if the social issue that the class wants to study is a city zoning law that limits the number of persons to six individuals who could live in a single-family, three-bedroom house, have students collect the following types of information about the subject.
   - Newspaper clippings
   - Radio broadcasts
   - Editorials
   - Internet sites
   - Interviews with zoning commissioners
   - Interviews with the mayor and city council members
   - Interviews with residents of subdivisions
   - Interviews with residents from another town
   - Interviews with zoning commissioners from other areas

6. Have students bring to class their information and discuss the social implications of the zoning restriction. You might ask the following questions.
   - Is a specific cultural group the focus of the restriction?
   - Is the restriction a safety concern?
   - Are the members of the zoning board a specific cultural group?
   - Does the language from the texts indicate biases?
   - Do the texts about the issue have underlying prejudices?
   - Are the media's messages balanced and neutral?
   - Is anyone being disenfranchised by this restriction?

7. Tell students that taking social action means acting responsibly—not making false accusations, but presenting a reasoned, thoughtful account of the facts. Have students use the facts they have collected to develop a "white paper" about the topic to present to the people in power—in this case, the zoning commission.

8. Explain to students that their social action may or may not bring results, but, as members of a democracy, they should continue to use critical literacy skills to further social action whenever possible.

SECTION **7.4**

web resources

CHAPTER 7

Taking Social Action
Reproducible, 40

RETHINKING SCHOOLS

This site describes a nonprofit, independent publisher of educational materials, which advocates the reform of elementary and secondary education with a strong emphasis on issues of equity and social justice.
www.rethinkingschools.org

Activities *and* Journal Entries *for* Teacher Educators

Activities

1. In content area groups, identify the content standards in your discipline that relate to critical literacy. List them on a shared document, such as a Google document or a wiki, so that you have a sense of how students in your classes will be exposed to critical literacy throughout the school day. Draw conclusions about the strength of the critical literacy instruction in your region. Contact policy makers to advocate for increased critical literacy instruction, if appropriate.

2. Select a strategy from this chapter and adapt it to your discipline.

3. Students will have different abilities to think critically. Some ELLs, for example, may not have a background in questioning authority. Select a strategy from this chapter and show how you will differentiate the strategy for students with various experiences in thinking critically.

4. Develop a list of print-based and online resources that you could use as documents to teach critical literacy.

5. Investigate how cultural groups value critical literacy differently.

6. Respond to this scenario: Your district is planning to close one high school that is the most culturally diverse. Use your disciplinary expertise to develop a group of lessons that have students respond to this situation. For example, English teachers could have students learn about the issue and write an editorial; social studies teachers could have students look at the historical background of the school, and so on.

Journal Entries

1. Reflect on what you know about critical literacy and what you still need to learn. Write about the kind of professional development you might need in order to increase your knowledge.

2. Taking social action is an important aspect of critical literacy. How can you expand your teaching to reach the world outside your classroom?

3. As you read in this chapter, texts are never neutral, including this one. What perspective do you think the authors used as they wrote this chapter? Think about what you agree with and what you disagree with. Select one of your ideas and write about it.

8 Studying

IRA Standards: 1.1, 2.1, 2.2, 4.2, 5.3

Learning Goals

The reader of this chapter will:

- Understand the theories and research on studying
- Understand how studying relates to improved academic performance
- Understand the value of learning to study in the disciplines
- Recognize the purpose of specific reading behaviors (i.e., skimming, scanning, and precise reading)
- Learn instructional strategies that help students learn and remember content

Questions to Consider

1. What are the theories and research about studying that relate to your discipline?
2. Why is it essential for students to learn to study in the disciplines?
3. How can you incorporate study strategies into your discipline?
4. Why is it important for students to use various types of reading behaviors (i.e., skimming, scanning, and precise reading)?

OVERVIEW

Studying is a unique skill, different from the reading strategies presented in other chapters of this book. When students read, they focus attention on the text; then they use their ability to process print to construct meaning. While reading, students rely on textbook features and use their ability to reason in order to fulfill their reading purposes. Studying is different. When students study, they read, understand, learn, and remember information from texts for a specific task (Anderson & Armbruster, 1984).

To illustrate the difference between reading and studying, think about textbook passages you assign students to read in preparation for class discussion. You expect them to read, understand, and remember information that they can apply to a general discussion about the topic. You expect students to know some of the content information. When you assign students studying tasks, your expectations are often different. You expect students to identify the important ideas in the text, to learn and remember those ideas, to be able to understand the relationship between the information they studied and past material, and to retrieve that material in certain ways for a test or a performance.

Research reveals that studying has a strong relationship with academic success (Credé & Kuncel, 2008; Tuckman, 2003). Credé and Kuncel (2008) determined that studying includes three constructs: 1) study skills—students' knowledge of study strategies and ability to manage time and resources; 2) study habits—students' engagement in regular studying (routines) in environments conducive to studying; and 3) study attitudes—students' positive attitudes toward studying. They found that study skills, study habits, and study attitudes are not dependent on high cognitive ability. In other words, students of varying abilities can learn to study effectively.

Recent research on memory indicates that spacing study tasks is superior to massing study tasks (Kornell, Castel, & Bjork, 2010; Taylor & Rohrer, 2009). When studying a particular skill, spacing or distributing practice across multiple episodes results in improved academic achievement. Massing study tasks (cramming) is less effective than planning study tasks over time. Other literacy research notes the connection between metacognition and studying. Developing effective study skills depends on students' ability to assess accurately what they know or don't know (Pashler, Balin, Bottge, Graesser, Koedinger, McDaniel, & Metcalfe, 2007). Studying also requires students to adapt their study behaviors to the demands of specific learning tasks (Credé & Kuncel, 2008).

Study strategies can facilitate students' ability to learn, understand, retain information, and help them develop their own individualized approaches to learning content information.

> Utilizing study strategies involves helping learners formulate purposes for learning, providing guidance through a learning experience, and then helping learners to reflect on what has been learned. Examples of study strategies include the use of reference skills; note taking; outlining; reading and interpreting diagrams, charts and graphs; varying the reading rate; and exercising effective time management (Misulis, 2009, p. 16).

Studying has two basic components: knowing what to study and knowing how to study. Students need to be aware of the learning task. If studying is to accomplish a specific task, students must understand the task. Generally, you will be the one who determines the studying task. For example, you might ask students to study material for a test, a performance, or a presentation. Your role is to make sure that students understand the nature of the task. Then students need to identify the subsets of the task and set study goals to accomplish each one. As students decide what to study, they may survey the materials and use flexible reading strategies to determine what information to learn and remember. They may set goals, manage their study time, and monitor their studying effectiveness. Once students have determined what they should study, they need to use study strategies to learn and remember the material for the specific study task.

Knowing what to study is not enough; students also need to know how to study. When students study to read and remember, they need to focus attention on the material, encode that information, and learn the material in such a way that they can retrieve it for the task. Students need to read the text information and form it into their own words so that it makes sense, and they are able to repeat that information in any one of a variety of forms for a test. To do this, students need to learn how to use study strategies. The following strategies are generally considered useful for most students who are studying (see Block & Pressley, 2002).

- Preview text
- Predict
- Skim or scan text
- Read slowly and carefully
- Reread difficult sections
- Paraphrase
- Relate new information to existing knowledge
- Create mental images
- Develop questions
- Highlight, underline, or take notes
- Outline
- Create a diagram
- Summarize

Because studying is task directed and people learn in different ways, study plans and methods tend to be idiosyncratic. For example, students who are studying a history text could be faced with five new vocabulary words, eight pages to read, three charts, two graphs, and five pictures. Some students prefer to read the text in sequential order, taking detailed notes using the Cornell notetaking method found on page 238. Other students prefer scanning the chapter and using the REAP strategy, taking annotative notes. Still others may use the REST strategy and take notes along with writing their own comments and questions. Because there isn't one correct way to study, you should present students with a variety of study strategies and let them choose those strategies that work best for them (Simpson & Nist, 2002).

Studying in schools is often assigned so that students learn material for a culminating activity such as a test or a performance. Students should know, however, that studying is a useful life skill. Even though students are not formally graded in their everyday life the same way they are in schools, they still have many opportunities to study: to read and learn to perform a specific task. For example, students who are learning to drive will read the driver's manual, learn driving skills from an adult, and practice driving. Students are actually studying; they are reading and learning in order to perform a specific task. Therefore, as you teach students how to study for your class, also tell them that they can use the skills they are learning for many important activities in which they will engage as adolescents and adults.

Study strategies are very important to master during adolescence (Peverly, Brobst, & Morris, 2002). The amount of information to be learned increases as students progress through the grades. Study skills make a difference. They are viewed as academic enablers—critical tools for learning and fundamental for academic competence (Gettinger & Seibert, 2002). Adolescents need teachers to provide explicit instruction and intentional practice in studying. Unfortunately, many students enter college unprepared to meet the studying demands (Pressley, Yokoi, van Meter, Van Etten, & Freebern, 1997). In college, studying is part of the hidden curriculum that relies on students' metacognition, motivation, and interest (Nist & Simpson, 2000). For these reasons, it is important to give your students many opportunities to learn, use, and master study strategies.

Learning to Study

BACKGROUND

Studying is generally a self-directed activity. Students can be taught a variety of study strategies, but they need to assume responsibility for their own studying. Content area teachers can assist students in learning how to take responsibility for disciplinary learning by helping them to develop study plans, manage their study time, and monitor their study habits.

Adolescence is a critical developmental time for teaching students to assume responsibility for their own learning (Peverly, Brobst, & Morris, 2002). Many adolescents do not understand the relationship between studying and achievement. They do not think about the consequences of their actions—academic achievement from their use of study strategies. Teachers are uniquely positioned to help adolescents see the explicit connection between their studying and their academic performance. It is important to help students learn that studying takes time, effort, and attention. Students will need to make study plans, set study goals, and use study strategies to accomplish their goals.

One of the most effective ways to teach a study strategy is by integrating the strategy into the course content (Allgood, Risko, Alvarez, & Fairbanks, 2002). Teaching students how to learn is equally important for all students—high-achieving students (Stanley, Slate, & Jones, 1999), average students, struggling students (Burke, 2002a), and those students who learn differently (Deshler, Schumaker, Lenz, Bulgren, Hock, Knight, & Ehren, 2001). Teachers need to introduce students to study strategies that will help them maximize their learning.

Many content area teachers use Graphic Organizers to help their students organize content and study for tests (Barry, 2002). Graphic Organizers are visual representations of how the ideas in text are organized and connected. This research-supported reading strategy has also been shown to promote thinking (Lee & Spratley, 2010). Students of all abilities in various types of classrooms can use them effectively to organize and study content area information. (Refer to Chapter 6, Section 6.2 Graphic Organizers for specific directions, reproducibles, and examples.)

Even though studying is generally an individual endeavor, students should study with friends at times. Middle and high school students are social beings. Therefore, students should be encouraged to study in groups for part of their study time. Certainly, there are times when solo studying is best, but many adolescents learn better when they can share ideas with their peers. Consequently, you should encourage students to learn how to plan, manage, and monitor their individual studying, but you should also encourage students to spend some of their study time learning from each other.

Section **8.1** INSTRUCTIONAL STRATEGY 1

Preplan–List–Activate–Evaluate (PLAE)

Research indicates that students who construct and implement an effective plan of study do better on tests than students who do not have a study plan (Nist & Simpson, 1989). For that reason, Nist and Simpson (1989) created PLAE, a study strategy to help students create goals and plan what to do during study time. PLAE incorporates the following methods necessary for strategy control and regulation: goal setting, understanding of a variety of strategies, the ability to select appropriate study strategies, the ability to activate and monitor a plan of action, and the ability to evaluate a study plan. When students employ PLAE, they **P**replan or define their tasks and goals, **L**ist or select the strategies they will use, **A**ctivate or implement the study plan, and **E**valuate the plan's effectiveness after they receive feedback.

Directions

1. Tell students that you will be demonstrating a study strategy that they can use in all subject areas to improve their learning of content material. Use examples from your content area or use the following example.

2. Display PLAE where it can be seen by the entire class. Tell students that PLAE is an acronym for **P**replan, **L**ist, **A**ctivate, and **E**valuate.

PLAE Study Plan

Preplan—Preplan or define study tasks and goals.
List—List or select strategies to accomplish study tasks and meet study goals.
Activate—Activate or implement the study plan using appropriate strategies.
Evaluate—Evaluate the effectiveness of the study plan.

From Nist, S. L., & Simpson, M. L. (1989). PLAE, a validated study strategy. *Journal of Reading, 33*, 182–186.

---

3. Identify a study goal that students will need to accomplish in the near future. Tell students that you will be using the following example to demonstrate the **P**replan stage of PLAE.

Study Goal

For French class you will be asked to learn vocabulary and language structures associated with various foods and grocery shopping. We will have a mock grocery store with food to sell. To demonstrate your knowledge, you will be evaluated on your ability to conduct a conversation in French. Students in the fourth-year French class will play the roles of the shopkeepers.

4. Divide the class into groups of three or four students. Have students create a list of tasks designed to accomplish the study goal. After students have developed lists, have them discuss their ideas with the whole group. A sample list follows.

Study Tasks

- Scan your French book, looking for the chapter that discusses the vocabulary of grocery shopping.
- Create note cards or write notes with the terms to learn.
- Memorize the vocabulary.
- Practice the new vocabulary with classmates in conversations about grocery shopping.

5. Tell students that the next step in PLAE is to list their prior knowledge of successful study strategies. Have students discuss the strategies they could use to accomplish their study tasks.

6. Have groups of students discuss possible study options. Then have students brainstorm strategies that they could use to accomplish each task. Students should individually decide which study strategy to use. Ask students to write their study plans on index cards. An example of a study plan follows.

Study Plan

Skim section 1 from chapter 6.
Identify words to learn.
Memorize new words.
Practice new words in dialogue with classmates.

7. Have students activate their study plans. Each day, ask students whether they were able to accomplish their study goals.

8. After students have completed their study plans and have demonstrated their learning, have them evaluate their study plans. For students to evaluate their study plans, they need to identify the outcome of the culminating event. Then ask students to determine whether their grades were higher or lower than they expected.

If the grades were lower, have students reread their study plans, think about whether they implemented the plans, and list reasons why their grades were not as high as they expected. Students should evaluate not only their final grades but also the effectiveness of their studying. If they identify a weak point, students should revise future study plans.

CHAPTER 8

SECTION 8.1

web resources

Preplan-List-Activate-
Evaluate (PLAE) Study Plan
Reproducible, 1
Social Studies Example, 2

Section **8.1** INSTRUCTIONAL STRATEGY 2

Managing Studying

Teaching students all of the strategies in the world will not necessarily help them learn content information. Students also need to learn how to manage their study time. Middle and high school students often have full schedules. However, they need to make time to study and manage their study time so that they can learn the necessary material from your content area. Middle and high school students need to assume the responsibility for managing their own study time, but you can help them understand the factors involved in using time wisely.

Directions

1. Tell students that you will be discussing effective techniques for managing study time. Explain that even though many of them know how to study, unless they manage their study time they will not use their study time effectively.

2. Write the following list of Tips for Managing Study Time so that it can be seen by the entire class. Discuss each of the items on this list with the students. Tell students that if they follow these suggestions they will have more productive study sessions.

Tips for Managing Study Time

- Study in a comfortable environment with good lighting and minimal distractions.
- Set study goals for each study time. List the goals and estimate the amount of time each study goal will take.
- Determine whether short periods or long periods of study time are best.
- Schedule study time at your best time for learning (e.g., early morning).
- Keep a pencil or pen available when studying to summarize, underline, or write down key notes or ideas.
- Keep a positive attitude during study time. Do not try to rush through studying. Become engaged in learning.
- Use study questions or create self-questions while studying. Keep your mind focused.
- Actively read and study. Monitor your attention to the task.
- Relate what you are studying to your life.
- Compliment yourself for productive study periods.

Based on Risko, V. J., Fairbanks, M. M., & Alvarez, M. C. (1991). Internal factors that influence study. In R. F. Flippo & D. C. Caverly (Eds.), *Teaching reading & study strategies at the college level* (pp. 237–293). Newark, DE: International Reading Association.

Monitoring Study Habits

As students study, they need to constantly monitor the effectiveness of their study time. You can teach students how to manage their study sessions, but they need to independently monitor their use of those management techniques as they study. When students monitor and manage study time and subsequently experience success as a result of these efforts, they will continue to use study strategies (Allgood, Risko, Alvarez, & Fairbanks, 2002). Because students may not be aware of the need to monitor studying, you can teach them ways to become aware of their progress.

Directions

SECTION **8.1**
web resources
Study Skills Self-Assessment
Reproducible, 3

1. Tell students that they should become aware of the study strategies they use and should make changes so that studying is more productive. Tell students that one way to increase self-awareness is to complete a survey about study habits.

2. Duplicate and distribute the Study Skills Self-Assessment reproducible found on the website. Have students answer the questions by circling the number that best describes their study habits. After students have completed the survey, have them reflect on their strengths and weaknesses and make a plan to change any habits that interfere with learning. Have students take the survey periodically so they can monitor changes in their study habits.

Project Journals

Many secondary school students have large projects to accomplish, either individually or in groups. One of the biggest difficulties with projects is managing the work. "A project journal is a device used by students to plan, organize, develop, and implement their ideas" (Stephens & Brown, 2000, p. 156). It can also be used to help them plan how to study large amounts of material.

Directions

1. Tell students that they will be keeping a project journal with their assignment and that the entire class will decide upon the format for the project journal.

2. Duplicate and distribute the Project Journal reproducible found on the website. Explain to students that the format you're showing them is only one way to use a project journal and that project journals need to reflect the task assignment and goals.

3. Discuss the assignment you have given to students, explaining each of the components of the students' responsibilities. You might say something like the following, using a social studies example.

   Your assignment is to work in groups to learn and understand each of the constitutional amendments in the Bill of Rights. Then you will choose one amendment and provide a historical background that explains how that amendment was conceived. This assignment will consist of two parts. First, you will be given a quiz on the Bill of Rights. Your individual grade will be the average of the grades for the group's members. Second, you will need to develop a pamphlet, cartoon, or newspaper article explaining one amendment. You will have two weeks to finish the assignment and will have two class periods to work on it.

4. Ask students if they understand the assignment. Then divide the class into groups and have them discuss what tasks they will need to accomplish as in the example that follows.

- Identify each of the amendments in the Bill of Rights.
- Write them on index cards.
- Memorize the amendments and quiz each group member.
- Select one amendment.
- Use source material to determine the amendment's historical background.
- Develop a pamphlet, cartoon, or newspaper article.

CHAPTER 8

SECTION 8.1

web resources

Project Journal Reproducible, 4

5. Discuss additional sections of the project journal such as a timeline, individual group members' tasks, and group assessment of progress.

6. Use students' ideas to develop a project journal that can be used with the entire class. Once students have become accustomed to using this strategy, allow groups to develop their own unique project journals.

Readers Needing Additional Support

For students who struggle with text, provide accommodations and adaptations (Lenz & Deshler, 2004) to ensure successful learning experiences. An accommodation varies how students learn the content. For example, increase the time allotted to complete the study task or allow the use of computer and/or assistive technologies (e.g., Franklin Language Master, Kurzweil 3000, audiotapes). An adaptation varies the content that the student learns. For example, select reading materials at the students' ability levels or choose visually rich reading materials.

SURF THE WEB

HOW TO STUDY
The How to Study website is a free study skills resource. It includes brief articles about studying, remembering, taking tests, note-taking, language arts, math, and college.
http://www.how-to-study.com

ITOOLS
iTools offers a comprehensive set of Internet tools. The Search Tools section includes numerous search engines, web directories, discussion forums, and video search capabilities. The Language Tools section provides access to several dictionaries, vocabulary tools, and text translators. Research Tools connects to multiple encyclopedias, newspapers, magazines, and topic directories as well as biographies and quotations.
http://www.itools.com

LEARN MORE
The Learn More website focuses on supporting student learning from K to college. The site provides a set of general study skill guidelines for middle school and high school students.
http://www.learnmoreindiana.org

STUDY GUIDES AND STRATEGIES
The Study Guides and Strategies website includes study guides and resources for high school and college students. The site includes information on preparing to study, effective study skills, literacy skills, and test-taking skills.
http://www.studygs.net

Assessing Student Learning

Ask Topic Questions

Goal: *To help students learn how to study.* Helping students focus on the importance of studying in the content areas is critical. To check their knowledge of studying, you can ask them to develop probing questions about the topic (Angelo & Cross, 1993). To assess students' understanding of studying, you can use a technique called Ask Topic Questions (Tuttle, 2009). After students have discussed the importance of studying in the content areas, ask them to write five probing questions about studying. Tell students not to ask factual questions (e.g., what is . . .), but write questions that explore their understanding (e.g., how does . . .). Once students have developed five probing questions, invite them to share their questions with one another. Alternatively, you can ask students to exchange and respond to their peers' questions.

Understanding Textbook Features

GOAL

To help students understand the features of textbooks

BACKGROUND

Many students have difficulty studying because they don't understand how to read textbooks. They approach studying like they do reading novels—begin at the first paragraph and read lightly until the end. Textbooks, however, are not meant to be read like novels; they have features such as headings, subheadings, and indexes to help readers gain information.

Some texts have features that make them "considerate" or "friendly" for students (Armbruster, 1984; Armbruster & Anderson, 1988, 1995). "Inconsiderate" or "unfriendly" texts do not have these features, such texts have other characteristics that cause students to work especially hard to comprehend the text. These characteristics include an organization that is hard to decipher, a writing style that is too difficult, passages that are too long, and/or graphics that are difficult to understand (Olson & Gee, 1991; Smith, 1992). When students are required to read texts that are "inconsiderate" or "unfriendly," or texts they simply can't read (Allington, 2002), many students decide not to expend the effort required to comprehend the material. All students warrant "texts that are coherent, well-structured, appropriate for students' age and grades, and designed to include a variety of text features" (Sheridan-Thomas, 2008, p. 167).

Teaching middle and high school students about textbook features and how to use them is important across the disciplines. You can teach students strategies to help them understand textbook features, which can help them study more effectively. Struggling students, in particular, need explicit instruction on how to make the most use of textbook features (Sheridan-Thomas, 2008). Once your students know how to approach a textbook, they are better prepared to learn and remember as they study.

Section **8.2** INSTRUCTIONAL STRATEGY 5

Book Tour

A Book Tour is a strategy that helps students become familiar with text features. Many students are unfamiliar with the features of content area texts that assist the reader with comprehension. Book Tours "front-load" or guide readers through features that warrant special attention and can help students as they learn from textbooks (Buehl, 2001).

Directions

1. Tell students that a Book Tour is like a guided tour through a museum, a historical mansion, or an art gallery; it helps readers pick out certain features of the text. Ask students whether they've experienced a guided tour. Have them share their experiences.

2. If none of the students has experienced guided tours, create an example of taking a visitor on a guided tour through your school as in the following example.

   As you enter the building, you'll notice the signs to the administrative offices. Here you'll need to sign in and take a visitor's badge. Now we'll move down the hall toward the gymnasium. In the display cases to your right, you'll see the trophies students have won for participating in sporting events. Of special note is the first place trophy for girls' basketball. Last year they won the state tournament.

3. Explain to students that you're going to take them through a tour of their textbook and that it will be similar to other guided tours.

4. Open your textbook and point out the features that are important to your content area subject. The following list includes some of the features that you might emphasize.

Authors	Cartoons	Index
Table of contents	Margin notes	List of references
Titles and subtitles	Bolded vocabulary words	Appendices
Graphs and charts	Chapter outlines	Footnotes
Pictures	Chapter questions	Glossary
Primary sources		

5. After you've given students a Book Tour, have them create their own Book Tour for students in other classes by developing a survey using the book features they have learned. Have students exchange papers and tour the book again to become even more familiar with the text.

Section **8.2** INSTRUCTIONAL STRATEGY 6

Textbook Survey

Students who know textbook features study more efficiently. Textbook Surveys can help students internalize their knowledge about textbooks, which helps them learn from texts.

Directions

1. Tell students that knowing textbook features helps them read and study from their textbooks. Describe the features of the textbook using Book Tours (Instructional Strategy 5).

2. Then tell students that you're going to give them a Textbook Survey so that they can think more deeply about text features.

3. Duplicate and distribute the Textbook Survey reproducible that can be found on the website. Ask students to complete the survey independently.

4. After students have finished the Textbook Survey, facilitate a classroom discussion about each of the items on the survey. In this way, you'll be using the survey as a teaching tool rather than as an assessment device.

5. Encourage students to elaborate on their answers to the survey. Acknowledge instances where students need further instruction about textbook features and use those times to teach students more about their textbook.

SECTION **8.2**
CHAPTER 8
web resources
Textbook Survey Reproducible, 5

Section **8.2** INSTRUCTIONAL STRATEGY 7

Textbook Scavenger Hunt

A Textbook Scavenger Hunt is an innovative way for students to survey their textbooks. This strategy helps students to become knowledgeable about the content and format of their books. It provides them with authentic practice in using their books as references. You can develop a Textbook Scavenger Hunt for your particular textbook that invites students to seek specific information or treasures by using the table of contents, index, glossary, and other features.

Directions

1. Develop a Textbook Scavenger Hunt to help students use the textbook's features and locate specific information in the textbook. Try to use all of the reference features (index, subject index, author index, table of contents, glossary, appendices, and answer sections). Modify the reproducible that can be found on the website to guide the development of your Textbook Scavenger Hunt.

2. Tell students that to improve their studying they need to understand how to find information in their textbooks. Explain that they need this search for information to be effective and efficient.

3. Introduce the Textbook Scavenger Hunt strategy. Distribute the Textbook Scavenger Hunt that you have developed.

4. Explain to students that by working through the Textbook Scavenger Hunt, they will become familiar with the features and content of their textbooks. You can have students complete the Textbook Scavenger Hunt in cooperative groups, pairs, or alone.

CHAPTER 8

SECTION 8.2
web resources
Textbook Scavenger Hunt Reproducible, 6
Math Example, 7

Section **8.2** INSTRUCTIONAL STRATEGY 8

THIEVES

THIEVES (Manz, 2002) is a strategy for students to use when previewing textbook chapters. This strategy prompts students to search systematically through the assigned chapter and respond to a set of questions. You can teach students to follow the acronym THIEVES as they preview a chapter. Encourage your students to "steal" as much information as possible from the chapter.

Directions

1. Explain to students that effective readers preview textbook chapters before they begin reading the chapter. Explain that a thorough preview will improve their understanding of the chapter.

2. Tell students that the THIEVES strategy is a systematic way for students to "steal" a lot of information from the chapter. Duplicate and distribute the THIEVES reproducible that can be found on the website. Introduce the THIEVES acronym and tell students that THIEVES stands for **T**itle, **H**eadings, **I**ntroduction, **E**very first sentence in a paragraph, **V**isuals and vocabulary, **E**nd-of-chapter questions, and **S**ummary.

3. Model the THIEVES strategy using an example chapter from your content area or use the science example provided on the website.

4. Tell students to skim the assigned chapter and follow the THIEVES steps to gather information from the chapter.

CHAPTER 8

SECTION 8.2
web resources
THIEVES Reproducible, 8
Science Example, 9

Readers Needing Additional Support

Help students recognize and use features of their textbooks. Gather copies of content area textbooks or ask students to bring their textbooks to class. In small groups, have students identify and use the various features of their textbook. Provide copies of instructional strategies (e.g., Textbook Survey or THIEVES) for students to use. Allow students to discuss the features and how they can be used when studying.

THIEVES

Title
What is the title?
What do I know about this topic?
How does this topic connect with the other chapters?
Does the title express a point of view?
What do I think I will be reading about?

Headings
What does this heading let me know I will be reading about?
What is the topic of the paragraph beneath the heading?
How can I turn this heading into a question that may be answered by the content?

Introduction
Is there an opening, perhaps italicized?
Does the first paragraph introduce the chapter?
What does the introduction let me know I will be reading about?
Do I already know anything about this content?

Every First Sentence in a Paragraph
Read the first sentence of each paragraph.
What do I think this chapter is about?

Visuals and Vocabulary
Are there photographs, drawings, maps, charts, or graphs?
What can I learn from these visuals?
How do captions help me to understand the meaning?
Is there a list of key vocabulary terms and definitions?
Are there important words in boldface type throughout the chapter?
Do I know what these words mean?
Can I tell the meaning of these words by reading the sentences?

End-of-Chapter Questions
What do the questions ask?
What information do these questions earmark as important?
What information do I learn from the questions?
Keep the end-of-chapter questions in mind and note where the pertinent information is located in the text.

Summary
Read the entire summary.
What do I understand and recall about the topics in the summary?

Adapted from Manz, S. L. (2002). A strategy for previewing textbooks: Teaching readers to become THIEVES. *The Reading Teacher, 55*, 434–435.

| **Assessing Student Learning** | **Exit Sheet** |

Goal: *To help students understand the features of textbooks.* Students need to understand the various features of content area textbooks. To check their understanding of textbook features, you can ask students to share what they know. One simple technique to use is an Exit Sheet (Tuttle, 2009). After you have taught students about textbook features and how to approach a textbook, ask them to identify what they learned on an Exit Sheet. Give the students one or two minutes at the end of the class session to write what they learned on an Exit Sheet—a 3 x 5 card or half sheet of paper. Collect the Exit Sheets and scan them before the next class to get a sense of students' responses. Once you have reviewed their responses, consider instruction that reviews or extends what students know about textbook features.

Reading Flexibly

GOAL

To help students develop the ability to read flexibly

BACKGROUND

Reading flexibly is a necessary skill when studying. To understand text, students use different processes for different purposes. For example, students may skim the text to get the gist of it, or they may read the text with the intent of retaining the information for a long period of time (RAND Reading Study Group, 2002).

Flexible readers modify their reading rates and their choice of strategies to fit different kinds of texts for different purposes. Flexibility can be viewed as an aspect of metacognition (i.e., thinking about thinking). Good readers are metacognitively aware. They know when comprehension is failing and when it is time to apply fix-up strategies, including an adjustment of reading rate. The rate at which students read material is influenced by at least four factors: 1) the speaking-listening rate to which they have become accustomed; 2) prior knowledge or familiarity with the material; 3) the rate at which they can receive and think about incoming information; and 4) their purpose for reading the material (Manzo & Manzo, 1990a). Additionally, reading rate is affected by the organization of the text and the author's writing style.

According to many authors, including Crawley and Mountain (1995), there are three types of reading behaviors: skimming, scanning, and precise reading. Skimming is used to gain an overview or a general idea of text. This level of reading is appropriate for previewing a chapter in a textbook or deciding whether to choose a particular library book by skimming the book jacket. Scanning is used to locate specific information or to answer a question. For example, when looking up a phone number in the directory, we scan the page until we get close to the name we are seeking. At that time, we probably begin to do precise reading. Precise reading requires analyzing words or an author's ideas in a purposeful and deliberate manner. This type of reading is used when we read textbooks for the purpose of learning and retaining information or when we read websites.

The widespread use of the Internet and related technologies redefines the nature of literacy (Leu, 2000). Internet reading requires students to incorporate the three traditional levels of reading (skimming, scanning, and precise reading) and incorporates one more: scrolling. When students read websites, they use scrolling, scanning, skimming, and precise reading, recursively. The following strategies can provide opportunities for your students to increase their reading flexibility while maintaining adequate comprehension.

Section **8.3** INSTRUCTIONAL STRATEGY 9

Skim–Away

Skimming involves reading quickly over material to gain a general impression of its content. When readers skim, they preview material and start to forge links with their background knowledge as they gain a general impression of the text. According to Fry (1978), skimming is usually done at rates of about 800 to 1,000 words per minute. The following strategy is designed to develop students' ability to skim a text selection.

Directions

1. Tell students that this reading strategy is one they can use to get an overall idea about the contents of the chapter or text. Explain that when readers skim they are reading text quickly to get a main idea. To demonstrate skimming, use an example from your content area or the following social studies example.

2. Ask students to open their history text and turn to the chapter on Ancient Greece. Tell students that they are going to skim the first section of the chapter to get a sense of the chapter's contents and to begin to think about the main idea of the chapter. Tell students that, as they do this, they are activating their background knowledge about the chapter's subject. Allow about three minutes to complete this activity. Tell them that, as they skim, they should do the following things.

   - Read the chapter title and glance over the headings and subheadings included in the chapter as they slowly turn the pages.
   - Think about the focus of the chapter as they skim over the maps, charts, and illustrations.
   - Quickly read the section review.

3. After students have completed skimming the first section of the chapter, ask them to close their books and write a paragraph that includes everything they can recall from the first section. Invite students to share their paragraphs and talk about the techniques they used as they skimmed. An example of a student's paragraph follows.

   > This section is sort of a preview about the battle between the Persians and the Athenians for the city of Athens. It looks like the chapter will focus on the geographic setting of Greece and include lots of information about the Bronze Age, the Dark Ages, and the Greek Gods. There are several photographs of Greek art works, a map of Greece during the Bronze Age, and a great photograph of the Acropolis. The section review includes some vocabulary words and questions about the contents.

4. Discuss with students the value of skimming before they read a chapter. Tell students that when they have skimmed the first section, they have the gist, or the general idea, of the chapter and are prepared to scan it more carefully for precise information.

Section **8.3** INSTRUCTIONAL STRATEGY 10

On Your Mark, Get Set, SCAN!

Scanning is used by readers to locate specific information. Readers use scanning when they look up a number in the phone book or a word in the dictionary. In scanning, readers know what information they are seeking and work at a speed of about 1,500 words per minute. This speed usually results in 100% accuracy in obtaining the desired information (Crawley & Mountain, 1995). The following strategy uses scanning as a way for students to experience finding specific information within a selection of text.

Directions

1. Tell students that this reading strategy involves scanning their texts as they look for specific information. Explain that when readers scan they move their eyes quickly down the page until they locate the information they are seeking. Tell them that it is important that they read quickly and try to skip words or descriptions that do not seem pertinent to the information for which they are looking.

2. Ask students to open their history text and turn to the chapter on Ancient Greece or use an example from your content area.

3. Look over the chapter and pick out facts that students can locate as they scan. Try to pick out facts that are important to the contents. Write 5 to 10 questions, based on text information. Allow five minutes for the completion of this activity. Tell students that they are going to scan the first section of the chapter to find answers to the following questions.

- How did geography shape Greek civilization?
- How much of Greece is covered with mountains?
- Describe briefly the life of the Minoans.
- What was the main business of the Bronze Age kings?
- When did the Olympic Games begin?
- What are myths?

4. Ask students to work as quickly as possible to locate the answers to the questions. Tell them to write down the answers but not to worry about spelling at this time. Remind them that it is not necessary to read every word in the text to obtain the information they need to complete the activity. Say to students, "On your mark, get set, scan!" as they begin the activity.

5. After students have completed the scanning activity, invite them to share their answers and to discuss the techniques they used as they located information. Encourage them to practice using scanning with other textbook assignments in order to increase their reading efficiency.

Section **8.3** **INSTRUCTIONAL STRATEGY 11**

SCAN and RUN

SCAN and RUN (Salembier, 1999) is an effective strategy for supporting general and special education students to comprehend informational text. The SCAN and RUN strategy helps students to monitor their reading comprehension before, during, and after reading the text. The mnemonic SCAN and RUN consists of seven cues that guide students to understand the assigned text. Before reading, students use the first four cues: **S**urvey the headings and turn them into questions; **C**apture the captions and visuals; **A**ttack boldface words; and, **N**ote and read all of the chapter questions. During the reading, students use the last three cues: **R**ead and adjust speed as needed; **U**se word identification skills such as sounding out, looking for other word clues in the sentence, or breaking the word into parts; and, **N**otice and check parts you don't understand and reread or read on. After reading, students answer questions at the end of the assigned passage and share their understanding in class discussion.

Directions

1. Tell students that skilled readers monitor their comprehension before, during, and after reading. Explain that using strategies for reading will help them comprehend their assigned texts.

2. Introduce the SCAN and RUN strategy. Duplicate and distribute the SCAN and RUN reproducible that can be found on the website.

3. Describe the meaning of each of the seven cues:

> **S**urvey the headings and turn them into questions.
> **C**apture the captions and visuals.
> **A**ttack boldface words.
> **N**ote and read all of the chapter questions.
>
> **R**ead and adjust speed as needed.
> **U**se word identification skills such as sounding out, looking for other word clues in the sentence, or breaking the word into parts.
> **N**otice and check parts you don't understand and reread or read on.
>
> Tell students that they will use the SCAN cues before reading and RUN cues during reading.

CHAPTER 8

SECTION 8.3

web resources

SCAN and RUN Reproducible, 10

4. Model the use of SCAN and RUN using an example from your content area.

SCROL

SCROL (Grant, 1993) provides students with an opportunity to use skimming, scanning, and precise reading as they study a chapter of text. Students will scan the table of contents to locate the appropriate chapter, skim the headings of the chapter as they preview it, and carefully read the chapter in order to construct an outline of its contents. Grant (1993) identified four advantages to using SCROL.

1. Students increase comprehension by activating their background knowledge prior to reading.
2. Students are guided in understanding the relationships among ideas in the text.
3. Students use content structure as a method for remembering text information.
4. Students' motivation for reading text is increased.

Directions

1. Tell students that good readers use three levels of reading: skimming, scanning, and precise reading. Explain that all of these levels are incorporated into a strategy called SCROL.

2. Explain to students that when they scan they are looking for specific information and they should read quickly down a page. When they locate information they want to read, they may want to skim it to determine if it is information they are seeking. Then they begin to do precise reading. Model the SCROL strategy for students using examples from your content area or use the example provided below.

   Scan the table of contents in your text on careers and look for the page number for chapter 10, "How to Get Jobs and Work Experience." When you find it, open your books to the appropriate page.

3. Tell students that SCROL stands for **S**urvey, **C**onnect, **R**ead, and **O**utline. As you direct students' attention to chapter 10 in their texts, model how to use SCROL.

4. Ask students to skim the chapter and **S**urvey the headings. As they skim, they should look at the headings, subheadings and illustrations to get the main idea of the chapter. Tell them to consider what they already know about the topic, "How to Get Jobs and Work Experience." Tell students that when they see the heading "newspaper advertisements" they probably already know that newspaper advertisements are a good place to look for jobs. As they survey the chapter, they are skimming it for general information.

5. After students have surveyed the chapter, ask them to share some of their ideas about the chapter's contents as you write their ideas where they can be seen by the entire class. For example, one student might say, "This chapter is going to tell us about work permits. I think work permits are necessary if we want to get a job and we're under 15 or 16. I'm not sure which." Another student might say, "There's a section called Distributing a Flier. This sounds interesting. Maybe it's going to tell us how to make up our own fliers when we're looking for a job."

6. Invite students to **C**onnect the headings to one another. Ask them to look for key words in the headings to help them make the connections. As they do this, tell them that they are using scanning because they are looking for specific information.

7. Ask students to continue to scan the headings and to offer suggestions about the chapter's contents. For example, one student might say, "There are also sections about entrepreneurship and private jobs, so the chapter must have some information about working on your own." At this point, students have used skimming to preview the text and scanning to find text topics.

8. Now ask students to **R**ead the text, looking for words and phrases that explain the headings. As they do this, explain that they are employing precise reading or reading in a purposeful manner.

9. After students have finished reading the chapter, explain that they should **Outline** the chapter by listing the headings and writing under the headings any details that they remember from their reading. An example follows.

Newspaper Advertisements
- Classified advertising by employers
- Help-wanted section
- Read carefully before responding
- Place an ad for a job in situation wanted

10. Direct students to look back at the text to determine the accuracy of their outlines. As they do, point out to them that, once again, they are scanning the chapter to look for specific information. If they have written down incorrect information or wish to add additional information, they should revise their outlines.

Newspaper Advertisements
- Classified advertising lists available jobs.
- Help-wanted advertisements are for full-time jobs or adult skills.
- Some ads are for teenagers over the age of sixteen.
- Situation wanted ads should be brief but include essential information.

11. To conclude this strategy, review with students the different types of reading (skimming, scanning, and precise reading). Point out that they used all three types as they employed the SCROL strategy.

Section **8.3** INSTRUCTIONAL STRATEGY 13

Reading Flexibly on the Internet

Media literacy, defined as "the understanding and production of messages through physical devices," incorporates six components: the ability to access, analyze, synthesize, interpret, evaluate, and communicate messages (Flood & Lapp, 1995, p. 3). Successful integration of these components is necessary for adequate comprehension. "New literacies" such as blogs, bulletin boards, e-mail, listservs, presentation software, spreadsheets, virtual worlds, web browsers, and wikis also require students to integrate these components, and highlight the need for flexible reading. Students must be able to vary their reading rates as they navigate information sources on the Internet to determine the quality and relevancy of the information. This means that as students scroll down the screen, sometimes they skim or scan, and often they use precise reading to analyze ideas and words.

Directions

1. Model the use of flexible reading on the Internet for students by using the following example or an example related to your content area. Display the following Internet activity for the entire class, or, print a copy of a web page or several web pages for each student.

2. Tell students that they need to use various strategies when reading on the Internet. They will use scrolling, skimming, scanning, and precise reading as they locate and evaluate information and determine its relevancy to their search. Review and define, if necessary, any of these terms.

3. Open an Internet address from your content area or use the following science example. http://library.think-quest.org/TQ0312238/cgi-bin/view.cgi. This address opens a website titled *Of Mind and Matter—The Mystery of the Human Brain*. Tell students that you are researching how long-term memory works.

4. Show students that the website has several sections for them to skim as they scroll down the screen and look for information about how memory works. As they skim, they read quickly over the topics. They will see the following choices: Anatomy, Function, Disorders, Psychology, and Interact! These topics give the students a general idea about the information that is available through this website. Although they have several choices

of web pages, none of them appears to relate directly to long-term memory. A logical choice, at this point, will probably be the page labeled Function. Click on the Function link.

5. Tell students to scan the Function page in order to find information about long-term memory. As they do, students will see that Memory is one of the choices. Click on the Memory link. Ask them to scan the Memory page for information about long-term memory. Point out to students that the type of reading they did on this web page was slower and more precise because they were trying to locate a specific piece of information—long-term memory.

6. Tell students to read the information about long-term memory. Ask students to answer the following questions as they read this section of the web page.

   ● What is required to get information from the short-term to long-term memory?
   ● What do scientists think is important for long-term memory?
   ● How can long-term memories be categorized?

7. Point out to students that, to answer these questions, they need to scan the paragraphs; however, if they wish to take notes on the material or analyze some of the information, they will need to use precise reading. Such reading is described as slow, careful reading for the purpose of learning or studying.

8. Guide students in conducting their own Internet research project. They should use flexible reading rates as they encounter web pages.

Readers Needing Additional Support

For students who struggle with text, preselect Internet websites with text sections of varied length and complexity. Have students work in pairs to identify places within the website where they will need to vary their reading rates. Then allow time for students to skim, scan, and use precise reading to gain an understanding of the text.

SURF THE WEB

AN EXPLORATION OF TEXT SETS: SUPPORTING ALL READERS
Using multiple strategies, this site helps students to explore and read texts of varying complexity.
http://www.readwritethink.org/classroom-resources/lesson-plans/exploration-text-sets-supporting-305.html

THINKQUEST LIBRARY
The ThinkQuest Library includes more than 5,000 web-based projects created by students from around the world. The library includes a wealth of resources on a wide range of topics for students.
http://www.thinkquest.org/pls/html/think.library

Assessing Student Learning

Questions

Goal: *To help students develop the ability to read flexibly.* Developing the ability to read flexibly is necessary for effective studying. Students need to know that they will use different types of reading for different purposes. To help students recall when to use various types of reading, pose a series of questions. Appropriate questions will allow the teacher to check student understanding and encourage student engagement (Tuttle, 2009). During a discussion of reading (i.e., skimming, scanning, and precise reading), ask students questions about these reading types and when they should be used. Possible questions include: When would you use skimming? How would you use scanning? In what instances would you use precise reading? Answers to these questions will gauge students' understanding about the use of skimming, scanning, and precise reading.

Summarizing Content Information

GOAL

To help students learn content information by summarizing

BACKGROUND

The goal of studying is to learn content information. All of the reading strategies and skills in this book can have a positive impact on learning; however, students can go through the motions of preparing a study plan, reading flexibly, and taking notes without learning the material. To learn content material, students need to be able to translate ideas into their own words and retrieve that material to accomplish a task. When students use their background knowledge to make predictions, take notes, and summarize content material, they have a better chance of really learning (Caverly, Mandeville, & Nicholson, 1995).

A skill that helps students read more effectively and learn disciplinary topics is annotation (Zywica & Gomez, 2008). An annotation is a note of comment or explanation that helps to improve content understanding. It requires students to focus on important aspects of content within the text and build students' ability to "read to learn." When annotating text, students pose questions, identify main ideas, make predictions, and note reactions (Lee & Spratley, 2010). Importantly, students can use their annotations as study guides.

When students study to learn content material, they need to encode the ideas in the text. One of the best ways to encode text is to write summaries of the material. A content area summary is defined by the following features:

"a. it is short

b. it tells what is most important to the author

c. it is written 'in your own words'

d. it states the information 'you need to study'" (Friend, 2001, p. 320).

The process of summarization entails drawing on prior knowledge of the topic, organizing new information, and forming connections among related topics. Four components of summarization are:

"1. identify and/or formulate main idea

2. connect the main ideas

3. identify and delete redundancies

4. restate the main ideas and connections using different words and paraphrasing"
   (National Institute for Literacy, 2007, p. 23).

Summarizing is beneficial because it gives students the opportunity to rethink the content material and process it deeply.

You can teach students to write summaries of content material and to summarize independently as they study. Teaching students to write microthemes and to use GRASP facilitates learning the skill of summarizing. Your goal, however, is to have students automatically summarize as they read. Students reading about the particles in matter in their science text, for example, first read an introduction that reviews ideas presented earlier in the text. Then the text presents a short experiment, and finally it explains a diagram of particles in solids, liquids, and gases. When students read these two pages, they should summarize each section before reading the next section. Summarizing during reading is one of the most effective strategies students can use as they learn content information.

Read-Encode-Annotate-Ponder (REAP)

One way to take notes is to make annotations on note cards, in a learning log, or on the computer. Annotative notes are at the heart of the REAP strategy (Eanet & Manzo, 1976). When students employ REAP, they **R**ead text passages, **E**ncode the message by translating the passage into their own words, **A**nnotate or write their messages in their notes, and **P**onder the messages they have written. Annotations can take various forms. Students can write a summary annotation that condenses the main ideas of a passage into one or two concise statements. A second type of annotation is a thesis annotation that states the main point the author has tried to relate. A third type of annotation is a critical annotation. A critical annotation answers the question "So what?" Students' critical annotations first state the author's thesis and then state an opinion about that thesis. A final type of annotation is a question annotation. For this type of annotation, students write a question about a significant aspect of the passage.

REAP can also be used by students to improve their comprehension of content material available on the Internet (Manzo, Manzo, & Albee, 2002). As students read information on the Internet, encourage them to use the REAP strategy to make annotations about the information they find. As your students use the strategy, they begin to think about the content material from various perspectives—a critical goal of the REAP strategy.

Directions

1. Tell students that you will be demonstrating a study strategy that they can use as they read textbook material and learn content information. To demonstrate the REAP strategy, use an example from your content area or the following example.

2. Identify a passage that you want students to read. Tell them to read the passage independently. After they have read the passage, tell students to identify the main points and restate them in their own words. The following is an example of a textbook passage and an encoded message based on that passage. Write the passage and message where they can be seen by the entire class.

   Investing in Savings Accounts

   When you invest your money in savings accounts, the money is essentially risk-free; it has the greatest safety of any investments you might choose. Even though banks might fail, as long as your investment in a bank is insured by either the Federal Deposit Insurance Corporation (FDIC) or the Federal Savings and Loan Insurance Corporation (FSLIC), your savings are risk-free. Even if the bank fails, your money is insured. Bank savings accounts are virtually risk-free investments; however, money invested in banks does not return a high rate of interest.

   Encoded Message

   This paragraph is about investing in savings accounts. When you invest in savings accounts your money will not accrue much interest, but it will be safe.

3. Distribute note cards to students. After students have practiced encoding, or restating, the main points of the passage, have them write their restatements on the cards. Tell students that there could be many different ways to write a summary and that one type of message is not superior to any other type.

4. Divide the class into groups of three or four students. Have students share their statements with each other. Then have them ponder, or think about, the different types of messages represented by the group.

5. Tell students that there are four main types of annotations: summary annotations, thesis annotations, critical annotations, and question annotations. Write an example of each type of annotation where it can be seen by the entire class. Use examples from your content area or the examples that follow. Have the students identify the types of annotations they have written. Then remind students to use the REAP strategy as they study content information.

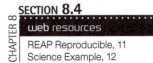

SECTION 8.4

web resources

REAP Reproducible, 11
Science Example, 12

REAP Annotations

Summary Annotation
Money invested in banks is insured, so it is virtually risk-free.

Thesis Annotation
Investing money in banks has low risks and low returns.

Critical Annotation
Investing money in banks has low risks and low returns. I don't think money that is not needed to pay bills should be invested in banks. The low risks don't compensate for the low returns.

Question Annotation
I thought that there was a ceiling on the amount of money that is insured by the banks. Are all savings entirely insured?

EXAMPLE

Section **8.4** INSTRUCTIONAL STRATEGY 15

Summary Microtheme

To learn content information, students need to process that information deeply. One way to process information is to create a short summary of a passage in a textbook or a section of notes. A Summary Microtheme (Brozo & Simpson, 1995) is a type of summary that can be used in content area classes to help students process and learn material. A microtheme can be used in a number of ways. Teachers can assign microthemes to get a general picture about how well students understand main concepts; teachers can use microthemes to hold students accountable for learning a concept; and students can use microthemes to process information as they study.

Directions

1. Explain to students that a microtheme is a way for them to summarize a passage or concept to learn the material.
2. Tell students that you will be modeling an example of a microtheme. To demonstrate how to write a microtheme, use an example from your content area or use the examples that follow.
3. Identify a concept that you want students to understand. Locate a passage of text that explains the concept. Distribute copies of the passage to students. The following example is a passage about the chemical reaction that takes place when hair is curled or straightened.

   The curliness of your hair depends on how disulfide bonds are joined between parallel protein chains. When a person gets a permanent, curls are created or removed in three steps. Here's the chemical recipe. First, break the disulfide links between protein chains. Next, use a form (curlers, rollers, etc.) to curl or uncurl the hair. Third, rejoin the disulfide links between protein chains in their new orientation.

4. Distribute note cards to each student. Ask students to read the passage and write a microtheme, or a short summary about the passage. After students have written a microtheme, write your own summary where it can be seen by the entire class. Explain how you arrived at your summary by thinking aloud. Then have students compare their summary to yours. Many different summaries should be considered correct. An example of a Summary Microtheme about the preceding passage follows.

   A chemical reaction of breaking and reforming disulfide bonds is necessary to permanently change the curliness of hair.

5. Tell students that as they study they should stop occasionally and write a Summary Microtheme about the text. Remind students that by processing material they will remember it better.

6. An example of a Summary Microtheme based on a literature example follows.

Literature

Summary Microtheme

Daedalus was exiled from Athens, so he sailed to Crete where he was befriended by King Minos. King Minos would not allow Daedalus to leave Crete, so Daedalus married and had a son, Icarus. Since Daedalus was homesick for Athens, he built wings for himself and Icarus. As they flew toward Athens, Icarus ignored his father's warning and soared too close to the sun. The heat melted his wings, and Icarus fell into the sea.

EXAMPLE

7. Microthemes can be used in a number of ways. Students can use microthemes to practice identifying and summarizing information they have learned. You can use microthemes to assist students in processing information, or you may decide to evaluate or grade the microthemes that students write. A rubric is an appropriate assessment tool for the evaluation of Summary Microthemes. A six-point rubric that you can use or adapt to score Summary Microthemes follows.

Summary Microtheme Evaluation Rubric

6 A summary that is scored a "6" meets all of the criteria for accuracy, comprehensiveness, and clear sentence structure. The main points in the text should appear correctly in the summary with all main points developed. The summary should be as comprehensive as possible and should read smoothly from beginning to end with appropriate transitions between ideas. The sentence structure should be clear and varied, without vagueness or ambiguity, and without more than one grammatical error.

5 A summary that is scored a "5" should be accurate and comprehensive, but it may lack perfect sentence structure. The summary may be clearly written but be somewhat unbalanced or less thorough than a "6" summary. It may show that the student has a minor misunderstanding of the material. A "5" summary should have no more than two grammatical errors.

4 A summary that is scored a "4" is one that is good but not excellent. It reveals a generally accurate reading of the passage with a clear sense of the main points of the material, but it will be noticeably weaker than a summary that is scored a "5" or a "6." The summary may be weak in its content, organization, or conventions but not all three.

3 A summary that is scored a "3" is strong in at least one area of competence, and it portrays a fairly clear and accurate view of the material being summarized. A "3" paper is either unbalanced or lacks the clarity and precision of a top-ranked summary. The sentence structure of a "3" summary frequently prevents the inclusion of sufficient ideas for good comprehensiveness.

2 A summary that is scored a "2" is weak in all areas of competence, either because it is so poorly written that the reader cannot understand the content or because the content is inaccurate or disorganized.

1 A summary that is scored a "1" fails to meet any of the areas of competence.

Guided Reading and Summarizing Procedure (GRASP)

Summarizing text passages is a complex skill that takes guidance and practice. All too often, students are asked to summarize complex text without really understanding what a summary is or how to compress many ideas into a brief synopsis. Students can practice summarizing passages by using Summary Microthemes (see Instructional Strategy 15), or you can also teach students how to summarize using the **G**uided **R**eading **A**nd **S**ummarizing **P**rocedure (GRASP) (Hayes, 1989). The goal of teaching GRASP is to enable students to summarize independently when they try to understand texts and when they study to learn text material.

Directions

1. Provide students with a short passage of text that they can read easily. Explain that they will be writing a summary of the passage. You can use an example from your content area or the following example about Texas independence.

    > In the 1820s, Americans began migrating into Mexican territory. Stephen Austin received permission from the Mexican government to found a colony of about 300 settlers in what is now east Texas. Austin led the first group of American settlers into the territory in 1822. By 1824, over 2,000 settlers lived in the area.
    >
    > Soon other agents arranged contracts for Americans to settle in Texas. By 1830 over 7,000 Americans lived in the area, more than twice the number of Mexicans in the territory. Worried that it was losing Texas through immigration, Mexico passed a law in 1830 prohibiting settling there.
    >
    > The Americans continued to move into the territory. As their numbers increased, the Americans demanded more political freedom. They declared independence for the Republic of Texas in 1836. Under the leadership of William Travis, the Americans began to fight for freedom. At the battle of the Alamo, the Mexicans routed the Americans. At a later battle, however, Sam Houston led the Americans to victory. Texans elected Sam Houston as their first president late in 1836.

2. Ask students to read the passage independently with the purpose of remembering all that they can. After all students have finished reading, ask them to tell you what they remembered. List the items they volunteer where they can be seen by the entire class. The following examples are taken from the preceding passage.

    Students' first recollections

    Americans moved into Mexican territory.
    Austin was the leader of the settlers.
    Mexico began to discourage settlers.
    Americans continued to move into the area.
    Americans declared independence.
    Mexico won at the Alamo.
    The Americans won the next fight.

3. Have students reread the passage with the purpose of making additions and corrections to the list. Revise the list as needed.

Students' first recollections	Additions/corrections
Americans moved into Mexican territory.	During the 1820s, Americans moved into Mexican territory.
Austin was the leader of the settlers.	There were over 2,000 settlers by 1824.
Mexico began to discourage settlers.	Mexico passed a law prohibiting more settlers.
Americans continued to move into the area.	Americans continued to move into the area.

Americans declared independence.	In 1836 Americans declared independence.
Mexico won at the Alamo.	Mexico won at the Alamo.
The Americans won the next fight.	Under the leadership of Sam Houston, the Americans beat the Mexicans.

4. Ask students to organize the remembered information. Suggest categories for the list they generated. List the categories and ask students to divide the items on the list into categories. The following example is based on the preceding passage.

Category: Settling Mexican Territory

During the 1820s, Americans moved into Mexican territory.

There were over 2,000 settlers by 1824.

Mexico passed a law prohibiting more settlers.

Americans continued to move into the area.

Category: War for Independence

In 1836 Americans declared independence.

Mexico won at the Alamo.

Under the leadership of Sam Houston, the Americans defeated the Mexicans.

In 1836 Texas elected its first president, Sam Houston.

5. Using the outline generated by categorizing the information, ask students to write a summary of the material. You might suggest that students begin with a main idea statement for the first main heading with the details as subheadings. An example summary paragraph is shown below.

Summary

During the 1820s Americans began settling Mexican territory, which is now east Texas. By 1824 there were over 2,000 settlers. Americans kept moving into the territory. Then Mexico passed a law prohibiting more settlers. Americans, however, continued to move into the area. By the 1830s the Americans began to want independence from Mexican authority. In 1836 the Americans declared independence. Mexico and the Americans went to war. Mexico won the famous battle of the Alamo, but the Americans won the war.

Section **8.4** INSTRUCTIONAL STRATEGY 17

Paraphrasing

Paraphrasing (Kletzien, 2009) encourages readers "to use their own words and phrasing to 'translate' the material to their own way of saying it" (p. 73). An important strategy for use with content area texts, paraphrasing is viewed as a precursor to summarizing text. The Paraphrasing strategy includes 1) an explanation of the strategy, 2) modeling the strategy using think-alouds, 3) guided practice of the strategy, and 4) independent use of the strategy. When paraphrasing text, students learn to monitor their understanding and assess what they know about a topic (Kletzien, 2009). Students can use the Paraphrasing strategy as they read and study any of their content area texts.

Directions

1. Tell students that as they read assigned texts they need to paraphrase the content. Explain that paraphrasing is "putting the content into one's own words" (Kletzien, 2009, p. 73). Let students know that using the Paraphrasing strategy will help them to understand the main idea and details of the text.

2. Introduce the Paraphrasing strategy. Explain that paraphrasing is a strategy that many good readers use while reading. After reading a passage, these students pause and put what they have just read into their own words. The strategy allows students to check their understanding of the passage and will help them to re-

member the content. (If students cannot put the content into their own words, they can reread the text passage.)

3. Model paraphrasing by thinking aloud after you read a passage. Ask the following questions aloud to model your thought process: What was this passage about? What is the main idea? What are the important details? What does this passage tell me? Then, rephrase the passage into your own words. To make sure that students understand the strategy, model numerous passages from your content area text.

4. Once students understand how paraphrasing works, ask them to participate with you in paraphrasing a text passage. Guided practice affords students with opportunities to practice the strategy with your support.

5. Once students are able to use paraphrasing under your guidance, have them practice the strategy in pairs. Partners can take turns asking, "What was the passage about?" and prompting the rephrasing of the passage.

6. After students are comfortable using paraphrasing in pairs, provide opportunities for students to practice using paraphrasing independently. Assign passages from students' content area text. Have them rephrase what passages mean in their own words. You can ask students to share their restatements orally or have them write their restatements for your review.

7. Remind students that understanding is the goal of reading and paraphrasing can help them achieve this goal when reading their content area text.

Readers Needing Additional Support

Have students listen to books on tapes as they follow along in the text. Adjust the speed of the tapes as needed to support the students. At the end of each paragraph, direct students to pause the tape and stop reading. Ask the students to paraphrase what they have read or listened to by stating the main idea and related details. Have students resume their simultaneous listening/reading of the next paragraph and paraphrase its content. After students become proficient at verbalizing the main idea and details, have them write down the main idea and details. In addition, allow students to use multiple forms of expression (Orkwis & McLane, 1998) such as concept maps, illustrations, or software (e.g., Inspiration) to represent the main ideas and details.

SURF THE WEB

PARAPHRASING: WRITE IT IN YOUR OWN WORDS
Online handout from the Online Writing Lab (OWL) at Purdue University describes the process of paraphrasing. (Available in html and pdf)
http://owl.english.purdue.edu/owl/resource/619/01/

QUOTING, PARAPHRASING, AND SUMMARIZING
Online handout from the Online Writing Lab (OWL) describes the appropriate uses of quoting, paraphrasing, and summarizing. (Available in html and pdf)
http://owl.english.purdue.edu/owl/resource/563/01/

SCALING BACK TO ESSENTIALS: SCAFFOLDING SUMMARIZATION WITH FISHBONE MAPPING
This lesson from the ReadWriteThink website guides students to summarize main ideas and related details from text using fishbone mapping.
http://www.readwritethink.org/classroom-resources/lesson-plans/scaling-back-essentials-scaffolding-277.html

Assessing Student Learning

Shrinking Text

Goal: *To help students learn content information by summarizing.* Summarizing content information is a key to effective studying. Students need to be able to summarize as they read content area texts. Once students know how to summarize content area text, they will be more adept at learning content information. To determine the extent to which students can summarize text, teachers can use an informal activity: Shrinking Text. Before assigning a text passage, tell students that they are going to summarize a reading passage in pairs. Distribute one large note card (4 x 6 or 5 x 8) to each student pair. Have students read the passage independently and then work with their partner to summarize the passage. Have the students "shrink the text" by writing a brief summary of the passage on the large note card. After the student pairs have completed "shrinking the text," invite them to share their summaries with another pair. Once the pairs have shared, collect and review their summaries to get a sense of their ability to summarize text.

Taking Notes

BACKGROUND

Taking notes facilitates learning in at least two ways: by the process of taking notes and by the product, or the notes themselves (McKenna & Robinson, 1997). When students take notes, they use many cognitive processes that aid learning. First, students select what information to take down as notes. Then, they condense the information into words, phrases, or sentences. Finally, they write the notes in some type of organized form. These processes are ways to learn content material.

The notes that students write are the product of the note-taking activity. These organized, selected phrases from the text help students as they review the major concepts to learn. The product of taking notes is important; however, it is the mental process involved in taking notes that produces the learning (Herrell & Jordan, 2002). Double entry note taking, for example, requires students to pose questions, make observations of patterns in the text, summarize, and make connections (Lee & Spratley, 2010). Students' cognitive engagement during the act of note taking helps them to become more adept at reading disciplinary text.

Students also need to be encouraged to use their notes when studying in the classroom or at home. Written notes can be used to cue their memory of important information and ideas (Pashler, Balin, Bottge, Graesser, Koedinger, McDaniel, & Metcalfe, 2007). The structure of note-taking strategies such as Note Cue Cards and Cornell Note-Taking supports student learning by prompting students to recall main ideas and supporting details, major terms and definitions, and critical disciplinary concepts.

Most students know that note taking can help them study and remember important information; however, they will not automatically know how to take effective notes. Brown (2005) reports that students' perceptions of their note-taking abilities differ from their actual note-taking abilities. For example, students tend to make lists rather than using more organized or effective note-taking strategies. Effective note taking helps students to sort the unimportant information from the important and to see connections between main ideas and supporting details. If students are not taught note-taking strategies, they may not select important information to record nor write their notes in an organized manner (Stahl, King, & Henk, 1991). To help students become effective note takers, you should teach them how to use some of the following note-taking strategies.

There are many types of note-taking strategies, some using paper and pencil and some electronic. Taking notes is an activity that is individualistic; different students prefer different types of notes. Therefore, you should teach several types of note-taking strategies and encourage students to use the ones that are most helpful to them.

Section **8.5** INSTRUCTIONAL STRATEGY 18

Note Cue Cards

Note Cue Cards (Manzo & Manzo, 1990b) have two instructional purposes: they help students identify important information in texts, and they facilitate discussion of key terms and concepts after reading. Note Cue Cards contain questions, answers, and comments written on note cards by the teacher about the ideas presented in a passage. When you use Note Cue Cards, you are able to guide students' attention to ideas and information as they read. After students read the text, Note Cue Cards focus the discussion on important ideas and information.

Note Cue Cards scaffold learning for struggling readers by identifying key terms in the text and modeling the thinking-questioning process readers use as they learn from text.

Directions

1. Choose a passage that is important for students to read and learn. Prepare enough prereading Note Cue Cards so that each class member has at least one card. Some cards should have questions, some cards should have answers to the questions, and some cards should have comments about the topic. For example, say:

> Today we're going to read a section about human rights in our civics textbook. This section is important because it describes the basis for our rights in the United States.
>
> Question: What are some of the limits on the rights of the American people?
> Answer: The government can establish laws to restrict certain rights to protect the health, safety, security, and moral standards of a community.
> Comment: The restriction of rights must be reasonable and must apply to everyone equally.

2. Explain that you will be using Note Cue Cards to help students identify the important information in the text and to facilitate discussion and learning. Distribute the cards to students. Ask students to preview the identified passage of the text, read the cards, and think about how their cards apply to the text.

3. Ask a student to read a question card. After a student has read a question, ask students to read a card that would answer the question, and then ask for a comment card.

4. Have students read the passage of the text. After students have read the text, distribute more Note Cue Cards. You may decide to give students blank cards, so they can write their own questions, answers, and comments. For example, here are some student-generated Note Cue Cards.

> Question: How are an individual's rights limited for the common good?
> Answer: The rights of any individual may be limited to prevent interfering with the rights of others.
> Comment: Americans do not have unlimited rights.

5. Continue class discussion using Note Cue Cards. Explain that using Note Cue Cards helps students know what information to look for as they read. Discuss the ways the cards are used (i.e., questions, answers, and comments). Explain that, as they read independently, students should create self-questions similar to the questions written on the Note Cue Cards. They should ask themselves questions about the contents of texts, they should try to answer those questions, and they should make comments as they read.

6. Later, students could be invited to prepare Note Cue Cards on another section or chapter in the text.

Section **8.5** INSTRUCTIONAL STRATEGY 19

Record–Edit–Synthesize–Think (REST)

Record-**E**dit-**S**ynthesize-**T**hink (REST) (Morgan, Meeks, Schollaert, & Paul, 1986) is a note-taking strategy that takes into account the integration of textbook readings, lectures, and class discussions. When students use REST, they record what they have read in the text or heard in class, edit those notes by condensing them and deleting irrelevant material, synthesize notes by recording information stressed both in class and the textbook, and think about the notes while studying and learning the content information. REST can be used when teachers assign textbook reading before class discussion, or it can be used when class discussion precedes textbook reading.

Directions

1. Tell students that you will be demonstrating a study and note-taking strategy that they can use to learn content material. Use an example from your content area or the following examples.

2. Identify a concept that will be the topic of a class discussion and will be assigned to students to read. Have students read the passage independently or in groups.

3. Have students record notes from the reading on the left half of a sheet of paper in a manner similar to the following example.

Science

REST

Notes from text (pp. 17–19)	Notes from class
■ St. Paul's Island in the Bering Sea near Alaska	
■ 41 sq. miles	
■ 1911—25 reindeer introduced	
■ no predators	
■ 1937—reindeer population increased to 2,000	
■ by 1950 no more reindeer	

Summary

EXAMPLE

4. After students have recorded notes from their reading, present a lecture or conduct a class discussion about the topic. Tell students to write notes from the lecture or class discussion on the right half of the paper as in the following example.

Science

REST

Notes from text (pp. 17–19)	Notes from class
■ St. Paul's Island in the Bering Sea near Alaska	■ food capacity of island limited
■ 41 sq. miles	■ interdependence involves limiting factors
■ 1911—25 reindeer introduced	■ no data on reindeer population in 1941–1942
■ no predators	■ carrying capacity—maximum population of a particular species that the habitat can support
■ 1937—reindeer population increased to 2,000	
■ by 1950 no more reindeer	

Summary

EXAMPLE

5. Tell students that lectures and class discussions may repeat information that students have read in their text and written in their notes. Some of the contents of lectures and class discussions, however, will be different. Tell students that both types of notes are important to study. After students have recorded notes from the class lectures or discussions, have them edit their notes and delete information that is redundant or irrelevant.

6. Explain that the next step in REST is to synthesize the information from textbook reading and class discussions. Tell students to read both columns of their notes carefully, looking for a synthesis of the information from both sources. Have students write the synthesis of the notes at the bottom of the sheet as in the following example. After students have synthesized their notes, they should think about their summary and study the content information.

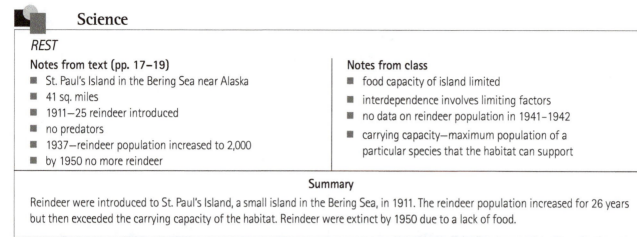

REST

Notes from text (pp. 17–19)
- St. Paul's Island in the Bering Sea near Alaska
- 41 sq. miles
- 1911–25 reindeer introduced
- no predators
- 1937—reindeer population increased to 2,000
- by 1950 no more reindeer

Notes from class
- food capacity of island limited
- interdependence involves limiting factors
- no data on reindeer population in 1941–1942
- carrying capacity—maximum population of a particular species that the habitat can support

Summary

Reindeer were introduced to St. Paul's Island, a small island in the Bering Sea, in 1911. The reindeer population increased for 26 years but then exceeded the carrying capacity of the habitat. Reindeer were extinct by 1950 due to a lack of food.

EXAMPLE

7. REST can also be used as a note-taking strategy when students first hear a lecture or a class discussion. Students using REST to take notes from a class discussion should record notes on the right half of the sheet of paper. When they edit their notes, they should add questions and notes on the left half of the paper to direct their reading. After reading the textbook passage, students should synthesize both of the sources by writing a summary at the bottom of the page. The example on the website shows notes taken from a lecture and class discussion on the right side of the paper and notes and questions about a future reading assignment on the left side.

CHAPTER 8
SECTION 8.5
web resources
REST English Example, 13

Section **8.5** INSTRUCTIONAL STRATEGY 20

Cornell Note-Taking

Cornell Note-Taking (Pauk, 1974) is similar to the REST strategy (see Instructional Strategy 19) in that it is a two-column note-taking strategy. With Cornell Note-Taking, however, notes from textbook reading or class discussions are written on the right side of the page, and key words that organize the notes are written on the left. Cornell Note-Taking is an excellent strategy for topics that can be organized with main ideas and details as opposed to cause-effect and problem-solution structures.

Directions

1. Tell students that you will be demonstrating a note-taking strategy that can help them study and learn content information. Use an example from your content area or use the following example to model Cornell Note-Taking.

2. Identify a topic that would be organized with the structure of main idea-details. Be sure students understand this type of text structure. Conduct a class discussion or have students read a passage from a textbook about the topic.

3. Distribute sheets of paper that have a vertical line drawn approximately three inches from the left side of the paper or use the reproducible found on the website. Tell students that they should take detailed notes about the topic of the reading assignment or class discussion by writing their notes on the right side of the sheet of paper as in the following example.

Literature

Cornell Note-Taking

Key words	Notes from reading or class discussion
	■ literature in early 20th century
	■ depict life as it is: brutal, difficult
	■ expansion of West, after Civil War
	■ growth of industry
	■ books increased
	■ Stephen Crane (1871–1900)
	■ "An Episode of War"
	"The Open Boat"
	The Red Badge of Courage

E X A M P L E

4. Divide the class into groups of three or four students. Have students share the notes they wrote on the right half of the paper. Then ask students to generate ideas for key words to write on the left side of the paper.

5. Tell students to independently decide which key terms would be appropriate to write on the left side of their notes, as the following example illustrates.

CHAPTER 8

SECTION 8.5

web resources

Cornell Note-Taking
Reproducible, 14
Science Example, 15

Literature

Cornell Note-Taking

Key words	Notes from reading or class discussion
Realism in literature	■ literature in early 20th century
Historical factors	■ depict life as it is: brutal, difficult
	■ expansion of West, after Civil War
	■ growth of industry
	■ books increased
Crane's works	■ Stephen Crane (1871–1900)
	■ "An Episode of War"
	"The Open Boat"
	The Red Badge of Courage

E X A M P L E

Section **8.5** INSTRUCTIONAL STRATEGY 21

Power Notes

Power Notes (Santa, Havens, & Maycumber, 1996) is a note-taking strategy for students to use with assigned readings. Similar to outlining, the Power Notes strategy requires students to organize information in a hierarchical manner. Power Notes, however, are simpler for students to use because they do not require a complicated coding system. With Power Notes, students analyze the text and then code a main idea or topic with a "1," a detail with a "2," and an example with a "3." Once students have constructed their Power Notes, they can use them for studying or for developing a written paper. Encourage your students to use Power Notes to code main ideas, supporting details, and examples.

Power Notes

1. Main Idea or Topic
   2. Detail
   2. Detail
      3. Example
   2. Detail
      3. Example
      3. Example
1. Main Idea or Topic
   2. Detail
      3. Example

Directions

1. Tell students that good readers analyze the text as they read. Explain that analyzing the text will help them organize the content and improve their understanding of the text.

2. Explain that the Power Notes strategy is a systematic way for them to organize the information from the text. Introduce the idea that Power Notes will allow them to take charge of the information in the text.

3. Model the Power Notes strategy using an example from your content area or use the visual arts example provided on the website.

4. Have students practice analyzing and organizing information from your content area. One suggestion is to select the key concepts and vocabulary terms from a current area of study. Create sets of note cards with these concepts and vocabulary terms. In cooperative learning groups, ask students to analyze the note cards and organize them by power levels. Prompt students to discuss the concepts and related vocabulary terms. By organizing and discussing the note cards by power levels, students will be rehearsing (studying) the content. Next, instruct students to write a set of Power Notes on their own paper for further review.

5. After students are comfortable with the format of the Power Notes, direct them to create Power Notes for an assigned reading. Remind students that making and reviewing Power Notes will help them organize information and improve their understanding of the content.

6. In addition to being a study strategy, help students understand that Power Notes are useful for developing an organized written assignment.

SECTION **8.5**

CHAPTER 8 | web resources

Power Notes Visual Arts Example, 16

Section **8.5** INSTRUCTIONAL STRATEGY 22

Double Entry Diary

Double Entry Diary (Tovani, 2000) guides students to monitor their understanding of text using a two-column format similar to Cornell Note-Taking (see Instructional Strategy 20). This strategy provides students with a framework for responding to assigned reading when marking the text is not an option. According to Gomez and Gomez (2007), double entry note-taking has been used successfully to help high school science students rework their texts and improve their understanding of science. First, students select and note specific passages from the text in the left-hand column of their paper. Then they react and record their responses to the passage in the right-hand column of their paper. The Double Entry Diary is a versatile study tool that can be used for questioning, clarifying ideas, determining importance, making inferences, and recording other thoughts.

Directions

1. Tell students that successful readers think about the text as they read. Explain that you are going to share an instructional strategy that gives them a structure for their thinking.

2. Explain that the Double Entry Diary strategy is a note-taking strategy that helps students to structure their thinking. Tell students that it is a two-column note-taking format that will help them monitor their learning.

3. Introduce the Double Entry Diary strategy. Duplicate and distribute the Double Entry Diary reproducible that can be found on the website. Alternatively, you can direct students to fold a piece of notebook paper in half lengthwise.

4. Explain that a Double Entry Diary consists of two columns. In the left column, students note specific information from the text, such as a direct quote or a summary. In the right column, students record their critical thoughts or inferences about the information. Explain that the right column provides students with space to make conscious connections with the text.

5. Model the Double Entry Diary strategy using an example from your content area or use the language arts or social studies examples found on the website.

6. Focus on one comprehension skill (questioning, clarifying ideas, determining importance, making inferences) at a time. Student responses can be elicited with prompts such as:

   This reminds me of . . .
   I wonder . . .
   I think . . .
   This is important because . . .
   This confuses me because . . .

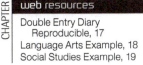

CHAPTER 8

SECTION 8.5

web resources

Double Entry Diary
   Reproducible, 17
Language Arts Example, 18
Social Studies Example, 19

7. Prompt students to use the Double Entry Diary strategy when studying or reading challenging text.

Readers Needing Additional Support

> Give students who struggle with text opportunities to identify and note important information in text. Provide photocopies of the text and encourage them to highlight or mark important information. Have partners discuss the information they identified. Ask students to write down the important information and supporting details using one of the note-taking strategies (e.g., Cornell Note-Taking). After students complete their note-taking, encourage them to use their notes for studying the content.

SURF THE WEB

DEVELOPING AN OUTLINE
Online Writing Lab (OWL) at Purdue University provides resources to support the development of an outline. Resources include an online handout and a sample outline.
   http://owl.english.purdue.edu/owl/resource/544/1/

NOTE MAKING
The note making section of Jim Burke's website, englishcompanion.com, is a user-friendly resource for teachers and students. The site includes a variety of note making formats and examples.
   http://www.englishcompanion.com/Tools/notemaking.html

INSPIRATION SOFTWARE
Inspiration software allows teachers and students to create graphic organizers such as concept maps and flow charts. This unique program uses multiple modes—visual diagrams and outlines.
   www.inspiration.com

Simple Concept Map

Goal: *To help students learn how to take notes from texts.* Taking notes can help students study and remember important information. When teachers prompt students to take notes as they read content area text, they provide a vehicle for students to process content information. To assess students' prior knowledge of note taking, prompt students to share their experiences with note taking using a Simple Concept Map. Prior to instruction on note taking or a note-taking strategy, have students write the word "note taking" in the center of a sheet of paper (8.5 x 11). Then, ask them to share their previous experiences with note taking by building a Simple Concept Map from the word "note taking." After students have created a Simple Concept Map about note taking, ask students to share their note-taking experiences and concept maps in small groups (three to four students). Once students have shared, collect and review their concept maps to determine the extent of their experiences with note taking. Use this information when planning the instruction of note-taking strategies. After teaching one or more of the note-taking strategies, repeat the Simple Concept Map activity. Compare students' experiences and understanding before and after instruction. As time permits, invite students to compare their two concept maps.

Activities *and* Journal Entries *for* Teacher Educators

Activities

1. In small content area disciplinary groups, have students think about learning to study in their discipline. As part of this discussion, ask students to collaborate on the development of a two-column note-taking chart that compares study strategies that helped them learn disciplinary content with study strategies they would consider teaching their students. In the left-hand column, have students list "Study Strategies Used" to help them learn content information. In the right-hand column, have students list "Study Strategies to Consider." Tell students to be prepared to explain their reasons for listing strategies in the "Study Strategies to Consider" column. After completing the two-column note-taking chart, invite the students to share their charts with the other disciplinary groups. Once all the groups have shared, post their charts where they can be viewed by the entire class. Then, invite students to look across the charts and discuss the similarities and differences noted by the disciplinary groups.

2. Tell students that they are going to engage in some collaborative brainstorming to explore ways to promote study groups in the disciplines. To begin, encourage students to recall a time when they engaged in a study group. Ask them to think about how this study group functioned, and what made it successful or problematic. Then, in pairs, have students note their prior experience with study groups, including what made the study group successful or problematic, on a sheet of paper. Once students have completed their collaborative brainstorm, ask them to select an item from their brainstorm to share with the entire class. After the pairs have shared, discuss ways that the students can help their students develop successful study groups.

3. Tell students that they are going to engage in a modified jigsaw activity to examine the note-taking strategies presented in the text. Divide the class into five interdisciplinary groups. Give each group a sheet of chart paper that is titled with one of the following note-taking strategies: Note Cue Cards, Read-Edit-Synthesize-Think, Cornell Note-Taking, Power Notes, and Double Entry Diary. As members of an interdisciplinary group, have students review and discuss the text pages associated with their assigned note-taking strategy. Tell them to prepare a chart that includes 1) a description of the note-taking strategy, 2) an example of the strategy, and 3) an explanation of when to use the strategy. Once the groups have completed their charts, provide class time for them to teach their peers about the note-taking strategy. Then, post the charts where they can be viewed by the entire class.

Journal Entries

1. How is studying different from other reading strategies?

2. Why is it essential for students to learn how to study in your discipline?

3. How do you plan to make study strategies that support students' ability to learn content information an integral part of your discipline?

References

Agnew, M. L. (2000). DRAW: A motivational reading comprehension strategy for disaffected readers. *Journal of Adolescent & Adult Literacy, 43,* 574–576.

Ajayi, L. (2009). English as a second language learners' exploration of multimodal texts in a junior high school. *Journal of Adolescent & Adult Literacy, 52,* 585–595.

Alexander, S. (1997). Nadia the willful. *The language of literature* (pp. 23–27). Evanston, IL: McDougal Littell.

Allan, C. B., & Lutz, W. (2000). *Life without bread: How a low-carbohydrate diet can save your life.* Los Angeles: Keats.

Allen, J. (1999). *Words, words, words: Teaching vocabulary in grades 4–12.* York, ME: Stenhouse.

Allgood, W. P., Risko, V. J., Alvarez, M. C., & Fairbanks, M. M. (2002). Factors that influence study. In R. F. Flippo & D. C. Caverly (Eds.), *Handbook of college reading and study strategy research* (pp. 201–219). Mahwah, NJ: Erlbaum.

Allington, R. L. (2002). You can't learn much from books you can't read. *Educational Leadership, 30*(3), 16–19.

Almasi, J. (2003). *Teaching strategic processes in reading.* New York: Guilford Press.

Alvermann, D. E. (1991). The discussion web: A graphic aid for learning across the curriculum. *The Reading Teacher, 45,* 92–99.

American Institutes for Research. (2005). *Reading framework for the 2009 National Assessment of Educational Progress: Pre-publication edition.* Washington, DC: Author.

Anderson, T. H., & Armbruster, B. B. (1984). Studying. In P. D. Pearson (Ed.), *Handbook of reading research* (Vol. I) (pp. 657–679). New York: Longman.

Angelo, T. A., & Cross, P. K. (1993). *Classroom assessment techniques: A handbook for college teachers* (2nd ed.). San Francisco: Jossey-Bass.

Antes, R. L. (1989). *Preparing students for taking tests* (Fastback 291). Bloomington, IN: Phi Delta Kappa Educational Foundation.

Anzaldua, G. (1993). *Friends from the other side: Amigos del otro lado.* San Francisco: Children's Book Press.

Argueta, J. (2001). *A movie in my pillow: Una pelicula en mi almohada.* San Francisco: Children's Book Press.

Armbruster, B. B. (1984). The problem of inconsiderate text. In G. Duffy, L. Roehler, & J. Mason (Eds.), *Comprehension instruction* (pp. 128–143). New York: Longman.

Armbruster, B. B. (1986, December). *Using frames to organize expository text.* Paper presented at the annual meeting of the National Reading Conference, Austin, TX.

Armbruster, B. B., & Anderson, T. H. (1988). On selecting "considerate" content area textbooks. *Remedial and Special Education, 9*(1), 47–52.

Armbruster, B. B., & Anderson, T. H. (1995). Producing "considerate" expository text: Or easy reading is damned hard writing. *Journal of Curriculum Studies, 17,* 247–274.

Artley, A. S. (1975). Teaching word meaning through context. *Elementary English Review, 20,* 68–74.

Ash, G. E. (2005). What did Abigail mean? *Educational Leadership, 63*(2), 36–41.

Au, K. H. (1993). *Literacy instruction in multicultural settings.* Fort Worth, TX: Harcourt Brace Jovanovich.

Baker, L., & Brown, A. (1984). Metacognitive skills and reading. In P. D. Pearson (Ed.), *Handbook of reading research* (Vol. I) (pp. 353–394). New York: Longman.

Balcells, J. (1997). The enchanted raisin. *The language of literature* (pp. 347–354). Evanston, IL: McDougal Littell.

Banks, J. A., & Banks, C. A. M. (2001). *Multicultural education: Issues and perspectives* (4th ed.). New York: Wiley.

Barry, A. L. (2002). Reading strategies teachers say they use. *Journal of Adolescent & Adult Literacy, 46,* 132–141.

Baumann, J. F., & Kame'enui, E. J. (1991). Research on vocabulary instruction: Ode to Voltaire. In J. Flood, J. Jensen, D. Lapp, & J. Squire (Eds.), *Handbook of research on teaching the English language arts* (pp. 604–632). New York: Macmillan.

Baumann, J. F., Kame'enui, E. J., & Ash, G. E. (2003). Research on vocabulary instruction: Voltaire redux. In J. Flood, D. Lapp, J. R. Squire, & J. M. Jensen (Eds.), *Handbook of research on the teaching of the English language arts* (2nd ed.) (pp. 752–785). Mahwah, NJ: Erlbaum.

Beach, R., & O'Brien, D. (2007). Adopting reader and writer stances in understanding and producing texts. In L. S. Rush, A. J. Eakle, & A. Berger (Eds.), *Secondary school literacy* (pp. 217–242). Urbana, IL: National Council of Teachers of English.

Bean, T. W. (2000). Reading in the content areas: Social constructivist dimensions. In M. L. Kamil, P. B. Mosenthal, P. D. Pearson, & R. Barr (Eds.), *Handbook of reading research* (Vol. III) (pp. 629–644). Mahwah, NJ: Erlbaum.

Bean, T. W., & Moni, K. (2003). Developing students' critical literacy: Exploring identity construction in young adult fiction. *Journal of Adolescent & Adult Literacy, 46,* 638–648.

Bean, T. W., Readence, J. E., & Baldwin, R. S. (2008). *Content area literacy: An integrated approach* (9th ed.). Dubuque, IA: Kendall Hunt.

Bean, T. W., Sorter, J., Singer, H., & Frazee, C. (1986). Teaching students how to make predictions about events in history with a graphic organizer plus options guide. *Journal of Reading, 29,* 739–745.

Beck, I. L., & McKeown, M. G. (2006). *Improving reading comprehension with Questioning the author: A fresh and expanded view of a powerful approach*. New York: Scholastic.

Beck, I. L., McKeown, M. G., Hamilton, R. L., & Kucan, L. (1997). *Questioning the author: An approach for enhancing student engagement with text*. Newark, DE: International Reading Association.

Beck, I. L., McKeown, M. G., & Kucan, L. (2002). *Bringing words to life: Robust vocabulary instruction*. New York: Guilford Press.

Beers, K. (2003). *When kids can't read: What teachers can do*. Portsmouth, NH: Heinemann.

Benne, B. (1988). *Waspleg and other mnemonics: Easy ways to remember hard things*. Dallas, TX: Taylor.

Berglund, R. L., & Johns, J. L. (1983). A primer on uninterrupted sustained silent reading. *The Reading Teacher, 36,* 534–539.

Biancarosa, C., & Snow, C. E. (2006). *Reading next—A vision for action and research in middle and high school literacy: A report to Carnegie Corporation of New York* (2nd ed.). Washington, DC: Alliance for Excellent Education.

Blachowicz, C. L. Z. (1986). Making connections: Alternatives to the vocabulary notebook. *Journal of Reading, 29,* 543–549.

Blachowicz, C. L. Z., & Fisher, P. (2000). Vocabulary instruction. In M. L. Kamil, P. B. Mosenthal, P. D. Pearson, & R. Barr (Eds.), *Handbook of reading research* (Vol. III) (pp. 503–523). Mahwah, NJ: Erlbaum.

Blachowicz, C. L. Z., & Fisher, P. (2004). Putting the fun back in fundamental: Word play in the classroom. In J. F. Baumann & E. J. Kame'enui (Eds.), *Vocabulary instruction: Research to practice* (pp. 218–237). New York: Guilford Press.

Blachowicz, C. L. Z., & Fisher, P. (2006). *Teaching vocabulary in all classrooms* (3rd ed.). Upper Saddle River, NJ: Prentice Hall.

Blachowicz, C. L. Z., & Ogle, D. (2001). *Reading comprehension: Strategies for independent learners*. New York: Guilford Press.

Block, C. C., & Pressley, M. (Eds.). (2002). *Comprehension instruction: Research-based best practices*. New York: Guilford Press.

Block, C. C., & Pressley, M. (2003). Best practices in comprehension instruction. In L. M. Morrow, L. B. Gambrell, & M. Pressley (Eds.), *Best practices in literacy instruction* (2nd ed.) (pp. 111–126). New York: Guilford Press.

Bloom, B. S. (Ed.). (1956). *Taxonomy of educational objectives. Handbook I: Cognitive domain*. New York: David McKay.

Bloome, D., & Egan-Robertson, A. (1993). The social construction of intertextuality in classroom reading and writing lessons. *Reading Research Quarterly, 28,* 304–333.

Bluestein, N. A. (2010). Unlocking text features for determining importance in expository text: A strategy for struggling readers. *The Reading Teacher, 63,* 597–600.

Blum, R. (2010, June 13). U.S. beats England, 1–1. *The Columbian.*

Boslough, J. (1985). *Stephen Hawking's universe*. New York: Avon Books.

Bourdieu, P., & Passeron, J. C. (1977). *Reproduction in education, society and culture*. Los Angeles: Sage.

Boyd, F. B., & Ikpeze, C. H. (2007). Navigating a literacy landscape: Teaching conceptual understanding with multiple text types. *Journal of Literacy Research, 39,* 217–248.

Brashares, A. (2001). *The sisterhood of the traveling pants*. New York: Delacorte.

Brine, M. D. (1995). Somebody's mother. In E. H. Sword & V. McCarthy (Eds.), *A child's anthology of poetry* (p. 16). New York: Harper Collins.

Brookhart, S. (2010). *Assess higher-order thinking skills in your classroom*. Alexandria, VA: Association for Supervision and Curriculum Development.

Brophy, J. (1986). Teacher influences on student achievement. *American Psychologist, 41,* 1069–1077.

Brown, A. L. (1997). Transforming schools into communities of thinking and learning about serious matters. *American Psychologist, 52,* 399–414.

Brown, A. L., & Palincsar, A. S. (1984). Reciprocal teaching of comprehension: Fostering and monitoring activities. *Cognition and Instruction, 1,* 117–175.

Brown, R. (2005). Seventh-graders' self-regulatory note-taking from text: Perceptions, preferences, and practices. *Reading Research and Instruction, 44*(4), 1–21.

Browne, A. (1986). *Piggybook*. New York: Alfred A. Knopf.

Brozo, W. G., & Simpson, M. L. (1995). *Readers, teachers, learners: Expanding literacy in secondary schools* (2nd ed.). Columbus, OH: Merrill.

Brozo, W. G., & Simpson, M. L. (1999). *Readers, teachers, learners: Expanding literacy across the content areas* (3rd ed.). Upper Saddle River, NJ: Prentice-Hall.

Buehl, D. (2001). *Classroom strategies for interactive learning* (2nd ed.). Newark, DE: International Reading Association.

Buehl, D. (2009). *Classroom strategies for interactive learning* (3rd ed.). Newark, DE: International Reading Association.

Burke, J. (2001). Making notes, making meaning. *Voices from the Middle, 9*(4), 15–21.

Burke, J. (2002). *Tools for thought: Graphic organizers for your classroom*. Portsmouth, NH: Heinemann.

Burns, R. (1995). My heart's in the highlands, my heart is not here. In E. H. Sword & V. McCarthy (Eds.), *A child's anthology of poetry* (p. 42). New York: Harper Collins.

Capote, T. (1994). Miriam. *Literature & language*. Evanston, IL: McDougal Littell.

Carman, R. A., & Adams, W. R. (1972). *Study skills: A student's guide to survival*. New York: Wiley.

Carnegie Council on Advancing Adolescent Literacy. (2010). *Time to act: An agenda for advancing adolescent literacy for college and career success*. New York: Carnegie Corporation of New York.

Carr, K. S., Buchanan, D. L., Wentz, J. B., Weiss, M. L., & Grant, K. J. (2001). Not just for the primary grades: A bibliography of picture books for secondary content teachers. *Journal of Adolescent & Adult Literacy, 45,* 146–153.

Carroll, L. (1871). *The walrus and the carpenter.* Reprinted from *The hunting of the snark and other poems and verses.* New York: Harper & Brothers, 1903.

Carroll, L. (1871). *Through the looking glass, and what Alice found there.* New York: Random House.

Cartwright, K. B. (2009). The role of cognitive flexibility in reading comprehension: Past, present, and future. In S. E. Israel & G. G. Duffy (Eds.), *Handbook of research on reading comprehension* (pp. 115–139). New York: Routledge.

Cassidy, J., Valadez, C. M., Garrett, S. D., & Barrera, E. S. (2010). Adolescent and adult literacy: What's hot, what's not. *Journal of Adolescent & Adult Literacy, 53,* 448–456.

Caverly, D. C., Mandeville, T. F., & Nicholson, S. A. (1995). PLAN: A study-reading strategy for informational text. *Journal of Adolescent & Adult Literacy, 39,* 190–199.

Champe, P. C., Harvey, R. A., & Ferrier, D. R. (2005). *Biochemistry* (3rd ed.). New York: Lippincott Williams & Wilkins.

Chapman, C., & King, R. (2003). *Differentiated instructional strategies for reading in the content areas.* Thousand Oaks, CA: Corwin.

Cheney, L. (2005). *A time for freedom.* New York: Simon & Schuster.

Christensen, L. (2000). *Reading, writing, and rising up: Teaching about social justice and the power of the written word.* Milwaukee, WI: Rethinking Schools.

Christensen, L. (2009). *Teaching for joy and justice.* Milwaukee, WI: Rethinking Schools.

Chun, C. W. (2009). Critical literacies and graphic novels for English-Language Learners: Teaching *Maus. Journal of Adolescent & Adult Literacy, 53,* 144–153.

Ciardiello, A. V. (2007). *Puzzle them first! Motivating adolescent readers with question-finding.* Newark, DE: International Reading Association.

Coiro, J., & Dobler, E. (2007). Exploring the online reading comprehension strategies used by sixth-grade skilled readers to search for and locate information on the internet. *Reading Research Quarterly, 4,* 214–257.

Collins, B. (2002). *Sailing alone around the room.* New York: Random House.

Collins, J. L. (1998). *Strategies for struggling writers.* New York: Guilford Press.

Comber, B. (2001). Classroom explorations in critical literacy. In H. Fehring & P. Green (Eds.), *Critical literacy: A collection of articles from the Australian Literacy Educators' Association* (pp. 90–102). Newark, DE, and South Australia, Australia: International Reading Association and Australian Literacy Educators' Association.

Common Core Standards Initiative. (2010). Retrieved October 1, 2010, from http://www.corestandards.org/

Costello, B., & Kolodziej, N. J. (2006). A middle school teacher's guide for selecting picture books. *Middle School Journal, 38*(1), 27–33.

Countryman, J. (1992). *Writing to learn mathematics.* Portsmouth, NH: Heinemann.

Courtney, G. (2003). *Vocabulary acquisition.* St Charles, IL: Author.

Crawley, S. J., & Mountain, L. (1995). *Strategies for guiding content reading* (2nd ed.). Boston: Allyn & Bacon.

Credé, M., & Kuncel, N. R. (2008). Study habits, skills, and attitudes. The third pillar supporting collegiate academic performance. *Perspectives on Psychological Science, 3,* 415–453.

Cronin, D. (2000). *Click, clack, moo: Cows that type.* New York: Simon & Schuster.

Cummings, e. e. (1995). maggie and milly and molly and may. In E. H. Sword & V. McCarthy (Eds.), *A child's anthology of poetry* (p. 62). New York: Harper Collins.

Cummins, J. (1979). Cognitive academic language proficiency, linguistic interdependence, the optimum age question and some other matters. *Working Papers on Bilingualism, 19,* 121–129.

Cunningham, A. E. (2005). Vocabulary growth through independent reading and reading aloud to children. In E. H. Hiebert & M. L. Kamil (Eds.), *Teaching and learning vocabulary: Bringing research to practice* (pp. 45–68). Mahwah, NJ: Erlbaum.

Cunningham, J. W. (1982). Generating interactions between schemata and text. In J. A. Niles & L. A. Harris (Eds.), *New inquiries in reading research and instruction.* Thirty-first yearbook of the National Reading Conference (pp. 42–47). Rochester, NY: National Reading Conference.

Cunningham, P. M. (2000a). Big words for big kids: The morphology link to meaning and decoding. In K. D. Wood & T. S. Dickinson (Eds.), *Promoting literacy in grades 4–9: A handbook for teachers and administrators* (pp. 282–294). Boston: Allyn & Bacon.

Cunningham, P. M. (2000b). *Phonics they use* (3rd ed.). New York: Longman.

Cunningham, P. M. (2006). What if they can say the words but don't know what they mean? *The Reading Teacher, 59,* 708–711.

Cunningham, P. M., & Hall, D. P. (1994). *Making big words: Multilevel, hands-on spelling and phonics activities.* Torrance, CA: Good Apple.

Cunningham, P. M., & Hall, D. P. (1997). *Making more big words: Multilevel, hands-on phonics and spelling activities* (2nd ed.). Parsippany, NJ: Good Apple.

Curran, M. J., & Smith, E. C. (2005). The Imposter: A motivational strategy to encourage reading in adolescents. *Journal of Adolescent & Adult Literacy, 49,* 186–190.

Curtis, A. (2003). *Word smart for the GRE.* New York: Random House.

Damico, J., Baidon, M., Exter, M., & Guo, S. J. (2009/2010). Where we read from matters: Disciplinary literacy in a ninth-grade social studies classroom. *Journal of Adolescent & Adult Literacy, 53*, 325–335.

Dana, C., & Rodriguez, M. (1992). TOAST: A system to study vocabulary. *Reading Research and Instruction, 31*, 78–84.

Daniel, M. (2006, Feb.). *Taking all children to the head of the class: Bilingual learners explore cultural nuances in text.* Paper presented at the National Association of Bilingual Education Annual Conference, Phoenix, AZ.

Daniel, M., & Lenski, S. (2007). The importance of critical literacy for English Language Learners. *Illinois Reading Council Journal, 35*(2), 32–36.

Davis, S. J. (1990). Applying content study skills in co-listed reading classrooms. *Journal of Reading, 33*, 277–281.

Deighton, L. C. (1959). *Vocabulary development in the classroom.* New York: Teachers College Press.

Delpit, L. (1992). Education in a multicultural society: Our future's greatest challenge. *Journal of Negro Education, 61*, 237–249.

Denner, P. R., McGinley, W. J., & Brown, E. (1989). The effects of story-impressions as a prereading/writing activity on story comprehension. *Journal of Educational Research, 82*, 320–326.

Denti, L., & Guerin, G. (2004). Confronting the problem of poor literacy: Recognition and action. *Reading & Writing Quarterly, 20*, 113–122.

Deshler, D. D., Palincsar, A. S., Biancarosa, G., & Nair, M. (2007). *Informed choices for struggling adolescent readers: A research-based guide to instructional programs and practices.* Newark, DE: International Reading Association.

Deshler, D. D., Schumaker, J. B., Lenz, B. K., Bulgren, J. A., Hock, M. E., Knight, J., & Ehren, B. (2001). Ensuring content area learning by secondary students with learning disabilities. *Learning Disabilities Research & Practice, 16*(2), 96–108.

deTrevino, E. B. (1989). The secret of the wall. *The language of literature* (pp. 390–401). Evanston, IL: McDougal Littell.

Donovan, M. S., & Bransford, J. D. (2005). Introduction. In M. S. Donovan & J. D. Bransford (Eds.), *How students learn: History, mathematics, and science in the classroom* (pp. 1–28). Washington, DC: National Academies Press.

Dowhower, S. (1989). Repeated reading: Research into practice. *The Reading Teacher, 42*, 502–507.

Draper, R. J., Smith, L. K., Hall, K. M., & Siebert, D. (2005). What's more important—literacy or content? Confronting the literacy-content dualism. *Action in Teacher Education, 27*(3), 12–21.

Duffy, G. G. (2002). The case for direct explanation of strategies. In C. C. Block & M. Pressley (Eds.), *Comprehension instruction: Research-based best practices* (pp. 28–41). New York: Guilford Press.

Duke, N. K. (2000). 3–6 minutes per day: The scarcity of informational texts in first grade. *Reading Research Quarterly, 35*, 202–224.

Duke, N. K., & Pearson, P. D. (2002). Effective practices for developing reading comprehension. In A. E. Farstrup & S. J. Samuels (Eds.), *What research has to say about reading instruction* (3rd ed.) (pp. 204–242). Newark, DE: International Reading Association.

Eanet, M., & Manzo, A. V. (1976). REAP—A strategy for improving reading/writing/study skills. *Journal of Reading, 19*, 647–652.

Edmonds, M. S., Vaughn, S., Wexler, J., Reutebuch, C., Cable, A., Tackett, K. K., & Schnakenberg, J. W. (2009). A synthesis of reading interventions and effects on reading comprehension outcomes for older struggling readers. *Review of Educational Research, 79*, 262–300.

Edmunds, K. M., & Bauserman, K. L. (2006). What teachers can learn about reading motivation through conversations with children. *The Reading Teacher, 59*, 414–424.

Edwards, E. C., Font, G., Baumann, J. F., & Boland, E. (2004). Unlocking word meanings: Strategies and guidelines for teaching morphemic and contextual analysis. In J. F. Baumann & E. J. Kame'enui (Eds.), *Vocabulary instruction: Research to practice* (pp. 159–176). New York: Guilford Press.

Eeds, M., & Cockrum, W. A. (1985). Teaching word meaning by expanding schemata vs. dictionary work vs. reading in context. *Journal of Reading, 28*, 492–497.

Ehlers-Zavala, F. (2008). Teaching adolescent English language learners. In S. Lenski & J. Lewis (Eds.), *Reading success for struggling adolescent learners* (pp. 74–89). New York: Guilford Press.

Ehrenreich, B. (2001). *Nickel and dimed: On (not) getting by in America.* New York: Metropolitan Books.

Eugenides, J. (2002). *Middlesex.* New York: Pecador.

Fang, Z. (2008). Going beyond the Fab Five: Helping students cope with the unique linguistic challenges of expository reading in intermediate grades. *Journal of Adolescent & Adult Literacy, 51*, 476–487.

Fehring, H., & Green, P. (Eds.). (2001). *Critical literacy.* Newark, DE, and South Australia, Australia: International Reading Association and Australian Literacy Educators' Association.

Ferroli, L., Beaver, K., Hagan, R., & Moriarty, A. (2000, March). *Interventions for getting middle school readers caught up.* Presentation at the 32nd Illinois Reading Council Conference, Springfield, IL.

Ferroli, L., Cooper, L., & Zimmerman, L. (2001, March). *The compare-contrast procedure in word identification.* Presentation at the 33rd Illinois Reading Council Conference, Springfield, IL.

Fillmore, L. W. (2005, January). *Changing times, changing schools: Articulating leadership choices in educating bilingual students.* Paper presented at the annual meeting of the National Association for Bilingual Education, San Antonio, TX.

Fisher, D., & Frey, N. (2004). *Improving adolescent literacy: Strategies at work.* Upper Saddle River, NJ: Merrill Prentice Hall.

Fisher, D., & Frey, N. (2008). Student and teacher perspectives on the usefulness of content literacy strategies. *Literacy Research and Instruction, 47*, 246–263.

Fisher, D., & Ivey, G. (2005). Literacy and language as learning in content-area classes: A departure from "every teacher a teacher of reading." *Action in Teacher Education, 27*(2), 3–11.

Fisher, J. B., Schumaker, J. B., & Deshler, D. D. (2002). Improving the reading comprehension of at-risk adolescents. In C. C. Block & M. Pressley (Eds.), *Comprehension instruction: Research-based best practices* (pp. 351–364). New York: Guilford Press.

Flanigan, K., & Greenwood, S. C. (2007). Effective content vocabulary instruction in the middle: Matching students, purposes, words and strategies. *Journal of Adolescent & Adult Literacy, 51*, 226–238.

Flood, J., & Lapp, D. (1995). Broadening the lens: Toward an expanded conceptualization of literacy. In K. A. Hinchman, D. J. Leu, & C. K. Kinzer (Eds.), *Perspectives on literacy research and practice* (pp. 1–16). Chicago: National Reading Conference.

Flood, J., Lapp, D., & Fisher, D. (2002). Parsing, questioning, and rephrasing (PQR): Building syntactic knowledge to improve reading comprehension. In C. C. Block, L. B. Gambrell, & M. Pressley (Eds.), *Improving comprehension instruction: Rethinking research, theory, and classroom practice* (pp. 181–198). San Francisco: Jossey-Bass.

Fractor, J. S., Woodruff, M. C., Martinez, M. G., & Teale, W. (1993). Let's not miss opportunities to promote voluntary reading: Classroom libraries in the elementary school. *The Reading Teacher, 46*, 476–484.

Frank, A. (1995). *Anne Frank: Diary of a young girl*. New York: Doubleday.

Franzak, J. K. (2006). Zoom: A review of the literature on marginalized adolescent readers, literacy theory, and policy implications. *Review of Educational Research, 76*(2), 209–248.

Freire, P. (1970). *Pedagogy of the oppressed*. New York: Continuum International.

Freire, P. (1985). *The politics of education: Culture power, and liberation*. New York: Bergin & Garvey.

Freire, P., & Macedo, D. (1995). A dialogue—Culture, language and race. *Harvard Educational Review, 65*, 377–402.

French, F. (1986). *Snow White in New York*. New York: Oxford University Press.

Friend, J. (2001). Teaching summarization as a content area reading strategy. *Journal of Adolescent & Adult Literacy, 44*, 320–329.

Fry, E. (1968). A readability formula that saves time. *Journal of Reading, 11*, 513–516.

Fry, E. (1978). *Skimming and scanning*. Providence, RI: Jamestown.

Galica, G. S. (1991). *The blue book: A student's guide to essay examinations*. New York: Harcourt Brace Jovanovich.

Gambrell, L. B., Palmer, B. M., Codling, R. M., & Mazzoni, S. A. (1996). Assessing motivation to read. *The Reading Teacher, 49*, 518–533.

Garan, E. M., & DeVoogd, G. (2008). The benefits of Sustained Silent Reading: Scientific research and common sense converge. *The Reading Teacher, 62*, 336–344.

Garcia, G. E. (1991). Factors influencing the English reading test performance of Spanish speaking Hispanic students. *Reading Research Quarterly, 26*, 371–392.

Gardner, M. (1994). The dinner party. *The Saturday Review of Literature 25*. New York: General Media Communications.

Garrett, J. (2003). *The art of black & white photography*. New York: Sterling.

Gay, G. (2000). *Culturally responsive teaching: Theory, research & practice*. New York: Teachers College Press.

Gee, J. P. (1993). What is literacy? In L. M. Cleary & M. D. Linn (Eds.), *Linguistics for teachers* (pp. 257–265). New York: McGraw-Hill.

Gee, J. P. (2004). Language in the science classroom: Academic social languages as the heart of school-based literacy. In E. W. Saul (Ed.), *Crossing borders in literacy and science instruction: Perspectives on their practice* (pp. 13–32). Newark, DE, and Arlington, VA: International Reading Association and National Science Teachers Association.

Gee, J. P. (2005). *An introduction to discourse analysis: Theory and method* (2nd ed.). New York: Routledge.

Gere, A. R. (Ed.). (1985). *Roots in the sawdust: Writing to learn across the disciplines*. Urbana, IL: National Council of Teachers of English.

Gettinger, M., & Seibert, J. K. (2002). Contributions of study skill to academic competence. *School Psychology Review, 31*, 350–365.

Gilbert, P. (2001). (Sub)versions: Using sexist language practices to explore critical literacy. In H. Fehring & P. Green (Eds.), *Critical literacy: A collection of articles from the Australian Literacy Educators' Association* (pp. 75–83). Newark, DE, and South Australia, Australia: International Reading Association and Australian Literacy Educators' Association.

Gillet, J., & Kita, M. J. (1979). Words, kids, and categories. *The Reading Teacher, 32*, 538–546.

Gipe, J. P. (1979). Investigating techniques for teaching word meanings. *Reading Research Quarterly, 14*, 624–644.

Gipe, J. P. (2010). *Multiple paths to literacy: Assessment and differentiated instruction for diverse learners, K–12*. New York: Pearson.

Giroux, H., & McLaren, P. (1992). Writing from the margins: Geographies of identity, pedagogy, and power. *Journal of Education, 174*(1), 7–30.

Glencoe/McGraw-Hill. (2004). *Biology: The dynamics of life* [online student edition]. Retrieved January 30, 2006, from http://www.glencoe.com/sec/science/biology/bio2004

Gomez, L. M., & Gomez, K. (2007). Reading for learning: Literacy supports for 21st-century work. *Phi Delta Kappan, 89*, 224–228.

Grant, R. (1993). Strategic training for using text headings to improve students' processing of content. *Journal of Reading, 36*, 482–488.

Graves, M. F. (1986). Cost and benefits of different methods of vocabulary instruction. *Journal of Reading, 29*, 596–602.

Graves, M. F. (2006). *The vocabulary book: Learning & instruction*. New York: Teachers College Press.

Graves, M. F., Juel, C., & Graves, B. (2003). *Teaching reading in the 21st century* (3rd ed.) Boston: Allyn & Bacon.

Graves, M. F., & Prenn, M. C. (1986). Costs and benefits of various methods of teaching vocabulary. *Journal of Reading, 29*, 596–602.

Green, P. (2001). Critical literacy revisited. In H. Fehring & P. Green (Eds.), *Critical literacy: A collection of articles from the Australian Literacy Educators' Association* (pp. 7–14). Newark, DE, and Norwood, South Australia: International Reading Association and Australian Literacy Educators' Association.

Greenwood, S. C. (2004). *Words count: Effective vocabulary instruction in action.* Portsmouth, NH: Heinemann.

Greenwood, S. C. (2010). *The power of words.* Portsmouth, NH: Rowman & Littlefield Education.

Gunning, T. G. (2008). *Developing higher-level literacy in all students: Building reading, reasoning, and responding.* Boston: Allyn & Bacon.

Guthrie, J. T. (2004). Classroom contexts for engaged reading: An overview. In J. T. Guthrie, A. Wigfield, & K. C. Perencevich (Eds.), *Motivating reading comprehension: Concept-oriented reading instruction* (pp. 1–24). Mahwah, NJ: Erlbaum.

Guthrie, J. T., & Davis, M. H. (2003). Motivating struggling readers in middle school through an engagement model of classroom practice. *Reading & Writing Quarterly, 19,* 59–85.

Guthrie, J. T., Hoa, L. W., Wigfield, A., Tonks, S. M., Humenick, N. M., & Littles, E. (2007). Reading motivation and reading comprehension growth in later years. *Contemporary Educational Psychology, 32,* 282–313.

Guthrie, J. T., & Knowles, K. T. (2001). Promoting reading motivation. In L. Verhoeven & C. E. Snow (Eds.), *Literacy and motivation: Reading engagement in individuals and groups* (pp. 159–176). Mahwah, NJ: Erlbaum.

Guthrie, J. T., & Wigfield, A. (2000). Engagement and motivation in reading. In M. L. Kamil, P. B. Mosenthal, P. D. Pearson, & R. Barr (Eds.), *Handbook of reading research* (Vol. III) (pp. 403–422). Mahwah, NJ: Erlbaum.

Gutierrez, M. V. (2009/2010). "I thought this U.S. place was supposed to be about freedom": Young Latinas engage in mathematics and social change to save their school. *Rethinking Schools, 34*(2), 36–39.

Hackmann, D. G. (1997). *Student-led conferences at the middle level.* ERIC DIGEST. Champaign, IL: Clearinghouse on Elementary and Early Childhood Education.

Haggard, M. R. (1986). The vocabulary self-collection strategy: Using student interest and world knowledge to enhance vocabulary growth. *Journal of Reading, 29,* 634–642.

Hancock, D. R. (2001). Effects of test anxiety and evaluative threat on students' achievement and motivation. *Journal of Educational Research, 94,* 284–290.

Hansen, J. (2009). Multiple literacies in the content classroom: High school students' connections to U.S. history. *Journal of Adolescent & Adult Literacy, 52,* 597–606.

Harmon, J. M., Hedrick, W. B., & Wood, K. D. (2005). Research on vocabulary instruction in the content areas: Implications for struggling readers. *Reading & Writing Quarterly, 21,* 261–280.

Harris, T. L., & Hodges, R. E. (1995). *The literacy dictionary: The vocabulary of reading and writing.* Newark, DE: International Reading Association.

Hart, G. (2005). *James Monroe.* New York: Times Books/Henry Holt.

Hartman, D. K. (1995). Eight readers reading: The intertextual links of proficient readers reading multiple passages. *Reading Research Quarterly, 30,* 520–561.

Hayes, D. A. (1989). Helping students GRASP the knack of writing summaries. *Journal of Reading, 33,* 96–101.

Heffernan, L., & Lewison, M. (2005). What's lunch got to do with it? Critical literacy and the discourse of the lunchroom. *Language Arts, 83,* 107–117.

Heffernan, L., & Lewison, M. (2009). Keep your eyes on the prize: Critical stance in the middle school classroom. *Voices from the Middle, 17*(2), 19–27.

Hemmrich, H., Lim, W., & Neel, K. (1994). *Primetime!* Portsmouth, NH: Heinemann.

Herber, H. L. (1978). *Teaching reading in content areas* (2nd ed.). Englewood Cliffs, NJ: Prentice-Hall.

Herrell, A., & Jordan, M. (2002). *50 active learning strategies for improving reading comprehension.* Columbus, OH: Merrill Prentice Hall.

Herrera, S. G., Perez, D. R., & Escamilla, K. (2010). *Teaching reading to English language learners: Differentiated literacies.* Boston: Allyn & Bacon.

Hibbing, A. N., & Rankin-Erickson, J. L. (2003). A picture is worth a thousand words: Using visual images to improve comprehension for middle school struggling readers. *The Reading Teacher, 56,* 758–770.

Hidi, S., & Baird, W. (1988). Strategies for increasing text-based interest and students' recall of expository text. *Reading Research Quarterly, 23,* 465–483.

Hidi, S., & Renniger, K. A. (2006). The four-phase model of interest development. *Educational Psychologist, 41*(2), 111–127.

Hinton, S. E. (1967). *The outsiders.* New York: Puffin.

Hoffman, J. V. (1979). The intra-act procedure for critical reading. *Journal of Reading, 22,* 605–608.

Holdaway, D. (1979). *The foundations of literacy.* New York: Ashton Scholastic.

Hughes, C. A., & Deshler, D. D. (1993). Test-taking strategy instruction for adolescents with emotional and behavioral disorders. *Journal of Emotional & Behavioral Disorders, 1,* 189–198.

Hughes, C. A., & Schumacher, J. B. (1991). Test-taking strategy instruction for adolescents with learning disabilities. *Exceptionality, 2,* 205–216.

Hughes, C. A., Schumacher, J. B., Deshler, D. D., & Mercer, C. D. (1988). *The test-taking strategy.* Lawrence, KS: Edge Enterprises.

Hughes-Hassell, S., & Rodge, P. (2007). The leisure reading habits of urban adolescents. *Journal of Adolescent & Adult Literacy, 51,* 22–33.

Hunt, L. C., Jr. (1970). The effect of self-selection, interest, and motivation upon independent, instructional, and frustrational levels. *The Reading Teacher, 24,* 146–151, 158.

Illinois State Board of Education. (2010). Illinois Report Card. Retrieved August 10, 2010, from http://www.isbe.stateil.us/research/htmls/report_card.htm

International Reading Association & National Council of Teachers of English. (1996). *Standards for the English language arts.* Newark, DE, and Urbana, IL: Author.

Irwin, J., & Baker, I. (1989). *Promoting active reading comprehension strategies.* Englewood Cliffs, NJ: Prentice-Hall.

Ivey, G. (1999). Reflections on teaching struggling middle school readers. *Journal of Adolescent & Adult Literacy, 42,* 372–381.

Ivey, G., & Broaddus, K. (2000). Tailoring the fit: Reading instruction and middle school readers. *The Reading Teacher, 54,* 68–78.

Ivey, G., & Broaddus, K. (2001). "Just plain reading": A survey of what makes students want to read in middle school classrooms. *Reading Research Quarterly, 36,* 350–377.

Ivey, G., & Fisher, D. (2006). *Creating literacy-rich schools for adolescents.* Alexandria, VA: Association for Supervision and Curriculum Development.

Jackson, A. W., & Davis, G. A. (2000). *Turning points 2000: Educating adolescents in the 21st century.* New York: Teachers College Press.

Jackson, S. (1943). After you my dear Alphonse. *New Yorker Magazine.* New York: Conde Nast Publications.

Jacobs, V. A. (2008). Adolescent literacy: Putting the crisis in context. *Harvard Educational Review, 78*(1), 7–39.

Jacobson, J. M. (1998). *Content area reading: Integration with the language arts.* New York: Delmar.

Jeong, J., Gaffney, J. S., & Choi, J. O. (2010). Availability and use of informational texts in second-, third-, and fourth-grade classrooms. *Research in the Teaching of English, 44,* 435–456.

Jensen, E. (2009). *Teaching with poverty in mind.* Alexandria, VA: Association of Supervision and Curriculum Development.

Jiminez, R. J. (1997). The strategic reading abilities and potential of five low literacy Latina/o readers in middle school. *Reading Research Quarterly, 32,* 224–243.

Johns, A. (1997). *Text, role, and context: Developing academic literacies.* New York: Cambridge University Press.

Johns, J. L. (2008). *Basic reading inventory* (10th ed.). Dubuque, IA: Kendall Hunt.

Johns, J. L., & Lenski, S. D. (2010). *Improving reading: Interventions, strategies and resources* (5th ed.). Dubuque, IA: Kendall Hunt.

Johnson, D. D. (2001). *Vocabulary in the elementary and middle school.* Needham Heights, MA: Allyn & Bacon.

Johnson, D. D., & Pearson, P. D. (1984). *Teaching reading vocabulary* (2nd ed.). New York: Holt.

Johnson, G. B., & Raven, P. H. (2004). *Biology.* New York: Holt, Rinehart & Winston.

Johnson, H., & Freedman, L. (2005). *Developing critical awareness at the middle level.* Newark, DE: International Reading Association.

Kame'enui, E. J., Dixon, S. W., & Carnine, R. C. (1987). Issues in the design of vocabulary instruction. In M. G. McKeown & M. C. Curtis (Eds.), *The nature of vocabulary acquisition* (pp. 129–145). Hillsdale, NJ: Erlbaum.

Kamil, M. L. (2003). *Adolescents and literacy: Reading for the 21st century.* Washington, DC: Alliance for Excellent Education.

Kamil, M. L., Borman, G. D., Dole, J., Kral, C. C., Salinger, T., & Torgesen, J. (2008). *Improving adolescent literacy: Effective classroom and intervention practices: A practice guide* (NCEE #2008-4027). Washington, DC: National Center for Education Evaluation and Regional Assistance, Institute of Education Sciences, U.S. Department of Education.

Kane, S. (2007). Does The Imposter strategy pass the authenticity test? *Journal of Adolescent & Adult Literacy, 51*(1), 58–64.

Kasten, W., & Wilfong, L. G. (2005). Encouraging independent reading with ambience: The Book Bistro in middle and secondary school classes. *Journal of Adolescent & Adult Literacy, 48,* 656–664.

Katz, C. A., Polkoff, L., & Gurvitz, D. (2005). Shhh . . . I'm reading: Scaffolded independent-level reading. *School Talk, 10*(2), 1–3.

Kincheloe, J. L. (2007). *Critical pedagogy primer.* New York: Peter Lange.

King-Shaver, B., & Hunter, A. (2003). *Differentiated instruction in the English classroom.* Portsmouth, NH: Heinemann.

Klare, G. R. (1963). *The measurement of readability.* Ames, IA: Iowa State University Press.

Klemp, R. M. (1994). Word storm: Connecting vocabulary to the student's database. *The Reading Teacher, 48,* 282.

Kletzien, S. B. (2009). Paraphrasing: An effective comprehension strategy. *The Reading Teacher, 63,* 73–77.

Kornell, N., Castel, A. D., & Bjork, R. A. (2010). Spacing as the friend of both memory and induction in young and older adults. *Psychology and Aging, 25,* 498–503.

Krashen, M. R. (2004). *The power of reading: Insights from the research* (2nd ed.). Portsmouth, NH: Heinemann.

LaBerge, D., & Samuels, S. J. (1974). Toward a theory of automatic information processing in reading. *Cognitive Psychology, 6,* 293–323.

Laffey, D. G., & Laffey, J. L. (1986). Vocabulary teaching: An investment in literacy. *Journal of Reading, 29,* 650–656.

Langer, J. A. (1981). From theory to practice: A prereading plan. *Journal of Reading, 25,* 152–156.

Langer, J. A. (2001). Literature as an environment for engaged readers. In L. Verhoeven & C. E. Snow (Eds.), *Literacy and motivation: Reading engagement in individuals and groups* (pp. 177–194). Mahwah, NJ: Erlbaum.

Langer, J. A. (2002). *Effective literacy instruction: Building successful reading and writing programs.* Urbana, IL: National Council of Teachers of English.

Langer, J. A. (2004). *Getting to excellent: How to create better schools.* New York: Teachers College Press.

Larson, R. E., Hostetler, R. B., & Edwards, B. E. (1997). *Precalculus with limits: A graphing approach.* Boston: Houghton Mifflin.

Lee, C. D., & Spratley, A. (2010). *Reading in the disciplines: The challenges of adolescent literacy.* New York: Carnegie Corporation of New York.

Lee, P., & Alley, G. R. (1981). *Training junior high LD students to use a test-taking strategy.* Lawrence, KS: Institute for Research on Learning Disabilities.

Leiner, K. (2001). *Mama does the mambo.* New York: Hyperion.

Lenski, S. (2008a). Teaching from a critical literacy perspective and encouraging social action. In S. Lenski & J. Lewis (Eds.), *Reading success for struggling adolescent learners* (pp. 227–245). New York: Guilford Press.

Lenski, S. D. (2001). Intertextual connections during discussions about literature. *Reading Psychology, 22,* 313–335.

Lenski, S. D. (2008). Struggling adolescent literacy: Problems and possibilities. In S. Lenski & J. Lewis (Eds.), *Reading success for struggling adolescent learners* (pp. 37–57). New York: Guilford Press.

Lenski, S. D. (2008b). Using picture books to explore cultural messages. In C. S. Rhodes, L. B. Wolf, & J. Darvin (Eds.), *From contemplation to action: Promoting social justice through children's literature* (pp. 109–123). East Rockaway, NY: Cummings & Hathaway.

Lenski, S. D., & Ehlers-Zavala, F. (2004). *Reading strategies for Spanish speakers.* Dubuque, IA: Kendall Hunt.

Lenski, S. D., Houshmand, R., Pearson, R., & Teague, A. (2007). Multi-genre text sets: Combining nonfiction and literature. *Oregon English Journal, 19*(1), 19–24.

Lenski, S. D., & Johns, J. L. (1997). Patterns of reading-to-write. *Reading Research & Instruction, 37,* 15–38.

Lenski, S. D., & Nierstheimer, S. L. (2002). Strategy instruction from a sociocognitive perspective. *Reading Psychology, 23,* 127–143.

Lenz, K., & Deshler, D. D. (2004). Teaching content to all: Evidence-based inclusive practice in middle school and high school. Boston: Allyn & Bacon.

Leonardo, Z. (2004). Critical social theory and transformative knowledge: The functions of criticism in quality education. *Educational Researcher, 33,* 11–18.

Leu, D. J., Jr. (2000). Literacy and technology: Deictic consequences for literacy education in an information age. In R. F. Flippo & D. C. Caverly (Eds.), *Handbook of college reading and study strategy research* (pp. 743–770). Mahwah, NJ: Erlbaum.

Leu, D. J., Jr., Mallette, M. H., Karchmer, R. A., & Kara-Soteriou, J. (2005). Contextualizing the new literacies of information and communication technologies in theory, research, and practice. In R. A. Karchmer, M. H. Mallette, J. Kara-Soteriou, & D. J. Leu, Jr. (Eds.), *Innovative approaches to literacy education: Using the internet to support new literacies* (pp. 1–10). Newark, DE: International Reading Association.

Levoy, M. (1997). Aaron's gift. *The language of literature* (pp. 185–192). Evanston, IL: McDougal Littell.

Lewis, C. S. (2000). *The lion, the witch and the wardrobe.* New York: Harper Trophy.

Lewkowicz, N. K. (2000). On the question of teaching decoding skills to older students. In D. W. Moore, D. E. Alvermann, & K. A. Hinchman (Eds.), *Struggling adolescent readers: A collection of teaching strategies* (pp. 189–196). Newark, DE: International Reading Association.

Luke, A., & Dooley, K. (in press). Critical literacy and second language learning. In E. Hinkel (Ed.), *Handbook of research in second language teaching and learning* (Vol. II). New York: Routledge.

Luke, A., & Woods, A. (2009). Critical literacies in schools: A primer. *Voices from the Middle, 17*(2), 9–18.

Lyman, H. B. (1997). *Test scores and what they mean* (6th ed.). Boston: Allyn & Bacon.

Mackey, M. (1997). Good-enough reading: Momentum and accuracy in the reading of complex fiction. *Research in the Teaching of English, 31,* 428–458.

Mallette, M. H., Henk, W. A., Waggoner, J. E., & DeLaney, C. J. (2005). What matters most? A survey of accomplished middle-level educators' beliefs and values about literacy. *Action in Teacher Education, 27*(3), 33–42.

Manz, S. L. (2002). A strategy for previewing textbooks: Teaching readers to become THIEVES. *The Reading Teacher, 55,* 434–435.

Manzo, A., Manzo, U., & Albee, J. J. (2002). iREAP: Improving reading, writing, and thinking in the wired classroom. *Journal of Adolescent & Adult Literacy, 46,* 42–47.

Manzo, A. V. (1969). The ReQuest procedure. *Journal of Reading, 13,* 123–126, 163.

Manzo, A. V., & Manzo, U. C. (1990a). *Content area reading.* New York: Macmillan.

Manzo, A. V., & Manzo, U. C. (1990b). Note cue: A comprehension and participation training strategy. *Journal of Reading, 33,* 608–611.

Marzano, R. J. (1992). *A different kind of classroom: Teaching with dimensions of learning.* Washington, DC: Association for Supervision and Curriculum Development.

Marzano, R. J., & Pickering, D. J. (1997). *Dimensions of learning teacher's manual* (2nd ed.). Alexandria, VA: Association for Supervision and Curriculum Development.

Mathison, C. (1989). Activating student interest in content area reading. *Journal of Reading, 33,* 170–176.

Mayer, R. E. (1996). Learning strategies for making sense out of expository text: The SOI model for guiding three cognitive processes in knowledge construction. *Educational Psychology Review, 8,* 357–371.

McCombs, B. L., & Barton, M. L. (2001). Motivating secondary school students to read their textbooks. In J. A. Rycik & J. L. Irvin (Eds.), *What adolescents deserve: A commitment to students' literacy learning* (pp. 72–81). Newark, DE: International Reading Association.

McCormack, R. L., & Pasquarelli, S. L. (2010). *Teaching reading: Strategies and resources for grades K–6*. New York: Guilford Press.

McDonald, A. S. (2001). The prevalence and effects of test anxiety in school children. *Educational Psychology, 21*, 89–101.

McKenna, M. C., & Robinson, R. D. (1997). *Teaching through text: A content literacy approach to content area reading* (2nd ed.). New York: Longman.

McLaughlin, M., & Allen, M. B. (2002). *Guided comprehension: A teaching model for grades 3–8*. Newark, DE: International Reading Association.

McLean, C. A., Boling, E. C., & Rowsell, J. (2009). Engaging diverse students in multiple literacies in and out of school. In L. M. Morrow, R. Rueda, & D. Lapp (Eds.), *Handbook of research on literacy and diversity* (pp. 158–172). New York: Guilford Press.

McNamera, T., Miller, D., & Bransford, J. (1991). Mental models and reading comprehension. In R. Barr, M. L. Kamil, P. Mosenthal, & P. D. Pearson (Eds.), *Handbook of reading research* (Vol. II) (pp. 490–511). White Plains, NY: Longman.

Meltzer, J., & Hamann, E. T. (2004). *Meeting the literacy development needs of adolescent English language learners through content area learning. Part one: Focus on motivation and engagement*. Providence, RI: Education Alliance at Brown University.

Mercurio, M. L. (2005). In their own words: A study of suburban middle school students using a self-selection reading program. *Journal of Adolescent & Adult Literacy, 48*, 130–141.

Misulis, K. E. (2009). Promoting learning through content literacy instruction. *American Secondary Education, 37*(3), 10–19.

Mitchell, M. (1936). *Gone with the wind*. New York: Macmillan.

Moje, E. B. (2000). *"All the stories they have": Adolescents' insights about literacy and learning in secondary schools*. Newark, DE: International Reading Association.

Moje, E. B. (2007). Developing socially just subject-matter instruction: A review of the literature on disciplinary teaching. *Review of Research in Education, 31*, 1–44.

Moje, E. B. (2008). Foregrounding the disciplines in secondary literacy teaching and learning. *Journal of Adolescent & Adult Literacy, 52*, 96–107.

Montelongo, J., Herter, R. J., Ansaldo, R., & Hatter, N. (2010). A lesson cycle for teaching expository reading and writing. *Journal of Adolescent & Adult Literacy, 53*, 656–666.

Moore, D. W., Bean, T. W., Birdyshaw, D., & Rycik, J. A. (1999). Adolescent literacy: A position statement. *Journal of Adolescent & Adult Literacy, 43*, 97–112.

Moore, D. W., & Moore, S. A. (1986). Possible sentences. In E. K. Dishner, T. W. Bean, J. E. Readence, & D. W. Moore (Eds.), *Reading in the content areas: Improving classroom instruction* (2nd ed.) (pp. 174–179). Dubuque, IA: Kendall Hunt.

Moore, D. W., & Moore, S. A. (1992). Possible sentences: An update. In E. K. Dishner, T. W. Bean, J. E. Readence, & D. W. Moore (Eds.), *Reading in the content areas: Improving classroom instruction* (3rd ed.) (pp. 196–202). Dubuque, IA: Kendall Hunt.

Moore, D. W., Moore, S. A., Cunningham, P. M., & Cunningham, J. W. (1994). *Developing readers and writers in the content areas K–12* (2nd ed.). New York: Longman.

Moore, D. W., Moore, S. A., Cunningham, P. M., & Cunningham, J. W. (2006). *Developing readers and writers in the content areas K–12* (5th ed.). Boston: Allyn & Bacon.

Morgan, R. F., Meeks, J. W., Schollaert, A., & Paul, J. (1986). *Critical reading/thinking skills for the college student*. Dubuque, IA: Kendall Hunt.

Morrow, L. M. (2003). Motivating lifelong voluntary readers. In J. Flood, D. Lapp, J. R. Squires, & J. M. Jensen (Eds.), *Handbook of research on teaching the English language arts* (2nd ed.) (pp. 857–867). Mahwah, NJ: Erlbaum.

Morsy, L., Kieffer, M., & Snow, C. E. (2010). *Measure for measure: A critical consumer's guide to reading comprehension assessments for adolescents*. New York: Carnegie Corporation of New York.

Mukhopadhyay, S., Powell, A. B., & Frankenstein, M. (2009). An ethnomathematical perspective on culturally responsive mathematics education. In B. Greer, S. Mukhopadhyay, A. B. Powell, & S. Nelson-Barber (Eds.), *Culturally responsive mathematics education* (pp. 65–84). New York: Routledge.

Musnick, D., & Pierce, M. (2004). *Conditioning for outdoor fitness* (2nd ed.). Seattle: Mountaineers Books.

Nagy, W. E., & Anderson, R. C. (1984). How many words are there in printed school English? *Reading Research Quarterly, 19*, 304–330.

Nagy, W. E., & Herman, P. A. (1987). Breadth and depth of vocabulary knowledge: Implications for acquisition and instruction. In M. G. McKeown & M. E. Curtis (Eds.), *The nature of vocabulary acquisition* (pp. 19–35). Hillsdale, NJ: Erlbaum.

Nagy, W. E., & Scott, J. A. (2000). Vocabulary processes. In M. L. Kamil, P. B. Mosenthal, P. D. Pearson, & R. Barr (Eds.), *Handbook of reading research* (Vol. III) (pp. 269–284). Mahwah, NJ: Erlbaum.

National Assessment of Educational Progress. (1997). *Report in brief: NAEP 1996 trends in academic progress*. Washington, DC: Author.

National Association of Secondary School Principals. (2005). *Creating a culture of literacy: A guide for middle and high school principals*. Reston, VA: Author.

National Governors Association Center for Best Practices and Council of Chief State School Officers. (2010). *Common Core State Standards Initiative*. Retrieved June 28, 2010, from http://www.corestandards.org/

National Institute for Literacy. (2007). *What content-area teachers should know about adolescent literacy* (NICHD 2007-00-00). Washington, DC: National Institute of Child Health and Human Development and the Office of Adult and Vocational Education, U.S. Department of Education.

National Reading Panel (NRP). (2000). *Teaching children to read: An evidence-based assessment of the scientific research literature on reading and its implications for reading instruction.* Washington, DC: National Institute of Child Health and Human Development.

National Reading Panel (NRP). (2006). *Report of the National Reading Panel: Teaching children to read: An evidence-based assessment of the scientific research literature on reading and its implications for reading instruction.* Washington, DC: National Institute of Child Health and Human Development.

Neufeld, P. (2005). Comprehension instruction in content area classes. *The Reading Teacher, 59,* 302–312.

Newton, R. M., & Newton, E. (2005). A little Latin and . . . a lot of English. *Adolescent Literacy in Perspective,* June, 2–7. Retrieved August 9, 2010, from www.ohiorc.org/adlit/ip_content. aspx?reclID=159&parentID=158

Nist, S. L., & Simpson, M. L. (1989). PLAE, a validated study strategy. *Journal of Reading, 33,* 182–186.

Nist, S. L., & Simpson, M. L. (2000). College studying. In M. L. Kamil, P. B. Mosenthal, P. D. Pearson, & R. Barr (Eds.), *Handbook of reading research* (Vol. III) (pp. 645–666). Mahwah, NJ: Erlbaum.

Nourie, B. L., & Lenski, S. D. (1998). The (in)effectiveness of content area literacy instruction for secondary preservice teachers. *The Clearing House, 71,* 372–374.

O'Brien, D. G., & Dillon, D. R. (2008). The role of motivation in engaged reading of adolescents. In K. A. Hinchman & H. K. Sheridan-Thomas (Eds.), *Best practices in adolescent literacy instruction* (pp. 78–96). New York: Guilford Press.

Oczkus, L. (2003). *Reciprocal teaching at work: Strategies for improving reading comprehension.* Newark, DE: International Reading Association.

Oczkus, L. (2004). *Super six comprehension strategies: 35 lessons and more for reading success.* Norwood, MA: Christopher-Gordon.

Oczkus, L. (2010). *Reciprocal teaching at work: Powerful strategies and lessons for improving reading comprehension* (2nd ed.). Newark, DE: International Reading Association.

Ogle, D. M. (1986). K-W-L: A teaching model that develops active reading of expository text. *The Reading Teacher, 39,* 564–570.

Ogle, D. M. (2011). *Partnering for content literacy: PRC2 in action.* New York: Pearson.

Ogle, D. M., & Blachowicz, C. L. Z. (2002). Beyond literature circles: Helping students comprehend informational texts. In C. C. Block & M. Pressley (Eds.), *Comprehension instruction: Research-based best practices* (pp. 259–274). New York: Guilford Press.

Olson, M. W., & Gee, T. C. (1991). Content reading instruction in the primary grades: Perceptions and strategies. *The Reading Teacher, 45,* 298–307.

Oracle ThinkQuest. (2003). *Of mind and matter.* Retrieved August 12, 2004, from http://library.thinkquest.org/TQ0312238/cgi-bin/view.cgi

Orkwis, R., & McLane, K. (1998). *A curriculum every student can use: Design principles for student access.* Reston, VA: ERIC Clearinghouse on Disabilities and Gifted Education.

Padak, N., Newton, E., Rasinski, T., & Newton, R. M. (2008). Getting to the root of word study: Teaching Latin and Greek word roots in the elementary and middle grades. In A. E. Farstrup & S. J. Samuels (Eds.), *What research has to say about vocabulary instruction* (pp. 6–31). Newark, DE: International Reading Association.

Paris, S. G. (2009). Constrained reading skills—so what? In K. M. Leander, D. W. Rowe, D. K. Dickinson, M. K. Hundley, R. T. Jimenez, & V. J. Risko (Eds.), *58th yearbook of the National Reading Conference* (pp. 34–44). Oak Creek, WI: National Reading Conference.

Paris, S. G., & Lindauer, B. K. (1976). The role of inference in children's comprehension and memory for sentences. *Cognitive Psychology, 8,* 17–227.

Parks, R. (1997). *I am Rosa Parks.* New York: Penguin Books.

Pashler, H., Balin, P., Bottge, B., Graesser, A., Koedinger, K., McDaniel, M., & Metcalfe, J. (2007). *Organizing instruction and study to improve student learning* (NCER 2007–2004). Washington, DC: National Center for Education Research, Institute for Education Sciences, U.S. Department of Education.

Pauk, W. (1974). *How to study in college.* Boston: Houghton Mifflin.

Paul, R. W. (1993). *Critical thinking: How to prepare students for a rapidly changing world.* Santa Rosa, CA: Foundation for Critical Thinking.

Paulson, E. J., & Armstrong, S. L. (2010). Situating reader stance within and beyond the efferent-aesthetic continuum. *Literacy Research and Instruction, 49,* 86–97.

Pérez, A. I. (2002). *My diary from here to there: Mi diario de aquí hasta allá.* San Francisco: Children's Book Press.

Perkins, D. N. (1994). *Knowledge as design: A handbook for critical and creative discussion across the curriculum.* Pacific Grove, CA: Critical Thinking Press and Software.

Peverly, S. T., Brobst, K. E., & Morris, K. S. (2002). The contribution of reading comprehension ability and meta-cognitive control to the development of studying in adolescence. *Journal of Reading Research, 25,* 203–216.

Pinkus, L. M. (Ed.). (2009). *Meaningful measurement: The role of assessments in improving high school education in the twenty-first century.* Washington, DC: Alliance for Excellent Education.

Pitcher, S. M., Albright, L. K., DeLaney, C. J., Walker, N. T., Seunarinesingh, S. M., Headley, K. N., & Dunston, P. J. (2007). Assessing adolescents' motivation to read. *Journal of Adolescent and Adult Literacy, 50,* 378–396.

Pitcher, S. M., Martinez, G., Dicembre, E. A., Fewster, D., & McCormick, M. K. (2010). The literacy needs of adolescents in their own words. *Journal of Adolescent & Adult Literacy, 53*, 636–645.

Poe, E. A. (1974). The purloined letter. In *The American tradition in literature* (pp. 844–860). New York: Grosset & Dunlap.

Poe, E. A. (1979). The purloined letter. In *An Edgar Allan Poe reader: Adapted classic tales* (pp. 45–56). New York: Globe.

Powell, R., Cantrell, S. C., & Adams, S. (2001). Saving Black Mountain: The promise of critical literacy in a multicultural democracy. *The Reading Teacher, 54*, 772–781.

Pressley, M. (1995). More about the development of self-regulation: Complex, long-term, and thoroughly social. *Educational Psychologist, 30*, 207–212.

Pressley, M. (2000). What should comprehension instruction be the instruction of? In M. L. Kamil, P. B. Mosenthal, P. D. Pearson, & R. Barr (Eds.), *Handbook of reading research* (Vol. III) (pp. 545–561). Mahwah, NJ: Erlbaum.

Pressley, M. (2002). Comprehension strategies instruction: A turn of the century report. In C. C. Block & M. Pressley (Eds.), *Comprehension instruction: Research-based best practices* (pp. 11–27). New York: Guilford Press.

Pressley, M., El-Dinary, R. B., Gaskins, I., Schinder, T., Bergman, J. L., Almasi, J., & Brown, R. (1992). Beyond direct exploration: Transactional instruction of reading comprehension strategies. *Elementary School Journal, 92*, 513–535.

Pressley, M., Yokoi, L., van Meter, P., Van Etten, S., & Freebern, G. (1997). Some of the reasons preparing for exams is so hard: What can be done to make it easier? *Educational Psychology Review, 9*, 1–38.

Protopopescu, O. (2003). *Metaphors and similes you can eat and 12 more poetry writing lessons*. New York: Scholastic.

RAND Study Group. (2002). *Reading for understanding: Toward an R&D program in reading comprehension*. Santa Monica, CA: Author.

Raphael, T. E. (1982). Questioning-answering strategies for children. *The Reading Teacher, 36*, 186–191.

Raphael, T. E., & Au, K. H. (2005). QAR: Enhancing comprehension and test taking across grades and content areas. *The Reading Teacher, 59*, 206–221.

Rasinski, T., Padak, N., Newton, R. M., & Newton, E. (2007). *Building vocabulary from root words*. Huntington Beach, CA: Teacher Created Materials.

Raz, O. (2005). *The bread for life diet: The high-on-carbohydrate weight-loss plan*. New York: Stewart, Tabori & Chang.

Reasoner, C. (1976). *Releasing children to literature* (Rev. ed.). New York: Dell.

Reinking, D. (2001). Multimedia and engaged reading in a digital world. In L. Verhoeven & C. E. Snow (Eds.), *Literacy and motivation: Reading engagement in individuals and groups* (pp. 195–221). Mahwah, NJ: Erlbaum.

Reutzel, D. R., Fawson, P. C., & Smith, J. A. (2003, December). *Teaching comprehension strategies using information texts*. Paper presented at the annual meeting of the National Reading Conference, Scottsdale, AZ.

Ricci, G. J., & Walgren, C. (1998, May). *The key to know "Paine" know gain*. Paper presented at the 43rd annual convention of the International Reading Association, Orlando, FL.

Richardson, J. (2000). *Read it aloud*. Newark, DE: International Reading Association.

Risko, V. J., Fairbanks, M. M., & Alvarez, M. C. (1991). Internal factors that influence study. In R. F. Flippo & D. C. Caverly (Eds.), *Teaching reading & study strategies at the college level* (pp. 237–253). Newark, DE: International Reading Association.

Robinson, H. A. (1975). *Teaching reading and study strategies: The content areas*. Boston: Allyn & Bacon.

Roe, B. T., Stoodt-Hill, B. D., & Burns, P. C. (2011). *Secondary school literacy instruction: The content areas* (10th ed.). Belmont, CA: Wadsworth.

Rosenbaum, C. (2001). A word map for middle school: A tool for effective vocabulary instruction. *Journal of Adolescent & Adult Literacy, 45*, 44–49.

Rosenblatt, L. (1978). *The reader, the text, the poem: The transactional theory of the literacy work*. Carbondale, IL: Southern Illinois University Press.

Rosenblatt, L. (1994). The transactional theory of reading and writing. In R. B. Ruddell, M. R. Ruddell, & H. Singer (Eds.), *Theoretical models and processes of reading* (4th ed.) (pp. 1057–1092). Newark, DE: International Reading Association.

Ruddell, M. R. (2005). *Teaching content area reading and writing* (4th ed.). Hoboken, NJ: Wiley.

Ruddell, R. B. (2002). *Teaching children to read and write: Becoming an influential teacher* (3rd ed.). Boston: Allyn & Bacon.

Ryan, R. M., & Deci, E. L. (2000). Intrinsic and extrinsic motivations: Classic definitions and new directions. *Contemporary Educational Psychology, 25*, 54–67.

Sadler, C. R. (2001). *Comprehension strategies for middle grade learners: A handbook for content area teachers*. Newark, DE: International Reading Association.

Sakta, C. G. (1998/1999). SQRC: A strategy for guiding reading and higher level thinking. *Journal of Adolescent & Adult Literacy, 42*, 265–269.

Salembier, G. B. (1999). SCAN and RUN: A reading comprehension strategy that works. *Journal of Adolescent & Adult Literacy, 42*, 386–394.

Sales, G. C., & Graves, M. F. (2005). *Teaching reading comprehension strategies*. (U.S. Department of Education Project Number R3055040194). Minneapolis, MN: Steward Incorporated.

Samuels, S. J. (1979). The method of repeated readings. *The Reading Teacher, 32*, 403–408.

Samuels, S. J. (2006). Toward a model of reading fluency. In S. J. Samuels & A. E. Farstrup (Eds.), *What research has to say about fluency instruction* (pp. 24–46). Newark, DE: International Reading Association.

Sandmann, A. L. (2005). What's a nice poem like you doing in a place like this? *School Library Journal, 51,* 16–19.

Santa, C. M., Dailey, S. C., & Nelson, M. (1985). Free-response and opinion proof: A reading and writing strategy for middle grade and secondary teachers. *Journal of Reading, 28,* 346–352.

Santa, C. M., Havens, L. T., & Maycumber, E. M. (1996). *Creating independence through student-owned strategies* (2nd ed.). Dubuque, IA: Kendall Hunt.

Saul, E. W., & Dieckman, D. (2005). Choosing and using information trade books. *Reading Research Quarterly, 40,* 502–513.

Schiefele, U. (1992). Topic interest and levels of text comprehension. In K. A. Renninger, S. Hildi, & A. Krapp (Eds.), *The role of interest and development* (pp. 151–212). Hillsdale, NJ: Erlbaum.

Schraw, G., Bruning, R., & Svoboda, C. (1995). Source of situational interest. *Journal of Reading Behavior, 27*(1), 1–17.

Schumm, J. S., & Mangrum, D. T. (1991). FLIP: A framework for content area reading. *Journal of Reading, 35,* 120–124.

Schwartz, R. (1988). Learning to learn vocabulary in content area textbooks. *Journal of Reading, 32,* 108–118.

Scieszka, J. (1995). *Math curse.* New York: Viking.

Scott, S. W. (1995). Lochinvar. In E. H. Sword & V. McCarthy (Eds.), *A child's anthology of poetry* (pp. 244–245). New York: HarperCollins.

Sejnost, R., & Thiese, S. (2001). *Reading and writing across content areas.* Arlington Heights, IL: Skylight Professional Development.

Service, R. (1995). The cremation of Sam McGee. In E. H. Sword & V. McCarthy (Eds.), *A child's anthology of poetry* (pp. 246–249). New York: Harper Collins.

Shanahan, T., & Shanahan, C. (2008). Teaching disciplinary literacy to adolescents: Rethinking content-area literacy. *Harvard Educational Review, 78*(1), 40–59.

Sheridan-Thomas, H. K. (2008). Assisting struggling readers with textbook comprehension. In K. A. Hinchman & H. K. Sheridan-Thomas (Eds.), *Best practices in adolescent literacy instruction* (pp. 164–184). New York: Guilford Press.

Siegel, M., & Fernandez, S. L. (2000). Critical approaches. In M. L. Kamil, R. Barr, P. D. Pearson, & P. Mosenthal (Eds.), *Handbook of reading research* (Vol. III) (pp. 141–151). Mahwah, NJ: Erlbaum.

Simpson, M. L. (1986). PORPE: A writing strategy for studying and learning in the content areas. *Journal of Reading, 29,* 407–414.

Simpson, M. L., & Nist, S. L. (2000). An update on strategic learning: It's more than textbook reading strategies. *Journal of Adolescent & Adult Literacy, 43,* 528–541.

Simpson, M. L., & Nist, S. L. (2002). Encouraging active reading at the college level. In C. C. Block & M. Pressley (Eds.), *Comprehension instruction: Research-based best practices* (pp. 365–378). New York: Guilford Press.

Singer, J., & Shagoury, R. (2005/2006). Stirring up justice: Adolescents reading, writing, and changing the world. *Journal of Adolescent & Adult Literacy, 49,* 318–339.

Sis, P. (1996). *Starry messenger: Galileo Galilei.* New York: Farrar, Straus & Giroux.

Smith, D. (1992). Common ground: The connection between reader-response and textbook reading. *Journal of Reading, 35,* 630–634.

Smith, F. (1986). *Insult to intelligence: The bureaucratic invasion of our schools.* New York: Arbor House.

Smith, M. W., & Wilhelm, J. D. (2006). *Going with the flow: How to engage boys (and girls) in their literacy learning.* Portsmouth, NH: Heinemann.

Smolkin, L. B., & Donovan, C. A. (2005). Looking closely at a science trade book: Gail Gibbons and multimodal literacy. *Language Arts, 53*(1), 52–61.

Snow, C., & Moje, E. (2010). Why is everyone talking about adolescent literacy? *Phi Delta Kappan, 91*(6), 66–69.

Soares, L. B., & Wood, K. (2010). A critical literacy perspective for teaching and learning social studies. *The Reading Teacher, 63,* 486–494.

Spinelli, J. (2000). *Stargirl.* New York: Alfred A. Knopf.

Spor, M. W., & Schneider, B. K. (1999). Content reading strategies: What teachers know, use, and want to learn. *Reading Research and Instruction, 38,* 221–231.

Stahl, N. A., King, J. R., & Henk, W. A. (1991). Enhancing students' notetaking through training and evaluation. *Journal of Reading, 34,* 614–622.

Stahl, S. A. (1986). Three principles of effective vocabulary instruction. *Journal of Reading, 29,* 662–668.

Stahl, S. A., Hynd, C. R., Glynn, S. M., & Carr, M. (1996). Beyond reading to learn: Developing content and disciplinary knowledge through texts. In L. Baker, P. Afflerbach, & D. Reinking (Eds.), *Developing engaged readers in school and home communities* (pp. 139–163). Mahwah, NJ: Erlbaum.

Stanley, B., Slate, J. R., & Jones, C. H. (1999). Study behaviors of college preparatory and honors students in the ninth grade. *The High School Journal, 82,* 165–171.

Stauffer, R. G. (1969). *Directing reading maturity as a cognitive process.* New York: Harper and Row.

Stephens, E. C., & Brown, J. E. (1994). Discussion continuum. *The Journal of Reading, 37,* 680–681.

Stephens, E. C., & Brown, J. E. (2000). *A handbook of content literacy strategies: 75 practical reading and writing ideas.* Norwood, MA: Christopher-Gordon.

Stevens, L. P. (2001, December). *A critical discourse analysis of two science teachers' literacy practices*. Paper presented at the National Reading Conference, San Antonio, TX.

Stevens, L. P., & Bean, T. W. (2007). *Critical literacy: Context, research, and practice in the K–12 classroom*. Thousand Oaks, CA: Sage Publications.

Stratton, A. (2004). *Chanda's secrets*. New York: Annick Press.

Taylor, B. M., & Beach, R. W. (1984). The effects of text structure instruction on middle-grade students' comprehension and production of expository text. *Reading Research Quarterly, 19,* 134–146.

Taylor, K., & Rohrer, D. (2010). The effects of interleaved practice. *Applied Cognitive Psychology, 24,* 837–848.

Taylor, K., & Walton, S. (2002). Questioning the answers. *Instructor, 111,* 16.

Thayer, E. L. (1995). Casey at the bat. In E. H. Sword & V. McCarthy (Eds.), *A child's anthology of poetry* (pp. 278–279). New York: HarperCollins.

Tiedt, I. M. (2000). *Teaching with picture books in the middle school*. Newark, DE: International Reading Association.

Tobias, M. C. (1988). Teaching strategic text review by computer and interaction with student characteristics. *Computers in Human Behavior, 4,* 299–310.

Tomlinson, C. A. (2004). Differentiating instruction: A synthesis of key research and guidelines. In T. L. Jetton & J. A. Dole (Eds.), *Adolescent literacy research and practice* (pp. 228–248). New York: Guilford Press.

Tomlinson, L. M. (1995). Flag words for efficient thinking, active reading, comprehension, and test taking. *Journal of Reading, 38,* 387–388.

Tovani, C. (2000). *I read it, but I don't get it: Comprehension strategies for adolescent readers*. Portland, ME: Stenhouse.

Trabasso, T., & Bouchard, E. (2002). Teaching readers how to comprehend text strategically. In C. C. Block & M. Pressley (Eds.), *Comprehension instruction: Research-based best practices* (pp. 176–200). New York: Guilford Press.

Trelease, J. (2001). *The read-aloud handbook* (5th ed.). New York: Penguin.

Trivieri, L. A. (1993). *Precalculus mathematics: Functions & graphs*. New York: Harper Perennial.

Tuckman, B. W. (2003). The effect of learning and motivation strategies training on college students' achievement. *Journal of College Student Development, 44,* 430–437.

Turner, E. E., & Strawhun, B. T. (2006). With math, it's like you have more defense. In E. Gutstein & B. Peterson (Eds.), *Rethinking mathematics* (pp. 81–89). Milwaukee, WI: Rethinking Schools.

Turner, J., & Paris, S. G. (1995). How literacy tasks influence children's motivation for literacy. *The Reading Teacher, 48*(8), 662–673.

Tuttle, H. G. (2009). *Formative assessment: Responding to your students*. Larchmont, NY: Eye on Education.

Tyler, K. M., Uqdah, A. L., Dillihunt, M. L., Beatty-Hazelbaker, R., Conner, T., Gadson, N., Henchy, A., Hughes, T., Mulder, S., Owens, E., Roan-Belle, C., Smith, L., & Stevens, R. (2008). Cultural discontinuity: Toward a quantitative investigation of a major hypothesis in education. *Educational Researcher, 37,* 280–297.

United States Bureau of the Census. (1998). *Statistical abstract of the United States* (118th ed.). Washington, DC: U.S. Government Printing Office.

U.S. Department of Education Institute of Education Sciences. (2010). *National Assessment of Educational Progress,* Retrieved October 12, 2010, from The Nation's Report Card. http://nces.ed.gov/nationsreportcard/

Unrau, N. J. (1997). *Thoughtful teachers, thoughtful learners: A guide to helping adolescents think critically*. Scarborough, Ontario: Pippin.

Unrau, N. J. (2004). *Content area reading and writing: Fostering literacies in middle and high school cultures*. Upper Saddle River, NJ: Merrill Prentice Hall.

Unrau, N. J., & Schlackman, J. (2006). Motivation and its relationship with reading achievement in an urban middle school. *Journal of Educational Research, 100*(2), 81–101.

Untermeyer, L. (1997). The dog of Pompeii. *The language of literature*. Evanston, IL: McDougal Littell.

Vacca, R. T., Vacca, J. L., & Mraz, M. (2011). *Content area reading: Literacy and learning across the curriculum* (10th ed.). Boston: Allyn & Bacon.

Vasquez, V. (2003). *Getting beyond "I like the book": Creating space for critical literacy in K–6 classrooms*. Newark, DE: International Reading Association.

Vasquez, V. (2010). *Getting beyond "I like the book": Creating space for critical literacy in K–6 classrooms* (2nd ed.). Newark, DE: International Reading Association.

Vasudevan, L., & Campano, G. (2009). The social production of adolescent risk and the promise of adolescent literacies. *Review of Research in Education, 33,* 310–353.

Veciana-Suarez, A. (2002). *Flight to freedom*. New York: Orchard.

Verhoeven, L., & Snow, C. E. (2001). Literacy and motivation: Bridging cognitive and sociocultural viewpoints. In L. Verhoeven & C. E. Snow (Eds.), *Literacy and motivation: Reading engagement in individuals and groups* (pp. 1–20). Mahwah: NJ: Erlbaum.

Vivian, J. (1986). *Keeping bees*. Charlotte, VT: Williamson.

Vygotsky, L. S. (1978). *Mind in society: The development of higher psychological processes*. Cambridge, MA: Harvard University Press.

Walker, R. (2003). *Genes & DNA*. Boston: Kingfisher.

Wang, J. H., & Guthrie, J. T. (2004). Modeling the effects of intrinsic motivation, extrinsic motivation, amount of reading, and past reading achievement on text comprehension between U.S. and Chinese students. *Reading Research Quarterly, 39,* 162–186.

Wang, S., & Han, S. (2001). Six c's of motivation. In M. Orey (Ed.), *Emerging perspectives on learning, teaching, and technology.* Retrieved March 15, 2006, from http://www.coe.uga/epltt/6csmotivation.htm

Watkings, N. M., & Lindahl, K. M. (2010). Targeting content area literacy instruction to meet the needs of adolescent English Language Learners. *Middle School Journal,* 4(1), 23–32.

Weaver, C. A., III, & Kintsch, W. (1991). Expository text. In R. Barr, M. L. Kamil, P. Mosenthal, & P. D. Pearson (Eds.), *Handbook of reading research* (Vol. II) (pp. 230–245). White Plains, NY: Longman.

Wertsch, J. V. (1991). *Voices of the mind: A sociocultural approach to mediated action.* Cambridge, MA: Harvard University Press.

White, T., Sowell, J., & Yanagihara, A. (1989). Teaching elementary students to use word-part clues. *The Reading Teacher, 42,* 302–308.

Wigfield, A. (2004). Motivation for reading during early adolescent and adolescent years. In D. S. Strickland & D. E. Alvermann (Eds.), *Bridging the literacy achievement gap, grades 4–12* (pp. 86–105). New York: Teachers College Press.

Wilkinson, L., & Silliman, E. (1997). Alternative assessment, literacy education and school reform. In J. Flood & D. Lapp (Eds.), *Handbook for literacy educators* (pp. 6–76). Newark, DE, and New York: International Reading Association and Macmillan.

Wineburg, S., & Schneider, J. (2009). Was Bloom's taxonomy pointed in the wrong direction? *Phi Delta Kappan, 91*(3), 56–65.

Wink, J. (2001). *Critical pedagogy: Notes from the real world* (2nd ed.). New York: Longman.

Wittels, H., & Greisman, J. (1996). *The clear and simple thesaurus dictionary* (rev. ed.). New York: Grosset & Dunlap.

Wolfe, K., & Siu-Runyan, Y. (1996). Portfolio purposes and possibilities. *Journal of Adolescent & Adult Literacy, 40,* 30–37.

Wolk, S. (2010). What should students read? *Phi Delta Kappan, 91*(7), 8–16.

Wood, K. D. (1984). Probable passages: A writing strategy. *The Reading Teacher, 37,* 496–499.

Wood, K. D. (1988). Guiding students through informational text. *The Reading Teacher, 41,* 912–920.

Wu, Y., & Samuels, S. J. (2004, May). How the amount of time spent on independent reading affects reading achievement: A response to the National Reading Panel. Paper presented at the 49th annual convention of the International Reading Association, Lake Tahoe, NV. Retrieved July 23, 2010, from www.tc.umn.edu/~samue001/web%20pdf/time_spent_on_reading.pdf

Yolen, J. (1981). *Sleeping ugly.* New York: Coward-McCann.

Yopp, R. H., & Yopp, H. K. (2001). *Literature-based reading activities* (3rd ed.). Boston: Allyn & Bacon.

Yopp, R. H., & Yopp, H. K. (2007). Ten important words plus: A strategy for building word knowledge. *The Reading Teacher, 61,* 157–160.

Zaccaro, E. (2001). *Real world algebra: Understanding the power of mathematics.* Bellevue, IA: Nathan Levy Associates.

Zollman, A. (2009). Students use graphic organizers to improve mathematical problem-solving communications. *Middle School Journal, 41*(2), 4–12.

Zywica, J., & Gomez, K. (2008). Annotating to support learning in the content areas: Teaching and learning science. *Journal of Adolescent & Adult Literacy, 52,* 155–165.

Index

A

Abstract words, 50
Access to books, 31–32
Action, social, 207–208
Activating study plan, 212–214
Alliteration, 136–137
Alphabet books, 30–31
Alternative viewpoints, 189–193
  discussion continuum, 191
  discussion web, 190
  editorial perspective, 192–193
  options guide, 191–192
Annotative notes, 229–230
Anticipating known words, 80–81
Anticipation guide strategy, 16–17,
  124–125
Anticipation/reaction guide strategy,
  146–147
Ask the author strategy, 186–187
Assessment contexts, 10
Assumed identity, 54–55
Attitude, 25–32
  autobiography, 25–27
  classroom libraries, 31–32
  opinionnaire/questionnaire
    strategy, 27–28
  picture books strategy, 30–31
  sustained silent reading strategy, 28–30
Attribute web strategy, 129–130
Author, 183–188
  ask the author strategy, 186–187
  consider the source strategy, 184–185
  credibility of, 184–185
  identifying with, 186–187
  perspective guide, 185–186
  perspective of, 185–187
  purposes, 187–188
Author questioning strategy, 161
Autobiography, 25–27

B

Background knowledge, 51–55, 145–147
  exclusion brainstorming strategy, 53–54
  imagine that! strategy, 54–55
  knowledge rating scale strategy, 52–53
Bar graphs, 174–175
Biopoems, 127–128
Blogs, as new literacy, 44, 226–227
Bloom's taxonomy, 163–164
Bold contradictions, 41
Book tour strategy, 217–218
Bulletin boards, as new literacy, 226–227

C

Categories, developing, 64–65
CD-ROM encyclopedias, as new literacy,
  44–47
Character quotes, 125–126
Characterization, 127–130
  attribute web strategy, 129–130
  biopoems, 127–128
  missing person's report, 128–129
Characters, 21, 131–132
  power of, 204
  traits of, 129–130
Chart of connections, 166–167
Charts, 173–177
Clarifying, as thinking strategy, 201–202
Class discussion, 161
Classification of words, 66–67
Classifying challenge, 68
Classmate interaction, as they interview
  them, 27–28
Classroom libraries, 31–32
Cloze, 83–84
Collaboration, as motivational
  element, 136–137
Communication technology, 44–47
Compare-contrast procedure, 93–95
Complexity of text, 7
Concepts, relationship among, 64–65
Conceptual analysis, 64–65
Conceptual knowledge, 52–53
Conflict, 131, 133
Conflict-resolution paradigm, 133
Connections, 86–87, 165–169
  connections chart strategy, 166–167
  intra-act strategy, 168–169
  share what you know strategy, 167–168
Connotations, 75–76
Content area strategies, 9
Content area texts
  demands, 2
  features of, 217–218
Content predict-o-gram strategy, 36–37
Content vocabulary organization, 58–59
Context, 80–90, 107–108
  anticipating known words, 80–81
  for assessment, 10
  cloze, 83–84
  connections, 86–87
  contextual redefinition, 88
  definitions, 86–87
  of instruction, 8–9
  meaning prediction, 84–86
  predictions, 86–87
  word prediction, 81–83
  word questioning, 89–90

Contextual redefinition, 88
Contradictory statements, 41–42
Controversial issues, 192–193
Cornell note-taking, 238–242
Creation of interest, 16–24
Credibility, 184–185
Critical literacy, 200–208
  language, 204–205
  power graph, 204
  problematizing texts, 206–207
  reciprocal teaching plus, 201–202
  response sheet, 203
  social action, 207–208
Critical pedagogy, 180
Critical reading, 179–208
  alternative views, 189–193
  author's purpose, 183–188
  critical literacy, 200–208
  informed opinions, 194–199
  perspectives of author, 183–188
  qualifications of author, 183–188
Critical thinking, 30–31
Critiquing, as thinking strategy, 201–202
Cue cards, 235–236
Cueing system, 80–81
Cultural groups, 206–207
Cultural mix, 4–5
Cultures, represented in literature, 206–207
Curiosity, 33–38
  content predict-o-gram strategy, 36–37
  poetry prowess strategy, 37–38
  probable passages strategy, 34–36
  sentence creation strategy, 33–34

D

Decoding, 91–100
  compare-contrast procedure, 93–95
  foreign words, phrases, 99–100
  making big words strategy, 95–99
  repeated readings, 91–92
  two questions strategy, 92–93
Defining tasks, 212–214
Definitions, 56–62, 86–87
  four square strategy, 59–60
  graphic organizers, 58–59
  magic squares strategy, 57–58
  word storm strategy, 60–61
  word web strategy, 61–62
Deletions, word, 83–84
Demands, content area texts, 2
Denotations, 75–76
Derivatives, 110–119
Devices of literature, 136–137
Diagrams, 174–175
Dialectical journal, 155–156

Dictionary, 60–61, 105–108
    orientation, 104–105
    use of, 107–108
Digital texts, as new literacy, 44–47
Discipline, 3
Discussion continuum strategy, 191
Discussion web, 190
Distinguishing traits of character, 129–130
Diversity, 143, 181
Double entry diary, 240–242
Draw, read, attend, write strategy, 42–44
DRAW strategy. *See* Draw, read, attend, write strategy
Drawing inferences, 136–140
DVDs, as new literacy, 44–47

E

e-mail, as new literacy, 44, 226–227
Editorial perspective, 192–193
Electronic format, 104–105
Elements of fiction, 132
ELLs. *See* English language learners
Engagement, 13–47
    curiosity, 33–38
    interest, creation of, 16–24
    motivation, 39–47
    positive attitudes, 25–32
English language learners, 5–6, 110
Essential big words strategy, 110–113
Etymology, 99–100
Evaluating opinions, 195–197
Evaluating plan's effectiveness, 212–214
Examination of attitudes, 27–28
Exclusion brainstorming strategy, 53–54
Expository writing, 34

F

Fact, historical fiction, connecting, 137–140
Fifty essential big words strategy, 110–113
Figurative language, 73–74
Flexibility in reading, 222–227
    Internet, 226–227
    on your mark, get set, SCAN! strategy, 223–224
    SCAN and RUN strategy, 224
    SCROL strategy, 225–226
    skim-away strategy, 222–223
Fluency, word identification, 91–92
Footnotes, 102–103
Foreign words, phrases, 99–100
Four square strategy, 59–60

G

Gender, 206–207
General understanding, demonstrating, 144–149
    anticipation/reaction guide strategy, 146–147
    GIST strategy, 148–149

prereading plan, 145–146
    think, predict, read, connect strategy, 147–148
Generalizations, 125–126
GIST strategy, 148–149
Glossary, 60–61, 103–104, 107–108
Grammar, 131
Graphic features, 173
Graphic organizers, 58–59, 132, 151–152
Graphs, 174–175
GRASP. *See* Guided reading and summarizing procedure
Greek roots, 110–119
    fifty essential big words strategy, 110–113
    slash dash strategy, 117–119
    word spines strategy, 113–116
Guide words, 104–105
Guided reading and summarizing procedure, 232–233

H

Habits of study, monitoring, 215
Hierarchical information organization, 239–240
Historical fiction, 137–140
Humor, 37
Hyperbole, 136–137

I

Idea-maps, 152–153
Idea webs, 144
Identification of words, 91–92
Identifying with author, 186–187
Identity, 54–55
Imagine that! strategy, 54–55
Implementing study plan, 212–214
Implied meanings, 75–76
The imposter strategy, 41–42
In the feature, but not in the text strategy, 173
Inference chart, 157–158
Inferences, 123–126, 136–140, 155–158
Information technology, 44–47
Informational picture books, 30–31
Informational texts, 141–177
    connections, 165–169
    features of text, 170–177
    general understanding, 144–149
    interpretation, 155–159
    questioning texts, 160–164
    text structure, 150–154
Informed opinions, 194–199
    opinion-proof strategy, 195–197
    SOAPS + Claim strategy, 198–199
    state-question-read-conclude strategy, 194–195
    support your position strategy, 197–198
Inquiry questions, 163–164
Instructional contexts, 8–9

Interact with classmates, 27–28
Interest, creation of, 16–24
    anticipation guide, 16–17
    character, 21
    labels, 22
    paradox, 19
    people search strategy, 18–19
    predict-o-gram strategy, 21–22
    problem-solution scenario, 19
    problematic situation, 19–21
    setting, 21
    sketching, 22
    summary statement, 22
    that was then . . . this is now strategy, 22–24
Internet, 44–47, 226–227
Interpretation, 155–159
    inference chart strategy, 157–158
    it says—I say—and so strategy, 155–156
    ReQuest strategy, 157
    three-level guide, 158–159
Intertextual links, 168–169
Interviewing classmates, 27–28
Intra-act strategy, 168–169
IQs. *See* Inquiry questions
Irony, 136–137
It says—I say—and so strategy, 155–156

J

Journals, 61–62, 215–216
Judgments, reasoned, 194–195

K

K-W-L motivation strategy, 39–41
Knowledge rating scale strategy, 52–53
Known word anticipation, 80–81

L

Labels, 22–24
Latin roots, 110–119
    fifty essential big words strategy, 110–113
    slash dash strategy, 117–119
    word spines strategy, 113–116
Learning log, 229–230
Letter patterns, 93–95
Lexile framework, 7–8
Lines substituted for words, 83–84
Listing strategies, 212–214
Listservs, as new literacy, 226–227
Literacy, 200–208
    language, 204–205
    power graph, 204
    problematizing texts, 206–207
    reciprocal teaching plus, 201–202
    response sheet, 203
    social action, 207–208
Literacy devices, 136–137

Literary texts, 121–140
    characterization, 127–130
    literature, 136–140
    prior knowledge, 123–126
    structure, 131–135
Literature, 136–140
    fact, historical fiction, connecting,
        137–140
    literacy devices, 136–137
Long-term memory, 59–60
Longer words, pronunciation of, 93–95

M

Magic squares strategy, 57–58
Magnet words strategy, 67–68
Making big words strategy, 95–99
Managing studying, 214
Maps, 173–175
Maps of ideas, 152–153
Math puzzles, 57–58
Meaning, 91–100
    compare-contrast procedure, 93–95
    foreign words, phrases, 99–100
    making big words strategy, 95–99
    prediction, 84–86
    repeated readings, 91–92
    two questions strategy, 92–93
Meanings, 75–76
Memory, 59–60
Metaphors, 73–74, 136–137
Microtheme, summary, 230–231
Missing person's report, 128–129
Missing words, 83–84
Monitoring study habits, 215
Motivation
    communication technology, 44–47
    curiosity, 33–38
    draw, read, attend, write strategy, 42–44
    the imposter strategy, 41–42
    information technology, 44–47
    interest, creation of, 16–24
    K-W-L strategy, 39–41
    positive attitudes, 25–32
Motivational elements, 136–137
Multiple viewpoints, 192–193
Multisyllabic words, 93–95

N

NAEP. See National Assessment of
    Educational Progress
Narrative picture books, 30–31
Narrative writing, 34–36
National Assessment of Educational
    Progress, 141
Nation's Report Card, 141
Network trees, 59
New literacies, 44–47
Nontraditional forms, 37
Note cards, 229–230

Note-taking, 235–242
    Cornell note-taking, 238–239
    double entry diary, 240–242
    note cue cards, 235–236
    power notes, 239–240
    record-edit-synthesize-think strategy,
        236–238
Notebook, 61–62
Notes, annotative, 229–230

O

On your mark, get set, SCAN!
    strategy, 223–224
Onomatopoeia, 136–137
Opinion-proof strategy, 195–197
Opinionnaire/questionnaire strategy,
    27–28
Opinions, 194–199
    evaluating, 195–197
    opinion-proof strategy, 195–197
    SOAPS + claim strategy, 198–199
    state-question-read-conclude strategy,
        194–195
    support your position strategy, 197–198
Options guide strategy, 191–192
Organizing words, 66–67
Outlining, 151–152

P

Paradigm, 133
Paradox, 19
Paraphrasing strategy, 233–234
Pedagogy, 180
People search strategy, 18–19
Personal viewpoint, 54–55
Personality traits, 127–128
Personification, 73–74, 136–137
Perspective guide strategy, 185–186
Perspective of author, 185–187
Picture books strategy, 30–31
Pictures, developing, 73–74
PLAE strategy. See Preplan-list-activate-
    evaluate strategy
Plan of study, 212–214
Playful forms, 37–38
Poetry prowess strategy, 37–38
Point of view, 134–135
Positive attitudes, 25–32
    autobiography, 25–27
    classroom libraries, 31–32
    opinionnaire/questionnaire strategy,
        27–28
    picture books strategy, 30–31
    sustained silent reading strategy, 28–30
Power graph, 204
Power notes, 239–240
Power of characters, 204
Predict-o-gram strategy, 21–22
Predictions, 86–87, 201–202

Prefixes, 117–119
PreP. See Prereading plan
Preplan-list-activate-evaluate strategy,
    212–214
Prereading plan strategy, 145–146
Presentation software, as new literacy,
    226–227
Printed format, 104–105
Prior knowledge, 123–126
    anticipation guide strategy, 124–125
    character quotes strategy, 125–126
    story impressions strategy, 124
Probable passages strategy, 34–36
Problem-solution scenario, 19–21
Problematic situation, 19–21
    paradox, 19–21
Problematizing texts, 206–207
Processing informational texts, 142
Project journals, 215–216
Pronunciation, 92–95, 101–102, 105–106
    symbols for, 105–106
Purpose of author, 187–188

Q

Qualifications of author, 183–188
Question, answer relationship strategy,
    162–163
Questioning, as thinking strategy, 201–202
Questioning texts, 160–164
    inquiry questions, 163–164
    question answer relationship strategy,
        162–163
    questioning the author strategy, 161

R

Range of views, 191
Rate of learning, 71
Reaction guide, 146–147
Read-encode-annotate-ponder strategy,
    229–230
REAP strategy. See Read-encode-annotate-
    ponder strategy
Reasoned judgments, 194–195
Reciprocal teaching plus, 201–202
Record-edit-synthesize-think strategy,
    236–238
Record words, 61–62
Reference sources, 101–109
    dictionary, 104–105, 107–108
    footnotes, 102–103
    glossary, 103–104
    pronunciation strategy, 105–106
    right on the page strategy, 101–102
    thesaurus use, 108–109
    word mapping, 108–109
Reinforcement, 113–116
Relationship among concepts, 64–65
Relationship among words, 33–34, 63–68
    classifying challenge, 68
    magnet words strategy, 67–68

semantic feature analysis, 64–65
  word sort strategy, 66–67
Relationships between words, 92–93
Repeated readings, 91–92
Representation of cultures, 206–207
ReQuest strategy, 157
Resolution of conflict, 133
Response sheet for critical literacy, 203
REST strategy. *See* Record-edit-
  synthesize-think strategy
Retaining words, 59–60
Retention of words, 70
Right on the page strategy, 101–102
Root words, 110–119
  fifty essential big words strategy,
    110–113
  slash dash strategy, 117–119
  word spines strategy, 113–116

S

SCAN and RUN strategy, 224
Scanning text, 225–226
Scavenger hunt strategy for textbooks,
  218–219
School libraries, 31–32
SCROL strategy, 225–226
Search engines, as new literacy, 44
Self-collection, vocabulary, 70
Self-selected materials, 28–30
Semantic feature analysis, 64–65
Sentence creation strategy, 33–34
Settings, 21, 131–132
Share what you know strategy, 167–168
Signal words, 153–154
Significant relationships, 64–65
Similes, 73–74
Sketching, 22–24
Skim-away strategy, 222–223
Skimming text, 225–226
Slash dash strategy, 117–119
SOAPS + claim strategy, 198–199
Social action, 207–208
Sociocultural activity, reading as, 3–4
Software, as new literacy, 226–227
Source credibility, 184–185
Sources. *See* Reference sources
Speaker, occasion, audience, purpose,
  significance + claim strategy. *See*
  SOAPS + claim strategy
Specialized vocabulary, 60–61
Spelling, 92–93
Spreadsheets, as new literacy, 226–227
SQRC strategy. *See* State-question-read-
  conclude strategy
SSR strategy. *See* Sustained silent reading
  strategy
State-question-read-conclude strategy,
  194–195
Story impressions, 124
Story maps strategy, 132

Structure, 131–135
  conflict-resolution paradigm, 133
  story maps, 132
  what's your perspective? strategy,
    134–135
Structure of text, 150–154
  graphic organizers, 151–152
  idea-maps, 152–153
  signal words, 153–154
Struggling readers, 6–7
Study
  flexibility in reading, 222–227
  managing, 214
  monitoring habits, 215
  notes, 235–242
  preplan-list-activate-evaluate strategy,
    212–214
  project journals, 215–216
  study, 212–216
  summarizing, 228–234
  textbook features, 217–221
Study plan, 212–214
Study time, 214
Subtle contradictions, 41–42
Summarizing, 228–234
  guided reading and summarizing
    strategy, 232–233
  paraphrasing, 233–234
  read-encode-annotate-ponder strategy,
    229–230
  summary microtheme, 230–231
  as thinking strategy, 201–202
Summarizing passages, 230–233
Summary paragraph, 148–149
Summary statements, 22–24
Support your position strategy, 197–198
Sustained silent reading strategy, 28–30
SWYK strategy. *See* Share what you know
  strategy
Syllabication, 93–95
Synopsis, 232–233
Syntactic clues, 83–84
SYP strategy. *See* Support your position
  strategy

T

Technical vocabulary, 60–61
Text features, 170–177
  bar graphs, 174–175
  charts, 174–175
  in the feature, but not in the text
    strategy, 173
  previews, 171–172
  timelines, 176–177
Text preview, 171–172
Text structure, 150–154
  graphic organizers, 151–152
  idea-maps, 152–153
  signal words, 153–154

Textbook features, 217–221
  book tour strategy, 217–218
  scavenger hunt strategy, 218–219
  textbook survey, 218
  THIEVES strategy, 219–221
Textbook scavenger hunt strategy, 218–219
Textbook survey strategy, 218
That was then . . . this is now strategy,
  22–24
Theme, 132
Thesaurus, 60–61, 108–109
THIEVES strategy, 219–221
Think, predict, read, connect strategy,
  147–148
Thinking process, 155–156
Thinking strategies, 201–202
Three-level guide, 158–159
Time
  study, 214
  use of, 214
Timelines, 176–177
TOAST strategy, 71
TPRC strategy. *See* Think, predict, read,
  connect strategy
Traits of characters, 129–130
Transactional reading theory, 4
Two questions strategy, 92–93

U

Understanding, demonstrating, 144–149
  anticipation/reaction guide strategy,
    146–147
  GIST strategy, 148–149
  prereading plan strategy, 145–146
  think, predict, read, connect strategy,
    147–148
Unknown words, 61–62
Use of time, 214

V

Viewpoints, 54–55
  alternative, 191–192
  multiple, 192–193
  range of, 191
Views, 189–193
  discussion continuum strategy, 191
  discussion web strategy, 190
  editorial perspective, 192–193
  options guide, 191–192
Virtual worlds, as new literacy, 226–227
Vocabulary, 33–34, 49–76
  background knowledge, 51–55
  definitions, 56–62
  development, 61–62
  exclusion brainstorming strategy, 53–54
  imagine that! strategy, 54–55
  knowledge rating scale strategy, 52–53
  self-collection, 70
  TOAST strategy, 71

vocabulary, 69–76
word relationships, 63–68
word usage, 72–76

W

Web browsers, as new literacy, 226–227
Websites, as new literacy, 44–47
What's your perspective? strategy, 134–135
Wikis, as new literacy, 44, 226–227
Word deletions, 83–84
Word identification, 91–92
Word mapping, 108–109

Word prediction, 81–83
Word questioning, 89–90
Word relationships, 63–68
   classifying challenge, 68
   magnet words strategy, 67–68
   semantic feature analysis, 64–65
   word sort strategy, 66–67
Word sort strategy, 66–67
Word spines strategy, 113–116
Word storm strategy, 60–61
Word study, 77–119
   context, 80–90
   decoding, 91–100

   Greek roots, 110–119
   Latin roots, 110–119
   meaning, 91–100
   reference sources, 101–109
Word use, 72–76
   connotations, 75–76
   figurative language, 73–74
   metaphors, 74
   similes, 74
Word web strategy, 61–62
Wordless books, 30–31